A WORLD
of
DIFFERENCE

This book is dedicated to
Betty and David Greenglass
and Sawa Hiraki
With deepest appreciation

A WORLD *of* DIFFERENCE

GENDER ROLES IN PERSPECTIVE

Esther R. Greenglass, Ph. D.

Department of Psychology
York University
Toronto, Ontario

1807 1982

John Wiley & Sons

Toronto New York Chichester Brisbane Singapore

Canadian Cataloguing in Publication Data
Greenglass, Esther R., 1940–
 A world of difference

Includes indexes.
ISBN 0-471-79862-2 (bound)
ISBN 0-471-79949-1 (pbk)

1. Sex role.   2. Sex differences (Psychology).
I. Title.

HQ1075.G74   155.3'3   C82-094245-6

Cover design by Brant Cowie
Text design by First Image/Michael Gray
Typesetting by Artype Ltd.
Printed and bound in Canada by John Deyell Co.
10 9 8 7 6 5 4 3 2 1

Table of Contents

Preface

Even before I undertook any formal training in psychology, I was always fascinated by the psychological differences between the sexes. Sadly, my experience at university provided me with little insight into, let alone knowledge about, this subject. The psychology courses I took at both the undergraduate and graduate levels had little, if anything, to say about women. The theory and research in traditional areas of psychological inquiry that we studied were based mainly on men and their experiences. At best, the subject of psychological differences between the sexes was subsumed under the general topic of "individual differences". When psychologists were found to make statements about women, they were either unsubstantiated and often fallacious psychoanalytic assumptions as put forth by Freud, or they were generalizations about women's behaviour and psychology from research findings based on men. The message conveyed at that time was that the psychology of women, their unique experience, and how they differed from men psychologically were not important issues worthy of academic study.

With the resurgence of the Women's Movement during the sixties, there emerged an awareness of the need for the academic study of the psychology of women and psychological differences between women and men. There was a virtual explosion of research dealing with these issues in practically all academic disciplines, including psychology. At the same time, courses on the psychology of women and sex differences began to appear on campuses all over North America. Eagerly immersing myself in this new literature, I began to do research in areas relating to the psychology of women and to teach courses dealing with both the psychology of women and psychological differences between the sexes. Needless to say, these courses were long overdue and students not only greeted them eagerly, but also participated in class discussion with great enthusiasm. It was through discussion with my students over the years in these courses that many of my ideas for this book began to take form and coalesce. Their intellectual curiosity and personal involvement in many of the issues discussed in this book provided me with much of the incentive to put my ideas into print.

My approach is a feminist social psychological one, which is based on the belief that the individual's psychological functioning cannot be understood apart from the social context in which it is found. At the same time, according to the feminist approach, individuals should have the freedom to behave in ways that are not constrained by gender roles. But much of our behaviour and psychological functioning is affected by our gender role — whether that be feminine or masculine. In our society, the "meaning" of being a woman or a man is often the expression of unquestioned gender-role stereotypes that are imposed on the individual. One of the purposes of this book is to increase awareness of the constraints placed upon people by gender roles in many different areas of individual and social functioning. It thus constitutes the first step toward freedom to behave and *be* in ways that allow for greater fulfillment of one's potential. In this regard, recent research in women's studies has not only pointed out how the feminine gender role has restricted women and the realization of their potential; it has also increased awareness of both the restrictiveness of the masculine gender role and its deleterious effects on men.

The research included in this book is based on both Canadian and American data. While not denying the similarity between the Canadian and American experiences, I have attempted, where possible, to include specific Canadian data and research. In this way I hoped to make the book more relevant to the experiences of the Canadians who read it.

Many of the issues raised in this book are relevant to our own personal experiences. But it is important to point out that these same topics are, and continue to be, the object of empirical research. While it is difficult to maintain a completely objective perspective in most areas of scientific inquiry, in this area, particularly, much of our "knowledge" in the past has been derived from folk wisdom and common sense. It is precisely because of the unsubstantiated, ingrained, and tenacious nature of the belief systems surrounding many of these issues that I have documented this book so extensively with research data.

The present book represents my perspective on social areas that are relevant to the understanding of the differences in the psychological experiences of women and men. It is my hope that the ideas expressed here will stimulate students to do further research in this area which is of utmost importance to human social and psychological functioning. It is also my hope that this book will provoke a re-examination of many of the assumptions that people may hold regarding the psychological differences between the sexes.

. . . .

I could not have completed this book without the assistance and support of a great many people. They all took time from their busy schedules to help me in many different ways and for this I am most grateful.

Specifically, I would like to thank Morris Eagle, Norman S. Endler, Avis Glaze, Meredith Kimball, Gary J. McDonald, Sandra W. Pyke, Kjell

Rudestam, Vello Sermat, Irwin Silverman, Leo Spindel, Diana Wedlock, and Jeri D. Wine — all of whom took time to read all or parts of earlier drafts of the manuscript and generously shared their ideas with me on various topics. I especially wish to thank Cannie Stark-Adamec who spent many hours reviewing the entire manuscript in its earlier form. Her insights and ideas are an invaluable contribution to this book. Any errors I may have made are entirely mine and not a reflection on them whatsoever.

I wish also to thank the Consumer Income and Expenditure Division of Statistics Canada for providing me with valuable unpublished data. In particular, I wish to acknowledge Gail Oja for her encouragement and support. I want also to thank Randy J. Glasbergen and the other cartoonists for their contributions which have added much to the book and demonstrate that feminists do have a sense of humour. I would also like to acknowledge and thank Linda Lee who cheerfully typed much of the manuscript with speed and accuracy.

I am indebted to my graduate students, Rena Borovilos, Marsha Eisner, and Kathy Winthrope, who not only helped to compile an enormous amount of reference material but who also generously and cheerfully contributed their time and ideas in many different ways that helped bring this book to its final form. I especially wish to thank William G. McDonald, whose expertise contributed greatly to the chapter we coauthored in this book.

Special thanks go to the staff at Wiley for their conscientious, efficient, and accurate work on this book. I wish to thank Jim Rogerson, Editorial Director at Wiley, for his encouragement and support. In particular, I wish to express my gratitude to Kathryn Dean who guided the manuscript through numerous revisions and whose careful editing and profound sense of literature helped make a collection of ideas into a book.

My gratitude goes also to Condacy Moses and Lucy Spencer whose conscientious and loving care in my home during my absence gave me the many hours I needed to complete this book. I would also like to thank Linda and Susan Hiraki for sharing "mommy" with the book for what must have seemed an eternity. Lastly and first, I wish to express my loving gratitude to my husband and companion, George Hiraki, for his gentle strength and unwavering belief in me.

Esther R. Greenglass
Toronto, Ontario
March 1982

1

Introduction

Throughout the centuries, the differences between women and men have been a source of mystery and intrigue. Beliefs on the subject were based on folklore and folk myths, but emanated from such authoritative sources that few have questioned them. History and literature record characteristic views of the "nature" of women and men, views which continue to influence contemporary thinking about the sexes. Men and women alike have rarely been able to perceive women simply as human beings with the same range of qualities as those of men. Women have been viewed as mysterious creatures, and folk wisdom is replete with attempts to explain their nature. Ancient philosophers regarded women as essentially creatures of emotion and men as rational, intellectual beings. Men, then, were seen as having to exert authority over women and control them. Considered to be incarnations of virtue and deceit, chastity and lustful passion, women were thought to be a "necessary evil". This misogynist view has persisted to the present day. Many cultures warned men about the terrible consequences in store for those who yielded to female sexual mysteries and "power." At the same time, women were seen as deficient males, insignificant persons to be tolerated for the services they performed for men. Perceived in many cultures as the property of men, women were considered to have low social status and no personal rights. As a result, relationships between the sexes have never been equal. Here are some of the quotations on the subject that have been recorded:

> The glory of a man is knowledge, but the glory of a woman is to renounce knowledge.
>
> *Chinese proverb*

> Blessed are Thou, O Lord our God, King of the Universe, that I was not born a woman.
>
> *Morning prayer of the Orthodox Jew*

> Men are superior to women on account of the qualities in which God has given them pre-eminence.
>
> *the Koran, the sacred text of Islam*

1

Charm is a woman's strength just as strength is a man's charm.

Havelock Ellis

Why can't a woman be more like a man?

Professor Henry Higgins from "My Fair Lady"

A woman has to be twice as good as a man to go half as far.

Fannie Hurst

These and other similar proverbs and quotations, though based on folklore, represent the beliefs that have been held by countless numbers of people for centuries. While the basic assumptions of these beliefs are being challenged today, contemporary issues raised about women's role are not so different from those discussed in the past. Among the notions still commonly held are these:

1. Men are more important than women.
2. Men's work is superior to that of women.
3. Women's place is in the home, while men's place is outside the home.
4. Women exist for the pleasure and benefit of men.

There can be no doubt that women and men differ — both biologically and psychologically. According to the traditional view, women and men should serve different social functions because of their obvious biological differences. Social roles have been organized universally around the woman's ability to bear children and the man's greater potential for physical strength. These two major biological differences, then, can be seen as the origin of the evolution of differing roles for women and men. Traditional thinking about the sexes has been marked by the tendency to draw direct inferences about *social differences* from biological ones. But this kind of reasoning contains a biological fallacy, as pointed out by Margrit Eichler,[1] a sociologist, in her critique of the "double standard" in behaviour expectations for women and men. This consists in trying to explain social facts by biological ones without careful consideration of the culture through which such biological differences are expressed. For humans, since the meaning of a biological sex difference varies according to the culture through which it is mediated, a social difference cannot be explained by a biological sex difference. For example, while men, on the average, tend to have more muscle tissue than women, the male's predisposition to greater physical strength is greatly exaggerated in Western industrialized countries, where boys more than girls are encouraged, motivated, and, at times, forced to take part in physical activities, particularly sports. Thus, what started as a natural tendency toward somewhat greater muscular strength is greatly increased through a cultural factor — namely, physical activity. But in countries where women customarily carry the physical burden, the women's muscles are better developed than the men's. In this case, as in others, the role of the cultural environment becomes a critical variable in understanding social and psychological differences between the sexes. This is not to deny that there are obvious biological differences between women and men which result in psychological phenomena that are unique to one's sex. Biological events such as menstruation, pregnancy, and ejaculation result in psychological reactions that are specific to women or men. But, in the majority of instances, the size of the observed differences in behaviour between women and men is very small and need not limit their behavioural potential.

Traditionally, psychologists, like others, shared the assumption that any differences between women and men — both psychological and behavioural — were natural and normal. For the most part, the male-dominated profession of psychology did not regard empirical demonstrations of the obvious as scientifically necessary. Woolley,[2] writing in a respected psychological journal in 1910, said of the topic of research on sex differences:

> There is perhaps no field aspiring to be scientific where flagrant personal bias, logic martyred in the cause of supporting a prejudice, unfounded assertions, and even sentimental rot and drivel, have run riot to such an extent as here (p. 340).

Although conventional psychology did not ignore differences between women and men completely, the topic was subsumed under the heading of the study of individual differences in psychological functioning. And even when differences between women and men were examined, which was not often, the tendency was to view male responses as normative and to explain female behaviour in terms of deviation from or similarity to the male model. Most often, psychologists advanced theories of human behaviour and attempted to verify them empirically in studies which relied predominantly on men and boys as participants. [3-5] In one study, for example,[6] the number of participants in all-male psychological research was found to be almost five times the number of participants used in all-female research reported in five prestigious psychology journals. Moreover, findings based on male participants only were generalized to females, the assumption being that females would behave in the same way under the same conditions. In the absence of systematic knowledge of the psychological differences between them (particularly at that time), this practice of generalizing from males to females appears to have been based more on faith than on scientific data. Investigators attempted to justify the exclusion of females from psychological research on the grounds that it was difficult to obtain sufficient numbers of male and female participants to analyze differences between them. Female participants were excluded also because they behaved "inconsistently" — female participants did not behave in ways that conformed to the male models developed by psychologists.

More significant, however, is the fact that the majority of psychologists were simply not interested in studying differences between men and women. As recently as the early 1970s, the programme committee of the Canadian Psychological Association appeared to regard an interest in the psychology of women and psychological differences between men and women as illegitimate at worst, irrelevant at best.[7] Such topics were avoided both in the CPA's journals and in their convention programme. In 1972, a group of women psychologists, myself included, submitted a proposal for a symposium to the programme committee of the Canadian Psychological Association for presentation at its annual convention in Montreal. After repeated unsuccessful attempts to pass the committee's screening, we presented an underground independent symposium at the same convention, which drew considerable interest and was extremely well attended.

Since the early 1970s, interest in and knowledge about both the psychology of women and differences between men and women have grown at a phenomenal rate. This is partly a function of the resurgence of the Women's Liberation Movement in both Canada and the United States in the late sixties. The new feminism shed more light on the role of women in society and on the inequities surrounding women in economic, social, and political spheres. At the same time, the movement focused society's attention on the necessity to re-evaluate traditional assumptions about the nature of differences between women and men. This has resulted in an increased awareness among social scientists (particularly women) of the need for a scientific study of differences between women and men. Women's studies courses sprang up virtually everywhere — in departments of sociology, anthropology, political science, and psychology all across North America. They provided a forum for the critical evaluation of the position of women in society and the examination of conventional presuppositions about the differences between the sexes. Likewise, since the late 1960s, research has produced a wealth of studies in a variety of disciplines which challenge many of the assumptions traditionally held about women.

The psychology of women has begun to attain a respectable position as a field for scholarly analysis. For example, in 1974, the American Psychological Association formally recognized the growing scientific interest in the study of women when its Council of Representatives approved the formation of the Division of the Psychology of Women. And in 1976, the Canadian Psychological Association's Interest Group on Women and Psychology (IGWAP) was organized and is now the largest of the association's 14 interest groups. The first meeting of the Canadian Institute on Women and Psychology,[8] held in Ottawa in 1978, would not have occurred without the prior establishment of IGWAP. In addition, many psychologists (predominantly women) participate in the interdisciplinary Canadian Research Institute for the Advancement of Women, founded in 1976 and devoted to promoting research on women. In both the United States and Canada, new journals which specialize in the publication of this material have been established. Among these are the *Psychology of Women Quarterly, Sex Roles,* and *Signs,* in the United States, and *Canadian Women's Studies, Resources for Feminist Research,* the *International Journal of Women's Studies,* and *Atlantis,* in Canada. These publications present empirical studies, book reviews, and critical evaluations, all bearing on the topics of women, differences between men and women, and the roles they play in society.

The goal of the present book is to evaluate critically the social and psychological functioning of women and men, from a feminist perspective. In this regard, it should be pointed out that feminist scholarship can be as objective as any other kind of scholarship that has a particular theoretical basis. A truly value-free science does not exist anywhere. A feminist perspective, as employed here, is not antimale. On the contrary, it is based on assumptions of equality between women and men. Firstly, it starts from the premise that women and men have the same potential for individual development. Secondly, it rejects the idea that members of either sex can make significant choices as long as there are rigidly prescribed roles for women and men and social penalties for those who deviate. Thirdly, by probing for the origins of these roles and by examining social and psychological differences between women and men, this perspective points to ways of ultimately overcoming the differences and, thus, increasing the freedom of choice of individuals. Fourthly, the feminist perspective is grounded in an affirmation of the intrinsic worth of human diversity, which can be achieved only when people have the opportunity to explore their own options, rather than being constricted by traits thought to be the only ones appropriate for members of their sex.

While the focus of this book is on the social and psychological aspects of the roles enacted by women and men, these aspects cannot be understood apart from a full appreciation of the socio-political meaning of these roles, as defined by a patriarchal society such as ours. Accordingly, analyses in this book frequently refer to the social, economic, and political differentials associated with the roles of women and men, and the historical and present-day effects of social, economic, and political discrimination against women, which are an integral part of explanations of women's social and psychological functioning. It is only by inclusion of the socio-political dimension that it will be possible to discern where and how changes in socially assigned roles will have to occur if individuals (both women and men) are to achieve their potential.

Although extensive information has been compiled in many countries about the social roles assigned to women and men, discussion in this book will be based on North American — and especially Canadian — information and experience. In many instances, descriptions of feminine and masculine social roles will be applicable to countries other than those on this continent, but the word "society" will be used to refer to North American society and, often, to Canadian society in particular.

Some of the questions that are raised and discussed in this book are presented below:

> The passivity that is the essential characteristic of the "feminine" woman is a trait that develops in her from the earliest years. But it is wrong to assert a biological datum is concerned; it is in fact a destiny imposed upon her by her teachers and by society.
>
> *Simone de Beauvoir*

> It makes no difference whether pink is for girls and blue for boys, emotionality for girls and rationality for boys, or the other way round. What does make a difference is that a difference is made.... It is the bifurcation by sex that is the fundamental fact.
>
> *Jessie Bernard,* Women and the
> Public Interest

What is the essence of masculinity and femininity? To what extent are behavioural and psychological differences functions of biology? And what are the roles of social factors, influences, and expectations on the development of behaviour seen as appropriate for women and men?

. . . .

> Women are wiser than men because they know less and understand more.
>
> *James Stephens*

> Very learned women are to be found in the same manner as female warriors; but they are seldom or never inventors.
>
> *Voltaire*

> A woman is more influenced by what she suspects than by what she knows.
>
> *Bob Edwards*
> *(writer)*

> We must start with the realization that, as much as women want to be good scientists or engineers, they want first and foremost to be womanly companions of men and to be mothers.
>
> *Bruno Bettelheim*

The observation that women are less likely than men to be found as achievers in professional, artistic, political, and academic spheres has led many to the conclusion that women are less intelligent than men. Is this true? What are the intellectual differences between women and men? What are the factors contributing to these differences?

. . . .

To a great percentage of men a strictly monogamous life is either irksome, painful, disagreeable or an utter impossibility, while the number of women who are not satisfied with one mate is exceedingly small.

William J. Robinson

Nice, single girls *do* have affairs, and they do not necessarily die of them! They suffer sometimes, occasionally a great deal. However, quite a few "nice" girls have affairs and do not suffer at all!

Helen Gurley Brown

What is the nature of the differences in sexuality between women and men? Has the "sexual revolution" affected women and men equally?

. . . .

Women should remain at home, sit still, keep house, and bear and bring up children.

Martin Luther

The institution of marriage makes a parasite of woman, an absolute dependent. It incapacitates her for life's struggle, annihilates her social consciousness, paralyzes her imagination and then imposes its gracious protection, which is in reality a snare, a travesty on human character. . . .

Emma Goldman

How does marriage as a social institution affect women and men? While the structure of the family is undergoing tremendous change, what are the implications of these changes for women, men, and the relationship between them?

. . . .

The insistence that femininity evolves from necessarily frustrated masculinity makes femininity a sort of "normal pathology".

Judith Bardwick

Women tend to make their emotions perform the functions they exist to serve, and hence remain mentally much healthier than men.

Ashley Montagu

Who is mentally healthier — men or women? Are the origins of psychopathology the same in women and men?

. . . .

While women represent half the global population and one-third of the labor force, they receive only one-tenth of the world income and own less than one percent of the world property. They also are responsible for two-thirds of all working hours.

> *Kurt Waldheim, UN Secretary General,* Report to the UN Commission on the Status of Women

Whether women are better than men I cannot say — but I can say they are certainly no worse.

> *Golda Meir*

While women are increasingly entering the labour force, they still tend to be found in lower-paying and less prestigious jobs than men. Why?

. . . .

A young mother has taken her toddler shopping in a large supermarket. The child, an attractive three-year-old dressed in jeans and a sweater, is seated in its mother's shopping cart where it smiles at passing fellow shoppers. A stranger passing the pair in one of the aisles smiles back and says to the child, "Hello, what a cute little boy!" The stranger is greeted with a surprised and unamused look from the mother. The child shouts indignantly, "I'm not a boy; I'm a girl!"

The indignation aroused by this mistaken identification should not come as a surprise, since learning that one is either a male or a female is one of the first and most important things one learns as a young child. How do children learn that they are either female or male? What are the psychological implications of this knowledge for children?

. . . .

Gender-Role Differences: Stereotypes, Behaviour and Biology

Being born male or female in our culture means a great deal more than simply differing biologically. The sex of the newborn largely determines the nature of the experiences, attitudes, behaviours, feelings, and reactions of others that await the developing youngster. These are not randomly determined. In every society, there are norms or general rules that prescribe the behaviour and attitudes appropriate to members of a given sex group. These are conveyed and taught to the child beginning in infancy and continuing throughout the process of socialization. Not only does this ensure uniformity in behaviour and attitudes among members of a given sex group, but it also serves to prepare children for the roles they will enact as adults in their families and in their future employment. For example, the fact that so many adult women, despite differences in their intelligence, ability, and skills, are found in the housewife-mother role, is no accident. It is the inevitable result of a lifelong socialization programme designed to prepare females in our culture for this role. While childhood socialization is largely devoted to teaching the young girl the behaviours and attitudes necessary for her future domestic-maternal role with a de-emphasis on other possible roles, socialization of the young boy involves the inculcation of attitudes and behaviours thought to be necessary for his future occupational role. Very little of the male's socialization is aimed at preparing him for his parenting role.

In considering differences between the sexes, most psychological investigators and theorists differentiate between two sets of influences: the biological, which consists of genetic and physiological factors, and the environmental, including learning, social, and cultural determinants. The term *sex* has traditionally been used to refer sometimes to the biological aspect of an individual, and, at other times, to the socio-cultural characteristics of the person. Often, however, the investigator does not specify just what aspect of the individual is being referred to when the term *sex* is used. *Gender* has also been used differently by different people. We find that, at times, *gender* is used to refer to biological aspects of the person and, at others, it is employed to describe those aspects which result from learning. The inconsistent and ambiguous use of terms in the area of sex differences has thus made it very difficult indeed to know what writers mean when they use terms like "biological gender", "sex role", "gender role", or "sex-role identity".

In this regard, a number of psychological investigators, notably Reesa Vaughter,[1] Rhoda Unger,[2] and J. Martin Graham and Cannie Stark-Adamec,[3] have recently been drawing attention to the need for a clear, unambiguous definition of terms. Such a definition should distinguish between those aspects of "sex" associated with biological and physiological factors and those associated with social and cultural factors.[4] Thus, the following definitions are adopted and used in this book.

Definition of Terms

Sex is defined as a person's biological status, while *gender* refers to a person's learned or cultural status. Biologically, a person's sex may be female, male, or ambiguous (hermaphroditic). There are certain behavioural phenomena that follow from a person's biological status as a female or a male. So, for example, menstruation and gestation are sex-related female biological functions. Spermatogenesis and ejaculation are sex-specific male functions.

Gender and gender role are culturally assigned to a person on the basis of sex. While gender refers to one's status as feminine, masculine, or androgynous, *gender role* includes the prescribed behaviours, attitudes, and characteristics associated with gender status. *Gender-role identity* is the acceptance of oneself as feminine, masculine, or androgynous.

So while the attributes associated with *sex* are assigned on the basis of the person's biology, those attributed to *gender* are the result of learning in accordance with standards or prescriptions of the culture. Generally, a difference between males and females can be said to be due to *sex* and not *gender* when it meets the following criteria for biologically based determination: the sex difference occurs cross-culturally, it shows species continuity, it can be manipulated biochemically, and it appears early in development.[5]

Prerequisites for gender-role development seem to include learning sex and definitions of roles relating to sex, and learning to use sex as the salient cue for dichotomizing within a gender system. Not surprisingly, then, children's sex identity and their understanding of the conceptual system associated with sex develop earlier, more quickly, and are complete sooner than their gender-role identity and their understanding of the conceptual system associated with gender and gender role.[6,7] Knowledge of the culture's gender-role stereotypes is one of the most important factors in a child's development of gender-role identity.

Gender-Role Stereotypes

What are little girls made of? Sugar and spice, and everything nice; that's what little girls are made of.

What are little boys made of? Snips and snails, and puppy-dogs' tails;
that's what little boys are made of.

Nursery Rhyme

Sound familiar? These nursery rhymes are familiar because they have been
repeated in millions of homes. They are found in children's nursery rhyme
books and have been rehearsed in nursery schools for years. Through
simplicity and lyrical repetition, they convey to preschoolers the socially
prescribed characteristics for male and female children. What is more,
nursery rhymes constitute one of the ways in which children first learn
about how male and female children should behave.

Psychologists have found that there is substantial agreement in the
beliefs people hold regarding masculine and feminine gender roles.
Kagan,[8] a well-known psychologist, notes that the standards associated
with the roles assigned to girls and women emphasize "the ability to
experience deep feelings, to gratify love objects, and to elicit sexual arousal
in a male," while masculine standards emphasize "the ability to gratify a
love object . . . to be pragmatic, independent in judgment, and the ability to
control expression of fear" (p. 19). According to the gender-role
stereotypes operative in our society, women are supposed to be unaggressive physically, nurturant and caring toward others, friendly,
and attentive to their appearance. Men, on the other hand, are expected to
be physically and sexually assertive, independent, competent, and emotionally tough. In short, gender-role stereotyping is the promotion or
expression of commonly held beliefs about gender-role differences, sometimes to the point of caricature. Psychologists[9, 10] find that when respondents are asked to describe the characteristics of men and women in
general, men are viewed as being independent, objective, active,
competitive, adventurous, self-confident, and ambitious. Women are seen
as possessing the opposite of these traits. They tend to be described as
dependent, subjective, passive, not competitive, not adventurous, not self-
confident, and not ambitious. Women are further described as tactful,
gentle, aware of others' feelings, and able to express warmth. It would
appear, then, that among other things, the behaviour thought to be
appropriate for men will help them solve problems effectively, while the
behaviour prescribed for women should facilitate interpersonal relationships. What is more, it appears that people generally value masculine
characteristics more than feminine ones.[11, 12]

These results suggest that gender-role stereotypes consist of a
"political distribution" of traits whereby one group (males) is assigned a set
of traits that would facilitate their dominance and control of another
group (females), which, in turn, is assigned another, different set of traits
that would render them easily controlled. Moreover, the stereotypic
picture of men as the dominant gender group and women as the submissive
one is strikingly similar to the actual relative status of men and women in
our society.

All of us share stereotypes about masculine and feminine traits. These develop early in life. The child is consistently taught and gradually learns to associate selected attributes, behaviours, and attitudes with the concepts of masculine and feminine. Between the ages of three and seven years, the child gradually learns that people fall into one of two related categories: boys or girls, men or women, fathers or mothers.[13] One has only to see the anguish experienced by the "sissy" boy who is ridiculed by his male peers to be aware of the existence and operation of gender-role stereotypes and the psychological price of deviation. In contrast, the "tomboy" girl, while subjected to some ridicule, is accepted more readily. The "sissy" boy is probably ridiculed and punished more because he is seen as taking on a role which is lower in status than the one socially assigned to him. In contrast, the girl who is called a "tomboy" is seen as taking on a role which is higher in status because she is behaving in ways prescribed by the masculine gender role.

Gender-role stereotypes do have certain advantages, however. They serve a function in a society where continuity thrives on its members being able to predict with some certainty other people's behaviour. This can occur only when the members of a society internalize expectations of appropriate behaviour for men and women and regard them as generally agreed-upon guidelines for behaviour. Gender-role stereotypes also serve as a basis for judging other people's behaviour, and they may function as standards by which we all guide and evaluate our own behaviour and gender-role identity.

On the other hand, there are numerous disadvantages associated with the concept of stereotypes as they apply to women and men. Since they are generalized beliefs, it is assumed that if a person is of a particular sex, that person automatically possesses one genderized set of traits and lacks another. In all likelihood, an approach such as this will not produce an accurate depiction of an individual's personality. Thus, by their very nature, stereotypes cannot take into account the wide range of possible behaviours and traits that usually characterize the individual woman or man. Furthermore, whatever traits are usually thought of as distinctly masculine or feminine are also possessed by at least some members of the other sex. Finally, the all-or-none categorization involved in stereotyping is misleading because people are not so simple that they possess all of a particular trait or none of it. Results of psychological test taking show quite clearly that the majority of people will vary in the degree to which they possess a given characteristic.

One question frequently raised is this: Are gender-role stereotypes changing? Certainly the issue raised by this question is pertinent at a time when more and more people are accepting the tenets of the Women's Liberation Movement and equality between women and men has become a salient political and social issue. Research findings suggest that while there may not have been any recent substantial changes in gender-role stereotypes, women's evaluations of feminine traits are becoming more positive. One study,[14] for example, has found that college and high-school senior students were still perceiving men and women in the traditionally stereotyped manner: men were seen as aggressive, rough, dominant, and the like, while women were perceived as timid, sensitive, sociable, religious, and uncertain. But there is further research evidence that women are beginning to evaluate feminine traits more favourably than they did in the past. In 1960, for example, one investigator asked a group of college students to complete a series of statements about the opposite sex.[15] These are some examples of the statements used in the study: "I believe most women . . ." and "What I like least about men . . .". The results showed that women gave more favourable impressions of men than men gave of women. In more recent research,[16] however, female participants were found to assess feminine traits more positively than masculine ones. But male participants in the same study did not differentially value masculine and feminine characteristics. From this, it would seem that women are becoming more accepting of feminine characteristics that were not considered too socially desirable in the past. It may also be that women are beginning to see more value in their own attributes because of the impact of the Women's Liberation Movement which, among other things, encourages women to value themselves more as human beings. Evaluations of traditional stereotypes may be changing for men as well, since they tended to value feminine and masculine attributes to the same extent. All in all, the results of this study represent a considerable deviation from past research, which found that male and female participants evaluated masculine traits as more desirable than feminine ones.[17]

While everyone possesses stereotypic views of women and men, there are differences among people in the nature of these stereotypes, depending on whether or not their mothers have held outside employment. If a person's mother has worked outside the home, that individual tends to have a less stereotypic view of women.[18] Both men and women whose mothers have been employed tend to see very little difference between men and women in terms of warmth and expressiveness. Daughters of employed mothers also tend to see women as more competent than do daughters of more traditional full-time homemakers. However, men's judgements of competence do not seem to be altered by having an employed mother — probably because the mother is not the primary gender-role model for her son that she is for her daughter. Girls tend to identify more than boys (particularly as they get older) with their mothers and their mothers' activities. Apparently, these girls equate outside employment with competence in their mothers. In light of the growing numbers of wives and mothers entering the labour force, it is expected that the changes noted here will continue to develop.

Gender-Role Differences in Behaviour

On the basis of the earlier discussion about stereotyped attitudes, another question may now be raised: To what extent does *actual* behaviour correspond to these stereotypes? The answer to this question can be discovered by looking at some of the behaviours where differences between the sexes have been found. This examination of the behaviours that have been studied will not be exhaustive, but will represent those which most commonly come to mind when one thinks of "typical" gender-role differences.

Aggression and Dominance. Some of the stereotypic views about behavioural differences, such as greater aggressiveness in boys, have been borne out in research studies conducted during the last few decades. The central theme of aggression is the intent of one individual to hurt another — physically or psychologically. Most of the studies on aggression have been done with children as participants. Gender-role differences in aggressive activity have been found as early as the beginning of social play — at about two or two-and-a-half years when, in general, boys are more physically and verbally aggressive than girls.[19] The greater aggressiveness of boys does not appear to be limited to a specific situation, but can be found in a variety of settings. Specifically, boys have been found to engage in more negativistic behaviour, negative attention getting, antisocial behaviour, and physical aggression.[20-24] Boys have been observed to be not only more disruptive than girls in nursery school, but also more aggressive toward their peers.[25-27] So boys start off at a fairly early age being more aggressive than girls, beginning a trend that would seem to persist throughout childhood.

While young children — male and female — use aggression as a means of achieving dominance over others, as they get older, they substitute other, more complex social behaviours for achieving dominance. Not surprisingly, studies of dominance have revealed a greater tendency among men to try to dominate one another — most likely an outgrowth of the greater aggressiveness observed in boys in childhood. There is research evidence that by college age, male leaders use more authoritarian leadership methods than female leaders.[28] But being aggressive does not automatically ensure that anyone, a woman or a man, will be able to dominate others successfully. Successful dominance over others and effective leadership often depend on Machiavellianism — a disposition to view others as objects to manipulate in social interaction in order to achieve one's ends, and a tendency to do so given the opportunity. In this regard, flattery, bribery, deception, and even supporting other members of a group are techniques that may be used to gain one's ends. Thus, those who possess only stereotypically masculine traits of aggression and dominance are less likely to be good leaders than those who combine aggression and dominance with manipulative savvy. Indeed, a stereotypically masculine person who expresses physical and verbal aggression in a blatant or offensive manner may be an ineffective leader precisely because these behaviours will often produce exactly the opposite of the intended effect. The person who possesses power or the ability to influence, direct, or control others is probably well versed in techniques of psychological manipulation of individuals and groups. Here, also, a primarily aggressive style may interfere with, rather than facilitate, the effective wielding of power.

Dependency, Interdependence, and Independence. Girls and women are often thought to be more socially dependent and interdependent than boys and men. But to what extent is this conclusion supported by research data? Interpreting the data presents some problems in itself, since most of the research in this area makes no distinction between "dependency" and "interdependence". While "dependency" has been used variously to mean, among other things, the need for social approval and love in order to develop a sense of self-worth, "interdependence" is used here to refer to the ability to express interpersonal needs, particularly in emotional relationships and to relate meaningfully to others in interpersonal relationships.

There are those who argue that there are no differences in dependency between girls and boys in the early years.[29] This conclusion is based on a review of studies where the qualities used to define dependency include aspects of interdependence: proximity seeking and social responsiveness, for example. Other studies conclude that girls are more socially dependent than boys.[30] Girls have been found to seek help and/or information from others more than boys, and they have been found to maintain closer proximity to teacher or home, in addition to scoring higher on dependency scales in standard inventories.[31-37]

During childhood, dependency and interdependence are reinforced much more in girls than in boys. In their teenage and college years, girls and women have been found to be more dependent on others for approval and acceptance than boys and men.[38-42] The establishment of successful interpersonal relationships has been, and often still is, the most self-defining and rewarding achievement task for adolescent girls. While all very young children are dependent on adults for their physical well-being and for the knowledge that they are important, boys are discouraged from overt dependence on others for approval and acceptance. Although acceptance and approval remain important to the young boy, he is taught early in his childhood that they are contingent on his accomplishing something "worthwhile", such as excelling at sports. Because of prohibitions on remaining dependent as he did in the past, the young boy is forced to affirm himself in other ways, which leads him to seek achievements in the outer world and to value himself for these achievements according to objective criteria.[43] In the process of learning to evaluate himself against objective criteria, the developing boy is thus less directly dependent on others for his self-definition and sense of self-worth.

While boys are encouraged to develop greater independence and self-confidence, at the same time, they are not given as much opportunity as girls to develop a sense of interdependence. In learning to place less importance on the approval of others, they also learn to place less importance on interpersonal relationships in general. Trained to pursue goals other than interpersonal ones, boys and men do not develop a sense of interdependence to the same degree as girls and women. As a result of socialization pressures, many men may be unable to express their interpersonal needs in emotional relationships, thus making them more vulnerable to certain forms of psychopathology, since close emotional relationships are important to good psychological functioning (see Chapter 9).

While it is true that today women are seeking out and experiencing alternative sources of gratification to the traditional interpersonal ones, success, interpersonally, is nevertheless still of primary importance to them. While women probably remain more dependent and interdependent than men, there is a growing awareness of the desirability of men developing a greater sense of interdependence.

Anxiety. Are girls more anxious than boys? Early research findings reported in the 1930s and 1940s showed that, in general, girls were more anxious, fearful, and passive than boys and that girls had less self-confidence and lower opinions of themselves.[44] In later research, 8- to 11-year-old girls were found to be more anxious than boys when rated by their teachers.[45] While anxiety in young children is usually studied by having either teachers or investigators rate the child on various behavioural measures of anxiety, older children and adults participating in studies are asked to indicate how anxious they feel in certain situations. This method is known as the *self-report measure.* Like so many psychological measures, there are problems associated with it. For example, self-reports are often distorted by the respondent either as a result of memory loss or because of the respondent's need to present a certain image to the tester, an image which may or may not correspond with reality. However, many studies using self-report have had the same results: girls and young women are more fearful and generally more anxious than boys and young men.[46-50] Not only do girls and young women report that they experience more anxiety, but they are also more likely than their male counterparts to lack confidence in their ability to do well on a new task and, at times, they appear to have less control over what happens to them.[51]

However, another problem with self-report measures of anxiety raises some questions as to the validity of these research findings on anxiety. Could it be that girls obtain higher scores on these anxiety tests simply because they are more willing than boys to admit their true feelings of anxiety? Boys are taught fairly early in childhood that it is unmanly to admit to feelings of anxiety and fear. And, predictably, boys are less willing than girls to admit to weaknesses of various sorts.[52-54] Boys and young men may be more "defensive" than girls and young women when reporting their anxiety feelings and, as a result, may report lower anxiety than they actually experience. As far as self-reported anxiety is concerned, then, there is some question as to whether girls are "really" more anxious than boys.

Biological Factors, Sex and Gender-Role Differences

Gender-Role Identity:
The Role of Biology and Environment

According to the traditional view, a man's or woman's sense of masculinity or femininity is inherent, or almost entirely biologically determined. In human development, there is usually a consonance, or agreement, among the sex of the internal organs, the sex hormones, and the external genitalia. When a baby is born, the genitals usually clearly indicate whether it is a girl or a boy, and gender-role-appropriate rearing occurs.

In humans, 23 pairs of chromosomes are normally found in most cells of the body. Twenty-two of these pairs, the autosomes, carry genes that determine the various features of the individual. The remaining pair make up the sex chromosomes. In females, the sex chromosomes are a matched set (XX); males have one X and one Y chromosome. These are the chromosomes that carry the genetic material responsible for the individual's genetic sex. The genetic determination of sex, mediated by the Y chromosome, affects only the gonads — the testes and the ovaries. All other sexual differentiation is under hormonal control. During the first six or seven weeks of embryonic development, the structure of the gonads is undifferentiated — they are neither ovaries nor testes. At the same time, the basis of the male and female internal reproductive structures is present in two parallel systems of primitive genital ducts. The Mullerian duct system forms the basis of the fallopian tubes and the uterus; the Wolffian duct system represents the basis for the development of the male reproductive structures. Because the gonads are undifferentiated during the early weeks of embryonic life, it was thought in the past that the developing embryo was "neutral" or "bisexual". However, embryological research now suggests that the basic structure of the organism is female. "Something" must be added for male differentiation to occur,[55] and that is the Y chromosome. If a Y chromosome is present, the gonadal cells will differentiate as testes. The testes then begin production of two hormones which permit the foetus to develop further as a male. One of these inhibits the development of the Mullerian system, which, otherwise, would differentiate as female internal reproductive organs. The other is the androgenic hormone testosterone. The androgenic hormones, of which testosterone is the most potent, are called the male sex hormones because they are important in male sexual development. The male sex hormones promote the elaboration of the male Wolffian duct system. If the gonads that have elaborated as testes fail to initiate the secretion of the foetal hormones, the developing embryo proceeds to differentiate as a female, even though its genetic sex is XY. Thus, the development of female internal reproductive structures is not dependent on the presence of female hormones. In the absence of androgens, the Mullerian system will develop into fallopian tubes and a uterus, and the Wolffian system will become vestigial.

The external male and female genitalia develop from common embryonic structures. In humans, differentiation of the external genitalia begins around the eighth week of embryonic development; until then, the initial structures that will become the external genitalia are identical in males and females (Figure 2.1). These structures have the potential to differentiate as either female or male organs, depending on the influence of androgenic hormones. The undifferentiated genital tubercle will become a clitoris if androgens are absent; if androgens are present at a critical time, it will enlarge to form a penis. Without these hormones, the urethral folds remain separated to become the inner labial folds on either side of the vaginal opening; the presence of androgens causes the folds to fuse and form the urethral tube of the penis. Similarly, other tissues remain separated and become the outer labia of a female or form the scrotum of a male by fusing.[56]

Animal research has confirmed that elaboration of both internal and external sex structures is under hormonal control of the testes.[57] If the testes are removed from male embryos before they begin to differentiate as male, complete feminization of their development will occur. But the removal of ovaries from the female embryo has no effect on female differentiation. The female sex hormones (estrogen and progesterone) that are produced by the ovaries are not involved in the sexual differentiation of the female during foetal development.

Since female sexual differentiation proceeds innately if no gonads are present, some feminists have asserted that nature's basic form is female. The developing testes in males secrete hormones that initiate male differentiation. Thus, "embryologically speaking . . . it would be correct to say that the penis is an exaggerated clitoris rather than the reverse (p. 88)."[58] However, to argue that the female is therefore the norm for all human development merely perpetuates ideas of anatomical determinism and one-upmanship.[59,60]

In normal development, there is an agreement among chromosomes, internal and external sex organs, and the gender assigned to the child. Because biological and environmental (socialization) factors are influencing development in the same gender-role direction in normal

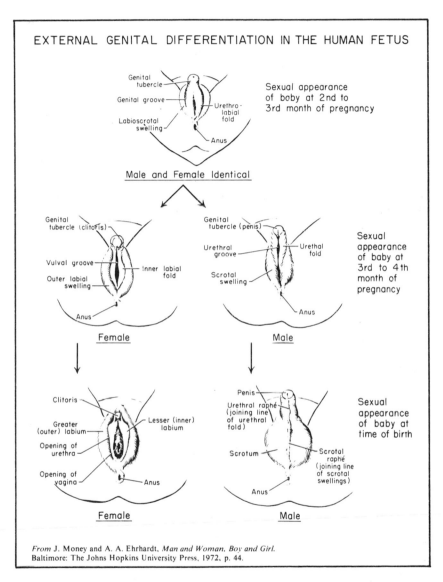

EXTERNAL GENITAL DIFFERENTIATION IN THE HUMAN FETUS

Sexual appearance
of baby at 2nd to
3rd month of pregnancy

Male and Female Identical

Sexual
appearance
of baby at
3rd to 4th
month of
pregnancy

Female   Male

Sexual
appearance
of baby at
time of birth

Female   Male

From J. Money and A. A. Ehrhardt, *Man and Woman, Boy and Girl.*
Baltimore: The Johns Hopkins University Press, 1972, p. 44.

Figure 2.1.   External Genital Differentiation in the Human Fetus
Three stages in the differentiation of the external genital organs. The male and the
female organs have the same beginnings and are homologous with one another.

development, it is difficult to assess the relative importance of the various factors in the formation of the child's gender-role identity.

There are some investigators, however, who have conducted a long programme of research on gender-role identity among people with *ambiguous* external genitalia. On the basis of their research with hermaphrodites, John Money and his associates[61-63] conclude that the acquisition of gender role and gender-role identity* is more dependent on the gender of rearing (environmental factors) than on biological determinants of sex, such as chromosomes or hormones. Hermaphrodites are people who may have both male and female tissues. True hermaphrodites are rare — they have one ovary and one testicle or a single organ containing both types of tissues and ambiguous-looking external genitalia. Pseudo-hermaphrodites (referred to below as hermaphrodites), who constitute most of the documented cases, have only one set of gonads (these may be testes or ovaries), but their external genitalia are either ambiguous in appearance or in conflict with internal sex organs and hormones. As Money and Tucker put it, "Hermaphrodites, also known as intersexes, are those in whom development of the sex organs took an incompatible turn at one of the forks in the road before birth (pp. 16-17)."[64]

How does this happen? In the case of the genetic male, the genitals of the hermaphrodite look ambiguous, or they resemble a clitoris, rather than a penis. One cause is found in a metabolic error that may prevent the genetically male foetus from producing the androgen that is critical for male development. A genetic defect may also cause the foetal organ cells to be insensitive to androgen, with the result that neither the internal reproductive male organs nor the external genitalia develop in the normal way.

A genetic female may develop into a hermaphrodite in one of two ways. A synthetic hormone administered to a pregnant woman may have a masculinizing effect. For example, one such hormone, progestin, was given to some pregnant women about 20 years ago to prevent miscarriage. Some of these women subsequently gave birth to babies with progestin-induced hermaphroditism. A genetic female may develop masculinized external genitalia if a malfunction of the adrenocortical glands causes the foetus to produce too much androgen. This is called adrenogenital syndrome.

When a hermaphrodite is born, there is usually a question as to whether the child is a boy whose testicles have not descended and who has a small open-guttered penis and an incompletely fused scrotum or whether the child is a girl with an enlarged clitoris and partially fused labia.[65] In these cases, the gender assigned to the child and subsequent rearing may or may not correspond to the genetic sex.

John Money and his coworkers use the term "gender identity" to refer to both the biological and cultural aspects associated with one's identity as male, female or ambiguous.

   In their research, Money and his associates have studied cases of matched pairs of congenital hermaphrodites who have the same apparent external genitalia at birth but are brought up according to different assigned gender roles.[66,67] For example, in one case, both children were genetic females with adrenogenital syndrome, which resulted in the genitals appearing masculine at birth.[68] The first child, originally thought to be male, was later reassigned as a girl. At two years of age, the child had surgery to correct her masculinized genitals. Later on, her behaviour was typically feminine except for her interest in "tomboyish" activities. The second child in the matched pair was misidentified at birth as male. Attempts to surgically masculinize the child's genitals were at first unsuccessful. The child was reared as a male all its life, and during this time "he" received appropriate surgery and androgen therapy. The child viewed itself as masculine, taking on its social, rather than its biological, identity (which was genetically female). Money notes that, in most of the cases, the socially imposed identity is the accepted one as long as there is no ambivalence about the child's gender-role identity. That is, if the parents are confused about the child's identity and are inconsistent in the way they treat the child, Money says that problems will likely result. On the basis of his studies, Money concludes that a person's psychosexual identity is established more in accordance with the gender assigned during rearing than with biological considerations such as chromosomes. There is a time period, however, after which it is supposed to be unwise to make a sexual reassignment because the child's gender-role identity has been established. This is called the critical period and is hypothesized as being between 18 months and 3 years. According to Money, then, the human is so amenable to the effects of learning and the environment that even the effects of biological factors on psychosexual identity can be completely reversed by early childhood training.

   But Money's position has not gone unchallenged. Among the criticisms levelled against him for the conclusion he has drawn from his research is the claim that one cannot generalize findings from people whose sex is ambiguous in the first place to people of unambiguous sex. But Money has supplied data which show that a reversal of biological sex assignment is also possible in people of unambiguous sex if it occurs early enough and if there is consistency in gender-role rearing. For example, one frequently cited case involves a set of male identical twins, one of whom was involved in an accident during circumcision in which his penis was destroyed.[69] He was reassigned as a female at 17 months and received surgical and hormonal treatment. The parents treated the two children differently and dressed them differently. The "girl", for example, was encouraged more to help with the housework. Not surprisingly, by age nine, the two children were showing stereotypically masculine and feminine characteristics.

   There are still many opponents of Money's view, who lay heavier emphasis on biological contributions in the development of gender role and gender-role identity and they cite numerous studies to support their view. [70,71] One well-known critic of Money asserts, for example, that just because Money has demonstrated that humans can be flexible in their psychosexual identification does not disprove that built-in biases must be overcome.[72] The controversy continues between those who place the greatest importance on biological predispositions and those who point to learning, experience, and training as key factors in the development of psychosexual identity. Nevertheless, Money's research demonstrates quite dramatically how malleable a human's gender-role identity can be.

The Role of Biology in Behaviour

In the past, many biologists assumed that a unidirectional causation existed between physiological factors and social behaviour. Those who have drawn heavily on biology to explain differences in behaviour between women and men have regarded the hormonal differentiation between the sexes as a basic determinant of sex-linked psychological characteristics and behaviours. Since there has been little research linking biological factors with psychological characteristics, statements on the subject remain hypothetical. However, it has been found that biological factors do play a role in certain general areas of behaviour, including aggression and maternal behaviour.

Aggression. The frequently observed association between the expression of physical aggression and being male has led many to hypothesize that male hormones play a significant role in aggressive behaviour. What is the evidence for a biological basis of male aggression? Research in this area has focused on how hormones affect the behaviour of rats and monkeys. In one type of study, pregnant females are injected with androgen and the behaviour of their female offspring is observed. These females have been found to show more threat (aggressive) behaviour and less withdrawal from others than normal female monkeys.[73]

It is difficult to generalize these results directly to humans, simply because there are few cases in human development where genetic females receive excess amounts of male hormones prenatally. When this does happen in humans, however, it can result from abnormal activity of the adrenal glands of the foetus, as well as from injection of masculinizing hormones during pregnancy. For example, in one study where 17 foetally androgenized girls (who suffered from an adrenal deficiency) were compared with their 11 normal sisters, the androgenized girls were "masculinized" in the following ways as they got older: they preferred playing with boys; they took little interest in traditionally feminine activities such as doll play; and they preferred outdoor sports. They also tended to initiate fighting more than their "normal" sisters.[74] Despite this consistency with the results reported earlier for monkeys, those for humans need to be interpreted cautiously for at least two reasons. First, the androgenized girls were receiving treatment with cortisone throughout childhood to correct the original adrenal condition. We do not know to what extent changes in the girls' behaviour were functions of this drug. Second and perhaps more important is the fact that reports of the girls' behaviours were given by their mothers. It is quite conceivable that, knowing their daughters had received abnormally high amounts of androgen, the mothers might have been predisposed to perceiving their daughters as "masculine". Nevertheless, research with animals suggests that sex hormones that are present before or at the time of birth may sensitize or "programme" the individual so as to affect behaviour in childhood as well as in adulthood.[75]

In talking about the role of biological factors in aggressive behaviour, we should look to the hormone-brain-behaviour system.[76] Observers have hypothesized that, at a very early developmental stage (prenatally), the hypothalamus of the brain becomes indelibly "sex-typed" through the action of sex hormones, with the result of predisposing the organism to "male" or "female" responses. The primary effect of prenatal androgens is frequently referred to as the development of a "male brain". This means that the brain's functions in controlling the production of hormones are set in a particular way, depending on the amount of testosterone present at a crucial period of prenatal growth. From this, it may be concluded that the presence of certain levels of androgens typically found in males may biologically prepare males more than females to learn aggression. Presumably, then, there is a sex-linked differential readiness to respond aggressively in the two sexes.

Girls and women, however, are capable of acting aggressively as well. For example, in the seventies, wives have been reported to be responsible for almost as much nonlethal violence within the family as husbands.[77,78] Some people have even argued that women are worse child abusers than men.[79,80] Although there is an association between male hormones and aggressive behaviour (mainly physical in nature), there are other important factors which contribute to an individual's aggressive behaviour. These consist of experiential and learning factors that exist throughout an individual's lifetime. Learning theory and the various propositions and deductions associated with it provide some insight into how aggressive behaviour may vary as a result of a person's experiences. For instance, a parent's use of physical and/or verbal aggression in disciplinary measures may well constitute a role model which children will follow, thus increasing their own aggressiveness. Similarly, when aggressive behaviour meets with positive sanctions in the form of approval, acceptance, and other positive reactions, it is likely to occur more frequently in the future. Conversely, if aggressive behaviour is punished or generally disapproved of, particularly by those important to the child, aggression should decrease, all other things being equal.

What, then, can be said about the generally greater aggressiveness of the human male? As was seen earlier, male hormones may create a greater readiness or predisposition in human males to act aggressively. This means that the human male may have a greater *potential* for aggressive behaviour, not that male hormones are the cause of aggressive behaviour. We cannot assume a unidirectional causation between biological factors (hormones) and behaviour because social experiences and learning are extremely important in shaping the developing child's behaviour. Young boys are often encouraged to play aggressively and are frequently provided with aggressive toys, such as guns and other weapons. On the other hand, girls' aggressive behaviour is not encouraged; it is either ignored or punished. Rather than being provided with toys that elicit aggressive behaviour, girls are usually given toys that evoke caretaking

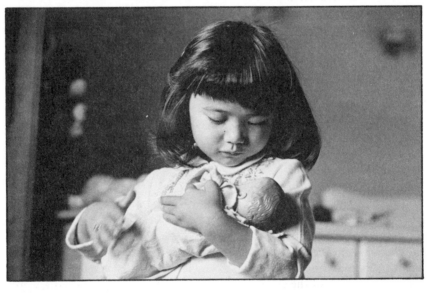

NFB PHOTOTHEQUE ONF ©

behaviour. In explaining the male's greater aggressive behaviour, then, two sets of factors — the biological and the environmental — have to be taken into account. If young boys are encouraged to be aggressive, as is the case when they are encouraged to play aggressively, their experience is congruent with their biological "readiness", and we should not be surprised to find boys behaving more aggressively than girls.

Maternal Behaviour. While it is a biological fact that only women can bear children, does it follow that women alone are capable of raising and nurturing them? The assumption that the biological mother must be the major responsible adult in the infant's life is related to the unsubstantiated theory that women have an instinct to mother which, for biological reasons, men do not share. From earliest recorded history to the present day, this assumption has been based on observations confirming that women, not men, are usually the ones who nurture and raise the children.

Since the rise of the Women's Liberation Movement, discussion has frequently centred on the mothering role and women: How necessary is this role to women's fulfillment? Is there such a thing as a maternal instinct? Now that the role of wife-mother is no longer seen as women's primary one and alternative roles have become available, these questions have acquired greater urgency and are frequently debated.

Is there a maternal instinct in humans? While not employed too frequently today, the word "instinct" was widely used in the past to refer to unlearned, patterned, goal-directed behaviour characteristic of a species, and usually was assumed to be tied to the presence of specific hormones. In general, evidence from studies using animals as subjects supports the concept of a maternal instinct in subhuman species. But as one progresses up the phylogenctic scale, biological factors play a decreasingly important role as determinants of behaviour, and learning and experience become more important. The concept of a maternal instinct in rats is supported by research indicating that female sex hormones associated with pregnancy and parturition seem to be implicated in the development of maternal behaviour. For example, when blood plasma taken from female rats that had recently given birth was administered to virgin females, the latency was reduced for these virgin animals to show maternal behaviour such as retrieving, nest building, and licking pups.[81] Although a virgin female will show such behaviour without hormonal treatment when given pups, the delay in the behaviour's appearance is two or three times as long as when maternal plasma has been given.

The development of maternal behaviour is also accelerated by early and continued exposure to the newly born animal. In the human baby's earliest days of life, its appearance and behaviour provide cues for the caretaker — mother, father, or other custodian — to respond by looking after the child. The rounded shape of the newborn's head, its plump cheeks, the smell of the skin, the hunger cry, and the exploring hands and mouth are just some of the signs that evoke care and attention for the baby. There is a special kind of intensive learning during the first minutes and hours after birth, which is a sensitive period for the development of attachment between mother and neonate.[82] This process is similar to, although much more complicated than, imprinting, the process described by Lorenz,[83] who observed geese and found that when the chicks hatched they followed the first large moving object they saw, whether it was their mother, another animal, or Lorenz himself. What is more, it has been noted that if these attachment mechanisms are interrupted for any reason, the young tend to develop abnormally. Although human newborn babies do not become attached to the first moving object that they see (e.g., the doctor and nurses who delivered them) attachment is formed very early (to their caretakers). Among rats, the stimulation from the pups during the first few days following parturition is crucial in establishing and maintaining the mother's responsiveness toward the pup.[84] If a mother is separated from her pups just after delivery for a period of two to four days, she will not effectively rear a substitute litter. "Parental" behaviour has also been found among virgin females and males with sufficient exposure to newborns. But, in contrast to the female that has given birth, and thus may be considered hormonally "primed", "parental" behaviour in males and in female virgins was not found to be readily aroused, appearing only after several days of exposure to the pups.[85] Evidence from animal studies suggests, then, that hormonal factors operate in concert with the eliciting properties of the young pup to maintain maternal behaviour. But it is also interesting to note that "maternal" behaviour can appear in animals that lack the hormones associated with pregnancy and parturition. The presence of the young is sometimes enough to evoke maternal behaviour.

Our present state of knowledge tells us very little about the potential of adult humans for nurturant behaviour towards infants. It is possible, however, that the hormones associated with pregnancy, childbirth, and lactation may contribute to a readiness to care for a young infant in a woman who has just given birth. However, since little is known about the role of hormones in initiating and maintaining maternal behaviour in humans, the suggestion that they are important would, at best, be speculative.

"Wendy and I were playing house. She muttered something about the 'alteration of biological history', handed me the kids, and split!"

Copyright © 1982, Randy Jay Glasbergen.

There is reason to question the existence of a maternal instinct in human females. While it may be true that the new mother is sensitive to the needs of her baby, it is also true that a woman who has just given birth to her first child and has not previously cared for an infant has great difficulty in the first days of the baby's life in establishing feeding, whether by breast or bottle. It has also been reported that new mothers often have to be taught how to hold, burp, bathe, and dress the baby.[86] But instinctive behaviour, which is supposed to come "naturally", would not have to be taught. Moreover, how can we explain the growing popularity of La Leche

League, an international breast-feeding organization, and the fact that increasing numbers of women are turning to it for advice on breast feeding if it is supposedly instinctive behaviour? If this most basic maternal behaviour has to be learned, the assertion that it is a function of instinct is disputable.

The assumption of a universal maternal instinct in females implies that any female is better equipped, for biological reasons, to care for the young than a male. But recent research suggests that even with little exposure to infants, the human male has more potential for nurturant

Courtesy Miller Services Ltd.

behaviour than was previously thought. For example, in one study of newborns who were observed in hospitals with both parents, fathers generally engaged in more nurturant interaction with the infants than did mothers.[87] When only one parent was present with the baby, fathers engaged in as much nurturant behaviour as the mothers, or more. Recorded behaviours included which parent initially took the child when it was brought into the room and the amount of looking, touching, rocking, holding, and smiling in the parent-child interaction. It is possible, of course, that the mothers may have interacted less with their newborns because of fatigue and discomfort following their labour and delivery. Nevertheless, the demonstration that fathers were able to behave in a variety of nurturant ways toward their newborns belies the traditional attitude that women have a monopoly on the "maternal instinct".

Not only is it possible that someone other than the mother is capable of nurturant behaviour toward a newborn; in addition, there is reason to believe that the skills needed to satisfy an infant's basic needs can be developed in alternative caretakers to the mother. For example, it has been shown that infants can actively initiate social interaction with their caretakers and can also modify their caretakers' behaviour.[88,89] So, contrary to traditional assumptions about the innate and unlearned quality of maternal behaviour, it appears that the behaviour necessary for infant caretaking is shaped, to some extent, by the infant itself. It follows, then, that the responses and skills required to satisfy the infant's needs can be developed in someone other than the mother so that she need not be the principal caretaker of her infant. Others who may care for the child as well include the father and/or other socially acceptable alternatives. In this regard, it is interesting to note that the major books and manuals telling women how to be "good" mothers have been written by men. This observation has led to the somewhat amusing conclusion that even though women have the babies, men have the maternal instinct.[90]

It is also important to note that, historically, women's drive for children has been modified by social conditions. When childbearing and childrearing provide the only socially acceptable adult roles for women, it is easy to assume the existence of a universal maternal instinct in women, simply because they are not occupying any role other than the maternal one. But when alternative social and occupational roles are available to women, along with more effective forms of birth control and legal medical abortion facilities, the birth rate drops and the number of childless women rises. The behaviour of the human animal is enormously plastic and variable, changing in response to altering social conditions. In fact, human beings' ability to adapt their behaviour to changing social conditions, rather than persist in the fixed behaviour that was previously thought to be a function of instinct, is one of the significant characteristics that sets the human apart from infrahuman species.

Femininity, Masculinity, and Androgyny

Until quite recently, few people questioned the basic assumptions that women were supposed to be feminine and men, masculine. These traditional attitudes about gender-role typing have been so ingrained that any deviations from culturally prescribed gender-role behaviour were considered maladaptive and undesirable. For years, people have taken it for granted that adjustment and psychological health depended largely on an individual's conformity to his or her gender role. While women have traditionally been encouraged to be sweet, cuddly, passive, and dependent, men have had to be tough, independent, brave, and assertive. But the assumption that high levels of gender-role typing are signs of good psychological adjustment has recently come under heavy attack. For example, it has been pointed out that the implicit cultural prescriptions requiring men to appear confident, decisive, in control, and to provide security for those presumed to be less competent, such as women and children, likely create undue pressure for the man.[91] This pressure is then expressed in anxiety, stress, or excessive competitiveness, and, perhaps, is also a major contributor to the occurrence of earlier death among men.

Although high masculinity has been related to better psychological adjustment in adolescent males, it is often accompanied by high anxiety and neuroticism, and low self-acceptance during adulthood.[92,93] Likewise, the restrictiveness associated with the prescriptions of the feminine gender role often precludes the expression of independence, assertiveness, and strength, all of which are necessary for individual self-expression. What is more, high femininity in girls and women has been correlated with high anxiety and low self-esteem.[94-96] Intellectual ability is also lower among people who have adopted traditional gender roles than among those who have not. Boys who are strongly masculine and girls who are strongly feminine tend to have lower overall intelligence, lower spatial ability, and lower creativity.[97] In effect, traditional gender roles impose the full burden of gender-role stereotypes and also prevent both women and men from expressing their best traits should those traits not coincide with the characteristics prescribed by their gender roles.

Even psychological measures of femininity and masculinity reflect the bias that they represent polar opposites. Traditional measures of psychological masculinity and femininity have been predicated on the assumption that they define endpoints of a unidimensional (single), bipolar continuum. Are the concepts of masculinity and femininity so simple that they can be scored on just one scale? Or are several scales necessary to describe them? The assumption of bipolarity also means that masculinity and femininity are opposites of each other and that the more feminine one is, the fewer masculine traits one has. Clearly, this is often not the case. Traditional psychological measures of masculinity and femininity have been shown to be inadequate because they fail to capture the full complexity of the human personality. To define masculinity as not feminine and femininity as not masculine precludes characterizing people as *both* feminine and masculine or as neither.

Androgyny and Beyond

Having become aware of the limitations of traditional conceptions of femininity and masculinity, feminists, social scientists, and feminist social scientists alike, began to search for a new standard of psychological health — one that allowed for the expression of the individual's best traits regardless of gender role. What was needed was a concept that took into account the coexistence of masculine and feminine characteristics in a woman or man. In modern thought, this idea was first expressed by Carl Jung[98] in his discussion of the concepts of animus and anima as unconscious archetypes: images of types of people that evoke emotional responses in the individual. The animus is the woman's masculine archetype and her unconscious male personality. The anima is the man's feminine archetype and his unconscious female personality. Jung felt that by integrating both feminine and masculine aspects into the conscious personality, women and men would reach their full potential. Jung's focus on the integration of the masculine and feminine aspects of one's personality can be regarded as a means of achieving androgyny.

The term androgyny, derived from the Greek roots *andro* (meaning man) and *gyn* (meaning woman), refers to the possession of both masculine and feminine characteristics. An androgynous person has both masculine and feminine traits. Sandra Bem [99] developed the first measure of psychological androgyny which treats masculinity and femininity as two separate dimensions. A person can obtain high scores on both scales, whereas on sex role* inventories used in the past, a person could receive only one score — toward one or the other end of the masculine-feminine continuum. The Bem Sex Role Inventory (BSRI) is a self-report measure consisting of 60 adjectives or descriptive phrases. Respondents are asked to indicate how well each describes them on a scale from one to seven. Twenty of the adjectives are stereotypically feminine and include such characteristics as affectionate, gentle, understanding, and sensitive to others' needs. Another 20 are stereotypically masculine. Some of the masculine adjectives are as follows: ambitious, self-reliant, independent, and assertive. Twenty additional adjectives are neutral — that is, not gender typed. Once the test has been taken, each respondent is given two scores: a masculinity score and a femininity score. An androgynous person is one who scores high on both masculinity and femininity.

The androgynous individual is said to possess the ideal personality. He or she is said to be adaptive, flexible, and effective in particular interpersonal contexts.[100–102] The androgynous person should also have an advantage in the intellectual area: both women and men who are androgynous would possess intellectual strengths associated not only with their own role, but also with other gender roles. The organizing ability required to receive information and understanding rests on a balance between assertiveness and the ability to suspend aggressiveness.[103] Androgynous women and men can show competence in behavioural spheres that

---

Sex role refers to gender role here.

are nurturant and emotionally expressive, as well as those characterized by assertiveness and independence. In other words, their competence is not limited to behaviours usually associated with their particular gender role. They are just as comfortable and competent engaging in activities associated with another gender role as they are doing same-gender ones. Bem and her research associates report that the androgynous man, when observed in experimental situations, plays with kittens and human infants, is not easily swayed in his opinions, and tends to be sympathetic toward a lonely student. Similarly, the androgynous woman could be independent and assertive or warm and responsive in the appropriate situations.[104-106] Thus, a man who is living up to his androgynous potential is able to express his feelings of tenderness and gentleness. He does not fear losing his masculinity in situations that require him to be passive or nurturant, as when he is with those who are helpless, such as small children or animals. The androgynous man is equally able to function in a protective role when that is required of him. An androgynous woman can also function equally well in different ways, depending on what the situation requires. Thus, not only can she retain the warmth and sensitivity typically associated with the feminine gender role, but she is also able to act with confidence and independence in competitive and other situations requiring behaviours usually associated with the masculine gender role.

Although androgyny has been thought to be associated with good adaptation, it may be more adaptive for women than for men. This was demonstrated quite dramatically in a series of studies [107] in which a total of 1404 college students (women and men) were given the Bem Sex Role Inventory to measure their role orientation. Their psychological adjustment was also assessed in a variety of areas. A pattern of findings replicated across such measures as gender-role identification, neurosis, introversion-extraversion, sexual maturity, helplessness, and self-esteem, to name only a few, indicated that flexibility and adjustment were generally associated with masculinity, rather than with androgyny, for both men and women. In no case were androgynous men found to be significantly more adaptive, flexible, or competent than masculine men. The women who were more masculine in orientation were also more adaptive, competent, and secure than their less masculine counterparts. A subsequent study in the same research programme revealed that both feminine and androgynous men wanted to become more masculine, whereas masculine men indicated little desire to change. As was the case with men, it was the feminine women who expressed the greatest desire to change in the direction of masculinity, with less desire for change indicated by androgynous women, and least by masculine women. So, the less masculine the person, the more desirable increased masculinity became. These results are to be expected, considering that we live in a society that values instrumental traits such as dominance, assertiveness, and independence — those typically associated with masculinity. Another consideration here is that people who possess masculine traits are probably considered more successful in society, since they likely receive more social rewards and, as a result, feel more confident. The findings should also lead us to question the advisability of current efforts to develop clinical techniques aimed at the "androgynization" of traditional men and women in a society that places greatest value on instrumental traits, those typically associated with masculinity.

Another problem with the androgyny construct centres around the question of whether it truly represents movement away from the restrictiveness of gender roles, toward the free expression of behaviour. It has been argued that the concept of androgyny does not really eliminate gender-role stereotypes, but combines them in a different way.[108] Essentially, feminine and masculine qualities are seen as coexisting in the androgynous personality. While allowing for individual expression, then, the idea of androgyny continues to perpetuate the concept of the duality of masculine and feminine characteristics.

Is it really necessary to think of personality traits as masculine or feminine? To what extent are these, in fact, artificial classificatory devices that have little to do with the reality of personality?[109] After all, personality is ultimately composed of a unique combination of psychological traits. It is possible to conceptualize personality without reference to organizing principles such as gender roles. Some have proposed that in order for individuals to be complete and to actualize their personal potential, they must transcend their gender roles.[110-112] According to theories of gender-role transcendence, conventional gender-role standards and gender-role identity are only stages in gender-role development that lead ultimately to the stage where no gender role exists — that is, to a transcendence of gender roles. While some consider androgyny to be the final stage of this process, others envisage the final stage as a unisex society. The ultimate identity of the individual would be a human one, freed, in effect, from the social expectations that accompany traditional gender roles. Although such a model is theoretically and psychologically appealing, it may represent a utopia at this particular stage in society's evolution. At the present time, the concepts of femininity and masculinity are firmly grounded in political and social differentiation that is ubiquitous throughout society.

Socialization of Girls and Boys: How Gender Roles Are Acquired

A person's gender role is a significant social fact. It is important because it has predictable consequences, not only for the individual, but also for the individual's relationships with others. Gender roles are so tightly woven into the fabric of society that no individual's development is free from their influence. In view of their importance — both psychologically and socially — it is relevant to raise certain questions about their development. For example, at what stage are gender roles acquired and what are the processes involved in their acquisition? What is the nature of these roles?

In the acquisition of gender roles, socialization is a key concept. As used here, socialization refers to the processes by which an individual acquires the attitudes, language, norms, and values necessary to function in a given society. It also involves continuous learning to perform various social roles throughout one's lifetime. Gender-role socialization refers to the processes by which an individual acquires the behaviours, attitudes, values, emotional responses, and personality characteristics defined as appropriate for his or her gender role. These vary from one culture to another.

As Margaret Mead[1] has demonstrated in her now-classic study of three New Guinea tribes, there may be marked differences in the specific behaviours and personality characteristics ascribed to males and females in different cultures. Among the Arapesh, for example, one of the cultures she describes, both males and females are socialized (and expected) to be loving, caring, gentle, nurturant, responsive, co-operative, and willing to subordinate themselves to the needs of others. Therefore, the personality characteristics that are inculcated in members of the Arapesh society are those defined as "feminine" traits in North America. Compare this culture with another New Guinea tribe, the Mundugumor, or headhunters, who expect their women and men to be aggressive, not nurturant. Additional predominant personality characteristics among these people are hostility, hatred, and suspicion. In a third culture, the Tchambuli, the women are typically dominant, impersonal, and managing, and the men are usually less responsible and more emotionally dependent — something of a reversal of stereotypes associated with the roles assigned to women and men in North American society. Aside from demonstrating the malleability of the human personality, Mead's study provides evidence that environmental (socialization) factors carry more weight than biological ones in determining what characteristics are considered to be masculine and feminine. Through the processes of selective reinforcement, personality can be shaped during socialization to conform to the expectations of a society's members. The demonstration of the importance of environmental factors as contributors to the shaping of personality does not, of course, rule out the influence of biological factors whose contribution to personality may not always be immediately obvious.

While Mead's study has been repeatedly cited as evidence of the plasticity of human personality and behaviour, other research findings dispute her results. For example, one investigator has argued that even among the Arapesh, it is the male who not only retained ultimate power in that society, but who also was solely responsible for organizing collective aggressive activity, including waging war.[2] The same investigator has disputed Mead's original findings that similar gender roles existed for women and men among the Arapesh.

Cross-cultural studies of gender roles can be very informative. Despite the tendency of most cultures to make their own definitions of gender-role-appropriate behaviour, there are some regularities in the definition of gender roles among various cultures. For example, most societies organize their social institutions around men and, as was discussed earlier, men in most cultures tend to behave more aggressively and to have greater authority than women. In many cultures, the division of labour falls along gender-role lines: men are most often assigned the physically strenuous and dangerous tasks, and they are often required to travel long distances from home to their various tasks. Women usually carry out domestic routines, look after the children, and minister to the needs of others. In most societies, cross-cultural regularities also exist in the personalities of boys and girls: while boys tend to engage in conflict and overt, observable aggression, girls are more frequently found to be affectionate, co-operative, responsive, and sociable.[3]

These cross-cultural regularities in behaviour may be partly the result of biological differences between females and males. For example, it is usually the male who possesses the potential for greater physical strength. The biological facts that only females can give birth and nurse the young caused females (in many societies) to remain close to home, at least while their offspring were young. Of course, while it is true that only the female can give birth to the young, even a nursing mother need not stay close to home all the time today. The combination of breast and bottle (to provide food while the mother is away from the infant during the day) can work remarkably well should the mother wish to return to her employment shortly after she gives birth. Within only a few weeks, the breasts adjust their milk supply to the needs of the mother-baby couple.

However, there are cultures, such as that of the Tchambuli, where the usual gender-role assignments do not apply or may even be reversed. And in many cultures, including our own, there are "normal" individuals who possess traits most commonly ascribed to another gender role than their own. Depending on factors in the person's environment, including others' expectations regarding gender-role-appropriate behaviour, personality can be shaped to develop in any of several directions.

An individual develops a gender role not within a vacuum, but within a dynamic social system which exerts a powerful influence on the direction that development takes. In order to get a comprehensive picture of how individuals acquire their gender roles, it is important to understand the influence of various social institutions, social forces, and groups of various kinds that make up this social system. These various influences gradually shape appropriate gender-role behaviour through the systematic application of positive and negative sanctions. While the influence of the social system is lifelong, much of our discussion of gender-role socialization will focus on the individual's early years (up to adolescence), since gender-role identity develops in the early years and stays with the individual throughout life. In this regard, the family must be viewed as one of the most significant agents of gender-role socialization.

The Family as an Agent of Gender-Role Socialization

It is in the family that society's expectations of gender-role-appropriate behaviour, as mediated by the parents, are first impressed upon the child. The child depends on its parents over a relatively long period not only for the satisfaction of its basic needs, such as food and shelter, but also for the fulfillment of its psychological needs, including the needs for acceptance and approval. This results in the parents being invested with an unparalleled amount of power. They control virtually all the child's resources, at least in early life. The parents' possession of such power over the child's material and psychological resources renders it relatively easy for them to shape their children's behaviour in the direction of their expectations, including those relating to gender-role-appropriate behaviour. And parents have certain preconceived ideas of how males and females should think, behave, and be. Based on social stereotypes, these ideas frequently act as guides for the parents' behaviour when they are interacting with their developing children. Parents also serve as role models for their children. Through their teaching and their examples, parents are preparing their children for the roles which they think the children will enact as adults. The discussion of the family as an agent of socialization will focus on the parents as role models, parent-child interactions, and the influence of toys and activities designated as appropriate for girls or boys.

Parents' Sex Preference

Long before the child's birth, parents start to discuss their preference for a girl or a boy, and frequently they discuss possible names for the child. "Pregnant couples" delight in predicting the sex of the child on the basis of such things as how high the woman is carrying and how hard the foetus is kicking. If, in the last trimester of pregnancy, the foetus is active, kicking,

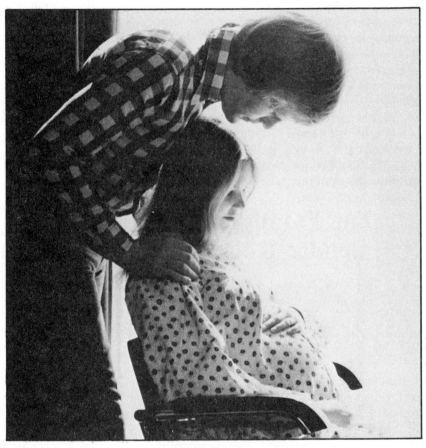

Courtesy Miller Services Ltd.

and moving a great deal, mothers have been reported to interpret these as signs that the child was a male.[4] But the wish to be surprised by the sex of the child when it is born is so strong in some couples that even when they can be informed of its sex beforehand by a procedure called amniocentesis, many couples choose not to be told. Amniocentesis involves withdrawing some amniotic fluid, which contains cells cast off from the foetus. The cells of the amniotic fluid are cultured and analyzed, and the resulting chromosomal study allows prenatal diagnosis of various chromosomal defects associated with the foetus, including Down's syndrome (also known as mongolism), which results in some degree of mental retardation.

The child's sex is also evident from the arranged set of chromosomes.

At birth, the most dominant characteristic used to describe the baby is its sex. While some birth announcements provide information on other physical characteristics of the infant (such as its weight) virtually all of them announce whether "it's a boy!" or "it's a girl!". Even before the child is born and certainly afterwards, parents, friends, and the social community are labelling and then responding to the child in a sex-differentiated fashion.

Parents do not want boys and girls to the same extent. Prospective parents tend to prefer boys, although this trend is less frequent now than it was in the past. In an American national-sample study reported in 1977, over 1500 married women under 40 and 25% of their husbands were asked whether they wanted to have boys or girls.[5] While most wanted children of either sex, the preference was still clearly for boys. Almost twice as many of the women preferred boys as preferred girls, and three to four times as many men preferred boys to girls. In the same study, prospective parents were asked why they wanted a boy or a girl. This type of question should yield information on the kinds of expectations people have for a son and a daughter. Some of the reasons given by the women for wanting a boy were to please their husbands, to carry on the family name (the husband's family name), and to be a companion to their husbands. Women wanted a girl in order to have a companion for themselves, and many of them said it would be fun to dress up a girl. They also said that girls are easier to raise, they are more obedient, and girls can help with the housework and the care of other children. Many agreed that girls stay closer to their parents and are sweeter and cuter. In view of prospective parents' preference for boys, as well as their different expectations for male and female children, it should not be surprising to learn that parents treat boys and girls differently.

Babies

All babies cry. This is a fact that can be verified by asking parents anywhere in the world. But how do people interpret crying behaviour? There is reason to believe that people may interpret a baby's crying differently, depending on whether the baby is a boy or a girl. In one study,[6] for example, a videotape of a nine-month-old crying baby was observed by a group of people, some of whom were led to believe it was a boy, while others were told it was a girl. The baby was videotaped reacting to a series of four stimuli: a teddy bear, a jack-in-the-box, a doll, and a buzzer. The results were that people attributed the baby's crying to different causes, depending on what they perceived was the sex of the baby. When the baby cried, the observers who thought it was a boy said that the baby was angry; those who thought it was a girl said that the baby was afraid. These impressions have important implications for how people would have treated the baby. Those who thought the baby was afraid, would have been more likely to hold and cuddle it than those who thought the baby was angry. In the latter case, people would likely have tried to restrain, discipline, or ignore the baby, rather than comfort it.

This raises the question of how parents view the behaviour of their male and female infants. Research suggests that as early as the infant's first day of life, parents tend to perceive their male and female babies in stereo-typed ways. In one study,[7] 30 sets of parents of newborns were asked to describe their infants. The daughters were described more often as little, beautiful, cute, weak, delicate, and as resembling their mother. Sons were described more often as firmer, larger-featured, better co-ordinated, more alert, stronger, and hardier. It is important to note, however, that because the male and female babies were equal in body dimensions and activity level, the actual viewing and holding of the babies could not have produced such different descriptions. This study illustrates well how preconceived gender-role stereotypes lead to different kinds of descriptions of male and female babies.

"It's not easy planning a dynamic, forceful, industrious future when everyone keeps referring to you as a 'itty bitsie peachy pie'."

Do parents treat male and female infants differently? Research has shown that, in some ways, they do. For example, parents tend to play more roughly and vigorously with their infant sons than with their infant daughters. In other words, both mothers and fathers seek to elicit gross motor behaviour more in their sons than in their daughters.[8-10] It would seem, then, that parents perceive their infant sons as sturdier or more able to withstand rough treatment than their infant daughters. The evidence, however, supports the opposite conclusion. Female neonates have been found to be physiologically more mature and more resistant to disease and injury.[11] Nevertheless, people, parents included, seem to persist in the belief that infant girls are more fragile. This assumption appears to extend beyond infancy into early childhood when parents of toddlers have been reported to be more apprehensive about their daughters' physical well-being.[12,13] From these observations, it does appear that parents' treatment of their female and male offspring is affected to some extent by cultural stereotypes or beliefs as to what girls and boys are supposed to be. It is interesting to note that differential parental behaviour toward sons and daughters has been recorded so early in the child's life.

For years psychologists and nonprofessionals alike have held the belief that parents talk to their daughters more than to their sons, beginning in infancy. It has been further assumed that, having received more verbal stimulation, girls' verbal development is more rapid during the early years. Recent evidence does not clearly support either of these beliefs, however. A discussion of differences between the sexes in verbal ability is found in Chapter 5. In Maccoby and Jacklin's[14] review of 22 studies which recorded parent-child verbal interaction, mainly with babies and preschoolers, no differences were found in either the kind or the amount of parents' vocalization to daughters and sons. As with vocalization, there is no clear-cut differential treatment of infant sons and daughters when parental warmth and nurturance are examined. Sometimes mothers are reported holding their three-month-old infant sons more;[15] but others have found that mothers touch their six-month-old daughters more frequently.[16] Maccoby and Jacklin examined nine observational studies involving mainly mothers and babies or small children. They found no sex differences in six of these studies in affectionate contact. Measures that were used include smiling, rocking, holding, and touching the child. In infancy, then, there does not appear to be any difference in parental warmth expressed toward children of the two sexes.

There are few consistent differences in the way parents treat their infant sons and daughters. One of the reasons more differences have not been found is that at this early stage, infants seem to be treated more as babies than as boys and girls. There are, after all, limitations to what parents are able to do with infants, simply because of their physical and intellectual immaturity. Parental handling at this early stage would centre more around basic caretaking activities and include some limited forms of play. As the child develops language skills and greater mobility, and asserts its independence more, parents and other caretakers find that they have to exert more control over the child, frequently for the child's safety. Consequently, as the child develops, its changing forms of behaviour often serve as cues to the parents who, in turn, must respond in an appropriate fashion. What is more, there are fairly clear-cut stereotypes regarding the behaviour parents expect in their male and female children. Throughout the child's development, these stereotypes appear to become increasingly salient as determinants of parental behaviour toward children.

Childhood

Boys' and Girls' Rooms: Is There Any Difference? In their efforts to assess how parents view and treat their developing youngsters, the majority of investigators use standard techniques of assessment, which include questionnaires, interviews, and observations of the parent and child interacting. Another, rather novel technique of assessing parental attitudes toward male and female children consists of looking at the furnishings and contents of the rooms parents provide for their children. How parents furnish the rooms of their sons and daughters, including the toys they provide, are indices of their expectations for their children's behaviour. If parents tend to furnish a child's room with dolls and stuffed animals, the behaviour expected of that child probably includes caretaking, nurturing, and playing house. On the other hand, when a child is provided with toys that consist primarily of blocks, puzzles, and toy tools, for example, the child can be said to be expected to engage in intellectual and physical manipulation of various elements of the environment.

These were the premises of a study[17] examining how parents furnished the rooms of 48 boys and 48 girls, who ranged in age from one month to six years. The boys' rooms contained toys that tended to fall into a restricted group: vehicles of all kinds, depots, educational-art materials, sports equipment, machines, and military toys. The toys in the girls' rooms formed a completely different group. Girls most often had dolls, doll houses, and domestic toys of all kinds. Notable by their absence in the girls' rooms were wagons, boats, and buses, while in the boys' rooms, there was an almost total absence of baby dolls and domestic toys. It would seem, then, that boys were provided with toys that encourage activities directed *away from* the home, while girls' rooms were furnished with objects that encourage activities *within* the home. By restricting their children's toys, depending on their sex, parents are conveying quite unambiguously just what their behavioural expectations are for their children. This is particularly true when children are young — under six years of age. While children may express their preference for certain toys, it is still usually the parent who makes the final decision about which toys to buy and how to furnish children's rooms. It is worth noting, however, that since the families in this study could afford to provide the children with their own rooms, they had probably achieved a fairly high socio-economic level. As such, it could be said that the sample was a select one and hardly representative of most of the population in terms of socio-economic class.

The fact that parents encourage different kinds of play in their sons and daughters by providing them with different types of toys is but one manifestation of the larger process of gender-role typing by which parents encourage their children to behave, think, and feel in ways defined by society as appropriate to a particular gender role.

Encouragement of Gender-Role Typing: Unequal Pressure on Boys.

> Tommy, the three-year-old son of a colleague of mine, is going to the zoo with his father. Just as the two prepare to leave, Tommy tells his father he has forgotten something and scurries up to his room. A few moments later, Tommy reappears with a pink ribbon in his hair. His father is aghast and shouts, "Take that thing out of your hair. No son of *mine* is going to the zoo with a ribbon in his hair." Tommy then bursts into tears and runs out of the room.

We would be hard-pressed these days to come up with an analogous anecdote about a three-year-old girl. Parents are much more likely to be found encouraging "masculine" behaviour in their sons than they are found insisting on "feminine" behaviour in their daughters.[18,19] A boy is generally found to be subjected to more disapproval for being a "sissy" than a girl is for being a "tomboy". Not only do little boys experience greater pressure to behave in a gender-role-appropriate way, but also this

*"Dad freaked out when he saw me playing with dolls.
So I told him I was a sultan and these were my wives."*

pressure is often enforced rather harshly.[20] In their review of close to 200 published studies dealing with the socialization of girls and boys, Maccoby and Jacklin[21] found that parents tend to use more physical and nonphysical negative reinforcements, as well as more praise, in pressuring their sons to behave in a "masculine" way.

Despite the well-known observation that fathers do not spend much time with their children, particularly when the children are young,[22,23] fathers play an important part in the development of a boy's gender role. Some have argued that fathers are much more concerned that their children develop appropriate gender-role behaviour than are mothers. For example, fathers have been reported to worry when their sons appear unaggressive and unwilling to defend themselves.[24] However, they rarely express concern when their daughters appear unaggressive.[25,26] While others maintain that mothers do not feel very strongly about their children behaving in a gender-role-appropriate manner, there is reason to believe that mothers, just as much as fathers, may be concerned about their *sons* growing up to be masculine. This comes from a study[27] of attitudes towards childrearing practices among mothers who were also feminists. The sample included women who held leadership positions in feminist organizations, as well as those who said they had personally been touched by the Women's Liberation Movement. In interviews, about one-third of the mothers said they had never given any serious thought to the application of nonsexist childrearing to boys. Even among the women who did not particularly disapprove of homosexuality, there was a lot of apprehension that their sons could become "unnecessarily" homosexual because of them. Interestingly, none of the women who also had daughters feared that a "liberated" upbringing would transform a girl into a lesbian. Despite their ideological beliefs, these mothers were unable to extricate themselves from a belief system that emphasizes the importance of masculinity in boys and tolerates little deviation from this norm. The results of the study are all the more compelling when one considers that these women were drawn from among people who have espoused equality between women and men. It may be inferred from this study that a survey of more conventional families would reveal that they would be even more likely to subscribe to the stereotype that a "liberated" upbringing may lead to reduced masculinity and, thus, homosexuality, in males. But, as will be discussed in Chapter 6, gender-role behaviour and sexual preference (male or female) are really independent dimensions of personality. Gay people may engage in the same range and diversity of gender-role behaviours as heterosexuals.

What Do Parents Expect of Their Sons and Daughters? On the basis of their review of research in the area of childhood socialization,

Courtesy Miller Services Ltd.

Maccoby and Jacklin[28] conclude: "Our survey of the research on socialization of the two sexes has revealed surprisingly little differentiation in parent behaviour according to the sex of the child. However, there are some areas where differential 'shaping' does appear to occur (pp. 338–339)." Nevertheless, the authors state that they found evidence that parents have a tendency to "shape" the behaviour of their sons and daughters in gender-role-appropriate ways by dressing them differently, by assigning them gender-role-differentiated chores and toys, and by encouraging interests along gender-role lines. This is most significant

Courtesy Miller Services Ltd.

information, which children utilize in the development of their gender-role identity, as well as in their cognitive construction of their gender role. In effect, then, through experience with parents, peers, and the outside world, children learn the behaviours, interests, and tasks associated with these roles.

The conclusion that parents do not differentially socialize their sons and daughters has not gone unchallenged. For example, Block[29,30] has reanalyzed many of the studies summarized by Maccoby and Jacklin and has come to different conclusions about many of the same issues. For one thing, Block argues, the studies that Maccoby and Jacklin considered involved primarily very young children for whom many of the measures were inappropriate because of their youth. Other researchers have found that in guiding their children in specific behaviours appropriate to their age group, parents clearly treat boys and girls differently. For example, in one study, sons were encouraged *more* than daughters to explore their environment independently.[31] When mothers of four-year-olds were asked in another study at what age they thought parents should expect or permit certain behaviours in their children, mothers of boys gave *younger* ages than mothers of girls for "independence-granting" items.[32] These included such things as crossing the street alone, being allowed to play away from home for long periods of time without first telling their parents where they would be, and using sharp scissors without adult supervision. But, interestingly, boys are *not* more advanced in many of the skills involved here and, if anything, are frequently more impulsive and less mature.[33]

Parents also see their female toddlers as needing help more than their male counterparts. Female toddlers are encouraged more to ask for help from parents and are rewarded more for following their parents around the house.[34] Parents have also been reported to feel that their daughters need more warmth and, in general, to feel more fear for girls than for boys.[35] These parental preconceptions are not restricted to very young children, but seem to continue to be an integral part of the parents' relationship with their daughters throughout their development. For example, parents whose children ranged in age from 3 to 20 years have reported that they feel greater warmth for and closeness toward their daughters, and they tend to restrict and supervise their daughters more.[36] Since it would seem that parents see their daughters as needing more guidance, protection, and warmth than their sons, it is not surprising to learn that girls and boys are treated differently by their parents in ways that coincide with these differential perceptions.

Implications for the Child. While parents are preparing and training their sons to mould their world, they train their daughters to be moulded by it. Not only are girls expected to be more dependent than boys, but their parents actually reward them for dependency behaviour, while depriving them of the independence training that boys receive. Boys experience a different form of deprivation in their training. The socialization of boys is directed more toward the encouragement of the development of a sense of independence. There is less emphasis in boys' socialization on the development of skills needed to express interpersonal needs, particularly in emotional relationships, and to relate meaningfully to others in interpersonal relationships — characteristics associated with interdependence.

As a result of gender-role differences in independence-dependency and interdependence training, the young girl is not as likely as the young boy to establish an early and independent sense of self. While both boys and girls form their first attachment to the mother, the girl's identification with her mother is consistent with both her sex and her gender role. The boy, on the other hand, has to be encouraged to separate from his mother, identify with his father, or learn some abstract concept of the masculine gender role. The desired behaviour that the boy must acquire is rarely defined as something he must do. Instead, undesirable behaviour is indicated negatively as something he should *not* do or be — anything, that is, labelled "feminine". Another factor contributing to the boy's separation from his parents, particularly his mother, is his greater tendency to be aggressive, which increases the likelihood of his coming into conflict with them. Pressure to separate his identity from that of his mother, combined with independence training, pave the way for the development of independence coping skills that are seen to be necessary for effective enactment of the masculine gender role in our society. Presented in this fashion, the very methods that train the boy to act independently prevent him from developing a greater sense of interdependence. If interdependent qualities are labelled "feminine" and associated only with the mother, the boy will find it less likely that these traits could exist in himself alongside his independent qualities.

Since girls are expected to be dependent and are often rewarded for dependent behaviour, they are likely to develop an inadequate sense of personal competence. They have probably received less encouragement than boys to "try their own wings". Girls are more likely to underestimate their own ability and more apt to lack confidence in their judgement when it is contrary to that of others. What is more, fathers have been found frequently to respond to their daughters in a gender-role-stereotyped manner.[37] This type of behaviour on the part of the father may actually impede a young girl's intellectual growth and independent achievement if the father sees these as masculine qualities not to be encouraged as much in girls. A father who treats his daughter in a fashion that elicits traditionally feminine behaviours may thus hinder her intellectual and academic development.

If girls are to be given equal opportunity with boys to become independently competent and self-confident, not only do they need encouragement and positive reinforcement of their independence strivings, but they may also need some maternal rejection to achieve a greater sense of separate self. This is not to imply, however, that mothers should be hostile to their daughters. One can encourage separation and independent functioning, even among toddlers, in a warm and loving relationship. Through gentle guidance and reinforcement of the young girl's independence efforts, she should come to value herself as a competent being. Conversely, if boys are to accept dependency needs both in themselves and in others and if they are to learn how to relate sensitively in interpersonal relationships, independence, dependency and interdependence cannot be presented as mutually exclusive characteristics. By encouraging and rewarding independent behaviours, *as well as* those that promote meaningful relationships, parents will be teaching their sons that they do not have to reject their own and other people's emotional needs in order to be independent.

In summary, if parents try to establish relationships with *both* their sons and daughters in which the youngsters can model their parents' independence efforts and be rewarded for them, they will have gone a long way towards fostering independence and self-confidence in their developing children. At the same time, if sons, as well as daughters, are not punished for showing dependent and interdependent qualities, parents will demonstrate that awareness and expression of emotional needs and independence can coexist in one person, and they will have had a great part in furthering the development of complete human beings.

Theories of the Development of Gender Roles

What are the processes through which the development of gender roles occurs? Several major theories have been offered to account for the development of gender-role behaviour and gender-role identity. These theories vary considerably in the emphasis they put on biological and social factors.

Psychoanalysis and Personality Development

Sigmund Freud (1856–1939) was the first to advance a major theory on personality, sex, and gender-role development. His theory of psycho-analysis, one of the most influential in the area of personality development, radically changed the way people looked at themselves and their experiences. Not only has psychoanalytic theory permeated psychiatry for the past five decades, but it has also affected the way in which society views human behaviour. Freudian theory has also had an influence of how psychologists have looked at differences between women and men. However, Freud's ideas, particularly those involving women and their psychological development, have never gone unchallenged. His theoretical conceptions of women have been and continue to be a source of heated controversy.

In order to understand his theory on the development of personality, it is important to consider some of the basic tenets of psychoanalysis. Two of the most important of these are the concepts of the *unconscious* and *psychosexual development*. Freud suggested that there are differing levels of awareness of feelings, thoughts, and personal experiences. In general, he saw the unconscious as operating according to the symbolic expression of wishes without regard to limitations of external reality.[38] He then postulated the existence of three mental structures:[39, 40] the *id* represents biological instincts or drives, primarily sexual and aggressive in origin, and seeks to discharge excitation according to the pleasure principle: the uninhibited pursuit of pleasure and the avoidance of pain. The *superego* represents the person's conscience and seeks to control behaviour and channel impulses in accordance with society's norms and standards. The *ego* he saw as reality oriented, trying to satisfy the urgent demands associated with the id within the limits imposed by a strict, uncompromising superego and the demands of external reality.

While a baby is born with an id, it has to develop a superego and an ego by progressing through "psychosexual stages".[41] Moreover, according to Freud, everyone passes through each of these stages, where the sexualized life force, or libido, focuses on a particular erotogenic zone of the body, an area which is sensitive to pleasurable stimulation. During the first, oral stage, erotogenous responses are centred around the mouth and lips. During the second year, the anal stage becomes ascendant, and sensuality is focused on bowel functioning. During the third, phallic stage, the focus of sensual pleasure shifts to the genital area: for the male, the penis; for the female, the clitoris.

During the phallic stage (from about 3 to 6 years of age), children develop the Oedipus complex, the resolution of which is important for appropriate gender-role identification and the establishment of a conscience. This complex derives its name from the Greek tragedy in which Oedipus unwittingly kills his father and marries his mother. According to Freud, the child wishes to possess the opposite-sexed parent and perceives the same-sexed parent as a rival. In the case of the boy, he is attached to his mother and wishes to possess her sexually and displace his father, who becomes a hated rival. At this stage, masturbation is gratifying to him, which accounts for the great value he puts on his beloved penis. But at about this time, when he discovers that females do not possess a penis, he is shocked and assumes that they have been castrated. He thinks that the same thing could happen to him. The panic of castration anxiety forces him to repress his sexual desire for his mother. He then yields to the father's authority and his feelings of rivalry are transformed into identification with the father. As a result, he feels he can retain his penis. Through identification with the father, he incorporates the father's standards into his newly formed superego. At the same time, he acquires other personality traits of the father. Another result of identification is the development of gender-role identity, which is discussed later in this chapter.

The girl, too, is emotionally attached to the mother during the first 3 years of life. She masturbates with her clitoris in the phallic stage. She then notices that boys have a "superior" organ to hers, and she falls victim to penis envy, which Freud said is of critical importance to her subsequent personality development.[42] She thinks that she has been castrated, views this as a personal wound to her self-esteem, and develops a permanent sense of inferiority. When she discovers her genital "inferiority", she abandons her mother as a love-object. In fact, she blames her mother for her lack of a penis. The girl's libido then shifts from her mother to her father, who now becomes a love-object, and her mother is seen as her rival. She then substitutes the wish for a child for her unattainable wish for a penis.[43] By transferring the object of her libido to the male and in equating penis with child, she partially resolves her penis envy and can then progress toward normal feminine functioning.

One major difference in the development of girls and boys centres around the "castration complex". The masturbating boy is already in the Oedipal stage when he sees that girls lack a penis — and fear of castration abruptly forces him to give up his mother in order to save his most valued penis. The masturbating girl is still in the phallic stage when she notices the boy's "superior" organ. Penis envy pushes her into the Oedipal stage, and there is no castration fear to make her give up her father abruptly. Without fear of castration, which is the major motive in the boy for resolving the Oedipus complex, the girl can remain indefinitely involved in its resolution — which may never be completely achieved. As a result, Freud said, she fails to develop a superego (conscience) that is as strong or as independent as that of the boy. She identifies with her mother, thereby taking on her feminine traits because she realizes the impossibility of gratifying her desire for her father and because she fears losing her mother's love (anaclitic identification). This supposedly occurs at about age six.

During the later years of childhood, the latency stage, Freud assumed that psychosexual development was relatively quiescent. During the genital stage, the final one, libidinal energy is focused in the genital area and heterosexual activity with peers substitutes for the unattainable parent.

Implications for Women's Personality. As a result of lingering penis envy, Freud believed that women develop a personality that is characterized by vanity and jealousy. The reasoning is thus: if a woman cannot have a penis, she will turn her entire body into an erotic substitute. Female jealousy, he said, was a displaced version of penis envy. As a result of penis envy, women also develop passivity and masochism as defining personality traits. He theorized that during the course of the Oedipus complex, girls begin to get less pleasure from "masculine masturbation" (clitoral masturbation) probably because they realize that, since they cannot compete with boys, it would be best to give up the idea of doing so.[44] Moreover, they have to give up their infantile gratification from masturbation of the clitoris and prepare for adult gratification through vaginal intercourse. For Freud, who put forth the "dual-orgasm" theory, the vagina was the "truly feminine" organ. The idea that vaginal sexuality is somehow more "naturally feminine" than clitoral sexuality persists today, as will be seen in Chapter 6. He went on to say that when a girl abandons her active (clitoral) sexuality, she gives up her active strivings in all other areas as well. The passive mode of vaginal sexual expression was supposed to generalize so that the girl generally eschews active, aggressive, and, hence, traditionally masculine behaviour, turning her repressed aggression inward and acquiring self-destructive attitudes and masochistic behaviour.[45]

Criticisms of Freud. Despite his extensive writings on women, Freud's theory predominantly emphasized male psychology. Moreover, his writings are replete with protestations of how little is known about women. As late as 1933 in his essay "Femininity", he wrote:

> Throughout history people have knocked their heads against the riddle of the nature of femininity... Nor will *you* have escaped worrying over this problem — those of you who are men; to those of you who are women this will not apply — you are yourselves the problem (p. 113).[46]

Most of Freud's assumptions regarding women have been criticized not only by those within the psychoanalytic camp, but by others as well. Neo-Freudians, political feminists, and psychologists have all criticized Freud for taking the male as the basic standard of health and normality. Kate Millett, a political feminist, states it very well. According to Millett, Freud fails

> to acknowledge that woman is born female in a masculine-dominated culture which is bent upon extending its values even to anatomy and is therefore capable of investing biological phenomena with symbolic force (p. 180).[47]

According to Freud's patriarchal viewpoint, female development is both second best and second rate.[48] The female is regarded as an inadequate male in every respect. It is this assumption that leads to many fallacies in his thinking about women.

The phrase "anatomy is destiny" reflects Freud's heavy reliance on biological factors in the explanation of behavioural and social phenomena. As was pointed out in Chapter 1, social behaviour cannot be explained by referring simplistically to biological factors. Clinical evidence has established that, at times, gender-role identity may even be different from the sex of a person as defined genetically. As was discussed in Chapter 2, there are documented cases where a genetically female child was reared as a boy and that child developed a masculine gender-role identity. Thus, contrary to Freud's assumptions, the effects of biological factors on psychosexual identity can be completely reversed by early childhood conditioning.[49]

Empirical work on many of Freud's assumptions about women has not given support to such ideas as penis envy and the Oedipus complex. For example, little evidence exists that girls and women envy male anatomy, while there is considerable evidence that women and girls envy the masculine gender role for its greater power and privilege — its greater socio-cultural advantages.[50] Neither does experimental evidence support the Oedipal shift from mother to father. In fact, most children (boys *and* girls) at ages four to six remain primarily attached to their mothers, particularly when the mother is the primary caretaker.

Freud's original dual-orgasm theory has also been the object of considerable criticism and recently has been disproven. According to Freud, if the woman did not experience a transfer in the location of her orgasm from the clitoris to the vagina, she was frigid and sexually immature. However, Masters and Johnson's[51] work on the anatomical and physiological sexual response in women has shown that there is no difference in orgasm whether induced by stimulation of the clitoris or the vagina. Their data has shown, furthermore, that all female orgasms, regardless of clitoral stimulation, include vaginal contractions. Thus, there is no evidence for two orgasms, a vaginal and a clitoral one (see Chapter 6).

In summary, then, Freud's views on women could be called distorted and one-sided. Blinded by the assumption of the innate superiority of the male, Freud completely ignored behaviour and experiences of women that contradicted his theory. Moreover, his apparent acceptance of the concept of biological determinism and his disregard for the influence of the larger socio-cultural environment resulted in a theory that reflected his personal bias more than the true nature of women.

Development of Psychoanalytic Theory. Dissatisfaction with Freud's theory as it pertained to women led some of his colleagues and "heirs" to make revisions of orthodox psychoanalytic theory and set forth their own. Two of these theorists will be discussed here.

Helene Deutsch was born in 1884 and received training in psychoanalysis. While working within a Freudian theoretical framework, she has greatly expanded some of the classical psychoanalytic concepts as they relate to women.[52,53] Deutsch shared many of Freud's beliefs about the psychosexual stages of development but modified two key Freudian concepts of female personality development: penis envy and the resolution of the Oedipus complex. Contrary to Freud's thinking, Deutsch did not view penis envy as the basis of a girl's essential conflicts, nor did she see it as the crux of a woman's development as a person. She viewed it as a secondary development, not exclusive to women, growing out of a general tendency of all children to want everything they do not have. As to the resolution of the Oedipus complex, Deutsch believed that detachment from the mother was never fully achieved. She held that the girl's pre-Oedipal relationship to her mother was extremely complex and important. In fact, Deutsch believed that development of the feminine identity grew out of a struggle against this tie with the mother.

Regarding women's sexuality, Deutsch believed that orgasm was a male phenomenon and that the function of the vagina was limited to a passive-receptive sucking one. She believed that intercourse for the truly feminine woman should exclude orgasm and consist only of relaxation without contractions of the vagina. She also believed that the clitoris was superfluous to sexuality in the healthy adult woman. However, as will be discussed in Chapter 6, research has shown that when women experience orgasm, they experience changes in the clitoris, as well as pulsations in the vagina. Further, in believing that masochism was basic to the feminine personality, Deutsch's theory was clearly misogynist.

Karen Horney was born in 1885 and also trained in classic psychoanalytic theory. Her writing provided a new dimension in psycho-analytic thinking about women and their psychological development. In particular, Horney was highly critical of Freud's male cultural bias. In 1926, in her paper "The Flight from Womanhood", she writes:

> Now, if we try to free our minds from this masculine mode of thought, nearly all the problems of feminine psychology take on a different appearance (p. 59).[54]

Horney believed that the paucity of knowledge about women derived from the male bias of psychoanalytic observers. The concept of "human being", she said, was identified with the concept of "man". She believed that women, too, possessed the same bias, since they had adapted themselves to the desires of men.

While not denying the prevalence of penis envy in women, she differed from Freud in the way she regarded it. For her, the source of penis envy was the greater ease with which a boy could handle the genital in masturbation and urination. She also saw this envy as emanating from the girl's awareness of the superior social status of the male. Horney viewed penis envy as an aspect of mutual envy that existed between women and men. She pointed out that it is not only women who envy the attributes of the other sex. Many of her male patients, she said, revealed envy of women's basic biological functions, such as pregnancy, childbirth, and nursing, and of certain parts of the female anatomy — the breasts, for example. She went on to say that men cope with this envy through repression and defence. By glorifying the male genitals, they compensate for their inability to give birth.

While not denying the prevalence of inferiority feelings in women, she argued against the importance Freud ascribed to them in women's personality. In discussing women's feelings of inferiority, Horney pointed out that social and cultural factors must be taken into account. In our masculine civilization, she said, all the professions are dominated by men. Since women are barred from accomplishment in the outside world, they have a social basis for their feelings of inferiority. For Horney, understanding the interaction of psychic and social factors was critical to the understanding of women's inferiority feelings.

Horney argued against psychoanalytic ideas about masochism in women.[55] She demonstrated that cultural factors, such as the widely held belief in women's inferiority, lack of effective outlets for expansiveness and sexuality, the economic dependence of women on men, and the restriction of women to roles built on emotional bonds, could account for the female's tendency toward masochism. Among other topics of importance to the psychology of women, Horney wrote on marriage, motherhood, and relationships between the sexes.

Other theorists writing within the psychoanalytic framework include Clara Thompson (1893-1958), Carl Jung (1875-1961), and Erik Erikson (1902-   ). While offering many positive insights about the psychology of women, many of the neo-Freudians shared with Freud negative and limited perceptions of women. The application of modern experimental methods to the study of women showed later that many of the assumptions held by psychoanalytic theorists about women and their "normal" functioning were erroneous. As Horney had pointed out, socio-cultural factors are critical to an understanding of the psychology of women.

Processes in the Development of Gender-Role Behaviour

Identification. According to psychoanalytic theory, gender-role identity is achieved through the process of identification: the tendency of children to identify with the same-sex parent. As discussed earlier, the boy's fear of castration motivates him to repress his desire for his mother and identify with his father, and thus resolve his Oedipal conflict. Instead of competing with his father, the youngster identifies with him. This is supposed to result in a lessening of the father's aggression ("he would not castrate someone who is like him") and it is also supposed to ensure the affection of the mother ("she has to love me now because she loves my father and I am like him"). Identification with the father is assumed to be critical for the boy's gender-role adoption, since the boy is taking over many of the father's personality characteristics. The girl, realizing the impossibility of gratifying her desire for her father and fearing the loss of her mother's love, identifies with her mother. The girl's identification with the mother is rooted in the girl's love and attachment to her mother, as well as her need to ensure that the dependency relationship with her mother continues.

In the process of identification with the same-sex parent, the child is seen attempting to emulate the parent's ways of behaving, thinking, and feeling. At the same time, the child attempts to adopt the parent's ideals, attitudes, and opinions. In short, the child is incorporating parts of the parent's personality into its own. But identification, as originally put forth by Freud, leaves a number of important points unexplained. For example, it does not provide reasons why the *power* of a model (the father) or the *nurturance* of another model (the mother) should affect the sexes differently. It has been shown that when more than one model is available, children will imitate the more dominant, powerful figure. And, other things being equal, children tend to choose to imitate the more nurturant model.[56-58] So, within a two-parent family, if the mother is the more nurturant figure, children of both sexes should imitate her. And, if the father is the dominant figure, then both boys and girls should imitate him. But this in itself should not make boys masculine and girls feminine.

Another criticism of identification theory relates to one of its basic assumptions — namely, that it is necessary for adult role models, themselves, to have clearly differentiated gender roles so that the child can distinguish what is masculine and what is feminine behaviour.[59] However, adult role models who exhibit stereotyped gender roles may impede, rather than facilitate, the child's gender-role identification. In fact, children may find it easier to identify with less differentiated and less stereotyped parental models.[60]

Social Learning Theory. Explanations of the acquisition of gender-role* behaviour using social learning principles are the most widely accepted today. Focusing mainly on observable behaviour, social learning theorists have formulated a set of hypotheses which describe and explain simple learning, first in rats and later in humans. Social learning theory is particularly useful in explaining the development of gender-role differences.[61] Stated simply, according to this theory, gender-role-appropriate responses are rewarded by parents and others and are therefore repeated in the future. Gender-role-inappropriate behaviour, or those responses that deviate from behaviour defined as appropriate to one's gender role, are likely to be punished and, as a result, become less frequent in the future and eventually do not occur again.[62]

The most pervasive point of view in social learning theory is that children's behaviour is "shaped" to conform to expectations of socialization agents such as parents and teachers. "Shaping" refers to the process of reinforcing successive approximations of some desired response. Young children learn very early that their parents or parent substitutes expect them to act in a manner appropriate to their gender role.

A child's behaviour is shaped in a variety of ways to produce a person who conforms to the requirements of his or her gender role. While rewards and punishments administered directly after responses have occurred are significant in this process, they are insufficient in themselves to account for behaviour that conforms to traditional role expectations. For one thing, it is unlikely that in each child's life there are *enough* instances of gender-role relevant behaviour manifested and consistently

---

*In this description of social learning theory, the term gender role is used. However, social learning theory and related research generally use the term sex role where gender role is used here.

reinforced in ways that coincide with gender roles, for this process to be paramount.

Learning principles in addition to reward and punishment are seen as central to the development of gender-role-appropriate behaviour. One of these is known as imitation, also referred to as observational learning, vicarious learning, and modelling. By observing a model's behaviour, usually the parent's, the child may acquire behaviour appropriate to his or her gender role. Bandura and his coworkers [63-65] have done extensive laboratory work on imitation, where they have shown that after exposure to aggressive models, children imitate many novel aggressive responses.

It is assumed that many of the child's responses (or behaviours) may also develop through imitation of the same-sex parent's behaviour. While this explanation is very appealing, it has not been confirmed by research findings. For example, in some experiments where children were given every opportunity to copy adults, they showed no consistent trends to mimic one sex more than the other. When researchers have looked for correlations between parents' personalities and those of their children, they have generally not found that children resemble the same-sex parent more than the opposite-sex one.[66]

It is difficult, however, to reconcile these research findings with everyday observations of small children's behaviour. It is well known that little girls are always dressing up in their mothers' clothes, wearing their shoes, mimicking their gestures, and frequently reproducing their mothers' behaviours in their attempts to be "little mommies" themselves. It may be that, at first, children observe and then imitate the behaviour of both parents and only as they get older do they select from their repertoire of behaviours those responses that have been directly rewarded. A parent, for example, may wittingly or unwittingly reward gender-role-appropriate behaviour by smiling or showing affection and approval. Similarly, parents will punish or simply not reward those behaviours not consistent with the child's gender role. While a three-year-old girl who dresses up in her mother's clothes may endear herself to her father, a three-year-old boy doing the same thing may find that his dressing up meets with disapproval if not a scolding. According to this explanation, then, gender-role typing would be a product of direct reinforcement of gender-role-appropriate behaviour.[67] While the *original* repertoire of children's behaviours might have come about partially as a conseqence of imitation or modelling, as children develop cognitively, they learn to select those behaviours appropriate to their gender role through direct experience with others.

In summary, then, the development of appropriate gender-role behaviour is seen by social learning theorists to be the result of direct reinforcement by external agents — in this case, the parents. While originally the behaviour occurs only because it has been rewarded by others, it is eventually internalized and regulated by the individual's own standards of gender-role-appropriate behaviour. When the child is young, the impact of the parents as socialization agents is greatest, since this is the time when the child is most dependent on parents for attention and affection. The child is, in effect, a "captive audience" for the parents' teachings according to social learning principles. Later on, other external agents become increasingly important in imparting the "message". While dealing extensively with the role of *external* factors in shaping gender-role-appropriate behaviour, social learning theory does not deal with cognitive (thinking) or affective (feeling) factors associated with this process. This is one of the major inadequacies of the social learning theory. When, for example, do children think of themselves as belonging to one gender group or another? How does their thinking about their gender-role identity affect their future gender-role development?

The processes of imitation and identification have in common the tendency to reproduce the behaviours, attitudes, and emotional reactions of models. There is, however, an important distinction between them: imitation usually refers to the reproduction of a model's discrete or separate responses; identification is used to mean the reproduction of something of a more global nature — that is, a model's complex integrated pattern of behaviours, attitudes, values, and feelings.

Cognitive-Developmental Theory. Unlike the social learning theory that emphasizes learning and external factors, the cognitive-developmental theory proposed by Kohlberg[68] views the child's thinking as the crucial factor in determining appropriate gender-role behaviour. Kohlberg's cognitive theory is similar to Piaget's developmental theory of intelligence in that it proposes that all children pass through developmental stages. The way they learn about appropriate gender-role bahaviour — theirs and others' — depends on the developmental stage they are at. According to the theory, as the child develops cognitively, his or her ideas about gender-role-appropriate behaviour also develop. This involves changes in the development of the child's perceptions of the physical and social world, including his or her sense of self.

By the age of two or three, children know their own sex labels (i.e., whether they are a "boy" or a "girl"). Children's basic self-categorization or label as boy or girl becomes the major organizer and determinant of many of their activities, values and attitudes. In the early stages of young children's cognitive development, they tend to see gender roles primarily in physical terms. A "female" is someone who carries a purse and has long hair. A "male" is someone with short hair who wears long pants. Since young children (less than six years old) have not as yet grasped the idea that a person's sex is a constant trait, it would not be unusual to find them thinking that if a boy changed his appearance, he could become a girl, and that a girl could become a boy in the same way.

At about six years of age, the child's identity as a boy or a girl becomes stabilized. This is at about the same time that the child begins to understand the principle of conservation — that physical properties are stable and invariant. Because children understand the concept of conservation by this point, they are able to grasp the idea that a person's sex remains a constant attribute throughout life. The child at this stage would not think, for example, that just because a girl cuts her hair, she has now become a boy. Once children have grasped the concept of constancy in their own self-concept (i.e., "I am a boy (girl)"), they acquire new values, behaviours, and attitudes related to this basic concept. Doing "girl" things for a young girl becomes rewarding simply because it coincides with the child's labelling of herself. Gender-role stereotypes for the young child come to acquire positive value and motivate the child to engage in behaviours consistent with his or her gender role. A boy sees masculinity as representing competence, strength, and power, and by acquiring the masculine stereotype, he presumably becomes motivated to enact a masculine role that coincides with the stereotype.

How does the theory account for the child's increasing tendency to behave in a manner appropriate for its gender role? Presumably, it is the knowledge of being a boy or a girl that motivates the child to discover how a boy or a girl should behave. Children find gender-role-appropriate behaviour rewarding because it coincides with their own label. As noted earlier, social learning theory maintains that children learn gender-role-appropriate behaviour because they are rewarded for doing so. According to cognitive-developmental theory, the tendency for young children is first to label themselves as "girl" or "boy" and then to seek out models that are in accordance with their gender-role concepts: modelling is seen as a consequence of labelling. In social learning theory, the opposite is assumed to occur.

Which is the better theory? One test of a good theory is how well it predicts events in the "real world". While little research has been done to validate the cognitive approach to gender-role development, it has been suggested[69] that the theory is inadequate because it cannot explain the wide range of degrees to which children adopt gender-role-appropriate behaviour. In any group of boys of the same age and intelligence, for example, there are wide variations in the degree of masculinity of their interests, attitudes, and behaviours. If this wide range of individual differences is to be explained, it is necessary to invoke the processes of selective reinforcement and modelling, which may vary considerably among children. The main strength of the cognitive-developmental theory is that it stresses the importance of cognitive growth and development in the evolution of the concept of gender role — factors which have been neglected in other developmental theories.

Summary

While volumes have been written about each of the three basic theories of gender-role development described above, our present purpose has been to describe the essence of each. While no doubt each theory contains some elements of truth, each also has certain flaws. The strength of social learning theory is that it represents a viewpoint which emphasizes environment, learning, and reinforcement.[70] Changes in the child's behaviour come about as a direct result of environmental actions and can be understood by knowing the reinforcement history in each case. However, this approach has not been very useful in generating many truly developmental studies because it is based on the assumption of continuity of behavioural mechanisms in going from immature to mature organisms.[71] One of the weaknesses of the social learning approach is that it does not deal with the cognitive and emotional factors associated with gender-role development. The way children think about themselves during the process of gender-role development and their feelings about it are obviously critical factors whose full impact on the process should be considered and assessed.

According to the cognitive-developmental theory, the gender (sex) label is an organizing rubric around which the child actively constructs his or her gender role. Through her or his experiences, the child learns those behaviours, interests, activities, and tasks that are defined as appropriate to gender-role categorization. The cognitive-developmental theory is much more comprehensive than the social learning theory, since it integrates the cognitive and behavioural factors associated with the developing child and relates them to external influences. However, this theory does not adequately explain the wide range of individual differences found among children of the same age and intelligence.

The concept of identification is an important one because of its emphasis on the process by which the child reproduces whole portions of the parent's personality, not just discrete responses. Thus, the concept of identification is useful in explaining our everyday observation that young children, in general, act, think, and feel very frequently just like their parents. In this way, the concept of identification complements the process of imitation as discussed in social learning theory. Obviously, then, identification is crucial in the development of gender-role-appropriate behaviour. Nevertheless, the concept of identification cannot explain how the different processes postulated for girls and boys do, in fact, result in femininity and masculinity. This is because children of *both* sexes will try to imitate both powerful and nurturant models. It is not just boys who identify with the powerful model or girls who identify with the nurturant model.

To sum up, then, a comprehensive theory of gender-role development will have to include aspects of all three theories if the complexity of the processes is to be fully represented. None by itself can do the job adequately.

Other Agents of Gender Role Socialization

In the early years of a child's life, the mother and father play a vital part in the development of the child's gender role and gender-role identity. As the child gets older, he or she is exposed to other influences which can be considered socialization agents in that they, too, have a major impact on the child's developing gender role. Some of these are books, television, the peer group, and the school system.

Books: Sexism in Print

... Bill said, "I will sit in front and steer the sled, Joan, you sit in the back so that you can hold on to me" (p. 41).[1]

He felt a tear coming to his eye, but he brushed it with his hand. Boys eight years old don't cry, he said to himself (p. 42).[2]

Bad luck follows me wherever I go. My girls are so stupid that they cannot learn to read or write (p. 133).[3]

These quotes are taken from children's books. The message is not so implicit: boys are stronger and more intelligent than girls. How typical are these quotes of children's literature? If they are typical, just what are the effects of this kind of communication on the developing child's gender-role identity?

Books are important socialization agents because symbolic behaviours represented in books may have effects on children similar to those resulting from actual interaction with the environment. Books not only convey information to children about the world around them and what children should and should not do, but also teach them the values that society accords to various behaviours and lifestyles. According to Margaret Mead, a culture has to get its values across to its children in such simple terms that even a behavioural scientist can understand them.[4] Books do provide children with gender-role models or examples of what they should strive for, along with clear instructive messages about normative or acceptable behaviour. In particular, the messages in children's books convey quite clearly the differential evaluation of females and males that is found in our society.

The Message in Children's Books

There is a consensus among those who have studied children's books about the nature of children's literature. Research on school readers, fairy tales, and picture books has resulted in four basic conclusions:

1. Females are consistently underrepresented in children's books.
2. Females are passive and males are active.
3. Males engage in a greater variety of activities than females.
4. Stereotyped masculine and feminine characteristics exist in children's books.

1. *The "Invisible" Female Character.* In picture books designed for young children, female characters are practically nonexistent. Not only are females underrepresented in the title, central roles, pictures, and stories, but there are also very few books about females.[5-7] Generally, studies of picture books show that the stories reflect a "man's world" — for example, a group of army officers interacting together or the adventures of two male animal friends.[8]

The trend toward the "invisible" female character observed in picture books designed for preschoolers continues with remarkable consistency in the readers given to children in elementary schools. In an American study of 134 elementary school readers and 2760 stories,[9] the following male/female ratios were obtained:

Boy-centred to girl-centred stories	5:2
Adult male main characters to adult female main characters	3:1
Male biographies to female biographies	6:1
Male animal stories to female animal stories	2:1
Male folk or fantasy stories to female folk or fantasy stories	4:1

What is the effect on girls who read these books and consistently find male characters as protagonists and female characters assigned to the background? The author's informal observation that some toddlers just learning to talk tend to use the word "boys" as a generic term for children suggests that even these little ones are getting the message: girls do not exist. And, if they do, they are not very important.

2. *Women and Girls are Passive; Men and Boys are Active.* Nowhere is this principle better illustrated than in fairy tales. In these stories, part of the generally accepted child folklore, a girl has only to be beautiful to get the reward—the boy. Girls frequently win the prize if they are "the fairest of them all". Boys, on the other hand, win if they are bold and active.[10] The prince forges his way through a jungle full of thorns and other dangers because he has heard of Sleeping Beauty's loveliness. She lies asleep in the ultimate state of passivity, waiting for her brave prince to awaken her and save her. Cinderella, too, leads a passive existence until her beauty captivates the prince during the ball. (She cannot even get to the ball by herself but has to be "sent" by her fairy godmother). In fairy tales, girls are not merely passive, they are also often victims and even martyrs.[11]

Cinderella, for example, is victimized by her ugly sisters, who keep her dressed in rags and hidden at home. In many of the fairy tales, the glamorous heroine is a passive victim who has to depend on others, such as men and fairy godmothers, to improve her lot.

Sleeping Beauty in Mrs. Craik's *The Fairy Book* 1863.
Engraving by C. H. Jeens after Joseph Noel Paton.

A recurrent theme in many children's books is the rescue activity — where the man or boy almost exclusively acts as the rescuer. The scenario goes something like this: the victim, predictably the girl, has to be rescued because she encounters mishaps, usually caused by bad luck. For example, in one Canadian school reader, Linda, we learn, is careless and gets lost. However, after she sheds a few tears, a police officer helps her.[12] In contrast, when boys crash their bikes or their rafts fall apart, for example, there is no rescue theme in the story. The boys, themselves, cope with the emergency, thus conveying the impression that boys are quite able to manage on their own.

In picture books, boys are often depicted as more adventurous and more independent.[13] While boys play outdoors in the real world, girls are frequently found indoors, in the kitchen, "watching the world go by". More often than not, girls are depicted as cut off from the world by a window, porch, or fence. Even when they are found outdoors, they tend to be represented as passive and immobile, often restricted from movement by their clothing — skirts and dresses prohibit more adventurous activity. In school textbooks, girls are typically depicted as passive, watching, weak, needing help, timid, incompetent, and docile. Boys are represented as brave, protective of girls, powerful, possessing initiative, competitive, independent, creative, and industrious.[14–16]

3.   *Women and Girls Serve; Men and Boys Have Fun.* With remarkable monotony, this theme is repeated in children's books: girls and women spend their time continually rehearsing their domestic roles. Domestic activities are portrayed primarily as a girl's preoccupation. One report found girls in domestic roles more than three times as often as boys.[17] Female characters are found so frequently engaging in domestic activities that one author has observed that one rarely sees female characters, animals included, without the perennial apron.[18] Could it be that by now the impressionable young child thinks that the apron is an integral part of the female anatomy?

Male characters, in contrast, are not usually found in the kitchen unless they are consuming something prepared for them by their mother or their sister. Most often, men and boys are found out of doors, having real adventures and leading exciting lives. Even if a woman is out of doors, she is usually engaging in a domestic activity. Boys and men engage in more varied activities than their female counterparts. For example, in one survey of 150 preschool books, sewing and cleaning were represented as activities almost exclusively associated with the feminine gender role, while car driving, fighting, making repairs around the house, gardening, reading, and engaging in water sports activities were depicted as predominantly associated with the masculine gender role.[19]

In most children's books, men and women are depicted in the same way as boys and girls. The impression conveyed is that the only worthwhile or available destiny for women is marriage, while men have the option of entering any occupation they choose. Fairy tales, for example, tend to focus on a girl's courtship, usually portrayed as the highlight of her life. But courtship is important only because it precedes that most important prize of all — marriage. The proverbial "and they lived happily ever after" implies that a happy, lifelong marriage is the girl's just reward for her beauty, passivity, and "femininity". While marriage is represented as rewarding for the man as well, he usually gets something more — power. This is because the princess he wins as a pretty wife is often part of a package deal, which also includes the kingdom.[20]

When women are portrayed in roles other than the marital one, they are usually restricted to a few, traditionally "female-typed" service occupations such as secretary, stewardess, teacher, waitress,[21,22] nun, nurse, or maid.[23] In contrast, men in children's books tend to be found in the more varied and prestigious roles of storekeeper, police officer, soldier, doctor, judge, security guard, and tailor.[24] With noteworthy consistency, children's books, from preschool to elementary school level, clearly convey the impression that women and girls are incapable of doing anything more worthwhile than serving others. For their male counterparts, however, anything is possible. It should not be too surprising to find in a later chapter of this book that vocational and professional aspirations among female high school students are considerably lower than those of male students. As the message in books is being continually rehearsed by children nearly every time they read, it cannot help but influence young people's career plans and the way they view their own future roles.

4. *Masculine and Feminine Gender-Role Stereotypes.* In children's books the attributes ascribed to gender roles are not only stereotyped, but they also convey the impression that men and boys are superior and women and girls are inferior. For example, male characters are often depicted as competitive and confident. Female characters are allowed to compete about half as often. One story taken from an elementary school reader[25] tells of a girl who swims against a boy and wins. But then he goes on to beat her five (!) times. If a girl wins at anything it is often a fluke or the result of a boy having taught her how to do something. A related theme depicts boys as autonomous individuals who engage in activities that promote their independence. Stories about girls behaving as independent agents are rare indeed.

While boys are depicted as confident, girls are portrayed as fearful about three times as often as boys.[26] In one story, two little girls stand on chairs and shriek for their younger brother to rescue them.[27] It is quite usual to find female characters depicted as dependent on male characters for help as well. Even mothers are at times portrayed as having to rely on male children for help. This is consistent with the frequent depiction of mothers as mental incompetents capable of functioning only in the kitchen. Often, even the younger son is portrayed as brighter than his mother. In one elementary school reader, a six-year-old boy was found to out-think a combination of two women.[28]

Generally, the stereotyped attributes assigned to male characters in children's books are ones highly valued in our society: independence,

From Rosemary Allison. The Pillow. Illustrated by Charles Hilder. Toronto: James Lorimer, 1979.

competitiveness, and competence, for example. Female characters are depicted not only as lacking these attributes, but also as possessing traits that are socially disparaged: fearfulness, dependency, and incompetence.

Have Children's Books Changed?

With the growth of the Women's Liberation Movement in the sixties, professionals and lay people alike have developed more awareness of the role of children's books in the perpetuation of gender-role stereotyping. During the last decade, both individuals and organizations have become vocal in their requests for changes in children's books. Feminist organizations in Canada and the United States continually publish lists of nonsexist books, and, in some cases, have published books themselves. For example, the Feminists on Children's Media, based in the United States, published "Little Miss Muffet Fights Back" — a booklet which lists more than 200 titles which the group thinks portrays girls and women positively.[29] Another American organization, The Feminist Press, published its first children's book in 1971. By 1975, it had produced seven children's titles with female protagonists who were depicted as active and adventurous. Certain companies that publish children's books have been moving in the same direction. In 1975, McGraw-Hill, for example, announced its intentions "... to eliminate sexist assumptions from [our] publications and to encourage greater freedom for all individuals to pursue their interests and realize their potential (p. 725)."[30] Government has also called for changes that would eliminate sexist portrayals of people and allow for the fulfillment of the individual's potential. For example, in 1972, the Ontario Government announced that it was taking steps to eliminate prejudiced references to Indians, Eskimos, and women in school texts.[31]

Despite concerted efforts of individuals and groups to bring about changes in children's books, little has, in fact, changed. In a comparison of "old" and "new" school readers, it has been found in one American study[32] that school readers published in about 1975 were not much different from their predecessors. They still featured more boy-centred stories and more illustrations of male characters, and male characters were still depicted in a greater variety of occupations than female characters. Although there were a few female characters who were clever, competent, and initiating, and although women were seen in a wider variety of occupations than in the past, most were cast in the role of mother. What is more, the creative aspects of the role were not emphasized — motherhood tended still to be depicted as an unimaginitive role. Despite government's vocal concern about biased readers being used in the schools, for the most part, the books being read in the school today are the same as those used in the past.

Structural and Psychological Implications of Books

Children's books present us with something of a paradox: on the one hand, they are supposed to convey normative expectations about gender roles and on the other, they communicate unrealistic information about the structure of the family and the employment world. Women tend to be represented in the domestic role to the exclusion of all others. Mothers are often portrayed as perfect servants, perpetually "on call". They rarely do anything but serve their families and are rarely seen holding outside employment. In reality, however, a substantial proportion of the female population holds outside employment and continues to do so after marriage and having children. In 1979, the participation rate of women in the Canadian labour force was 48.9%.[33] For married women, the rate was 47.4%.[34] Children's readers simply do not reflect reality.

Children's books also fail to portray single-parent families. Yet, it was reported in 1976 that 8.1% of Canadian families were single-parent families in which the lone parent was a woman.[35] The high divorce rate, which was reported to be 251.3 per 100 000 population in 1979 in Canada,[36] will probably remain high, leaving more families with one parent. This means that dependency on marriage on the part of either spouse is becoming less of an option — whether it be financial dependency, in the case of the woman, or domestic dependency in the case of the man.[37] Instead of perpetuating the belief that roles must be strictly segregated by gender, children's books should be directed toward the encouragement of developing competence in both employment and domestic roles in a single individual. At the present time, children's books continue to promote as ideal traditional roles suited to a societal structure which is becoming more or less obsolete.

From Robert Stewart. The Daddy Book. Pictures by Don Madden. New York: McGraw-Hill, 1972. Reprinted by permission of the publisher.

The media, particularly children's books and television, play a significant role in the child's developing gender-role identity by providing symbolic or live models that are imitated by children in observational learning. Research on the socializing effects of books has provided indirect evidence that the amount of achievement imagery in children's books during one period of time was highly correlated with measures of economic growth (or achievement in societal terms) when the children who had been exposed to these books reached maturity.[38] The greater achievement motivation demonstrated by boys in our society may derive in part from the fact that achievement imagery in books to which children of both sexes are exposed favours boys. In fact, it has been shown that gender-role stereotypes in children's stories can have an immediate effect on children's actual achievement behaviour.[39]

By perpetuating traditional gender-role models, books are also promoting the personality traits traditionally associated with the masculine and feminine gender roles in our society. The symbolic models provided in books promote expressive competence in girls and instrumental competence in boys.[40] As it is encouraged in boys, instrumental competence includes achievement orientation, dominance, and purposiveness, all of which are highly valued and presumably should lead to success. Expressive competence, on the other hand, is defined as the ability to be friendly, co-operative, and affiliative — traits which represent the antithesis of those which meet with approval, financial remuneration, and status in our society. As long as books continue to present children with masculine and feminine role models that exemplify such a narrow range of personality attributes, boys and girls will continue to regard stereotypic gender-role personality traits as ideal. In contemporary society, however, traditional gender-role demarcations in social life are gradually beginning to be eroded. If the individual is to function in an effective and satisfying way in society, the capacity to function equally well in instrumental and expressive ways must be encouraged in both sexes.

Television:
The Flickering Substitute Parent

Like books, television is a significant socializing agent. Because of its wide availability and ease of use, television is probably one of the most significant sources of media information. In a real sense, television has become an electronic babysitter. Children usually begin regular viewing at about the age of two or three years, when they watch an estimated two to three hours a day. Today's typical teenagers will have logged at least 15 000 hours of television.[41] By the time children reach the age of 18, they have probably spent more time watching television than being in a classroom or doing any other single activity, except perhaps sleeping.[42] In 1977, Dr. Benjamin Spock, the noted expert on babies and children, brought his stepdaughter and granddaughter to New York for some sightseeing. He confessed, "I couldn't get them away from the goddamned T.V. set. It made me sick (p. 64)."[43]

There is little doubt that television plays a key role in shaping children's attitudes, beliefs, and values, as well as their behaviour. For example, a good deal of research has demonstrated the relationship between televised violence and aggressive behaviour.[44-46] In laboratory experiments, children will usually imitate an aggressive adult that they observed in a film. Modelling (the process by which a person acquires social behaviours by copying or imitating the actions, attitudes, and emotional responses of others) and vicarious learning are two processes through which children, as well as adults, learn to reproduce what they see on television. In fact, symbolic behaviours portrayed on television are more immediate and compelling in presentation than those displayed in books.

The Message in Television

The message conveyed by television conforms in almost every respect to traditional gender-role stereotypes. This is illustrated well in an examination of Saturday morning cartoons — very popular programmes for children. To a great extent, the depiction of the sexes on T.V. is very similar to that found in children's books. For example, analyses of Saturday morning cartoon series show that not only do male characters outnumber female ones, but they are also found in a greater variety of occupational roles than female characters.[47,48] One study, for example, found that while occupational opportunities for male characters are unlimited, the occupations depicted for female characters are frequently limited to those of secretary, teacher, entertainer, or witch (see Table 4.1).[49] In addition to the fact that the number of female characters in the cartoon labour force underrepresents the actual number of women holding outside employment, negativism is frequently expressed in these cartoons toward women holding outside employment. For example, in one episode of "The Barkleys", Arney, the husband-father, blames his lateness for an important appointment on "those women" — in traffic and on the bus — and adds that they belong in the home.

The traits associated with male and female characters on T.V. more or less parallel those found in storybook characters. In general, female characters in cartoons are presented as timid, passive, weak, dependent, and incapable of initiating action.[50,51] Male characters are found more often as stable and intelligent people. Children's cartoons, for example, continue to perpetuate traditional gender-role stereotypes. While the man assumes complete financial responsibility, the woman is responsible for childcare and routine home maintenance. Women are depicted as needing men to lead them around, solve their problems, and, even more remarkably, they are often willing to subjugate themselves to cartoon males.

With the expansion of the Women's Liberation Movement and the corresponding increase in consciousness about the limiting effects of

TABLE 4.1
Variety of Vocational Roles Portrayed in
Observed Televised Cartoon Shows

MALES		FEMALES
superhero	spaceship pilot	girlfriend
mythological God	spaceman	musician-entertainer
professional villain	clothes store	singer-entertainer
king	manager	villain's daughter and assistant
sailor	salesperson	grandmother
fisherman	barber	aunt
fruit vendor	submarine captain	housewife-mother
musician-entertainer	fireman-firechief	secretary
singer-entertainer	ambassador	maid
cowboy	government minister	TV reporter
prospector	waiter	aquanaut-technician
clerk in hotel,	cook	"nanny"
bank, office	restaurant owner	assistant detective
military police	painter (artist)	teacher
hunter	judge	waitress
school principal	blacksmith	circus performer-horseback rider
warlock monster	clergyman (preacher)	movie star
business executive	orchestra conductor	witch
factory worker	television announcer	nurse
college student	television writer	
college professor	chauffeur	
foreman in factory	camera man	
physician	thief	
father (always with	newspaper editor,	
another job)	reporter	
son	newspaper boy	
grandfather	jail keeper	
uncle	clown in circus	
detective-inspector	circus performer-	
policeman-police chief	acrobat	
race car driver	rock group manager	
auto mechanic	pirate	
scientist	disk jockey	
helicopter driver	mailman	
tank commander		
(soldier)	cowboy, outlaw	
officer (soldier)	karate teacher	
pilot	grocer	
hotel manager	movie star	
crane operator	handyman	
astronaut	lawyer	
aquanaut-scientists	milkman	
congressman	college president, dean	
bus driver	prime minister	
park forest ranger	owner, gravel company	
inventor	circus owner, ringmaster	
	wrestler	

From R.M. Levinson, From Olive Oyl to Sweet Polly Purebread: Sex role stereotypes and televised cartoons. Journal of Popular Culture, 1975, 9, 566. Reprinted by permission of Journal of Popular Culture.

gender-role stereotypes, we would expect changes in the way gender roles are portrayed on children's T.V. programmes. In fact, very few changes have taken place. A comparison of the way the family was portrayed in 1963 and 1973 in "The Flintstones", "Roman Holidays", and "The Barkleys" reveals very few changes.[52] In all three series, the husbands were blue-collar workers and the wives were housewives. The personalities of the husbands and the wives were almost identical in the 1963 and the 1973 series. Even the plots were very similar — usually, they consisted of battles between the husbands and wives over some domestic conflict where the husband most often won.

Frequently, when the subject of sexist children's television programming is discussed, "Sesame Street" is held up as an exception in that it is thought to portray more "liberated" gender roles. Is this, in fact, the case? It is true that in contrast to most children's television programmes, "Sesame Street" will occasionally show female characters in nontraditional roles, such as those of plumber, firefighter, "mail person", for example. However, in many ways, "Sesame Street" does not differ from other children's television programmes in its portrayal of gender roles. For example, the masculine gender role is accorded greater social recognition than the feminine one, and there is considerable gender-role stereotyping in terms of role allocation. Jobs are held almost exclusively by men.[53] For example, Mr. Hooper works in his store, David works the soda fountain, and Luis operates his fixit shop. While Susan, one of the few female lead characters on "Sesame Street", may sometimes be referred to as a nurse, it is rarely that she is seen practising her skills. The message conveyed on "Sesame Street" is that the man is in the dominant social rank and the woman is in the subordinate one. This is brought out in a variety of ways. Not only do males compose the majority of the lead characters, but even the supposedly sexless nonhumans are more likely to have male voices. All-male scenes are the norm, as is the male authority voice-over. "Sesame Street" is generally held to be one of the best educational children's programmes presently broadcast. Thus, its misguided message about unequal masculine and feminine gender roles is being communicated to children authoritatively.[54]

Television Commercials

Children also watch television commercials. Since approximately 17% of T.V. air time is devoted to commercials,[55] by the age of 17, the average viewer has seen an estimated 350 000 commercials.[56] The differential portrayal of gender roles found in children's programmes is also evident in commercials. For example, an analysis[57] of commercials accompanying Saturday morning children's shows on three major American networks revealed that male characters, more than female ones, were depicted as independent agents, while female characters were presented in familial roles that defined them in relation to others.

The world for women in television commercials is clearly domestic. She is the product user. The woman is depicted as a compulsive cleaner whose entire waking hours are devoted to scouring everything in sight. If she is not preoccupied with becoming the world's best household drudge as well as an expert cook, the commercial shows her as feeling guilty. Despite the fact that women are the main consumers of the products advertised on television, men are presented as the authorities on the products being promoted, including everything from snowmobiles to toilet disinfectants.

Effects of Television Viewing

As would be expected, there is a relationship between television viewing and children's perceptions of gender roles. A great quantity of television viewing (25 hours or more per week) is clearly associated with stronger traditional gender-role development.[58] The more television children watch, the more stereotyped their perceptions of occupational gender roles become.[59] Thus, television teaches children to regard gender roles in highly traditional ways. The more the message is rehearsed, as is the case when children are heavy viewers, the greater the impact on the child's perception of gender roles.

The process through which this occurs appears to depend, in part, on whether the T.V. model viewed by the children is of the same or opposite sex. It has been found, for example, that nursery-school boys were more likely to reproduce nurturant, domestic, and artistic behaviours than leadership and problem-solving behaviours when the former activities were performed by a male model and the latter by a female one.[60] Children will reproduce more of the behaviours of a same-sex television model than an opposite-sex model, even when the same-sex model shows "gender-role-inappropriate" behaviour, such as a boy acting nurturantly. However, television is constantly promoting stereotypical masculine characteristics in boys by portraying males as solving problems and acting aggressively. Similarly, it is fostering traditionally feminine behaviour in girls by presenting female models who act dependently and expressively. Because of the very extent of its influence, television *could* act as an agent of change simply by portraying people engaged in socially desirable, non-gender-role stereotyped ways, such as by showing girls solving problems and boys acting nurturantly. The question that could be raised, then, is this: What exactly should be the role of television in this area? Is television simply supposed to reflect the status quo? Or do television programmers, particularly of children's shows, have a moral obligation to present gender roles as more flexible, in order to help developing children learn to cope better in a changing social world where the adoption of traditional roles most likely hinders an individual's social functioning?

The Peer Group

In the past, most children did not attend school until the age of five when they entered kindergarten. Today, however, there are play groups, nursery school, and daycare available from infancy on. Most three-year-olds attend some form of nursery school. Children are thus exposed fairly early in their lives to the peer group, one of the most important influences on a child's developing gender-role standards. It is probably not an exaggeration to say that we live in an age-segregated society, stemming partly from our age-graded school system. To a large extent, activities are carried out in age-related groups throughout an individual's lifetime. There are, in fact, organizations for everything in this group-oriented society, including self-help and help-others groups, as well as social groups and those formed on the job.[61] Groups, then, are very much part of social life. They serve an important function in that they monitor behaviour, convey to people what they are in relation to others, and allow people to assess their attributes relative to others.

The peer group is one of the first groups to which children must become attached if their needs for friendship are to be met. Either the child relates to the peer culture or he or she risks being rejected. Usually the peer group is composed of same-sex children, as cross-sex friendships in childhood are unusual. One of the most important functions of the peer group is that of mediator of the gender-role-stereotyped values of the culture. As such, the peer group disseminates stereotyped materials (e.g., records, clothes, posters) that originate in the adult culture. Girls' interest in folk heroines is often mediated by the peer group. In the 1980s they collectively "love" Olivia Newton-John, a singer and movie star. Interestingly, Ms. Newton-John personifies those traits that girls traditionally are supposed to strive for: prettiness, femininity, and the ability to entertain by singing and dancing. Groups of two or three girls will flock to her movies and they will also give and receive her records. A comparable folk hero for boys would be "The Fonz", who regularly appears on television.

The Peer Group, Values and Activities

In general, the peer culture emphasizes stereotyped features of gender roles; the values and norms of the group are those upheld by the stereotypes in the culture. Peer pressures on boys centre around physical activity and excellence in sports. In fact, boys are encouraged at an earlier age than girls to participate in organized peer group activities. Boys are encouraged to seek out playmates at an earlier age in the neighbourhood, and those parents who do not allow their sons to do so are accused of treating them like "sissies". Girls, in contrast, usually join groups later and less frequently. Their peer associations most often take the form of close friendships with one or two other girls. In general, despite the girl's association with the peer group, it tends to be less controlling of her behaviour than that of the boy. Her attachments tend more than the boy's to be to the family.

While the activities of girls' play centre around playing house, school, or hospital, boys are encouraged to engage in activities in teams that are in competition with other groups. There are important differences in the way physical activity is viewed here, which have significant implications for male and female peer groups. For example, a study[62] in four English-speaking countries found that physical activity was viewed as gender-role specific in all four countries. Male respondents saw physical activity as a challenge — allowing one to experience risk, thrill, or potential danger — and as a way of excelling physically. Female respondents had a positive attitude toward physical activity when it was seen as a social experience which enhanced personal health and physical fitness. If a boy does not excel in sports, he is seen as a deviant, and he will probably experience a decrease in self-esteem. But while girls may participate in sports, their participation is not nearly as critical to peer acceptance as it is for boys. Girls tend rather to engage in more individual-oriented sports such as swimming, skating, and gymnastics. Because girls do not have the team experience that boys do, they do not have as much opportunity as boys to develop a variety of team-related skills. In team sports, boys learn how to co-operate with others in order to achieve a common goal, as well as to subordinate their individuality to the team.[63] They learn leadership qualities by competing to become leader of their team. By developing these skills, boys become well equipped for the executive world, where team and leadership skills are required to climb the corporate ladder (see Chapter 8). While the acquisition of team skills may contribute to a boy's readiness to co-operate in various settings, they do not contribute to the development of the ability to relate meaningfully to others in emotional relationships.

The Peer Group in Adolescence

In adolescence, the peer group wields an even more powerful influence on the lives of girls and boys. While pressure on girls for early marriage is now decreasing, there is still considerably more pressure on adolescent girls to establish heterosexual relationships than to pursue a career. In this regard, the peer group provides substantial approval of a girl's popularity with boys. This, in turn, results in an increase in the adolescent girl's self-esteem. An adolescent girl's social standing among her peers depends more on her good looks and the boys who like her than on her achieving high grades in school. Marrying well is still seen as the goal that girls should strive for above all else. The female peer culture promotes this kind of thinking to the point of coercion. Boys are not encouraged to strive for marriage to the exclusion of other goals. The emphasis for boys is still on the achievement of physical excellence and on competition in sports. In adolescence, there is growing concern with the boy's future job or career and the preparation required for it. The values of the male adolescent peer culture are oriented toward the future just as those of their female counterparts, but the focus tends to be on the exploration of the skills and abilities necessary for a future occupational role. Relationships with girls also become important at this time insofar as they permit the adolescent male to explore his sexuality. Cross-sex relationships tend to be valued less as ends in themselves and more as means to an end in the male adolescent culture.

. . . .

The importance of the peer group as a continuing socializing influence on the development of the child's gender role, values, and behaviours should not be underestimated. Not only does the peer group communicate and disseminate gender-role information to the developing child, but it enforces conformity to gender-role standards among children and young adults who look to the peer group for approval and acceptance.

The Educational System

The educational system is one of the most important agents of gender-role socialization. This is because the developing child spends so much time in school, where the gender-role distinctions that were first learned in the home, then presented in books and on television, are further reinforced. This is accomplished through the curriculum, through guidance counselling, and by teachers. Beginning in the earliest grades, traditional gender roles are reinforced by the frequently observed practice of encouraging certain activities such as cooking and sewing for girls, and activities such as woodwork and mechanics for boys.[64] Even in "free schools", where there is no conscious attempt to enforce conformity to traditional gender roles, the policy of allowing children to "follow their own interests" frequently results in condoning stereotyped activities that children learn outside the school.[65]

As children progress through the school system, they learn that certain subjects such as English and Art are regarded as "girls' subjects" and others such as math, physics, and science, as "boys' subjects". In my own field of psychology, I have noticed how we have lost some excellent female students who wanted to become psychologists until they discovered that they had to take statistics courses throughout graduate school. Their anxiety when faced with the prospect of having to take mathematics courses rose so high that they avoided psychology completely and at the same time renounced their plans to go to graduate school. "Math anxiety", a concept that has been put forth to account for the avoidance of mathematics, primarily by women, is quite prevalent in the female population.[66] It is discussed further in the following chapter, where cognitive abilities and gender roles are explored. The mental block against mathematics experienced by many women is a prime example of how early gender-role expectations, based more on stereotyped beliefs than on reality, can function as an obstacle to an individual's pursuing her own interests.

The Role of Counsellors and Teachers

The educational system further perpetuates gender-role stereotypes through its guidance counselling. In the past, it was standard practice for counsellors to guide female students into "feminine" occupations and male students into occupations judged as appropriate for males. There is evidence that guidance counselling has not changed much in more recent times. In one study reported in 1977, for example, 300 high school counsellors were asked to select an appropriate occupation for six case studies (devised by the investigators) that could describe a young man or woman.[67] When the case study described a young woman, the counsellors chose occupations that paid less, required less education, and were more closely supervised than when the same case study described a young man. Could it be that guidance counsellors think that a young woman's primary goal is to get married and that they would therefore not want or need a well-paying job with considerable responsibility? If, in fact, guidance counsellors expect lower occupational aspirations among girls, as evidence suggests, they cannot help but communicate this to their students, implicitly and explicitly. The message becomes even more authoritative for the student, considering that it is being conveyed in a highly respected institution, the school, by a member of that system.

Teachers also play a major part in perpetuating traditional gender-role behaviour in their students. For example, gender-role stereotyping has been found to characterize the attitudes and expectations of both prekindergarten and secondary school teachers.[68,69] If a teacher consistently expects children to behave and think in stereotyped ways, we should not be surprised to find that they do. In fact, one study showed that preschool teachers reacted differently to their male and female pupils, particularly when the pupils behaved aggressively or dependently.[70] Instead of ignoring boys when they behaved aggressively, the teachers "rewarded" the boys' behaviour by drawing attention to it. Girls' "bad" or aggressive behaviour was treated quite differently. Instead of calling attention to the girls when they behaved aggressively, the teachers scolded them softly so the others could not hear. Girls were also encouraged more than boys to stay close to and depend on the teacher. So teachers tended to respond more to the girls when they were close to them than when they were farther away. However, they paid the same attention to boys whether they were nearby or not. While boys were encouraged to work independently, girls were rarely sent off to work on their own without the close supervision of the teacher. The reader should not get the impression that the teachers deliberately set out to inculcate traditional gender-role behaviour in their pupils. On the contrary, they were not aware that they were treating the girls and boys differently. Thus, their expectations and the accompanying behaviour can be said to be part of a traditional unnoticed and subtle ideology based on gender-role stereotypes and which can easily coexist with a conscious egalitarian philosophy.

Besides encouraging dependency in girls, teachers play a significant part in training girls to be obedient and docile.[71] Instead of rewarding initiative, parents and teachers alike reward neatness and cleanliness.[72] As these traits are being reinforced in girls both at home and in the classroom, it is not surprising to find them more prevalent among girls than boys.

. . . .¨. . . . .

In summary, then, the educational system can be regarded as a significant socializing agent of gender roles. In fact, traditional attitudes about gender roles pervade the entire system. Teachers, the curriculum, guidance counsellors, and books are all saying the same thing to students. But traditional gender-role behaviour is not immutable. It can be modified by changes in attitudes held by the authorities in the school. This was demonstrated in a comparative study of middle-class fourth graders, some of whom came from a "traditional" school and others, from a "modern" school.[73] In the modern school, which was characterized by more flexible and less traditional attitudes about gender roles, the girls generally showed less concern for approval than in the more traditional school. "Modern" school girls were also found to be as competent as boys in problem solving; in the traditional school, the boys were better.

If the educational system is to change its traditional attitudes regarding gender roles and move toward increasing flexibility, individuals within the system have first to confront their own beliefs and attitudes about the limitations and potential of males and females. In spite of all efforts to the contrary, teachers and school counsellors still bring certain prejudices to their work regarding feminine and masculine gender roles. It is important that school personnel have access to knowledge about the psychology and sociology of gender roles and gender-role socialization to counteract any unsubstantiated beliefs which may nevertheless be held tenaciously — and sometimes unconsciously. Some organizations have already been created to disseminate information and services relating to gender roles. For example, the Resource Center on Sex Roles in Education, established in Washington, D.C., in 1973, provides supportive services for individuals and groups working to reduce discrimination and stereotyping on the basis of sex in education. Among its activities have been the creation of a data bank of documents relating to sexism in the schools and the publication of materials, including supplementary teaching resources on gender-role stereotyping. Other educative efforts have been undertaken by the Feminist Press in New York State, which teaches courses on sexism in education to Long Island teachers and administrators. Ideally, courses on gender-role stereotyping and its effects on students should be provided in all teachers' colleges to make prospective teachers aware of their own attitudes and prejudices and to help them deal with students as individuals, not simply as members of a class — male or female. In fact, all educational personnel, including guidance counsellors and administrators, could benefit from these kinds of courses.

Gender-Role Differences in Cognitive Ability and Achievement

Achievement is highly valued in our society — particularly in intellectual areas. People who have prestige, status, and money are rated highly not only because of the power they possess, but also because they convey an ideal image of success and accomplishment — they have "made it". To be successful is to be "good"; to be a failure is to be "bad". Such is the message mercilessly driven home to children, beginning with the parents' earliest socialization efforts and faithfully carried on during the school years.

There are many factors that influence the extent of a person's achievements. One of these is just how much the person wants to accomplish something, whether it be completing a degree or composing a musical symphony. While some people do not really care much about achieving, there are others who want to achieve something so much that their anxiety also increases to the point that it has debilitating effects on their performance. Abilities also determine, to a great degree, the extent of a person's accomplishments. Research has documented that people differ greatly in their basic abilities, including general intelligence, verbal facility, and mathematical ability, for example. Obviously, then, a person who is high in mathematical ability stands a better chance of getting a Ph.D. in advanced mathematics than one whose ability is considerably lower, all other things being equal between the two.

Achievement can also be affected by a person's support system — that is, the extent to which people close and important to the person encourage his or her achievement efforts. The amount of help, encouragement, and opportunity available to a person may frequently be critical factors in whether or not a person's achievement efforts meet with success. A young woman born with the potential to be an intellectual genius, who is encouraged from earliest childhood to express her motivation to achieve in caretaking activities of others, is obviously not in an environment conducive to the fostering of her intellectual potential. This person's potential for intellectual achievement will have been wasted, since the environment did not provide the necessary opportunity and support for its realization.

The history of notable achievement has featured a disproportiona-

Mary Wollstonecraft Shelley
Author of *Frankenstein* (1818)

Mary Wollstonecraft Shelley has been known more for her association with a great poet than for her own literary work.

tely high number of men. This can be explained, in part, by the fact that history has been written by *men,* in accordance with *masculine* values, from a *masculine* perspective. Traditionally, women's "achievements" have been defined quite differently — famous women throughout history have been known for their great beauty or because they were the wife, mistress, or mother of a famous, highly achieving man. But creative achievement has always been considered a male stronghold. Even in these days of apparent liberation when women are beginning to make inroads into some traditionally masculine employment spheres, men are still disproportionately represented among those who are recognized as having produced outstanding achievements whether that be in the fields of literature, science, mathematics, medicine, or music. How is this to be explained? Are there any psychological reasons for women's relative obscurity in the area of notable achievement? Do women's cognitive abilities differ from those of men in any ways which would prevent them from achieving more? Or do women achieve less because they are less motivated to achieve than men? Finally, is there any evidence that women have less support from their environment than men in their creative and intellectual efforts? These are some of the questions to be dealt with in this chapter.

Cognitive Abilities

No matter how much a man or woman may want to be successful, success is very unlikely if that person lacks the necessary ability or aptitude. Early psychologists thought that most abilities, including intelligence, were innate (you were born with an ability or you were not). It was generally held by the "nativists" that there was little in the environment that could modify one's basic ability. According to the contemporary psychological view, however, abilities are not the direct result of inborn, preordained factors, but the product of a multitude of factors — not the least of which is the person's experience. This does not mean that innate (sometimes referred to as biological or genetic) factors are not important. However, their role has been redefined as one of setting the limits for a person's potential ability or intelligence. The realization of one's potential depends on the range and richness of the person's experience. A person may inherit the potential to be an intellectual genius, but if that person is not exposed to a richly stimulating environment, presenting vast opportunity for expressing intellectual curiosity, the chances are that the intellect will fail to even approach its potential. The discussion of abilities and the factors influencing them raises again the familiar psychological controversy, known as the "nature-nurture" problem: How much of a behaviour or a potential for behaviour, is due to inborn, hereditary factors, and how much is the result of environment (including learning)?

In considering abilities and how they differ in men and women, both hereditary and environmental factors must be taken into account. This is because men and women differ not only biologically, but also in the experiences to which they are subjected both as children (see Chapters 3 and 4) and as adults. But, in the past, when differences in abilities were observed between the sexes, biological (or genetic) factors tended to be invoked and were weighed more heavily than experiential ones. People were not unaware of the importance of experience in shaping and fostering abilities, but the bias was toward the belief that innate factors had a predetermined influence. Earlier research tended to support what many psychologists believed from the outset — that there were overwhelming differences between the sexes in most abilities and that these differences were caused by biological factors. But, at the time, research in this and in other areas of psychological inquiry was sadly inadequate in many ways. Samples were often small, since statistical techniques designed to handle large quantities of data had not yet been developed. Studies frequently lacked necessary controls. Of late, better research has demonstrated the importance of experience in shaping one's ability — in the areas of intelligence, verbal facility, and mathematical skill. While it does not completely rule out the influence of biological and innate factors, there is a growing body of research which links differences in certain abilities to differences in the experiences of men and women. Equally important is the recent observation that the abilities of women and men are tending to converge — differences in some abilities consistently noted in the past may be disappearing.

This is happening at a time when, in many ways, the experiences of women and men are converging. Gender-role distinctions are certainly not disappearing, but, at least among the younger members of society, there is some evidence of a decreasing conformity to traditional gender-role requirements in some areas. For example, the Women's Liberation Movement has contributed to a greater acceptance of so-called masculine behaviour in women in certain situations. Assertion, dominance, and leadership are no longer considered solely the man's domain. Similarly, certain sectors of society are beginning to become somewhat more tolerant of "maternal" behaviour in men — something that was taboo in the not-too-distant past.

The study of gender- and sex-related differences in abilities is critical not only because it will increase understanding of abilities in general, but also because it will give further insight into psychological differences between women and men. Of particular interest here is an examination of differences in cognitive abilities — those relating to the seeking, processing, and retention of information during the course of problem solving.

General Intelligence

When the discussion turns to cognitive differences between the sexes* one question always arises: Are males and females equally intelligent? Before the question can be answered, an acceptable definition of intelligence must be found. A psychologist who was asked this question would likely give an

---

* When differences in cognitive abilities have been studied, the only information typically available to the investigators has been the biological sex of the participants; hence, the phrases "differences between the sexes" and "sex differences" will be used frequently throughout this chapter.

operational definition: intelligence is what an intelligence test measures, usually including various forms of verbal and nonverbal skills. The typical intelligence test will therefore include several subtests designed to assess composite abilities. Some of these might be tests of memory, fluency, comprehension, and mathematical ability, for example. For the most part, studies have not found differences between the sexes on general I.Q. tests. Sometimes, however, girls have been found to score higher on general I.Q. tests than boys. When this happens, however, it is discovered that the particular I.Q. test that is used (and there are many) has concentrated heavily on verbal skills — skills in which girls typically excel. For the most part, however, I.Q. tests are well balanced — psychologists have standardized them so as to minimize sex differences. It is not surprising, then, to find that sex differences are minimal or nonexistent when such general I.Q. tests are used.

While studies of sex differences in general or composite ability are interesting, they do mask some of the important differences that exist in the degree to which either sex possesses specific cognitive abilities. Some of these include verbal, spatial, analytic, and mathematical abilities.

Verbal Ability

Psychologists, as well as lay people, have generally held that girls excel over boys in verbal ability from the time the first sounds are uttered. One of the most extensive reviews of sex differences in verbal ability suggests, however, that this may not be the case.[1] What is suggested instead is that there are distinct developmental phases in verbal ability where differences between the sexes may or may not be seen. While, in the past, it was thought that female infants vocalized more in the early babbling stage before age two, Maccoby and Jacklin's review finds that evidence of an advantage in female infants is not particularly strong or compelling. In the next phase, which extends from age three to about ten or eleven, boys and girls do not differ significantly in verbal abilities, which include reading vocabulary, reading comprehension, language, and other fluency tests. Although boys and girls perform similarly during this phase, it is nevertheless of interest to note that throughout the school years, it is boys, not girls, who seem to have many of the reading problems and speech difficulties. Around the age of ten or eleven, girls begin to outscore boys on a variety of verbal tests, including "low-level" measures such as fluency and "high-level" measures such as analogies, comprehension of different written materials, and creative writing. Throughout high school and possibly beyond, girls outscore boys on a variety of verbal tasks.

But there is some evidence to suggest that changes may be occurring in the verbal ability of men and women. The 1977 U.S. national sample of high school students taking college entrance tests does not show sex differences in verbal abilities.[2] Although national samples are not without their potential faults — that is, they may be contaminated by sampling problems, it is important to continue to monitor gender- and sex-related differences in ability in order to determine changing trends.

Spatial Ability

Visual spatial ability refers to the ability to manipulate visually or to make judgements about the spatial relationships of items located in two- or three-dimensional space. Psychologists use a variety of tests to assess visual spatial ability, including mazes, formboards, and block counting. Some differences between the sexes in this ability have been recorded. For example, starting in about junior high school, boys receive higher average scores than girls on psychological tests for visual spatial ability. While both boys and girls improve on these tests throughout high school, boys appear to progress at a higher rate than girls. As a result, it is not surprising that differences between the sexes in visual spatial ability are on the average larger than those in verbal abilities.

More than any other intellectual or social difference between the sexes, the ability to visualize spatial relationships has been associated with explanations invoking genetic (biological) factors. One of the theories most often cited (sometimes referred to as the X-linkage theory) can be outlined as follows: There may be a recessive gene on the X chromosome which has a positive effect on spatial perception. Males have only one X chromosome, and if they received the recessive gene, it would express itself and they would have superior spatial perception. On the other hand, females would need *two* recessive genes in order to have superior spatial perception, since they have two X chromosomes. So, according to this theory, since the chances of getting two recessive genes are less than those of getting only one, males on the average stand a greater chance of having superior spatial ability. The relationship between spatial ability and genetic factors has been tested by examining intrafamilial (within the family) correlations of performance on spatial tasks. The expectation in these studies is that since the male receives an X chromosome from the mother and not the father, there should be a greater correlation in performance on spatial ability tasks between sons and their mothers than between sons and their fathers. Data from several studies have, in fact, shown this to be the case.[3-5] However, more recent data have cast some doubt on the validity of the X-link hypothesis. Studies using much larger samples of participants than in the past have failed to find the correlations between parent and child originally reported.[6]

There is some question, then, as to whether or not there is a genetic linkage which predisposes males to superior visual spatial ability. But even if there were a genetic predisposition involved in spatial ability, learning and experience would still play a role in its development. For example, it is known that specific skills involved in the manifestation of this ability improve with practice.[7] Girls and boys are also known to engage frequently in different kinds of activities as a result of their differential play patterns. It is quite likely that differences in spatial ability may be related to these differences in the experience of girls and boys. As mentioned in Chapter 3, boys and girls are frequently given different classes of toys to play with. Boys, for example, are likely to be found playing with toys that lead to an enhancement of spatial skills. Of particular relevance here would be building toys, blocks, connector sets, and transportation objects, such as cars, trains, and planes. Girls' play activity tends to centre more around classes of toys which elicit behaviour of serving and caring for others, usually to the exclusion of the types of play in which boys are often found.

Another difference in the experiences of boys and girls which may be pertinent to spatial ability differences relates to their experience with mathematics. From a very early age, mathematics tends to be seen as a subject more appropriate for men and boys. This observation is supported by the popular stereotyped belief that "women have no head for figures" and is further reinforced by the lack of feminine role models among mathematics teachers, particularly as students progress to the higher grades in the educational system. In any event, girls are less likely to take advanced math courses in high school than boys. Because of the interrelationship between mathematical and spatial abilities, girls' relatively lesser exposure to mathematics may be a factor in their lower level of spatial ability. The interrelationship between the two abilities has been empirically demonstrated in studies showing that when the number of math courses taken by high school students is partialled out, sex-related differences in visual spatial ability are mitigated or disappear.[8,9] These results suggest that visual spatial ability may be a by-product of math learning, particularly in "higher" or more advanced mathematics classes. Since girls are starting to enrol in these classes more, and since these classes seem to teach spatial ability, it is quite possible that the differences in spatial ability that have been observed between the sexes in the past may disappear in the very near future.

In summary, then, the research evidence seems to point overwhelmingly to the importance of experience in the development of one's visual spatial ability. The frequently observed male advantage on tests of visual spatial ability may be due to boys' typical play and educational experiences, rather than to some inherent genetic factor. Therefore, by rendering the experiences of girls and boys more similar, beginning with the earliest play, they should increasingly show similar levels of visual spatial ability.

Analytic Ability

For a long time, professionals and lay people have shared the stereotyped belief that men are the more logical of the two sexes. Many people also believe that this accounts for the paucity of women in fields such as science, mathematics, and philosophy — presumably areas for which analytical thought is a major prerequisite.

But what does psychological research have to say on this question? According to psychologists, the analytic approach involves the ability to perceive an item as separate or distinct from the context in which it is found; it also involves the ability to restructure a situation. One of the most frequently studied analytic styles is called field dependence-independence,[10] a psychological concept which involves the ability to separate distinctive features from a competing background and to identify one feature of interest. Two of the best-known measures of field dependence-independence are the Rod-and-Frame Test and the Embedded Figures Test. For the Rod-and-Frame Test, participants are placed in a completely darkened room. All they can see are a luminous square frame and a luminous rod in its centre. The rod and the frame may be tilted to the left or the right, independently of each other. The participant's task is to indicate when the rod is truly upright and perpendicular to the ground, regardless of the position of the frame. The field-independent person can ignore irrelevant cues and accurately identify the true vertical position, while the field-dependent person is most affected by the context and, as a result, makes errors in identifying the true vertical position. In the Embedded Figures Test (EFT), the participant is asked to identify a simple design that is hidden in a camouflaging or more complex background. A field-independent person can identify the simple design quite easily and is unaffected by the distracting background; a field-dependent person has more difficulty ignoring the context in order to find the embedded design.

An extensive review of studies using these tests shows that in early childhood, boys do not consistently perform better.[11] But a male advantage reveals itself at the beginning of adolescence and continues into adulthood. Although several studies do not find significant differences in the performance of males and females, when studies do report differences, males usually perform better. Psychologists have thus concluded that males are superior in "analytic" thought.

Yet, additional findings suggest that, contrary to what was thought earlier, studies of disembedding may simply reflect sex differences in the ability to visualize.[12] Perhaps the sex difference after puberty is spatial in nature and has nothing to do with analytic ability in general. There is evidence to support such a conclusion. First, male participants do not perform better on nonvisual tasks that require disembedding. There is no difference between the sexes on an embedded figures test that asks participants to touch the stimulus instead of to look at it.[13] Nor were sex differences found when participants were given a test involving auditory disembedding, where they were required to focus on one voice and block out another one.[14] Rather than indicating that males have a relative superiority in analytic thought, earlier research findings may then be interpreted as indicating that males perform better at visual spatial tasks.

It is one thing to conclude (on the basis of research on field dependence-independence) that there are sex differences in the ability to disembed visually; it is quite another to suggest that these differences are indicative of personality differences between males and females. It was originally suggested, for example, that there is an integral relationship between cognitive style and personality variables.[15] The field-dependent person, it has been said, is less resistant to social pressures, more easily influenced, and more dependent than the field-independent one. It is true that the description of the field-dependent person is strikingly similar to that of the stereotypic woman in this culture and that the description of the field-independent person closely resembles that of the stereotypic man. But this raises a question as to how psychologists have concluded that there is a relationship between small differences in the performance of relatively simple tasks and the possession of intrinsic personality differences. The very fact that descriptions of field-dependent-independent "personalities" correspond so closely to stereotypical descriptions of women and men suggests that researchers may have been influenced by stereotyped preconceptions of masculinity and femininity in their interpretation of the data. It has been suggested, for example, that sex differences in field dependence-independence explain why women go into nursing and social work, while men aspire to occupations that enable them to express their assertive interests.[16] But the investigator who made this suggestion would be hard-pressed to substantiate such a broad generalization. While it is true that field dependence correlates with measures of interest in people and interpersonal situations, there is no evidence that characteristics defining masculinity and femininity derive from differing cognitive styles. It is precisely this kind of global reasoning that has frequently led people to fallacious beliefs about the potential abilities of women and men. In short, the research evidence to date fails to support the frequently voiced conclusion that boys and men are more analytical than girls and women.

Mathematical Ability

Another commonly held belief is that mathematics is a male domain, in which males are just naturally superior. What does the research in this area indicate? Among elementary school children, there are few differences between girls and boys in aptitude or achievement in mathematics. During the grade-school years, boys and girls are not very different in their early acquisition of quantitative concepts and their mastery of arithmetic.[17] Later on, at the secondary and post-secondary levels, when studies reported differences in mathematical ability, they usually favoured boys and men.[18] One possible reason for these findings is that boys and men usually take more advanced math courses in high school and college.[19-21] For example, in one study of an entrance class at the University of California at Berkeley, 57% of the entering men had four years of high school math, whereas only 8% of the entering women had the equivalent mathematical preparation.[22] While some state that males score higher in mathematical ability because of their greater average exposure to math courses, others argue that course taking is not the significant factor here. For example, Maccoby and Jacklin,[23] in their review of studies on mathematical ability, report that the male advantage showed up in research that compared math scores of male and female high school seniors after equating them on the basis of the number of math courses taken. Another factor that may be at least partially responsible for the frequently reported male superiority in mathematics has to do with their superiority on tasks assessing visual spatial perception. Since many mathematical problems involve spatial orientation, it is not clear whether differences in mathematical ability would be found if the visual spatial aspect of problems were removed.[24] So there is a real possibility that the reported male superiority in mathematics may reflect the male advantage in skills other than mathematical ability per se.

There is a plethora of research data pointing to the overriding influence of social factors and cultural norms on the development of differences in mathematical ability. For example, in the fall of 1976, the National Institute of Education (NIE) in the United States commissioned papers on three correlates of sex- and gender-related differences in mathematical aptitude and achievement. These included cognitive, biological, and social factors.[25-27] The consensus among the three papers was that social factors, more than biological (genetic) ones, are responsible for the observed differences. What are some of these factors? For one thing, as a result of social conditioning, many girls and women believe that mathematical ability is a uniquely male skill and thus their motivation to even attack math problems may be low; either they feel they will fail on these tests or, if they succeed in solving them, they may feel they are losing some of their femininity — a threatening and anxiety-provoking thought. However, when there is a clear association between the mathematical reasoning required by a particular problem and feminine concepts, women are less likely to feel threatened and will perform better than when the concepts of the problem are masculine in nature. In one study where adolescent and adult participants were presented with problems involving primarily mathematical or geometric reasoning, the males consistently obtained higher scores. If the problem involving identical logical steps and computations dealt with stereotypically feminine content, such as cooking or gardening materials, the females scored much better than if the problem dealt with topics considered to be "masculine", such as guns, money, or geometric designs.[28]

Another social factor that has been found to influence girls' performance on mathematical ability tests is the sex of the examiner. For example, girls have been found to do better on math tests when examined by a female examiner, rather than a male one.[29] It may be that a male examiner makes girls more anxious about their math performance — his presence may raise the salience of the stereotypic belief that mathematics is a "masculine" field and that girls do poorly in mathematics. Is it possible that girls' lower scores in math ability in high school are related to the preponderance of male teachers there?

Psychological factors have also been invoked to explain differences in mathematical ability between girls or women and boys or men. There are those who suggest that girls and women in particular are more prone to "math anxiety",[30] a concept that is used to explain avoidance of and poor performance in mathematics. Fear of mathematics, combined with the traditional social influences on women discussed earlier, probably contribute to the disproportionately large number of women and girls who avoid mathematics and math-related subjects. A rival explanation[31] contends that there are math-anxious boys and men too, but that they are more likely than math-anxious girls and women to pursue math courses because they see these as more useful or as unavoidable if they are to advance in their future careers. Girls, on the other hand, are less likely to see the relevance of math courses to their future careers, since they neither pursue careers in scientific and mathematical fields to the same degree as men, nor are they likely to be very aware of the relevance of mathematics and sciences to careers typically associated with women such as nursing, education, and the social sciences.[32] Despite the growing importance of mathematics to work in scientific and technical fields, many intellectually proficient students (mainly females) avoid math courses and, as a result, restrict themselves to a narrow range of possible careers.

Creativity

Throughout history, men have numbered much higher among those we call creative — scientists, artists, writers, and musicians. One would be hard-pressed to name a female Einstein, Rembrandt, or Mozart. Does this mean, then, that women are incapable of outstanding creative work? This question will be dealt with shortly. But in the meantime, it is important to consider other possible reasons for the relatively few women who have been labelled as highly creative. For one thing, as was mentioned earlier, it is quite possible that history, having been written by men, is biased because of the generally held belief that only men are capable of being intellectually creative. Women's creativity and their greatest contribution have traditionally been thought to lie in the area of reproduction. If one believed at the outset that women were incapable of unique and outstanding intellectual achievement, it would be difficult, if not impossible, to locate female geniuses in any intellectual field — whether it be science, art, or music. Because criteria of excellence in various creative fields have traditionally been established by men, work produced by women would have to conform to these man-made standards in order to qualify as creative. Sadly, what frequently happens is that when women do produce exceptionally unique work, it is described as a product of the "feminine" mind and, therefore, regarded as substandard.

What, then, is creativity? Most obviously, creativity prompts the formation of a unique work, which combines old perceptions in a new way or otherwise goes beyond the barriers of established convention. A creative work might consist of the development and proof of a new theory in science, a new work in literature, a unique symphony, or an original art

Maryon Kantaroff, a well-known Canadian sculptor.

concept. In psychological research, where there is a need to define precisely any behaviour that is being studied, many measures of creativity have been used. Two of these are the number of different ideas produced and the uniqueness of these ideas. One of the best-known measures used by psychologists to study creativity is Guilford's "Uses" Test.[33] This test requires that the participant list as many uses as possible for a familiar object such as a brick. Other verbal and nonverbal tests are used to assess creativity.

An examination of studies pertaining to verbal and nonverbal tests of creativity has revealed that girls and women are just as capable as boys and men of producing new and unique ideas. Among preschoolers and children in the earliest school years, there appear to be no differences between girls and boys in verbal tests of creativity. However, from age seven, girls and women do better on these tests.[34] This is not a particularly surprising finding, since measures of verbal creativity usually assess factors such as fluency, word uses, and other verbal skills in which females have been known to excel. Tests of creativity relying on nonverbal measures use picture construction tests, fantasy activity, and other nonverbal measures of originality of thought, and they tend not to show any trend toward the superiority of either group.[35]

How, then, can we account for the underrepresentation of women among creative geniuses? Have the social conditions surrounding women had some effect on their creativity? A brief look at history should prove informative. The situation of female artists is a case in point. Any list of the most well-known artists would likely include few women's names. Germaine Greer, the noted Australian feminist and author, has traced the history of women artists in a fascinating and informative book entitled *The Obstacle Race: The Fortunes of Women Painters and Their Work*.[36] In this book, she asks why there have been no female artists on a par with the greatest male artists. This may be partially accounted for by the conditions in which artists were forced to live in the past. As was the case for most people aspiring to high-level achievements, prospective artists had to undergo a long apprenticeship. Since apprentices were not allowed to marry, it was not unusual to find them consorting with prostitutes. What is more, they were frequently a lawless bunch of men — dirty and wild. Under these conditions, it is not surprising that people were reluctant to encourage a daughter's artistic aspirations. Greer adds that people were not willing to "waste" their daughters by allowing them to become artists, since, at least until the 18th century, a woman's reproductive potential was considered one of her most valued attributes. This all points to the fact that the training opportunities required to become an artist were simply not available to women.

However, as Greer points out, the obstacles did not stop there. Equally important to consider are the psychological obstacles that prevented and continue to prevent women from becoming artists. Painting, she says, is a libidinous business, in which artists must be able to acknowledge their erotic desires and channel them into their work. But as will be discussed in the next chapter, long-standing societal traditions have continually sought to deny, repress, and control women's eroticism. According to Greer, women cannot express spontaneous desire because it has been conditioned to appear only in response to men's initiative.

The paucity of prominent women in the realm of classical music can also be traced to the existence of external barriers, as well as internal, psychological obstacles. The kind of thinking that affected female musicians in the 19th century can be illustrated by the story of Clara Wieck. She was a brilliant pianist who could play Mozart and Hummel concertos by the age of nine, and by the age of eleven she had premiered her first composition. In 1840, she married Robert Schumann, one of the century's finest musical minds. They were regarded as a brilliant musical couple. Despite her obvious ability, she wrote in her diary that her "highest" wish was to be a dutiful wife. This, in fact, is what she turned out to be — she succeeded in "bringing" her husband to some of his best work.[37] But in doing this, her own musical gifts were left to languish, and she enacted the secondary role typically associated with women in the musical world.

In addition to the generally held belief that women were not suited to a career in classical music, there were external restraints that functioned to effectively bar women from a classical music career. For years, women were not allowed to play in orchestras, which deprived potential female symphony composers of necessary orchestral experience. They could perform, but only on "proper" instruments like the piano. They were effectively limited to only a few possible instruments, since they were not allowed to spread their legs into awkward positions or play anything that was considered unladylike. Despite the tremendous pressures to restrict women from the classical orchestral musical field, there have been

---

Canadian Female Music Composers

Historically, women have been discouraged, ignored, or dismissed as musically uncreative by the male-dominated musical establishment. Women do compose music seriously — they just don't get much credit for it. For example, in 1980, there were an estimated 150 Canadian women composers. Canada probably has one of the highest ratios of female to male composers of any western nation, and yet, during the 1980–81 concert season, only three of the 94 Canadian compositions performed by the symphony orchestras of the land were by women. It isn't that women have been idle. Leading composers such as Violet Archer, Jean Coulthard Adams, and Barbara Pentland have each turned out well over 100 compositions. When was the last time you heard one of them?

From *Toronto Calendar Magazine*, September 1981, p. 31.

exceptional women who have defied these pressures. Sarah Caldwell, for example, an opera conductor, won international acclaim conducting opera in Boston. And, in 1975, she became only the second woman — after Nadia Boulanger in 1939 — to conduct the New York Philharmonic Orchestra.

While it is true that in recent times there have been fewer social obstacles to women's participation in various creative fields, psychological factors are still functioning as internal barriers to the realization of women's creative potential. For example, research on highly creative female mathematicians suggests that the characteristics needed for creativity are antithetical to those included in the usual definition of the feminine gender role. In one study, a group of female mathematicians, described as between average and high in creativity, were compared to their less creative female counterparts.[38] The creative mathematicians were quite different from the others — they appeared to be less involved in social roles and in interpersonal relationships in general, and they showed a marked tendency to be more autonomous and more absorbed in their own inner life. The creative female mathematicians also tended to think in unusual ways, had fluctuating moods, genuinely valued intellectual matters, and were more rebellious and nonconformist than the others. The less creative women, on the other hand, spent more time on activities such as teaching, administration, and those involving the community or politics. The creative woman, then, is less likely to take on the traditional feminine gender role, which emphasizes interpersonal relationships. She tends to be much more independent. But, more importantly, the highly creative woman can and often does put her own intellectual needs ahead of those of others, something that would be very difficult for a woman who has internalized the traits traditionally associated with the feminine gender role.

Interestingly, even when women are found in fields such as the sciences, which offer the potential for creative behaviour, social pressures tend to pull them away from purely intellectual activities, such as research, toward activity judged as more appropriate for women — for example, teaching. But femininity per se does not appear to damage creativity, since, on the average, it has been reported that men who have more feminine characteristics are more creative. Evidence has shown that highly creative men (such as architects) achieve scores of higher femininity on conventional tests of masculinity-femininity. The converse does not seem to hold true: girls with more "masculine" interests are not necessarily more creative. The requirements for creative achievement in both women and men seem to be independence, a certain amount of narcissism, the ability to reject outside pressures and to find self-expression in directed research activity, and flexibility in general attitudes.[39]

The fact that women are underrepresented among those who have made outstanding intellectual achievements throughout history cannot be attributed to incapacity for creative thought. Rather, the demands and expectations associated with the feminine gender role are in direct opposition to those required of creative and outstanding achievement. When the expectations prescribed by the feminine gender role are reinforced by social sanctions, the obstacles for women become over-whelming.

Gender-Role Differences in Cognitive Abilities: What Do They Mean?

While it was generally held in the past that differences in cognitive abilities were due to sex (biological) factors, rather than gender (psychological) factors, more recent evidence suggests that few differences in cognitive ability can be traced back to sex-related factors only. While not ruling out the influence of inborn factors, research is pointing more to socio-cultural and psychological factors associated with gender roles as major determinants of cognitive ability. In general, when differences are found in cognitive abilities, they tend to be small, and there is much overlap in the distributions of scores obtained by all male and all female participants on the traits in question. Therefore, small average differences between female and male participants tell us very little about the extent to which an individual possesses a particular ability. It is important to remember also that when the average level of performance on a particular test differs for male and female participants, there are still some individuals in each group who deviate from the group average.

One of the difficulties frequently found in this area is the tendency to "overinterpret" any differences that are found. Differences on highly specific psychological tests of ability, whether due to sex- or gender-related factors, have been interpreted as indicating a fundamental difference in cognitive style. Such a conclusion is highly tentative and frequently is not substantiated with empirical data. What is more, it is erroneous to assume, as some investigators have, that the disproportionate number of women and men in various fields can be explained solely on the basis of differences on ability tests. In short, the data do not justify the rather broad and, at times, expansive conclusions that are often made in this field.

Apart from these problems of interpretation, recent findings have shown that gender-role differences in certain cognitive abilities are diminishing and, in some cases, disappearing. The increase in reported similarity between women's and men's abilities suggests that differences found in results of earlier studies are not due to inherent biological differences, as was assumed. An alternative interpretation is that the experiences which contribute to the development of cognitive abilities may be growing more similar for women and men so as to result in similar kinds of cognitive ability in them.

Achievement Motivation

It is almost axiomatic to suggest that in any successful accomplishment, ability is but one factor. Not to be forgotten or underestimated is a person's motivation to succeed at an accomplishment — the drive factor needed for successful accomplishment. Achievement and the drive for achievement are, in fact, watchwords of our society and our educational system. It is interesting to note, however, that while intellectual achievement in children of both sexes is rewarded and encouraged, after puberty, it tends to be regarded as an all-male preserve.

Achievement striving is seen not only as a masculine trait, but also as the sine qua non of "true masculinity", whereby competition comes to be regarded as *the* guiding principle of life. Similar thoughts have led one author to give the following description of what he calls "the male machine" — the masculine stereotyped personality:

> The male machine is...functional, designed mainly for work. He is programmed to tackle jobs, override obstacles, attack problems, overcome difficulties, and always seize the offensive. He will take on any task that can be presented to him in a competitive framework, and his most important positive reinforcement is victory (p. 1).[40]

© Joel Gordon 1976

For women, on the other hand, successful accomplishment external to the family may be considered possible, but it is not supposed to become the essence of a woman's life. Successful achievement for women may be just one of several other things in her life. Moreover, our society still regards marriage, children, and the ability to form and maintain good interpersonal relationships as the necessary components of femininity. In fact, because achievement motivation and the drive to succeed were formerly seen as antithetical to the feminine nature, psychologists in the past did not even consider them worth studying in women.

The Psychological Study of Achievement Motivation

The first and most well-known treatment of the subject of achievement motivation was undertaken almost 30 years ago by a group of psychologists.[41] They began with the assumption that human motives are readily expressed in a person's fantasy thoughts. By analyzing people's imaginative behaviour, then, they were able to assess individual differences in motives ranging from hunger, for example, to achievement and affiliation. Of particular interest to the psychological study of achievement was the procedure whereby participants were asked to tell stories about a picture or pictures found in the TAT (Thematic Apperception Test) cards. These stories were then analyzed for "achievement" imagery — that is, strong concern about performing well and measuring up to standards of excellence, as well as persistent and varying attempts to achieve. At the same time, it was assumed that people who express the most achievement imagery under standard testing procedures are the ones most highly motivated to achieve.

Early investigators working in this area defined the achievement motive as a relatively stable personality disposition to strive for success in *any* situation where standards of excellence apply. A high need for achievement was said to be reflected in stories that told of working toward a goal, wanting success, and feeling good about accomplishments. A low need for achievement was seen as reflected in stories ignoring these concerns.

Achievement Motivation in Men. Since psychologists who did the early work on achievement motivation tended to study men and boys, rather than women and girls, there has developed a considerable body of information on men who have high achievement motivation. One of the interesting findings that emerged from this early work had to do with the way the achievement motive was found to be aroused in an experimental situation. The early investigators found, for example, that the achievement content of the stories the male participant told about the various TAT cards could be increased when the experimenter stressed in the instructions the relationship between the stories the participant was asked to tell and the qualities of intelligence and leadership.[42,43] This is because men are generally expected to excel intellectually and they are supposed to possess leadership ability (if they are "real" men, that is). Psychologists then reasoned that if this were the case, they could arouse the achievement motive fairly readily by referring to these qualities in the experimental situation. Another finding reported in this early work was that high-achievement-motivated males preferred, selected, and, in fact, performed best *not* at very difficult tasks, but at tasks that were intermediate in level of difficulty.[44] (They did not like easy tasks either because they held insufficient challenge.) The early work also reported that men who were high in achievement motivation preferred tasks that held some element of risk for them. They also performed better and persisted longer at these kinds of tasks, provided that the outcome depended on their ability (rather than just on chance) and that the results of their efforts would be evaluated according to some standard of excellence.[45] These are just some of the many findings on psychological correlates of high need for achievement in men. Moreover, the early work in the area led to extensive theoretical and empirical efforts designed to increase our understanding of the determinants of achievement motivation and its development in men.

What about Achievement Motivation in Women? Notable by its relative absence in all this research and theory is the subject of achievement motivation in women. Is this because psychologists up to the 1960s did not think women possessed any degree of achievement motivation, since most women were found in the roles of housewife and mother, and those who were employed were generally not found in what were considered to be challenging occupations or professions? Many people, psychologists and lay people alike, probably assumed in the past (and in the absence of data) that most women simply were not motivated to achieve the way men were. Certainly, in their socialization, girls are not

I wanted to be an astronaut... but it's "MAN'S CONQUEST OF SPACE!"

I wanted to be a doctor... but it's "MAN'S FIGHT AGAINST DISEASE!"

I wanted to be the president... but it's "MAN'S STRUGGLE FOR POWER!"

Now all I want is a SELF-CLEANING OVEN....

generally rewarded or encouraged to achieve in the same way that boys are. In any event, when early investigations studied achievement motivation in women and girls (which was rare), results were inconsistent either with one another or with the theory and research data on men and boys that existed at the time. For example, the projective measures of achievement motivation that were used to assess achievement motivation in males were not found to correlate with either achievement effort or with academic and intellectual performance in females.[46] This is not to imply, as some people might have assumed, that achievement motivation is not found at all in women. As a matter of fact, in experimental studies where instructions did not stress either intelligence or leadership, no differences were found between men's and women's achievement motivation. But in studies where the instructions stressed intelligence or leadership, men showed an increase in achievement imagery; arousal conditions in which intelligence and leadership were stressed did not lead to similar increases in females.[47] It may be that achievement in intellectual or leadership roles is simply not as important to women as it is to men or that these types of roles may be psychologically more threatening to women because of fear of loss of femininity.

Rather than pursue their study of achievement motivation in women to discover why women were not showing the behaviours predicted by the original theory, early researchers more or less laid the matter to rest. For example, Atkinson, one of the pioneers in this area, wrote an over 800-page book on achievement motivation, entitled *Motives in Fantasy, Action, and Society,*[48] but treated the question of gender-role differences in achievement motivation only in a footnote, where he referred to it as an unresolved problem. McClelland,[49] another well-known researcher in the field, did not even mention achievement motivation in women in his book *The Achieving Society*. Achievement motivation in women was simply not regarded as a subject worth pursuing. There was obviously a need for further research to explain, for example, the lack of a consistent relationship between achievement motivation and achievement performance in female participants. Yet early researchers did not investigate the matter further.

It has been suggested that one of the reasons for the inconsistent results between men and women has to do with differences in the nature of their achievement motivation. Contrary to men, whose achievement motivation was aroused by instructions that stressed intelligence and leadership, instructions that stressed social skills were sometimes found to lead to increased achievement motivation in women. Since women were found to possess attributes related more to social interests than intellectual matters, their achievement motivation was aroused in experimental situations where the instructions stressed their *social acceptability,* rather than their intellectual or leadership ability. For instance, when female college students were informed in the instructions to an experiment about their social acceptance scores, which presumably reflected their degree of acceptance by the other members of the group, their achievement motivation scores were higher than in a neutral condition where no such instructions were given; differences were not found for male college students when they were exposed to these kinds of instructions.[50]

In light of these findings, two theories have been put forth to explain achievement behaviour. The first theory proposes that different needs are important for men's and women's achievement efforts and behaviour. According to this theory, women's achievement behaviour is motivated by affiliation needs, and men's, primarily by achievement needs. While men are supposedly striving to match or surpass some standard of excellence, women are presumably striving for social approval. To what extent is this theory supported by empirical work? For one thing, while it is true that women do score higher than men on scales that measure desire for affiliation,[51] there are no real differences between them in measures of achievement motivation. According to this theory, under neutral conditions, women should exhibit less achievement motivation — in fact, they do not. Furthermore, there is no evidence to support the contention that women's achievement efforts are more influenced by social reinforcement than men's.[52] So, all in all, the experimental evidence fails to support the first theory.

A second theory assumes that women and men have similar needs for achievement, but that there is a difference in the kinds of activities and goals on which they focus their achievement needs. According to this theory, social skills and interpersonal relations, themselves, are often important areas of achievement for women. So cultivating social skills and experiencing interpersonal success are important goals for women because they represent a type of achievement. The theory suggests, then, that men and women differ in the areas in which they strive to achieve. Women generally express their achievement needs in social and domestic areas; men, on the other hand, are seen achieving more in sports, mechanical areas, and intellectual and political ones. Support for the second theory is found in experimental data. For example, when experimental instructions stress the importance of social skills, achievement imagery in the stories told by women increases, but there has not been a corresponding increase in their purely affiliative ideas.[53] In wanting to achieve in social areas, then, women are demonstrating that they hold high standards of performance in spheres perceived as appropriate for their achievement.

Gender-Role Differences in the Motive to Avoid Success

Through socialization experiences, girls and boys learn to value and develop certain personality characteristics. For boys, the characteristics held up as being important are assertiveness, competitiveness, and independence, to name only a few. Girls, on the other hand, are discouraged from being *too* assertive, and they are not usually encouraged to be competitive. One acquaintance of mine actually punishes her seven-year-old daughter for being competitive with her peers. But, we may ask, what are the psychological implications for girls when they are socialized away from direct competition? From a purely practical standpoint, women are going to be at a severe disadvantage, compared to men, should they choose to enter certain intellectual and occupational spheres where the competitive spirit is an integral, if not necessary, component of success. For Matina Horner,[54] a psychologist well known for her work on achievement motivation in women, success, or even the thought of it, can have negative consequences for people, mainly women. Thus, she speaks of the motive to avoid success which, she says, many women have when approaching certain tasks, because of fear of feeling unfeminine or fear of being rejected by men should success result. Because of their socialization experiences, she argues, women are far more prone to fear of success than men. Horner goes on to suggest that if the motive to avoid success is greater in women, this might help to explain the inconsistency noted between the findings for women and men in the area of achievement motivation.

The experimental technique that Horner used to assess the motive to avoid success is now classic. To assess its presence or absence in women and men, she employed a projective technique, in which the participants (college students) were asked to write stories to verbal cues.

For the women in her sample, the verbal cue was:

> After first-term finals, Anne finds herself at the top of her medical school class.

The corresponding verbal cue for men was:

> After first-term finals, John finds himself at the top of his medical school class.

Horner then analyzed the stories written by the students, assuming that the stories they told indicated how they themselves felt about the prospect of success. Motive-to-avoid-success themes were registered when the imagery expressed serious concerns about success. These included stories in which the character tried to deny the success, was unhappy about doing well, or had negative experiences as a result of the high grades.

Horner found that more than 65% of the women wrote stories high in fear-of-success imagery, compared with less than 10% of the men. Horner classified the participants' stories into three main groups: fear of social rejection, concern about one's normality or femininity, and denial. An example of each of these themes is provided below:[55]

1. *Fear of Social Rejection.* This was the most frequent theme.

The negative consequences described in the story were rooted mainly in affiliation concerns, including fear of being socially rejected. They also included fears of isolation and loneliness as a result of success. Here is one example of this type of story:

> Anne has a boyfriend, Carl, in the same class, and they are quite serious. Anne met Carl at college, and they started dating about their sophomore year in undergraduate school. Anne is rather upset and so is Carl. She wants him to be higher scholastically than she is. Anne will deliberately lower her academic standing the next term, while she does all she subtly can to help Carl. His grades come up and Anne soon drops out of med school. They marry and he goes on in school while she raises their family (p. 60).

2. *Concern about One's Normality or Femininity.* Stories expressing this theme include expressed doubts of one's femininity, feeling guilty about success, and wondering about one's normality.

> Anne is completely ecstatic but at the same time feels guilty. She wishes that she could stop studying so hard, but parental and personal pressures drive her. She will finally have a nervous breakdown and quit med school and marry a successful young doctor (p. 61).

3. *Denial.* The theme here is one of denial of the possibility of Anne's success. Other themes try to absolve Anne of any responsibility for her success.

> Anne is a *code* name for a nonexistent person created by a group of med students. They take turns taking exams and writing papers for Anne...(p. 62).

Horner's major research findings led her to conclude that women are more afraid of success and are more likely than men to dread what they perceive to be its negative consequences. She went on to show that female college students who expressed "fear of success" performed more poorly on a test given in what she called a competitive situation* involving men than they did when they were alone.[56] On the other hand, the smaller group of women who showed little fear of success and the men performed better in the group situation than when alone. Presumably, the explanation is that a "competitive" situation elicits anxiety in the woman who has a fear of success and that this anxiety inhibits her performance when "competing" with a man. When performing alone, however, the anxiety would be considerably lower, so her performance would not be debilitated in the same way.

Horner's concept of the "motive to avoid success" caught on. Finally, there was an explanation that could apparently account for the frequent observation that women do not act or think like men in the area of

---

* *In fact, what Horner calls a competitive situation was not competitive at all. It simply consisted of female and male participants working on a task in the same room.*

achievement. Since her original work, dozens of studies all over the world have been asking women and men to tell stories about Anne and John. The essence of the mood that greeted and followed Horner's research is put very well in the following excerpt from an article in *Psychology Today:*

> Horner's conclusions, and the dramatic methods she used, captured both the popular and professional imagination. The media have recounted her findings widely . . . and almost everyone has tended to generalize from Horner's undergraduates to all women (p. 82).[57]

Notwithstanding its popular and professional appeal, the concept of the motive to avoid success is far from proven. For one thing, fear of success has not consistently been shown to be more prevalent among women. In one review of 61 studies, for example, the median rate of fear of success reported was 47% for women and 43% for men. And, in about one half of the studies with male participants, fear of success was more common among men.[58] Also, considering the plethora of studies in this area, it appears that the percentage of men and women showing fear of success depends on several factors, such as the time (year) they were tested, age of the participants, place of testing, etc.[59] Such wide variation makes us question whether we are dealing with a motive at all because a motive should remain fairly constant across a wide variety of situations.

If fear of success is not a motivational concept, then what was Horner measuring? It is possible that Horner was, in fact, assessing people's cultural stereotypes of appropriate behaviour for women and men. Viewed in this way, then, Anne's avoidance of success in a man's field is merely a reflection of the generally held belief that women should not attempt to succeed in traditionally masculine fields. So if stereotypes are the major influence in the kinds of stories people are telling, then *both men and women* (and not just women) should tell more "fear-of-success" stories about Anne than about John, thus reflecting the traditional belief that women find success more aversive.

This kind of reasoning led to another study very similar to Horner's, but this time asking both women and men to tell stories about Anne and John.[60] The results suggest that cultural stereotypes, not the individual's own motives, were the major influencing factors: both men and women told more stories indicating fear of success when they were given the sentence with Anne. (If the stories were really tapping a person's own motives, the expectation is that women would tell more stories indicating fear of success about both Anne and John than would men, thus reflecting their own stronger fear of success.) In fact, under these conditions, men told even more such stories (68%) than did women (51%) when talking about Anne. But only 21% of the men and 30% of the women indicated negative incidents when they were talking about John being in medical school. These results suggest, then, that "fear of success" may simply represent people's stereotyped reactions to successful women in a "man's" field. The reasoning can be extended one more step; if gender-role-appropriate success is the critical factor, then "fear-of-success" imagery should also be found when a man achieves success in a traditionally feminine field.

To test this postulate, male and female participants were asked in another study[61] to write five-minute stories in response to cues depicting a man's or woman's success in medical or nursing school. The results were that both male and female participants created stories reflecting fear-of-success imagery when presented with a woman in a nontraditional field for a woman, namely medicine. Similarly, both male and female participants told stories with negative consequences for a man in a nontraditional career field for men (i.e., nursing). The results thus showed that both men and women tended to express avoidance of activities seen as inappropriate to the person's gender role and that they anticipated negative consequences for people who violate gender-role norms in their choice of activities. The implications of these more recent research findings are critical in our interpretation of Horner's original concept. For one thing, "fear of success" would appear *not* to be a predominately female concern, as originally suggested by Horner. Instead of viewing "fear of success" as a motive, the research findings strongly suggest that it is more accurately seen as representing people's stereotyped reactions when confronted with others (both women and men) who engage in behaviours that do not conform to those prescribed by traditional gender roles.

Expectancy of Success and Achievement Motivation

It would appear, then, that since the fear-of-success concept does not constitute a valid explanation of the differences in achievement patterns observed between men and women, it is necessary to look elsewhere for possible explanations. One of the reasons that has been given for women's apparently lesser achievements is that they have lower expectancies of success than men in a variety of achievement areas.[62] This may be a function of the stereotyped cultural expectation that women are less competent than men. In fact, psychologists have demonstrated in various studies that the professional and artistic work of women is often perceived as inferior to that of men. In each case, the same work was being evaluated by two groups of participants. One group was told the work was produced by a man; the other group was led to believe it was done by a woman. In one study, using college women as participants, articles in various professional fields were evaluated less favourably when the alleged author was a woman than when it was a man.[63] Another study found that students rated identical paintings labelled with women's names less favourably than those with men's names, although the difference disappeared when the paintings were presented as contest winners.[64] The assumption of male superiority was further demonstrated, this time in a study that examined evaluations given female and male applicants for a job in the field of academic psychology.[65] In this study, identical résumés, with either a male or female name attached, were sent to numerous chairmen of psychology departments. Ten résumés were sent to each chairman, who was then asked to indicate how desirable each candidate was, as well as the rank at which each one would likely be hired. Despite their identical credentials, the women were consistently evaluated as lower and were offered significantly lower academic ranks than the men. These results are most interesting in view of the belief frequently espoused by psychologists that it is a scientific necessity that data be analyzed objectively. The results also provide rather clear-cut evidence that covert discrimination can and does occur in academic hiring practices. It would appear, then, that there is a stereotypical belief held by many people that women are less competent than men. This seems to hold true for various professional and artistic fields. In fact, in one study, there was not a single occupational category where college-aged judges even expected women to be more competent than men.[66]

If people generally believe that women are less competent than men regardless of the field they are in and the qualifications they possess, it is more than likely that this belief will be communicated to women through people's covert, as well as their overt, behaviour. Therefore, it should not be surprising to learn that women's expectations for success are very often lower than men's. Women are also expected to be less competent than men. Because these expectations are part of cultural gender-role stereotypes shared by men and women alike, many women come to believe them. If women continually get the message that they are less competent than men, it becomes almost a self-fulfilling prophecy. They eventually come to believe it and may even behave less competently.

Causal Attribution and Achievement Motivation

Another major reason for the differences in achievement patterns between men and women has to do with differences in the way they view the causes of their successful achievements. In general, when men are successful at a task, they tend to attribute their success to internal factors, particularly their *ability*; women attribute their successful achievement to *luck*.[67-69] Moreover, the causal attributions of people's success or failure have significant implications for their future achievement efforts. For example, men who possess high achievement motivation attribute their successes to their high ability and their effort, and they perceive their failures as due to their lack of effort.[70] Their attribution of failure to lack of effort should lead to their trying harder in the future, which has been noted in research.[71] So failure can have a highly motivating effect in the high-achievement-motivated man. The low-achievement-motivated man, however, is less likely to see his success as due to internal causes such as ability, but sees failure as caused by his low ability.[72,73] What this means, then, is that men with high achievement motivation probably feel more pride in their success and are motivated to work harder when they fail. But the low-achievement-motivated man should feel less pride in his success and he tends not to persist in failure situations.[74]

Women's causal attributions for both success and failure are different, however, which might explain why they seem to make less effort at achievement-related tasks. For one thing, women perceive luck more as a causal attribution of their successes as well as their failures.[75,76] When successful, women are also less likely than men to say it was because of their own ability.[77,78] What this means, then, is that women should feel less pride about their success than men because they are less likely than men to accept personal responsibility for their successes. (To think that your success is due to luck rather than ability really amounts to saying that you personally had very little to do with the success.) It is not terribly surprising to find fewer women than men attempting to excel in achievement situations if achievement per se is not as rewarding for them.

Another factor that may be responsible for turning women away from achievement-related tasks has to do with their typical response to failure. Research shows, for example, that women and girls, more than men and boys, are likely to attribute their failures to their lack of ability.[79,80] If someone believes she has failed at a particular task because of her low ability, she will be unmotivated to try the task again because, she may reason, she will just fail again. This is because low ability is an unchanging state. Trying the same task again tomorrow presumably will not result in any better outcome, since the ability should remain the same — low.

It would appear, then, that the reasons people generally give for their success or failure bear a significant relationship to their attempts at achievement in the future. Women have not been encouraged to the same extent as men to accept personal responsibility for their successes. This may explain why they experience less pride in their achievement efforts than men. As a result of finding achievement less rewarding, women probably reattempt achievement tasks less frequently. Finally, women's greater tendency to blame their failures on their low ability (something about which one cannot do very much) has probably contributed to their fewer achievement efforts. If women, like men, were encouraged to regard their failures as due to lack of effort, they would try hard to "do better next time".

The Feminine Gender Role and Achievement

The observation that women are less likely to be high achievers in professional, artistic, political, and academic spheres has led many to the erroneous assumption that women, compared to men, possess less achievement motivation. But, as was mentioned earlier, women and girls in our culture, notwithstanding the widely publicized ideology of the Women's Liberation Movement and its emphasis on the necessity of women developing assertiveness, are not expected to excel as intellectuals or as leaders. Instead, they are encouraged to *be* well liked, *be* nice, and get along well with others. Not only do girls and women strive to develop these qualities, but as was mentioned earlier, these become important spheres of achievement for women. Moreover, unlike the gender role prescribed for men, with its stress on achievement in intellectual, sports or mechanical endeavours, the traditional gender role prescribed for women calls for achievement in the areas of social skills and interpersonal relationships. In fact, success in interpersonal relationships comes to be seen as a measure of the woman's importance.

An interesting demonstration of how this can affect the individual woman's behaviour is found in a study that asked some of the female participants to work as a team with their boyfriends on a timed scrambled word task, while having others work in individual competition against their boyfriends.[81] In addition, all participants filled out a role-traditionalism scale which measured the extent to which the woman conformed to the feminine gender role as traditionally defined. The results were that women who adhered to the traditional role ascribed to women did better in the noncompetitive situation or team competition, while the more nontraditional women excelled in individual competition. These results suggest that more traditional women achieve at their highest level in those situations (noncompetitive) that might be viewed as compatible with traditional femininity. Less traditional women, on the other hand, appear to excel in situations that are characterized by greater competitiveness and, as such, might be described as more "masculine". Thus, achievement within the sphere of the traditional role ascribed to women is considered acceptable as long as it is a co-operative, rather than a competitive, venture.

Other differences noted between the two groups were that the traditionals had less interest in pursuing a career and lower educational aspirations than the less traditional women, who also rated themselves as more intelligent. Taken together, the results of this study suggest why so many women shun highly competitive occupational areas requiring years of training and opt instead for less competitive fields, where they can care for, help, or teach others. All of these latter activities, being congruent with the social role assigned to women are less likely to cause psychological dissonance, particularly for the woman who adheres to the ideology of the traditional role.

It would appear, then, that gender-role standards can be a significant influence on a person's achievement behaviour. Both the nature and kind of achievement striving seem to be affected by one's gender role. While the traditional masculine gender role stresses intellectual strivings and the necessity to excel as a leader in competitive situations, the traditional feminine gender role prescribes getting along with others and "being nice" as goals in themselves. Fulfillment, women and girls are constantly told, lies in having meaningful relationships with others. Competitive achievement is only for "tomboys" who, it is hoped, will eventually give it up. Fierce competition in a woman is not only *not condoned,* but it is often feared by others because it represents a departure from what our society has come to define as "normal" feminine behaviour. The man who strives to achieve fame, money, and power in business is admired — he is seen as goal-directed and ambitious and is respected as a result. The woman who tries to do the same is perceived as pushy, bossy, selfish, and, rather than being respected, she is criticized, and may therefore be prevented from succeeding.

Early Childhood Experiences and Achievement

Our brief look at the psychological study of achievement motivation has made it quite clear why psychologists who did the early work in the area failed to find consistent differences between female and male participants. Patterns of achievement strivings would appear to be quite different for them. The aetiology of this gender-role difference can be traced to early childhood. All children are dependent on adults for their physical, as well as their psychological, care. Boys as well as girls need the approval and acceptance of significant adults (e.g., parents, teachers) in their psychological growth. But there are significant differences in the way boys and girls are taught to get that positive reinforcement. Boys are taught very early that they must earn their masculinity by turning to achievements in the world. Girls, on the other hand, are not encouraged or rewarded to the same extent to give up their dependency behaviour. Their self-esteem remains dependent on the love of others.

Achievement patterns that we observe in adult men and women can be traced to childhood. While little boys are learning strategies for coping with their environment and at the same time developing feelings of self-confidence and independence, little girls learn how to achieve security through affiliative relationships. The reason little girls fail to develop a sense of mastery and effectance to the same degree as little boys is that they receive inadequate parental encouragement in early independence strivings. As discussed in an earlier chapter, boys are far more likely than girls to receive encouragement for independent behaviour and discouragement for dependent or clinging behaviour. Since the little girl has less encouragement for independence, receives more parental protectiveness, and experiences less pressure for establishing a separate identity from the mother, she does not have the same opportunity as the little boy to develop effective skills in coping with her environment *nor* is she likely to develop the same confidence in her ability. Lois Hoffman put it very well when she said:

She [the little girl] continues to be dependent upon adults for solving her problems and because of this she needs her affective ties with adults. Her mother is not an unvarying supply of love but is sometimes angry, disapproving, or unavailable. If the child's own resources are insufficient, being on her own is frustrating and frightening. Fears of abandonment are very common in infants and young children even when the danger is remote. Involvement in mastery explorations and the increasing competence and confidence that result can help alleviate these fears, but for girls they may continue even into adulthood. The anticipation of being alone and unloved then may have a particularly desperate quality in women. The hypothesis we propose is that the all-pervasive affiliative need in women results from this syndrome. Thus boys learn effectance through mastery, but girls are effective through eliciting the help and protection of others. The situations that evoke anxiety in each sex should be different and their motives should be different (p. 147-148).[82]

Human Sexuality: Implications for Gender-Role Differences

6

> Coitus can scarcely be said to take place in a vacuum; although of itself it appears a biological and physical activity, it is so deeply within the larger context of human affairs that it serves as a charged microcosm of the variety of attitudes and values to which the culture subscribes (p. 23).[1]

Historical Perspective

Throughout history, societies have always defined what is sexually appropriate and inappropriate for women and men. What is more, societal norms have historically prescribed certain sexual practices as pleasurable and acceptable, and others as repugnant. From an historical perspective, it is evident that attitudes towards sexuality are integrally related to society's normative structure regarding men and women, as well as to salient social institutional forms, such as traditional religion. As attitudes toward gender roles become more "liberal" and these roles are seen to embrace a greater range of behaviours, there is a corresponding increase in permissiveness in prevailing attitudes toward sexuality and in the mores surrounding sexual behaviour. Likewise, the liberalization of attitudes toward sexuality and sexual behaviour, itself, comes to have important implications for the psychology of the individual woman and man and for the relationship between them.

One of the most important structural influences on the definition of "acceptable" sexuality in the Western world has been that of Judeo-Christian religious teachings. Traditionally, the Church has sought to regulate (if not prevent) sexual behaviour in both women and men. In the Judeo-Christian religious heritage of Western societies, the Old and New Testaments prohibit sensuality in general and sexuality in particular. These prohibitions can clearly be seen in selections from *Genesis, Leviticus,* and *Exodus* in the Old Testament, and from *I Corinthians* in the New Testament. The teachings of the Church follow from a literal interpretation of the gospels that sexuality is sinful. Marriage is seen as the only context within which sexual expression can occur. In *I Corinthians,* while stressing the desirability of remaining chaste, St. Paul also acknowledges the urgency of sexual impulses and advises that one should marry only if they cannot be controlled:

> But if they cannot contain [their sexual impulses], let them marry: for it is better to marry than to burn (*I Corinthians*).

108

The Fall of Adam and Eve
Albrecht Dvrer
Germany (1471–1528)
Engraving
252 x 195 mm.
dated 1504
68.187, Centennial Gift of Landon T. Clay.
Courtesy, Museum of Fine Arts, Boston.

And, what is more, this view of sexuality had important implications for the way in which women were regarded. The defamation of sexuality led inevitably to the degradation of women — a perception that continues to infuse Western thought. Women were, in effect, regarded as agents of presumed "evil powers" in the form of the "subtle serpent" that tricked so-called honourable men into degradation. In fact, the early Christian Church regarded women as inferior to men. St. Paul, for example, instructed women to be submissive to their husbands, obeying them in everything.

There is a relationship between the view that the expression of sexuality is immoral and evil and men's belief in women's inferiority. In recognizing their strong, overwhelming sexual feelings, men had somehow to reconcile this knowledge with their perception of themselves as rational beings. The way they managed these feelings was by projecting them onto women: "Since she is attractive, she is tempting me and therefore *she* is evil." In this way the man successfully dissociated himself from any repugnant sexual feelings that he experienced. And, in the process of blaming women for their own eroticism, men could still retain their image of rationality and self-control: an image which was necessary for them to maintain their self-esteem. The expression "women are a necessary evil" probably had its basis in this long-held attitude.

Victorian Sexual Morality. The early 19th century in Europe was characterized by a repressive sexual morality known as Victorianism. So pervasive and influential were the attitudes and teachings of the Victorian Era on sexuality that one writer has been quoted by numerous others as saying, "Our culture is gradually convalescing from a sexually debilitating disease: Victorianism (p. 367)."[2] The widely held belief associated with Victorianism — that sexual behaviour should be engaged in as seldom as possible and certainly not enjoyed by women — may be seen as partially due to the teachings of early Christianity.

Victorianism really consists of a set of attitudes and directives regarding sexuality. Difficult as it may be to believe, Victorians, whose ideas dominated public morality in the early 19th century, regarded their bodies as a threat to respectability. So excessive was prudery at that time that patients, particularly women, refused to remove their clothes and submit themselves to medical examinations.[3] Sexual excitation was regarded as sinful and was condemned morally; chastity, continence (even in marriage), and self-control were valued and encouraged.[4] Sexual intercourse was generally regarded as an unfortunate procreative necessity; otherwise, it was seen as a waste of energy — a belief which formed the basis of the widely held attitude that more than one orgasm a week might debilitate a man. Masturbation was absolutely prohibited and was cited as a cause of all kinds of diseases, including insanity.

One of the most remarkable and well-known features of Victorian morality was the strict double standard of sexuality it advocated. Essentially, this meant that there was one set of rules for sexual behaviour for men and a different set of rules for women. While premarital sexual behaviour (usually with prostitutes) and extramarital sexual behaviour were tolerated, if not expected, in men, women were required to enter marriage as virgins and under no conditions were they allowed to have extramarital relations. Women were also denied any sexual drives; they were expected to remain passive in sexual intercourse and to show no pleasure. But, interestingly, this attitude presents a paradox considering another prevalent belief at the time — namely, that women were totally physical beings, instinctive and emotional by nature, constructed essentially for childbearing and nursing.[5] While women were not allowed to enjoy sexual behaviour of any kind, they were taught to tolerate their husband's sexual advances as part of their marital duty. The passage quoted below from a marriage manual published toward the end of the 19th century illustrates this very well:

> As a general rule, a modest woman seldom desires any sexual gratification for herself. She submits to her husband, but only to please him; and, but for the desire for maternity, would far rather be relieved from his attentions. The married woman has no wish to be treated on the footing of a mistress (p. 227).[6]

Because it was considered natural for men to be sexually aggressive, it was up to the wife to maintain propriety in the marriage bed by her lack of display of feelings.

Such was the Victorian morality. Needless to say, sexuality was conflict ridden, particularly for women. The situation was exacerbated by people's fear of venereal disease and the possibility of pregnancy because of lack of effective birth control.

Trends toward Liberalization. During the Victorian Era, sexuality, being shrouded in ignorance, remained a taboo subject. And Victorianism dominated thinking about sexuality until well into the 20th century when medical, social, and cultural changes led to a liberalization of sexual mores. For example, the trend toward the scientific study of sexuality and the dissemination of the results in scientific and lay circles alike did much to open up discussion in the sexual arena. It also served to dispel many of the myths that people held about the nature of sexuality. The first widely known attempt to study sexuality has its origins in the work of Havelock Ellis, whose *Studies in the Psychology of Sex*[7] were originally published between 1897 and 1910. He probably shocked his readers at the time with information that was based on data from cultural groups all over the world. He found that masturbation and other sexual responses were fairly common early in the lives of both girls and boys and that women's sexuality reached its peak later than that of men and continued to be strong late in life. According to Ellis, frigidity in women, which was quite common at the time, was the result of repression of sexual expression in girlhood. He was certainly ahead of his time when he wrote that a critical factor contributing to a woman's frigidity was the man's ignorance of the importance of stimulation of the clitoris, either directly or indirectly.

Another "shock" to the scientific community and to the public came in the form of Freud's now well-known theories of personality development. In his book *Three Essays on the Theory of Sexuality*,[8] published in 1905, he talked about the role of infant sexuality in the development of personality and adult sexuality. At that time, the idea that children were sexual beings was totally unacceptable. In effect, Freud's theory was based on the premise that human beings are filled with many conflicting emotions, desires, and impulses. Such an assumption constituted an affront to his readers — a challenge to the prevailing attitude that civilized *man* is a rational creature, unmoved by most emotions.[9] And when Freud talked about penis envy, incestuous desires in children, and castration fears, he could not help but offend the Victorians, who were not even able to accept the idea of eroticism in adults, let alone in children. Freud's work not only stimulated discussions about sexuality, but also demonstrated the importance of sexuality as an integral part of both normal and abnormal personality development.

Another key factor that led to greater liberalization of sexual mores was the contraceptive revolution of the late 19th century when the vulcanized rubber condom, the pessary cap, and the diaphragm made their appearance.[10] At first, these methods were used by about 20 to 30% of the population and eventually they became fairly widespread. Contraceptives were not new, however; they had been used for centuries, albeit their effectiveness in preventing pregnancy could very often be questioned. For example, the biblical method of withdrawal and Casanova's method of placing a hollowed-out lemon rind over the cervix, are just two that have been documented.

Since 1900, changes in sexual behaviour and sexual attitudes have been in the direction of greater liberalization. The changes that have occurred can best be described as an expansion of the concept of sexuality. The years since 1900 have seen greater liberalization of sexual behaviour and attitudes, changes that have been, in essence, an expansion of the concept of sexuality. In the 50 years from World War I to the late 1960s, there was a reduction in guilt feelings about sexual activity, and public discussion of sexuality increased. With the "sexual revolution" of the sixties came relatively more effective contraception, decreasing censorship, legalized abortion, acceptance of alternative forms of sexual expression, and an increase in the acceptance of hedonism. Instead of repressing their sexuality as they did in the past, men and women were encouraged to express it, as the range of acceptable forms of sexual behaviour significantly increased. But greater liberalization did not bring the utopia it had promised. With its emphasis on technique, the "sexual revolution" brought with it a new anxiety: fear of not performing adequately. Instead of liberating women, the greater permissiveness which characterized sexual attitudes led to their further sexual exploitation.

Marital Status, Sexual Behaviour, and Attitudes toward Sexuality

Sexual behaviour and attitudes toward sexuality have undergone dramatic changes in a relatively short time. It is probable that no other class of human behaviour or attitudes has changed so radically in just a few decades. The phrase "the sexual revolution" has been coined to refer to changes which cover everything from increased permissiveness toward alternative forms of sexual expression, to the almost complete disappearance of the female virgin, beyond a certain age. With the decline of the Church's influence, a proliferation of scientific studies of sexuality, and the growth of permissiveness in general, attitudes toward various forms of sexual expression and toward sexual behaviour, itself, have become much more liberal and flexible, particularly over the last few decades.

Premarital Sexual Behaviour among Men and Women

While the double standard has traditionally condoned, if not prescribed, sexual intercourse for the single male before marriage, the "good girl" was supposed to remain a virgin until she got married. Despite the prevalence of the double standard in people's attitudes, there is evidence that people's behaviour, particularly that of women, was quite different from prevailing attitudes. Not only was premarital sexual intercourse among women more prevalent than was generally thought, but it has steadily increased from the early part of the 20th century to the present. One of the first investigators in this area was Kinsey, who, in 1938, started to interview at least 10 000 people about their sexual behaviours and attitudes. He did not restrict himself to one or two groups, but included those in all walks of life, whose age, marital status, and social background varied widely. He found that 86% of the women born before 1900 had been virgins before marriage. However, by the 1950s, premarital coitus in women had increased — nearly half of the married women in Kinsey's sample had experienced coitus before marriage.[11] A U.S. national study of young unmarried women conducted in the early seventies[12] revealed that by the age of 19, almost one-half of those surveyed were no longer virgins, compared with about 18 or 19% of a comparable group in Kinsey's study. The rates of premarital coitus were considerably higher for males according to Kinsey's findings of the late forties — ranging from 68% of men with some college education, to 98% of those with only grade-school education.[13]

Other studies have found a continuing increase in premarital sexual intercourse in the 1960s and throughout the 1970s — particularly among women. For example, a U.S. national survey[14] of 2026 respondents found that only 41% of married women between the ages of 35 and 44 years had experienced premarital coitus, compared with 81% of the married women under age 25. The increase for men in rates of premarital sexual intercourse was less dramatic: 84% of married men 55 years old and older had experienced premarital coitus, compared with 95% of those between 18 and 24 years. Critics of these surveys are quick to point out that since the respondents were volunteers, they might have been "sexier" than those who would not volunteer to be in a survey on sexual behaviour. Or they may have tended to exaggerate their sexual experience and thus not have accurately reported their sexual behaviour. But since survey after survey[15-17] continued to show the same trend of increasing premarital sexual behaviour, one tended to hear fewer of these criticisms.

With an increase in premarital coitus has there also been an increase in the number of young people's sexual partners? Results of various surveys show that there has been little increase over the last few decades in the number of sexual partners reported by unmarried youth. For example, about 30 to 40 years ago, studies showed that from one-half to two-thirds of women who reported having had premarital coitus did so *only* with the man they eventually married.[18-20] More recently, a little more than half of the married women in a U.S. national survey were reported to have had premarital sexual intercourse with only one partner.[21] So a substantial number of women both in the past and more recently have had sexual intercourse only with the man they eventually marry. The situation with men is quite different. Although men have more sexual partners than women have before marriage, there is no evidence that this number has significantly increased over the years. For example, married men 35 years old and older have been found to have a median of six premarital coital partners, and the median for married males under 35 years old is still six.[22] Even with increased premarital sexual intercourse, there does not seem to have been an increase in the number of people's sexual partners. The findings that men sleep with more partners before marriage than do women probably reflect vestiges of the traditional double standard that condones premarital sexual activity in men while condemning it in women.

Although there tends to be a paucity of information relevant to the sexual behaviour and beliefs of Canadians, there are some data on the sexual behaviour reported by undergraduate college men and women in Canada. While fewer women than men report having had coitus premaritally, there is evidence that French-speaking students are more conservative in their sexual behaviour than their English-speaking counterparts.[23,24]

It is interesting to compare rates of premarital coitus in American and Canadian college students. Results of studies on sexual behaviour conducted between 1965 and 1977 suggest first that, in general, unmarried Canadian college students tend to be more conservative than unmarried American students.[25-28] While slightly more than one-half of male Canadian college samples surveyed have reported they were nonvirgins, the comparable rates in the U.S. samples were about two-thirds and higher. A comparison of American and Canadian female students reveals three main trends: firstly, since 1960, there has been an increase in female rates of premarital intercourse in both countries; secondly, in both countries, women tend to be less active sexually prior to marriage than men. Thirdly, women in the United States and Canada tend to resemble each other in their incidence of premarital sexual behaviour. As of 1975-77, about one-half of the female respondents on both American and Canadian campuses reported they were having premarital sexual intercourse, although Canadian women appear to have been somewhat more conservative sexually.[29,30] While these results are very interesting, they may not be indicative of national trends. No doubt, sexual activity varies as a function of numerous demographic factors including religion, region of the country, and cultural background.

Teenage Sexual Behaviour. Among those who engage in premarital sexual behaviour, young people under the age of 20 have attracted considerable attention from researchers in both Canada and the United States, partially because their sexual activity has increased in recent years and because of their high rates of pregnancy and sexually transmitted disease. Studies based on national probability samples in the United States show that while some teenagers have their first coital experience at the age of 12 or younger,[31] the older they are, the more likely they are to have had coital experience.[32,33] In a sample of about 400 U.S. adolescents (ages 13-19) in the early seventies, slightly less than 60% of the boys and 45% of the girls had experienced sexual intercourse.[34] In 1976, another American study of about 1500 single teenage girls found that while 18% were not virgins at the age of 15, by 19 years of age, 55% had experienced sexual intercourse.[35]

Canadian teenagers, like their American counterparts, are more likely to be nonvirgins the older they become. In 1976, a Canadian national survey of a representative sample of over 500 teenagers found that 30% of the boys had had sexual intercourse by the age of 15; by ages 16-17, the rate had risen to 41%.[36] The rates were much lower for girls: 8% of the 15-year-olds, compared with 18% of the 16-17-year-olds were nonvirgins. So, as we observed earlier, there is a trend for American youth to report more coital activity than their Canadian counterparts. While further research is needed here, it is probably true that the difference is due to many factors, including cultural, religious, and regional differences associated with each country.

There can be no doubt that the age at which adolescents are having their first coital experience is dropping.[37–40] One reason may be physiological; the onset of puberty has been appearing earlier. Improved nutrition, better medical technology, and better health in general all contribute to the earlier appearance of puberty. A girl today may expect to menstruate an average of some ten months earlier than did her mother.[41] About a century ago, a girl experienced her first menstrual period at about 17 years of age. In the past, young women and men were out of school and at work prior to reaching sexual maturity. Thus, they moved directly from the authority of their parents to the self-control required by adult economic responsibility. Today, one-third of all females now reach sexual maturity at or before 11 years of age. This has created new pressures for young women. With sexual maturation peaking in early adolescence and followed by many years of education and perhaps years of age segregation at university, young people are removed from the direct influence of their parents, and experience more social pressure from their peers. Youth today, many of whom do not experience pressure to be economically responsible for themselves while attending school, have the opportunity and time to re-evaluate society and its values, norms, and precepts. This has triggered unprecedented skepticism among youth, promoting greater exploration of sexuality and an increase in the individualization of moral judgements.[42] As a result, contemporary youth, both males and females, will be found engaging in more premarital sexual activity than did their parents. At the same time, they will be found "trying out" sexual relationships for the sake of a new experience.

Attitudes toward Premarital Sexual Behaviour

Not only has premarital sexual behaviour become more permissive over the years, but people's attitudes toward premarital sexual intercourse, particularly in women, have also become more liberal. Approximately four decades ago, moral objections to premarital sexual intercourse were fairly widespread. On the basis of interviews they conducted from 1938 to 1949, Kinsey and his associates[43] found that six out of ten college-educated men had moral objections to premarital sexual intercourse that were strong enough to have limited their own sexual behaviour. Noncollege men were less "moralistic"; nevertheless, one out of four of them felt the same way. But nine-tenths of the women in Kinsey's sample had moral views that prevented them from engaging in premarital coital activities. No doubt, people's greater moral objections to premarital sexual behaviour in the past were partly a function of their religious beliefs, which tended to be more influential in the past than today.

The changes in attitudes toward premarital sexual behaviour that have taken place may be summarized as follows:[44] there has been a shift in American standards (1) away from a belief in a strong "double standard" toward a belief in greater male-female equality, (2) toward a greater acceptance by men and women of premarital coitus in women, and (3) toward more "sex-with-affection" between people from similar backgrounds. Surveys of both college students and the general population in the 1970s reveal that a majority of people believe that premarital coitus is acceptable, as long as the two people are engaged, are in love, or care about each other.[45,46]

There is evidence that, at least among some groups, attitudes are moving away from the double standard toward a *single standard* of sexual behaviour for men and women. Among college students attending a large U.S. state-supported university, for example, attitudes toward premarital sexual behaviour in men and women became considerably more egalitarian from 1970 to 1975.[47] First, a man who had had coitus with many women was *more* likely to be seen as immoral by both male and female college students in 1975 than in 1970. And a woman who had slept with many men was *less* likely to be seen as immoral in 1975 than in 1970. This suggests that at least college students are indeed approaching a single premarital sexual standard. But to what extent can we generalize these results to the population at large? In the past, the sexual double standard was found to be more prevalent in the lower socio-economic groups.[48] If this is still true today, then the changes in attitudes described here may apply more to college youth than to youth in general.

While the double standard of sexual behaviour may be gradually giving way to a single standard for both sexes, there is still the feeling among many men that they want to marry a woman who has been "relatively unused" sexually.[49] A survey of 4066 American men selected as representative of all walks of life, ages, marital statuses, and backgrounds, found that one-third of the men preferred their wife to have had no sexual partner, other than themselves, before marriage. Another one-third of the sample said that their wife's prior sexual experience "would not matter". While 20% preferred their wife to have had sexual experience with "one or a few men she really loved", only 12% of the sample said that they preferred her to have had "a few casual affairs". What is more, at a time when it is supposed to be increasingly acceptable for people to have sexual relations for sheer enjoyment, only 2% of the men wanted to marry a woman who had had sexual relations with many other men. The investigators put it very well when they said:

> Fortunately... most men do not want to know [the number of sex partners the woman has had premaritally] — although they will invariably seek some verbal reassurance from the woman that there have not been *that* many (p. 296).[50]

Sexuality and the Performance Trap

During the sixties, along with a growing acceptance of premarital coitus in women, there was also a surge of interest in how to pursue sexual activity successfully, with a view to maximizing pleasure. At the same time, the market was suddenly flooded with books detailing the route to sexual pleasure for oneself and one's partner. For example, the best-seller, *The Sensuous Woman* by "J",[51] a graphic "how-to" book, might have been better subtitled *How to Get to a Man's Heart through His Genitals*.[52] Undoubtedly, the proliferation of these books contributed in part to a new openness about sexuality, becoming part of a growing body of information about the human body, particularly the woman's, which had been shrouded in ignorance for so long. While this new openness about sexuality had its benefits in terms of eliminating ignorance and allowing people to enjoy their sexuality, it also had its liabilities. Implicit in many of the books and articles written about sexual behaviour are performance demands — both on women and on men. Take the book *For Yourself* by Lonnie Garfield Barbach.[53] Its full title is *For Yourself — The Fulfillment of Female Sexuality: A Guide to Orgasmic Response*. It is an example *par excellence* of a book that stresses a woman's right to please herself. The glorification of multiple orgasms and prescriptions of what a truly "liberated" woman should be, have created somewhat unrealistically high standards of sexual behaviour.

Traditionally, as was pointed out earlier, women have not been expected to "perform" sexually, except possibly to simulate modest pleasure at appropriate moments. As the double standard breaks down and women begin to feel free to express their sexuality, they are no longer exempt from "performance" requirements. Today, women are already feeling the pressure to be skilled and experienced sexually. Changing attitudes toward virginity illustrate very well changes in attitudes that have occurred in recent years. While virginity was traditionally prized and clung to tenaciously, there is evidence in North American society that after age 20, it is being viewed with growing ambivalence and that some people even consider it an indication of undesirability and, to some extent, incompetence.[54] Today, women, as well as men, tend to be embarrassed if they are considered to lack either sexual experience or desire.

Sexual performance demands have important implications for the sexual roles that men and women enact. For one thing, two people frequently end up treating each other like an assembly of erogenous zones. Continually bombarded by descriptions in books of the parts of the body that should be stimulated, they end up adopting a clinical, depersonalized attitude about making love. They concentrate on each other not as creatures of love, but as sex objects to be worked on. Instead of having an honest relationship, they may try to act in ways that they perceive are expected according to these new sexual norms. A woman, for example, may fake orgasm because she may feel her partner needs her climax in order to feel adequate himself. Faking orgasm is similar to trying to make a favourable impression in order to "keep" a man. As long as women do this,

Courtesy Pieter Van Acker Miller Services Ltd.

Courtesy Miller Services Ltd.

however, they are not allowing themselves to learn what really pleases them. So the woman sacrifices the possibility of a wider range of feelings in order to flatter the man's ego.[55]

A paradox of our highly vaunted sexual freedom, according to Rollo May in his classic book *Love and Will,*[56] is a new form of puritanism, which he defines as consisting of three elements: first, a state of alienation from the body; second, separation of emotion from reason; and third, the use of the body as a machine — all of which are psychologically unhealthy. While, in the past, sin used to mean giving in to one's sexual desires, it now means not having full sexual expression. The contemporary "puritan" holds that it is immoral *not* to express your libido:

> A woman used to be guilty if she went to bed with a man; now she feels vaguely guilty if after a certain number of dates she still refrains; her sin is "morbid repression", refusing to "give". And the partner who is always completely enlightened (or at least pretends to be) refuses to allay her guilt by getting overtly angry at her (p. 46).[57]

This new puritanism brings with it a depersonalization of our whole language. Instead of "making love", we "have sex"; in contrast to "having intercourse", people "screw".

Implications for Traditional Gender-Role Behaviour. Despite the new "liberalism", many women still feel uncomfortable when they play an active sexual role. One of the reasons women may feel uncomfortable in the new role being prescribed for them has to do with the traditional feminine gender-role stereotype to which many women (and men) still subscribe. On the one hand, women are told to be sexy, to go out, in effect, and get their orgasmic due; but, at the same time, a woman may still feel the pressure to be traditionally feminine, pliant, accepting, and nonaggressive. The ambivalence generated by these conflicting prescriptions may create considerable anxiety, thus preventing the woman from "letting go" sexually.

The prevalent view is that the sexual revolution has liberated women from traditional gender-role prescriptions and from exploitation. It would be more accurate to say, however, that the sexual revolution has only partially modified behavioural prescriptions for women in a sexual relationship and that the use of contraceptives has fallen in line with conventional gender-role demands, leaving women vulnerable to both old and new kinds of exploitation. This is especially true for women who are just embarking on sexual relationships (premarital or extramarital) or whose sexual relationships have just ended.

The gender-role norms governing the sexual behaviour of women and men are largely carry-overs of views found in 19th-century Romanticism and Victorianism: the woman was an unattainable object for whom the man had an uncontrollable passion. The Victorian perception added a contradictory note to the portrait of the woman, who was also considered to be essentially a creature of emotion. Together, these attitudes constituted a stereotype that held sway over sexual relationships until well into the mid-20th century.

With the relaxation of sexual mores and the availability of more effective contraception, women are no longer seen as unattainable objects. Since it is the woman who risks pregnancy in a sexual relationship, she is expected to "protect" herself by taking responsibility for birth control. At the same time, the Romantic stereotype of men's uncontrollable sexual urges has survived the "revolution" intact, with all of its exploitative potential. This has led to men's assumption that women will be (should be) sexually available whenever men make their sexual overtures and that women will be the ones to take responsibility for the "inconvenience" of contraception, whether that be through the "pill", the I.U.D., or the diaphragm, for example. While it is true that fear of pregnancy has decreased as a result of the advent of more effective contraception, women are still less likely than men to engage in sexual behaviour for its own sake. Women more frequently view sexual behaviour with a man as an enhancement of the relationship and, compared to men, they are still more concerned with establishing a meaningful sexual relationship. Therefore, the chances of an unmarried woman becoming sexually involved with a man who has less emotional commitment continue to be great, a situation which also increases the possibility of her being sexually exploited.

Not only are women less likely than men to engage in purely sexual relationships, but the notion that they may be available for casual sexual relationships can be anxiety provoking for them. Many young women experience conflict about using the oral contraceptive pill after a love affair has ended, since it communicates their sexual availability. Consequently, they may discontinue using birth control, with the possibility that unwanted pregnancy may be more apt to occur in less serious relationships.[58]

Men, too, have not remained unaffected by the changes that have recently occurred. For example, men may feel at a disadvantage when approached sexually by a woman. This is because men have constructed a feminine ideal, which prescribes that women should be sexually accessible but not sexually demanding. While women are also expected to be docile and servile, they are not supposed to be totally uninteresting. Some men may not feel "masculine" when they are approached by women who are

Copyright © 1982, Randy Jay Glasbergen.

"Wearing your shirt open isn't sexy. Wearing your mind open is sexy!"

independent and able to express their eroticism. The reported increase in the incidence of impotence among men during the last few years has frequently been blamed on the increase in women's demands for high levels of sexual performance in men.[59] Sometimes a man is impotent when a woman takes the top position in sexual intercourse or when she plays an active sexual role.[60] Why are men "turned off" by women who try to initiate sexual activity? The psychological explanation must take into account the traditional longstanding definition of masculinity according to stereotypes. Very simply, the man is supposed to be in control of sexual encounters. When this control is threatened — that is, when a man is asked to "perform sexually" when he does not feel like it, he risks the possibility of not being able to "perform" at all. Many men have not learned to say "no" to a woman's sexual advances. Impotence, then, becomes a less painful way out of an impossible situation than having to refuse to have sexual relations — something a "real" man never does.

The newly liberated attitudes toward sexuality, with their emphasis on technique and a greater acceptance of all kinds of sexual behaviour, has led to a related problem known as sexual anorexia,[61] a condition involving a diminishing in sexual desire, voluntary celibacy, and intense sexual anxiety. Lack of sexual interest on the part of both women and men can be a defence against increased pressures and expectations to perform sexually. While some men may respond with impotence to the newly sexually assertive woman, others may withdraw psychologically by showing diminished sexual desire. Thus, rather than leading to increased fulfillment and pleasure, our newly found sexual freedom has resulted in a paralysis of feeling in many men and women. The normative requirements of gender roles as they were traditionally contracted are the antithesis of the expectations produced by the sexual revolution. These conflicts, though magnified by the sexual revolution, are just as much a product of prevailing stereotypical conceptions of gender roles. If individuals are to discover their sexuality and experience it fully, they will have to redefine their gender roles. If men are to fully experience their sexuality, they will have to give up their wish to control the sexual situation. With more experience at being sexually assertive, women should become more comfortable in their new role. As long as women feel they must be feminine in the traditional way, they will experience conflicting emotions, since the potential for enjoyment of their sexuality depends partly on their ability to articulate to their sexual partner just what pleases them. Instead of being a proving ground where the man and the woman vie for orgasmic track records, sexuality should be seen by both as a pleasurable experience which may or may not lead to orgasm.

Obstacles to Female Eroticism

There are other reasons why women have difficulty experiencing full eroticism in a sexual relationship with a man. Traditionally, women have always been told just how and in which part(s) of their bodies they should experience orgasm. The "correct" place, they were told, was in the vagina; the "other" orgasm, namely the one that resulted from clitoral stimulation, was not regarded as the "real thing" or as "naturally feminine". The original "dual-orgasm" theory was derived from psychoanalysis, as set out by Sigmund Freud (see Chapter 3). The clitoral orgasm, which resulted from masturbation of the clitoris (as practised in childhood), was supposed to give way later to the vaginal orgasm, which presumably characterized the mature woman. The mature woman, according to the "father of the vaginal orgasm"[62] is supposed to experience a transfer in the location of her orgasm or sexual response. According to Freud, if the shift did not occur, the woman was defined as frigid and sexually immature.

The idea that women experience two kinds of orgasm persists today. In fact, Freudian dogma on this point has been expressed in numerous books on sexuality that are read by millions. For example, in a very popular sex manual published in the late fifties, Robinson[63] says that the woman who experiences orgasm in her clitoris is suffering from a form of frigidity and, she adds, this type of frigidity is extremely common.

The widespread belief in the dual-orgasm theory of sexuality probably produced a great deal of frustration and unhappiness in women.[64] Physiologically, there is only one type of orgasm,[65] not a vaginal orgasm distinct from a clitoral one. Moreover, all female orgasms, regardless of clitoral stimulation, include vaginal contractions. Using photographic and instrumental observations during sexual intercourse and masturbation, Masters and Johnson have found that men and women experience orgasm in physiologically similar ways. In both sexes, the main physiological change in sexual arousal is that there is an increase in the flow of blood into the genital organs, which then become distended. This process is accompanied by irregular muscle contractions and then rhythmic movements. Research further showed that some women were able to experience multiple orgasms, given suitable conditions and effective stimulation. In direct contrast, men cannot have another erection after ejaculation, no matter how much they are stimulated, because of the refractory period that follows. Nevertheless, it has been reported that maybe about 20% of adolescent boys can experience multiple orgasm, something that declines with age.[66] Repeated climaxes may occur with or without ejaculation during a single act of sexual intercourse.

Masters and Johnson's research has been criticized for using participants who were not representative of the population at large. After all, just how many people would consent to being wired up, observed, and monitored while engaging in a most personal and private behaviour? While, admittedly, this is a valid criticism, the physiological reactions that were observed and recorded in the Masters-Johnson laboratory are probably indicative of sexually aroused individuals who are relaxed and comfortable with their surroundings. It is also true that there are wide individual variations in the conditions in which a person can experience sexual arousal. For some, these might include having coitus in a laboratory while being observed; for most others, the privacy of the bedroom may be the only suitable place where sexual arousal can comfortably occur.

Nevertheless, more recent research suggests that sexual intercourse is not an effective way for most women to experience orgasm. For example, in one study, only 30% of a sample of over 3000 women said they experienced orgasm on a regular basis during intercourse.[67] An additional 19% of the women said they required simultaneous clitoral stimulation by hand. Another 22% reported having orgasms only rarely during intercourse, and 29% did not experience orgasm at all. An overwhelming majority of the women (82%) said that they masturbated, almost all of whom said that orgasm was experienced regularly and easily in this way. So direct clitoral stimulation is necessary for most women to experience orgasm regularly. However, despite the association between manual stimulation of the clitoris and orgasm, the women in this study were reluctant to request manual stimulation of the clitoris from their sexual partners. The reason why more women may not have enlisted their sexual partners' assistance in experiencing orgasm is that, in this particular sample of women, there was a disproportionately high percentage of single women, including those living with a lover (41%). Only 38% were married. A single woman, probably not having known her sexual partner for as long as a married woman, may feel shy about asking him for extra stimulation. The unspoken message may be, "Your penis is not enough." Probably having known her husband longer, a married woman may have overcome her shyness and thus may more readily request clitoral stimulation from him.

Another reason why women are hesitant about requesting clitoral stimulation has an historical basis. Since intercourse has traditionally been defined as the basic form of sexuality and the only natural, healthy, and moral form of sexual physical contact, it has been taken for granted that intercourse should lead to orgasm in women. A related belief held by both women and men is that "...a man tends to be defined as [sexually] adequate to the degree that he is able to bring a woman to orgasm, preferably through the use of his penis ('Look, Ma, no hands!') (p. 87)."[68] A woman is defined as sexually adequate by the degree to which she can experience orgasm rapidly through the same method. A woman is labelled "sexually adequate", then, only insofar as she can make the man feel that *he* is sexually adequate. And, as we have seen, for many women, orgasm is not possible without clitoral stimulation. This implies that many women see themselves as sexually inadequate because of their inability to experience orgasm through sexual intercourse.

This narrow definition has had important implications for how men have perceived their adequacy as lovers as well. Since, traditionally, the penis has rarely provided an efficient means of producing a female orgasm, many men have been seen as having the problem of premature ejaculation — premature in that it occurs prior to the woman's orgasm. Thus, as long as penile stimulation is thought to be the answer to sexual satisfaction for women, both men and women will, at some time, experience a sense of failure as lovers.

Another inhibitor to women's experience of full eroticism is their perception of themselves as "sex objects" — a perception which functions to alienate women from their own bodies. Because women traditionally have not had access to power, money, or status except by attaching themselves to men who possessed them, sexual behaviour has been used as a commodity with which they have bargained for these things.[69] Moreover, women have been conditioned to sell their unique commodity to the highest bidder.[70] As a result, women are constantly striving to be attractive and, with some, it has become an obsession. Enormous amounts of time, energy, and money are invested in the cultivation of the popular

Image of Breasts Upsetting to Women

What one eleven-year-old did to help develop her breasts:

Bought a Mark Eden Bust Developer.
Slept on my back for four years.
Splashed cold water on them every night because some French actress said in
  Life magazine that that was what *she* did for her perfect bustline.
Ultimately, I resigned myself to a bad toss and began to wear padded
  bras.... And the bathing suits.... That was the era when you could lay an
  uninhabited bathing suit on the beach and someone would make a pass at
  it.

image. Having been taught that it is the facade that counts, women experiment from adolescence on until they find the one most flattering to them. It is not surprising, then, that many women become alienated from their bodies. Rather than experiencing satisfaction with their bodies in their natural state, women frequently try to change various parts of their bodies to conform to the norms of attractiveness set down by the society of that particular time.

Women are "playing to an audience" that only reinforces these norms of attractiveness by demanding stereotypical behaviour. Discussions of what "turns on" men are replete with catch phrases like "he's a tit man" or "an ass man", "he likes long legs", etc. Women, on the other hand, seem to be able to engage in sexual behaviour with fewer condiments — for the most part, they take men more or less as they find them. In contrast to men, women have not been found to have written treatises on how the "ideal" male should behave in fulfilling his role.[71] Germaine Greer, in her now-classic book, *The Female Eunuch,*[72] put it very well:

Until woman as she is can drive this plastic spectre out of her own and her man's imagination she will continue to apologize and disguise herself, while accepting her male's pot-belly, wattles, bad breath, farting, stubble, baldness, and other ugliness without complaint. Man demands in his arrogance to be loved as he is, and refuses even to prevent the development of the sadder distortions of the human body which might offend the aesthetic sensibilities of his woman (pp. 261-262).[73]

Women's criticisms of their bodies do not stop at the cosmetic. They are further alienated from their bodies by repugnance at their own genitals. In discussing the pervasiveness of "cunt-hatred" among both men and women, Greer points out that many women are embarrassed by cunnilingus and feel sure that men must find it disgusting:

> Vaginal secretions are the subject of a vast folklore; the huge advertising campaigns for deodorants and sweeteners of the vulvar area deliberately play upon female misgivings about the acceptability of natural tastes and odours .... The vagina is described as a *problem* preventing some of the niceness of being close. The excessive use of douches with chemical additives is actually harmful to the natural balance of organisms existing in the vagina ... (pp. 258-9).[74]

All of this leads women to be self-conscious, self-critical, and self-absorbed, rather than involved with their partners, while engaging in sexual behaviour. This cannot help but interfere with the woman's full range of potential feelings in a sexual relationship.

Sexuality and Marriage

The study of sexuality in marriage over the last four decades reveals an increase in married women's enjoyment of sexual behaviour. In their first years of marriage, 25% of the women studied by Kinsey never reached orgasm during coitus.[75] This percentage shrinks to 10% when all the years of marriage are considered. More recently, married women seem to be reaching orgasm more frequently. For example, a study of over 2000 married women in the early seventies revealed that 90% had achieved orgasm by age 25.[76] It should be pointed out, however, that these women, who were of all ages, tended to be employed and relatively highly educated, with the result that they were nonrepresentative of the population as a whole. But middle-American married women are also reporting that they experience sexual enjoyment. A 1974 survey of 100 000 *Redbook* readers, mainly from middle-America, reported that almost two-thirds of the wives were having orgasms "all or almost all of the time" during intercourse.[77]

Married couples, on the average, are having coitus about eight or nine times per month,[78] although there is a lot of variation in frequency, depending on the length of the marriage and the ages of the partners. For example, 25% of newly married wives have reported that they had coitus more than four times a week. This proportion dropped, however, to 5% for those who had been married eight years or longer.[79] There are many reasons for the decrease in frequency of sexual contact between spouses, among them being the presence of children and other familial responsibilities, a decrease in novelty and surprise associated with the other person, and general familiarity. While, in the past, wives might have regarded their conjugal sexual activity as a burden, according to two separate studies, the vast majority of contemporary American wives do not think that the frequency of coitus they are experiencing is too much.[80,81]

Not only are married women enjoying sexual activity more today than in the past, but they are also engaging in a greater variety of sexual activities other than intercourse (i.e., fellatio and cunnilingus). Three to four decades ago, "nice" women were not supposed to enjoy these activities — an attitude which no doubt inhibited women's participation in them. Nevertheless, half of Kinsey's married sample had experienced both cunnilingus and fellatio on at least one occasion.[82] In a more recent study conducted in the early seventies, 90% of wives under age 25 were reported to be participating in both acts.[83] Similar results were reported in the *Redbook* survey of the early seventies, in which fewer than 10% of the wives reported that they had never tried oral sex. Those who had tried it said that it enhanced their sexual relationship by providing variation in sexual expression.[84] Another means of achieving sexual variation is through the use of devices and aids such as vibrators and feathers. As would be expected, age is a very important factor related to their use. In one study, they were used as aids for sexual satisfaction by 26% of the women surveyed who were between the ages of 26 and 30 years, and by only 6% of the women past the age of 50.[85]

Changes in marital sexual activity have been paralleled by changes in extramarital sexual behaviour. Traditionally, adultery was viewed in much the same way as premarital sexual intercourse — tolerated, if not expected, in men, but condemned in women. In Kinsey's day, the double standard was very much in effect, as evidenced by his finding that by age 40, one-half of the men he surveyed reported having had an affair, as compared to only 26% of the wives. More recently, there has been evidence that younger couples, especially *women*, are starting to have affairs earlier. For example, in one study conducted in 1972, 26% of the wives had had extramarital coitus. Their average age was 34.5 years.[86] By age 40, then, many more women could be expected to have had at least one extramarital affair. Similarly, the *Redbook* survey found that 29% of all wives surveyed had had an affair — with many of them doing so earlier in marriage than was found in the past. From these results, it would appear that the traditional double standard is gradually being eroded as far as extramarital sexual activity is concerned. While the proportion of men having affairs has not changed much since Kinsey's day, they, too, are having affairs earlier in marriage than men did in the past.

While many people seek out affairs because of either boredom or unhappiness in their marriage, opportunity is a significant factor. Undoubtedly, the fact that men more frequently have held outside employment has contributed largely to their higher rate of extramarital sexual activity. The probability of women having affairs also seems to be determined in part by whether outside employment is held. The *Redbook* survey of the early seventies found that among wives in their late thirties, 53% of the employed women had had an affair, compared with only 24% of the housewives. We cannot conclude, however, that outside employment *causes* women to seek out affairs. Some of the factors that may be responsible for the higher incidence of affairs among employed women may be found in the employment situation itself. So, for example, the opportunity of meeting other men is simply greater when women are employed than when they are full-time housewives. And having something in common which results from working closely with another person could conceivably lead to emotional or sexual involvement. These, however, are some of the same factors that may predispose married men (most of whom are employed) to have affairs.

Over the last few decades, there have been significant changes in sexual behaviours and the attitudes associated with them. Norms regarding marital sexuality, like those pertaining to premarital sexual activity in women and men, are moving away from the double standard toward a single standard of behaviour for both. Younger wives in particular appear to be enjoying sexual behaviour more, experimenting more with different forms of erotic stimuli, and having affairs at younger ages, all of which renders them more similar to men in their behaviour. The result is that increasing numbers of younger married couples are probably experiencing more imaginative and varied sexual activity in marriage than did their predecessors.

Contraception and Abortion

While the study of sexuality has received considerable attention from social scientists, there has been much less attention paid to the consequences of sexual intercourse, particularly unwanted or unplanned pregnancy. While unplanned pregnancy is not the only consequence of heterosexual activity, it is one of the most salient concerns relating to sexuality in contemporary society. In this regard, it is important to understand some of the psychological aspects of contraceptive use and abortion. This discussion will centre around women because most of the research on use of contraceptives and effects of abortion has focused on women. Since pregnancy and abortion can be experienced only by women and since child-rearing is regarded as primarily the woman's responsibility, a more urgent demand is seen for research on women in these areas.

Despite the obvious relationship between heterosexual intercourse and pregnancy, statistics in both Canada and the United States show that teenagers in particular tend to use contraceptives sporadically if at all, and that, often, the types of contraceptives they use tend to be unreliable. According to one report, almost 700 000 teenagers in the United States become pregnant each year, resulting in 200 000 out-of-wedlock births and 300 000 abortions.[87] While the proportion of adolescents who use some kind of birth control has increased from 1971 to 1976, so has the proportion of teenagers who *never* use contraception. The percentage went from an estimated 17% in 1971 to 25% in 1976.[88,89] In one U.S. national study of adolescent sexuality, for example, nearly 60% of the teenaged males surveyed "sometimes, usually, or always" just trusted to luck that their partner would not become pregnant.[90] In contrast, national data from the United States suggest that married women (or couples) are far better contraceptors than the unmarried. In 1976, in the United States, 30% of couples where the wives ranged from 15 to 44 years old were sterile (due primarily to surgical sterilization), 49% used some other method of birth control, 13% were pregnant, postpartum, or seeking pregnancy, and 8% were not using any contraceptive.[91]

In Canada, too, there has been an increase in unplanned and unwanted pregnancies, particularly among young unmarried women. So, while the total number of births in Canada declined by about 130 000 from 1959 to 1972,[92] the number of illegitimate births rose by approximately 11 000 during the same period.[93] Not only are teenagers disproportionately represented among those who are having illegitimate births, but there is also evidence that their numbers are steadily increasing. In 1978, of all illegitimate births in Canada, 46% were reported to be for women between the ages of 15 and 19,[94] an increase of about 12% since 1960.[95] Similarly, among women having therapeutic abortions in Canada, the percentage of teenagers has been disproportionately high. In 1978, 30% of the abortions in Canada were performed on young women 15 to 19 years old.[96] Like the American findings, the Canadian national data indicate that effective contraceptive use increases with the age of the woman and tends to be greater among married women than among singles.[97] Because of the enormity of the problem of unwanted and unplanned pregnancy, we will now turn to an examination of some of the reasons why young people — particularly women — do not use contraceptives.

Contraceptive Use

One reason frequently given by young people for not using birth control is their belief that sexual intercourse should be spontaneous.[98] To *anticipate* sexual activity is synonymous with behaving improperly, while to respond to the magic of the moment with "spontaneous" sexual activity is to yield to the romantic norms of society.[99] While such an explanation for the nonuse of contraceptives may apply in some cases to the first coital experience, it seems less plausible when considering the young person who engages in sexual intercourse on a regular basis.

Some have maintained that young people's lack of knowledge is a significant obstacle to contraceptive use. For example, teenagers may mistakenly believe that they cannot get pregnant either because they are too young or because they have sexual intercourse too infrequently.[100–102] Even college students may be misinformed about how to prevent pregnancy, as was revealed in one study of questions submitted by students to a college newspaper, *The Michigan State University State News*. Here is a typical question:

> Over a period of about three months my girlfriend and I have had
> sexual intercourse about 15 times. In all of these encounters she claims
> never to have had an orgasm of any kind. With this in mind, we use no
> protection. Now she is pregnant! How? (p. 35).[103]

Others maintain, however, that many young women get pregnant even
when they have knowledge of contraceptive techniques.[104],[105] It has been
estimated that in urban America (and probably in urban Canada as well)
over 90% of unmarried pregnant early-adolescent girls, and virtually 100%
of unmarried pregnant adult women not only know about contraceptives,
but also know how to obtain and use them.[106]

More important than knowledge about contraceptives are the conflicts a person may experience with regard to his or her sexuality. If, then,
people are unable to acknowledge that they are sexual beings who will
probably engage in sexual behaviour, it comes to be regarded as a spontaneous event, and they will likely not take any preplanned birth control
measures. It has been shown, for example, that people are more likely to
use contraceptives when they are also able to accept their sexuality as a
natural function without guilt or anxiety. Conversely, a tendency to deny
one's sexuality is associated with nonuse of contraceptive measures. This
was shown in a study[107] which assessed people's use of contraceptives, as
well as their sexual attitudes. Participants were university undergraduates
who were shown a "sexually explicit" movie and then asked to rate it.
Using this technique, two groups were identified: erotophobes were those
who rated the film most strongly as pornographic, more explicit than they
expected, and even shocking; erotophiles were those who reacted in the
opposite way. Other important differences between the two groups were
that erotophobes, who felt that sexual behaviour was unimportant and disapproved of premarital coitus, were also less likely to use birth control
than erotophiles, who were less negative and anxious about sexuality. Presumably, a person's negative feelings about sexuality — their own and
others' — inhibit use of contraceptives. For this person, the expectation is
that intercourse will not occur. Because of their feelings of guilt and em-
barrassment, erotophobes have more difficulty not only in talking about
sexual behaviour and contraception, but also in obtaining contraceptives.
Presumably, they also dislike birth control measures that require them to
touch their genitals.

Inability to acknowledge and accept one's sexuality also inhibits
contraceptive use in more subtle ways. Many young women who engage in
premarital sexual behaviour act as if they do not know what they are
doing,[108] even though they may have factual knowledge, and thus they
avoid having to face the decision of using contraceptives. True emotional
awareness and acceptance of her sexuality would enable a woman to make
use of her factual knowledge about sexual activity and its possible consequences, allow her to make a rational appraisal of the situation, and use
contraception.

Young unmarried women who have undergone abortions report that when they were growing up, there was a "conspiracy of silence" surrounding their sexuality.[109] Sexuality was a taboo subject and took on an aura of secrecy. Young women who have experienced this during their upbringing, presumably internalize this conspiracy of silence by "not knowing" about their own sexual behaviour. Not being able to recognize openly and consciously what they are doing, sexually, these young women may frequently take chances with pregnancy.

This is only one of the problems caused by lack of communication about sexual behaviour. Its consequences go beyond the home, often extending to the educational system, which also tends to deny, rather than acknowledge, young people's sexuality. Not only is it necessary for those in positions of authority to accept the fact that teenagers are sexual beings, but it is also essential to provide forums for discussion of the consequences of sexual behaviour and the necessity of using contraceptive measures.

Contraceptive Use and Personality Factors. Despite the increased availability of contraceptives and a greater social acceptance of premarital coitus, not all sexually active women are equally likely to use contraceptives. There are personality differences between those who use contraceptives regularly and those who do not. This is a predictable finding, since contraceptive use is linked to the individual's behaviour in general, which is ultimately determined largely by that person's particular personality traits. It is not surprising to find, then, that among female university undergraduates, sexually active contraceptive users have been found to be more internalizing than those who do not use contraceptives.[110] (Internalizers are defined as those who show a greater tendency toward self-regulation than externalizers.) By this definition, internalizers could be expected to take self-protective measures when involved in premarital sexual intercourse. Women who use contraceptives have also been reported to be less dogmatic in their beliefs than those who do not use them.[111] (A person high in dogmatism is one who tends to resist accepting ideas that differ from his or her own.) Using contraceptives would therefore be more resisted by a highly dogmatic person because it represents a new idea.

There are other ways in which contraceptive users and nonusers have been found to differ. For one thing, women who define self-improvement, including improvement in their social status, as a priority among their goals, tend also to be "early acceptors" of contraceptives (those who use them before marriage as well as before their first pregnancy).[112] In addition, girls aged 13 to 17 who have never been pregnant and who are seeking contraceptive advice have been found to have greater scholastic interests than those who were either seeking to terminate an unwanted pregnancy or those who were in a home for unwed mothers.[113] Presumably, the same initiative that motivates young women toward education and achievement also impels them to seek effective contraceptives, all of which is part of their tendency to plan their lives. So a single woman aspiring toward self-improvement, who is ambitious and goal-directed, is also likely to engage in preplanned use of contraceptives if she is sexually active.

However, for the traditionally feminine woman, contraceptive use may present some problems. For example, she has been found to suffer more physical and psychological side effects from the use of contraceptives than the woman rated as less stereotypically feminine.[114,115] This may be the result of the contradiction between the implications of contraceptive use and the traditional feminine personality. On the one hand, contraceptive use usually requires orientation toward activity and initiative. On the other hand, the feminine woman is usually passive and dependent. The increase in problems in this group is likely related to a feeling that contraceptive use intrudes upon their typically passive and dependent lives. Moreover, it has been found that women who score high on passivity measures report more adverse side effects from the oral contraceptive pill and are sometimes resentful and hostile toward men for being absolved of the responsibility for contraceptive use.[116]

Even with knowledge of birth control, there are many young unmarried women who are having unprotected sexual intercourse. Contraceptive users should be distinguishable from nonusers on the basis of a number of psychological dimensions, among them being gender-role identity, motivation to achieve, as demonstrated by long-range academic and career plans, and the degree to which women accept their own sexuality.

Abortion and Its Effects

In the United States in 1978, 1 409 600 legal abortions were performed.[117] For the same year, in Canada, the number of abortions performed was 62 290.[118] Apart from differences in population, the discrepancy between these figures may be partly accounted for by the fact that abortion is not equally accessible to women in the United States and Canada. In the United States, abortion has been available on request since 1973 when the Supreme Court held that the states may not interfere with a woman's right to terminate a pregnancy by medically approved means in the first twelve weeks. In Canada, on the other hand, it is more difficult to obtain an abortion, since a woman must apply to a hospital therapeutic abortion committee, which may or may not approve her application. The situation is also rendered more difficult by the fact that as of 1978, only 20% of all Canadian hospitals had therapeutic abortion committees.[119]

In recent years, there has been a great deal of controversy surrounding the whole issue of abortion and its moral, religious, legal, and social psychological aspects. Being an emotionally charged issue, opinions relating to abortion tend to be either "for" or "against" it. Some people have suggested that instead of undergoing abortion, women should continue their unwanted pregnancies to term and then give up their babies for adoption. But there is evidence that when a woman is *forced* to carry an unwanted pregnancy to term both she and her child may suffer. In one Swedish study, for example, children who were born after their mothers were refused abortions were followed up until they were 21 years old.[120] They were compared with children who were born in the same hospital to mothers who had not applied for abortion. Children whose mothers were refused abortions generally had a more difficult time coping with many areas of their lives than the other children. Psychiatric disorders, delinquency, criminal behaviour, and alcoholism were also more prevalent among those whose mothers were refused abortions. These children received less schooling, and when they grew up, greater numbers of them were recipients of public welfare assistance and more were judged as unfit for military service.

There is also evidence that having a legal abortion is better for the *woman's* mental health than being forced to have a child against her wishes. In one study, conducted in Aberdeen, women who applied for legal abortions were psychologically tested at the time of referral for abortion and at the time of follow-up, 18 months later.[121] At the follow-up interview, comparisons were made between the mental health of those who were aborted and those who had been refused an abortion and forced to deliver the child. Women who had had abortions showed greater improvement in their mental health than women who had delivered. Women who had aborted not only had a greater lifting of feelings of depression and a decrease in hostility feelings, but also expressed fewer regrets than those who had delivered. From these findings, it would appear that the mental health of a woman faced with an unwanted pregnancy stands a greater chance of improving when the woman has an abortion than when she is forced, against her will, to deliver a child.

Those who oppose abortion on moral or religious grounds often point out, mistakenly, that abortion has damaging psychological effects on women — a conclusion that has not generally been supported by research. On the contrary, the predominant psychological reactions that have been found after abortion are relief, and happiness with the decision to have the abortion.[122,123] Few negative psychological reactions such as guilt, sadness, self-anger, or regret have been found in studies of women who have undergone abortion.[124-126] All things considered, women who have good coping strength *prior to* the pregnancy make relatively good adjustments after their abortions. While mild depression may occur in 10 to 20% of women, only 1 to 2% have been found to have serious problems, and these can usually be resolved with psychotherapy.[127] Certain factors, however, can predispose a woman to higher risk of experiencing psychiatric or psychological difficulties after an abortion. One of these is mental disturbance present before the abortion. In a Canadian study of 188 women who had had abortions, it was found that women with a history of psychiatric disturbance were three times as likely to have some form of mental disturbance after their abortions as those who did not report psychiatric difficulties in the past.[128] Similar results have been reported in other countries as well.[129-131] These results demonstrate that coping in general and coping with abortion in particular may be more difficult for the woman who has experienced some psychiatric disturbance than for the woman with no history of psychiatric disturbance.

Also influencing a woman's psychological reactions after abortion are her fertility plans — whether or not she plans to have children in the future.[132] Women planning to have children have been found to suffer more from neurotic symptoms afterwards than those planning not to bear children in the future. Specifically, women with fertility plans suffered more from physical complaints and from some perceptual and emotional instability, including ideas of persecution, broodiness, and mood fluctuations. The woman with fertility plans may also experience feelings of ambivalence about her abortion. Because these women were mainly young and single, they decided not to have a child at this time. However, these same women also expressed the wish to have a child (children) at some time in the future.

Among the issues frequently raised in the discussion of abortion and its consequences is the woman's relationship to her sexual partner. Does an abortion strengthen the relationship between a man and a woman? Or does an abortion lead to a deterioration in the relationship between the abortee and her sexual partner? Research shows that the future of this relationship after an abortion depends a great deal on the couple's marital status. The single woman is more likely to experience a break in the relationship with her sexual partner after an abortion than is her married counterpart. The percentage of women without husbands whose relationship deteriorated following abortion has been reported to range from 44% to as high as 77% of the samples studied.[133-136] The relationship of married women to their husbands does not seem to change as a result of their having had an abortion. The reason for this difference probably has to do with differing degrees of commitment between the man and the woman among those who are single and those who are married. In recent Canadian research, it has been found that there is an association between a woman deciding to have an abortion without consulting the man, and the breakup of the relationship later.[137] If an unmarried woman is unsure about committing herself to a man in the first place, that is, before the pregnancy, then gets pregnant, and subsequently decides to have an abortion without consulting him, this may leave her feeling that there is not much to the relationship, so she breaks up with him. The man, after realizing that his sexual partner has made the decision to have an abortion without consulting him, may also feel that there is insufficient caring or commitment for them to continue on together. In a marital relationship, however, there is likely to be more continuity and less chance of the relationship breaking up. A married woman's decision to have an abortion is most likely made with her husband and is simply part of the ongoing process of decisions that a married couple shares. In most marriages, then, the abortion event will not take on the importance that it can for the unmarried couple and, as a result, it is less likely to disrupt the relationship.[138]

Abortion, then, is not an isolated event in a woman's or a couple's life. Because of its implications both for individuals and for their relationships to others, abortion can be understood only within a social psychological context. The question should not be whether abortion is a good or bad thing. Rather, we should ask what is the meaning of abortion for the woman, for her relationship with her partner, and, if relevant, for the partner. In comprehending a woman's psychological adjustment after abortion, it is important to ask, further, to what extent she has psychologically assimilated the abortion experience.

. . . .

The consequences of heterosexual sexual activity can be far reaching, as we have seen. While unwanted and unplanned pregnancy is a significant social problem across North America, this discussion has certainly not exhausted all of the possible consequences of heterosexual sexual activity. Rather, the topics chosen for discussion represent some of the more salient concerns associated with this sexuality in our society. It would be unfortunate if our discussion gave the impression that fertility control is important only insofar as women are concerned. To date, however, there is considerably less research on contraceptive use among men, and, as was mentioned earlier, these issues are of more immediate concern to women. Nevertheless, the study of contraceptive use in men should not be neglected. Overpopulation and dwindling natural resources are significant international concerns. So the intelligent use of birth control should be a priority for men as well as women. And as men are increasingly expected to become more directly involved in childrearing, they should also be expected to take a more active role in the area of contraception.

Lesbianism and Male Homosexuality

Up to this point, the discussion has centred around heterosexual sexuality. Increasingly, however, heterosexuality is being seen as just one option or vehicle for the expression of human sexuality, and lesbianism and male homosexuality are being seen as valid optional lifestyles. Recent reconceptualizations of lesbianism and male homosexuality illustrate a diversity and range of potential of human sexuality that have not been acknowledged in the past. Lesbianism and male homosexuality are being conceptualized not as clinical entities indicative of psychopathology, but as subjects to be examined within the context of social issues.[139]

Recent reconceptualizations regarding lesbianism and male homosexuality are important issues in themselves, as well as in their implications for the study of gender roles in general. Accordingly, some important conceptual distinctions will be made here, concerning gender roles, gender-role identity, and sexual preference (male or female), which often have been confused in both the professional and lay literature. According to societal stereotypes, for example, homosexuality and the violation of gender-role stereotypes have been lumped together.[140] Beliefs about a person's sexual orientation have been inextricably tied to conceptions of that person's femininity and masculinity. Stereotypes have selectively attended to the "effeminate" gay man and the "masculinized" lesbian, thereby ignoring the full range of behaviour associated with gay people. For example, one study has found that a sample of 100 men rated the "typical male homosexual" as more delicate, more passive, more womanly, smaller, softer, and more yielding than heterosexual men.[141] Further research has shown that the gender-role identity of many homosexual men is not feminine, but tends to be more typically androgynous or expressive of characteristics of both gender roles.[142] And, contrary to the widely held stereotype, the partners in most lesbian couples do not assume rigidly defined masculine and feminine gender roles. Rather, the gender-role identification of both partners has been found to be predominantly feminine.[143,144] Research findings suggest, then, that gender-role behaviour and sexual preference (male or female) are really independent dimensions of personality, as are gender-role identity and sexual preference. Gay people may engage in the same range and diversity of behaviour as their heterosexual counterparts. What is more, the facility with which partners in a lesbian relationship may exchange gender roles contributes to a diversity and richness in relationships that cannot be found within a traditional heterosexual relationship.[145]

Changing Conceptions of Lesbianism and Male Homosexuality

Traditionally, male homosexuality and lesbianism have been seen as unnatural, abnormal, and deviant. These conclusions have been based on the assumption that heterosexuality is the "natural" emotional and sensual inclination. Psychologists and psychiatrists alike have used the term *homosexual* as a diagnostic label connoting a set of personality factors that implied psychopathology.[146] Several psychological theories have been offered to "explain" what disturbances in development would create such a "perversion". For the most part, beliefs regarding the causes of homosexuality have led either to suggestions for treatment to change homosexual orientation or to early family intervention to prevent its development.[147] All these theories failed to consider the basic question. Is homosexual behaviour deviant, unnatural, or abnormal?

The first and perhaps most influential work relevant to this question was that of Kinsey and his coworkers,[148,149] which demonstrated that homosexual behaviour was much more widespread than had previously been believed. Other research has reported that homosexual behaviour was found in almost all the human societies studied, including those similar to North America, which maintain strict cultural sanctions against homosexual behaviour.[150] Further data have indicated that some form of homosexual behaviour occurs in almost all species.[151]

Additional research has addressed the question of whether or not homosexuality per se is indicative of psychopathology.[152,153] It showed that trained clinicians, using standard projective techniques, could not differentiate the sexual orientation of homosexual nonpatients from that of nonhomosexuals who were also nonpatients, thus challenging the idea that homosexuality is an indication of psychopathology. What is more, the vast majority of gay people do not frequent therapists' offices, do not consider themselves in need of therapy, and reveal no signs of psychopathology on a wide range of psychological tests.[154-158]

It has only been within the last decade that homosexuality and lesbianism have begun to be recognized as normal alternative patterns of sexual functioning. This is the result primarily of the efforts of the Gay Movement in the United States and Canada, the influence of which has been particularly felt in the psychiatric and psychological professions. In 1973, the American Psychiatric Association removed "homosexuality per se" from the Diagnostic and Statistical Manual of Mental Disorders, and adopted a resolution strongly supporting gay civil rights. These decisions occurred only after the Association's general meetings had been disrupted for nearly two years by gay activists, who eventually succeeded in forcing a public hearing on homosexuality.[159]

In the following year, the American Psychological Association endorsed the actions of the psychiatrists and passed a resolution not only affirming the rights of gay people, but also urging "all mental health professionals to take the lead in removing the stigma of mental illness that has long been associated with homosexual orientations."[160]

The Women's Liberation Movement has also played an influential, though secondary, role in raising many issues relating to gay lifestyles. In challenging the prescriptions of traditional gender roles and their relationship to conceptions of mental health, feminists are confronting many of the issues of direct concern to lesbians and gay men. In particular, the issue of lesbianism has been a feature of emerging debates within the Women's Liberation Movement. Sexism, which has been shown to exist in psychotherapeutic relationships involving women, is especially relevant to the understanding of how lesbians are treated when they are in therapy. The lesbian is devalued not only as a woman, but also as a deviant — one who has departed from the norms of heterosexuality. This being the case, the lesbian is not likely to gain access to either self-definition or greater self-acceptance. In short, by questioning many of the assumptions related to traditional gender roles and focusing attention on the bias against women which exists both in psychology and in psychiatry, feminists have raised many important questions relevant to the reconceptualization and treatment of lesbians.

Despite social changes associated with lesbianism and male homosexuality during the 1970s, a recent study revealed that the majority of introductory psychology textbooks studied still portray homosexuality and lesbianism as deviant and abnormal.[161] Based on a sample of 48 textbooks, the study found that for every source of relevant information on male homosexuality or lesbianism, there were five sources of misrepresentative data. Moreover, these books failed to document accurately recent social changes associated with being gay. Summarizing the research findings, the investigator states:

> Instead of reproducing empirically sound research designed to remove the stigma of mental illness associated with homosexuality, it would appear that authors are perpetuating societal stereotypes, thereby inadvertently justifying the prejudice and discrimination encountered by gay people in their daily lives (p. 53).[162]

Differences between Lesbians and Male Homosexuals

While a good deal of research and study have been done on male homosexuals, very little has been written about lesbians. The reason for this probably lies in the relative status of women and men in our culture. Because North American culture values the male and the masculine role over the female and her socially ascribed role,[163-165] it has been considered imperative to search out the reasons for deviation from the norm of heterosexuality in males. When women have broken with traditional gender-role expectations, however, their deviation has not been imbued with the same importance — females and femininity are not as highly valued. Thus, women who deviate from traditional gender-role expectations may not be judged as harshly as men who break with the expectations associated with a more valued role. This hypothesis is consistent with the observation that lesbians are less likely to be defined as a social problem, less likely to be negatively stereotyped, and less likely to be rejected than male homosexuals.[166]

Historically, because lesbians have been perceived as female versions of male homosexuals, they have been seen as having been deprived of a political existence.[167] Recent research and writing frequently refer to the observation that the similarity between lesbians and male homosexuals is only a superficial one. The differences between them are a result of differences in socio-political and psychological factors. The lesbian experience is a *feminine* one with meanings and potentialities that emanate from the feminine gender role as it is found in our society.[168] While lesbians have often been grouped with male homosexuals in that they have been sexually stigmatized, there are important differences between them that justify treating them as distinct categories.

Firstly, there are noteworthy differences in the relationships of lesbians compared to those of homosexual men; often lesbians resemble heterosexual women more than homosexual men in their interpersonal behaviour. For example, both lesbians and heterosexual women are more likely than men — whether they are male homosexuals or heterosexuals — to see emotional involvement as important in a sexual relationship.[169] Lesbians are less likely to engage in sexual behaviour for its own sake — "casual" sexual relationships are less frequently observed among lesbians. Lesbians, compared to male homosexuals, more often form long-term relationships with a partner of the same sex[170] and are less likely to engage in sexual behaviour with people other than their steady partner,[171] indicating further that much of the sexual and courtship behaviour of lesbians closely resembles that of heterosexual women. One's experiences and feelings in this regard would therefore seem to have less to do with whether one's sexual preference is same-or opposite-sex than with whether one is a woman or a man. Gender-role prescriptions regarding women's orientation toward love are a major influence on lesbian relationships.

Secondly, women's lack of social, economic, and cultural privilege compared to that of men exerts a profound effect on the nature of lesbian relationships. One theory of lesbianism emphasizes the limitations imposed on women by societal definitions of the feminine gender role.[172] Women who feel compelled to reject the constraints of the feminine gender role as traditionally defined may find intimate relationships with other women more fulfilling than heterosexual ones. Accordingly, research has shown that lesbians care more than male homosexuals about having an egalitarian relationship with their sexual partner.[173] Thus, a woman's choice of a same-sex partner as a love-object will likely be largely influenced by her perception of the likelihood that she and her partner can establish and maintain an egalitarian relationship.

In one feminist analysis, Adrienne Rich[174] describes the sociopolitical implications of lesbianism. She rejects the idea that lesbianism simply refers to genital sexual expression between women. Rather, she uses the term *lesbian continuum* to refer to a range through each woman's life, of woman-identified experience, including the sharing of an inner life, personal experiences, and work. In addition, she sees this continuum as including other, more political relationships among women, including the bonding together against male tyranny, and the giving and receiving of practical and political support. Lesbianism also involves the rejection of patriarchal values, particularly as they pertain to heterosexual relationships.[175]

Thus, lesbianism and male homosexuality cannot be understood apart from our general knowledge of gender roles. Differences between lesbians and male homosexuals reflect, among other things, the differences associated with the social roles women and men are expected to adopt and subsequently enact in a variety of social contexts.

. . . .

In recent years, increased liberalization in sexual attitudes has resulted in growing acceptance of lesbianism and male homosexuality. There is a trend in psychological research that defines this orientation as a social issue, rather than a clinical entity. Yet, gay men and lesbians are still being stigmatized as minority groups, evidence of which is seen in denial of access to housing, in employment discrimination by the government, the educational system, and the armed forces, and in police entrapment.[176] The struggle of lesbian mothers to gain custody of their children has recently received greater public attention than in the past.[177]

Although, generally, lesbians are subject to dual discrimination — both as women and as lesbians — homosexual men and lesbians experience many of the same kinds of discrimination. The Gay Movement, which acts in the interests of both gay men and women, is becoming more visible in its endeavours to free its constituents from social, legal, and economic discrimination. Despite increased openness of gay women and men, many fears surrounding disclosure persist — fears associated with one's employment, family relationships, and acceptance by others. The psychological pain resulting from being stigmatized because of one's life-style is an ever-present reality for many lesbians and male homosexuals. But gay people, like heterosexuals, have the right to live with dignity, particularly in a pluralistic society. This will be possible only when societal attitudes change sufficiently toward the acceptance of the gay lifestyle.

7

The Family and Gender Roles

Despite recent social and attitudinal changes relating to the roles traditionally assigned to women and men, gender-role differences in behaviour
remain predominant in the nuclear family. The concept of a "unisex"
lifestyle may be appealing, particularly to the adolescent sector of society
— a fact which commercial bodies have exploited with fervour. However,
once two people marry and have children, this lifestyle is less likely to be
found. This is perhaps because marriage and, in particular, the presence of
children, almost always trigger a division of labour along traditional
gender-role lines. Of course, if gender roles were not polarized and if

"If your marriage is going to be an equal relationship,
how come he's dressed like Mr. Important and you look like
Little Mary Sunshine?"

women and men were more nearly androgynous in the larger society,
masculine and feminine roles within the nuclear family would likely not be
so distinct. As it is, the nuclear family is a microcosm of society, in which
traditional gender-role behaviour is intensified and perpetuated. Such
conformity to conventional norms may be the result of early conditioning
or it may simply represent the path of least resistance. Whatever the cause,
it has frequently been observed that the family remains a prime example of

an institution where traditional gender roles are repeatedly and continually enacted. While the traditional family as we know it — mother, father, and children — is becoming less common because of the growing divorce rate, there is evidence that people still seek out family forms that allow them to enact these traditional roles. This raises the question of why people marry in the first place.

Love and Marriage

Throughout history and in most societies, marriage has been based on practical and economic considerations. In the past, marriage represented not so much the joining together of two people, but the alliance of two families which were seen as stronger together than apart. Marriage became an established institution partly because it was pragmatic. Historically, no other unit or arrangement has been better able to meet the varied demands of reproduction, childcare, sexual gratification, and economic co-operation with as much efficiency as the nuclear family. The importance of marriage and the family to a given society's stability has been such that most societies have not left the task of mate selection to the partners, themselves. Instead, parents and matchmakers arranged marriages in accordance with practical and economic considerations. Nevertheless, even in societies where marriages have been arranged, prospective spouses were usually given some say in the matter.[1] So, for example, one member of a pair could veto a prospective partner if that person was seen as totally unacceptable. Moreover, most societies view congeniality as essential to two people's ability to function effectively in a marriage.

In present Western culture, everyone is expected to "fall in love",[2] and it is generally held that love should be the primary basis of marriage for everyone. The shift to free choice of spouses in America can be traced to the pioneering spirit that stressed individuality and to the gradual disappearance of an inherited aristocracy that had to control mate selection strictly to ensure its own survival. Although people contemplating marriage today do not entirely abandon the more sober considerations of social level, compatibility of temperament, and similarity of outlook,[3] love for the individual seems to be of central importance in people's wish to get married.

In spite of the "sexual revolution", one of the prime factors influencing people's wish for marriage remains some degree of romantic love. However, while women seem to be more romantic than men in that they place higher value on the emotional aspects of a sexual relationship than men, research suggests that women are much more practical than men in the area of marital mate selection.[4] Men seem to place more value on the relationship itself in their marital mate selection.

Evidence of women's more practical attitude toward prospective marital partners is found in the results of a study of attitudes toward love and marriage among 200 dating couples at the University of Michigan.[5] For example, women were less likely than men to agree with the following statement: "A person should marry whomever he loves regardless of social position." The same study showed that women were more likely than men to take economic considerations into account when selecting a prospective marital partner.

It should be noted, however, that, despite their pragmatism, women's marital mate selection is still influenced by the romantic ideal. Given the fact that romantic views of marriage still exist today, the women surveyed may have idealized men in higher socio-economic positions because of the higher status and prestige associated with these positions — precisely those that have been inaccessible to women for social and psychological reasons. By the same token, the men who agreed more with the statement that people should marry for love may have been equating love with sexual attraction. Nevertheless, women would seem to be far more pragmatic in their approach to marriage than men.

One possible reason for women's more pragmatic approach to marriage and selection of a prospective husband has to do with the relatively greater importance of marriage and children to their identity. For example, in one study of 200 students at the University of Wisconsin, only about one-third as many women as men said that they either did not plan to marry or were undecided about marriage.[6] Despite the increasing assimilation of the goals of Women's Liberation into the philosophy and lifestyle of many women today, particularly younger women, the research evidence suggests that the overwhelming majority of women continue to view their predominant goals in life as being those of marriage and motherhood. Apparently, marriage and motherhood are still of primary importance to women even as increasing numbers of them are incorporating career, marriage, and family plans into their projected lifestyle.[7] Moreover, in light of a woman's socialization, which still conditions her to regard her future identity fundamentally as that of wife and mother, a woman must choose carefully the man she eventually marries. Since it is still the woman, rather than the man, who most often takes on the mate's social and economic status, the woman tends to take into account more practical considerations in spouse selection. Courtship and dating are still serious enterprises for women. Since the man's identity and social status are based more on future achievements in his chosen occupation or profession, socio-economic or practical considerations would assume lesser importance in his selection of a marital partner.

While people today still want to marry someone with whom they are "in love", over the last 20 years there has been a gradual de-emphasis on the romantic aspects of relationships, and greater attention to immediate sexual gratification. This trend is illustrated very well in the changes that have occurred in popular songs. In the fifties, for example, singers were frequently found pining away for someone who was unattainable. In the song "In the Wee Small Hours of the Morning", Johnny Mathis lies awake thinking about a "girl", sure that he would be hers "if only she would call". Frank Sinatra's well-known "From Here to Eternity" also depicts a man's undying love for someone, despite her absence. In another tune popular with the youth of the fifties, Johnny Mathis promises his love until the "twelfth of never". In contrast, the songs of the sixties and seventies stress sexuality much more than romance. The theme of rejected lovers lamenting the loss of their one and only love was replaced by a new theme of sexual arousal and sometimes, gratification. In a song from the late seventies, for example, Rod Stewart asks, "Do Ya Think I'm Sexy?" In the same song, rather than asking the woman to spend her life with him, he asks her to spend the night with him. In the song "Dim All the Lights", disco queen Donna Summer, a popular female vocalist of the late 1970s, still portrays the passive female, asking her lover to "use" her, but spouse selection is not on her mind.

The changes in musical mores toward a demythologizing of romance partly reflects changes that are occurring in the attitudes of contemporary youth. In the past, romantic love was supported and encouraged by societal attitudes which stressed a future orientation. Strong prohibitions against premarital sexual behaviour and intermarriage also sustained the idealization of a "forbidden" person. But, as

Copyright © 1982. Randy Jay Glasbergen.

"If Cinderella wanted a date with the prince so badly, why didn't she just call him up and ask him out?"

pointed out in Chapter 6, prohibitions against premarital sexual activity are gradually diminishing, and an increasingly pluralistic society is coming to accept coupling of all kinds, including intermarriage between members of different religions and races, and homosexual pairing. Contemporary youths also feel less need to mould themselves into highly defined gender roles, as seen in a convergence in their dress and behaviour. The distance which traditionally existed between women and men and which made romantic love possible is gradually diminishing, thus allowing men and women to know each other better before marriage. Such changes among contemporary youth are also reflected in the growing number of couples who live together before marriage or who live together as an alternative to marriage. A new approach to mate selection is emerging. Based more on the couple's perceived compatibility and mutual satisfaction of needs, men and women are less likely to subscribe to the idealized fantasy that was fostered and prescribed by the romantic love ideal of the past.

The Traditional Nuclear Family

In the past, the roles of men and women in the traditional marriage and the family were predetermined and invariant. These roles, including the division of labour within the family, were thought to be determined by physiological differences and, thus, were considered natural and normal. The model of the family that prevailed in the social sciences assumed that the man played the instrumental role — that of breadwinner and protector, while the woman stayed in the home, enacting the roles of housekeeper and emotional mainstay. Social scientists considered that the family's main function was to socialize children, and that it was the only suitable agent for that socialization.

The Woman's Role in the Traditional Family. Until quite recently, the female life cycle has been equated with the family life cycle because most women marry at some point and most married women have children. In the traditional marriage, the woman's identity is defined not by her own interests, aptitudes, and instrumental skills, but by her duty to her family. The activities of the wife and mother are not just household tasks, but an expression of personal commitment to husband and children. Traditionally, that commitment has included subordination to the husband's traditional authority, at which the wife often chafes. Being economically and socially dependent on her husband, however, the traditional housewife often finds her identity submerged in that of her husband —lending credence to the adage that says: "When a man and woman marry, they become one, the man." Our social custom of requiring the woman to take the man's name on marriage (something which is not legally required) is symbolic of the process by which women in traditional marriages are identified with their husbands and not seen as individuals in their own right. This model of the traditional marriage persists today despite decreasing numbers of marriages where the husband is the sole breadwinner and the woman is a full-time housewife.

Assuming that the woman takes on the role of the traditional housewife, what is her social status? Not surprisingly, sociologists have relegated the role of housewife to a low-status category. The U.S. Bureau of the Census[8] classifies "housewife" in a group along with "student" and "looking for work", both temporary categories of conditional respectability and low economic status. Moreover, a housewife's status varies according to her husband's occupation, and her social standing can be closely predicted on the basis of his occupational standing.[9] In one Canadian study, Eichler[10] set out to determine whether or not it was possible to measure the prestige of the occupation of housewife empirically and to discover how the social status of the housewife was affected by her husband's occupation. Respondents in this study were asked to rank 93 occupations according to their personal evaluations of the social standing of each one. They did this by assigning each occupational title a score ranging from "1" to "9", with "1" indicating the lowest social standing and "9", the highest. While the occupation of "housewife" ranked 52nd in a total of 93 occupations, that of "physician" ranked at the top of the scale. Eichler went on to compare the social standing of the occupation of housewife with that of the 10 occupations which account for the greatest number of employed women in Canada. Of these, the occupation "secretary/stenographer" accounted for the highest percentage of the female labour force. She found that "secretary/stenographer" was almost equivalent in prestige to "housewife". The same study showed that when the husband's occupational status was higher than that of the occupation of housewife, the wife's prestige rose, but it was still not as high as the husband's. On the other hand, if the husband's social status was lower than that of "housewife", the wife lost prestige. These results suggest that the widespread practice employed by social scientists of categorizing a family's social status only on the basis of the man's occupation no longer corresponds to reality. Housewives would seem to have a certain amount of prestige in their own right. On the other hand, the results further indicate that a housewife's prestige depends also on her husband's social status. The housewife, being economically dependent on her husband, is in some ways, his employee. Dependence on another person for financial resources, as well as for prestige, cannot but hinder the development of the woman's self-image and sense of being an independent person in her own right.

The Traditional Mother. In our culture, the traditional mother is expected to put her child's needs before her own. Motherhood, as institutionalized in our society, assigns sole responsibility for childcare to the woman, particularly when children are young.[11] Furthermore, the normative prescriptions surrounding motherhood require 24-hour loving care, which is supposed to be the mother's exclusive activity. In her book *The Future of Motherhood,*[12] Jessie Bernard points out, however, that this is good for neither the mother nor the children. Citing cross-cultural studies, she says that in cultures where they were given the heaviest load of childcare, women were changeable in expressing warmth and were more likely to express hostility unrelated to their children's behaviour than women who could share childcare with others.[13] Mothers who reported that a great deal of their time was spent caring for children were somewhat more unstable in their emotional reactions to their children than mothers who did not have such exclusive responsibility. More maternal warmth and stability existed in mothers who had additional caretakers to ease their burden. As Bernard points out, the "smother love" which develops in many women who have no other channel for self-actualization has come to be resented by many children.

The role requirements of the housewife, with all of its demands, can also lead to psychopathology (see Chapter 9). Guilt is a major factor here. If their children are not bright, perfectly adjusted, socially adept, etc., mothers feel guilty — a predictable reaction if the woman is assigned exclusive responsibility for child socialization. Indeed, research shows that full-time housewives are more anxious and overly concerned about their children than women who combine a career with motherhood.[14] The same study reported good mental and emotional health among a larger proportion of the employed professional wives studied than for the full-time housewives. Perhaps the adverse effects of anxiety and guilt were mitigated by the beneficial effects of the employed wives' added income and increased financial security.

The Man's Role in the Traditional Family. Traditionally, the man's primary contribution to his family revolved around his role as breadwinner. Studies conducted in the 1960s suggest that marital happiness or satisfaction (for both spouses) is related more to how well the man performs in his role as breadwinner than how the woman performs in her role. A now-classic study[15] by Blood and Wolfe of 900 Detroit wives revealed that the higher the husband's social standing in the community, the greater the wife's satisfaction. The implications of this pressure on men to achieve are far reaching. Psychologically, a man's occupation is one of the few avenues through which he can "prove" his masculinity. And, undoubtedly, his self-esteem depends greatly on his success in his field. His success is also important to his wife if his social standing affects her satisfaction with their marriage. But pressures to achieve (see Chapter 5) have taken a heavy toll on men. Their shorter life span, resulting from heart attacks and untimely illnesses, has repeatedly been attributed to these kinds of achievement pressures.

But, we may ask, how much do men participate in day-to-day activities related to the family? While the average full-time female homemaker is devoting 35[16] to 60[17] hours a week to housework, an estimated one-quarter to two-thirds of husbands in the United States reportedly do no housework at all.[18] The most frequently cited study of the division of labour among married couples by Blood and Wolfe, mentioned above, reveals a division of labour along gender-role lines. They found that husbands did the lawn mowing, snow shovelling, and repairing, while wives did the housework and grocery shopping — a pattern which has

By Betty Swords. Reprinted from Male Chauvinist Pig Calendar 1974, copyright R/M Hurley.

"Well, I have to go to work, even if you don't."

persisted. Ten years later, it was found that men still take major responsibility for outside work.[19] Men's work around the house, then, tends to be confined to traditional masculine tasks.

What is the father's role in childcare? Until quite recently, there has been little consideration of the father's role during infancy. And, in our culture, it may even be considered inappropriate for fathers to be nurturant towards their infant children. In one study where 10 normal babies were monitored for a 24-hour period at two-week intervals from the time they were two weeks to the time they were three months old, fathers were found to spend an average of 37.7 seconds per day verbally interacting with their babies.[20] Other research suggests that fathers may not be regularly available to the child. For example, on the basis of interviews with 144 fathers with children from 9 to 12 months old, one study found that only 25% of them did any regular caretaking activities.[21] Fathers' play activity with a one-year-old does not seem much greater, as shown in another study, which found that middle-class fathers played an average of 15 minutes a day with them.[22] Taking families in which there were older as well as younger children, fathers reportedly spent between two and three hours a day in the company of their children and contributed 6 to 20 minutes to childcare on weekdays plus 30 minutes a day on weekends.[23] Childcare assistance from husbands usually consists of playing, "baby sitting", and discipline, rather than maintenance tasks such as feeding, changing diapers, and bathing. In general, then, these results suggest that in the traditional family, there is a sharp division of labour within the home along gender-role lines. As will be seen later, the situation changes little when the woman holds outside employment.

The Changing Nuclear Family

In the past, it was thought that the traditional family was the "natural" family form and that any other type of family structure was unnatural, deviant, and unhealthy. Since these beliefs were bolstered by religious teachings and a strong sense of community, powerful negative social sanctions were applied to those who deviated. With the weakening of religious as well as community ties (because of greater family mobility) and the emergence of various "liberation" movements, the traditional family has been challenged on a variety of fronts. In the 1960s, oppressed minorities such as students, Blacks, women (a "psychological" minority group), and lesbians and male homosexuals began to assert their rights to equality and, at the same time, to question middle-class values, the existence of which ensured the survival of the traditional family. At the same time, it was pointed out that other family forms were just as "natural". These included the communal family, the dual-career couple, the single-parent family, and the gay couple. Contemporary youth today are simply not living their lives as their parents did or as their grandparents did before them. Instead, they are evolving new family lifestyles that are responsive to their own needs, as well as to their social and economic surroundings. In the past, the stability and continuity of the family derived largely from the threat of severe economic and social sanctions imposed by the community on those who did not live in the prescribed family structure. Recently, however, marriage and family have been characterized by greater instability and fragility partly because they are based more today than in the past on mutual feelings — which are more subject to change. Modernization and "liberation" provide freedom not only to marry whomever one pleases, but also to dissolve one's marriage if it fails to provide happiness and equality for the spouses.

Clearly, the traditional family is on the decline. In 1972, traditional families, including man as breadwinner and woman as full-time homemaker (legally married) and their offspring, were estimated to comprise less than one-third of the families in the United States.[24] This figure diminished further to 16% of all American households in 1977.[25] At the same time, there has been a gradual increase in other family forms. For example, in the United States in 1977, 18.5% of all households included both father and mother as wage earners plus one or more children at home. Thirty percent consisted of married couples with no children or with none at home, and 7% were single-parent families.[26] The study of the ways in which the nuclear family is changing has far-reaching implications not only for understanding evolving gender roles, but also for the study of the social psychology of the individuals involved.

The Dual-Earner Family

> Superwoman gets up in the morning and wakes her 2.6 children. She then goes downstairs and feeds them a grade-A nutritional breakfast, and . . . then goes upstairs and gets dressed in her Anne Klein suit, and goes off to her $25,000-a-year job doing work which is creative and socially useful. Then she comes home after work and spends a real meaningful hour with her children, because after all, it's not the quantity of time, it's the quality of time. Following that, she goes into the kitchen and creates a Julia Child 60-minute gourmet recipe, having a wonderful family dinner discussing the checks and balances of the U.S. government system. The children go upstairs to bed and she and her husband spend another hour in their own meaningful relationship, at which point they go upstairs and she is multiorgasmic until midnight (p. 54).[27]

While in the not-too-distant past, the family in which both husband and wife held outside employment was considered an aberration, this family form is fast becoming an established alternative in contemporary society, as evidenced by the relatively rapid increase during the last few decades in the proportion of married women holding outside employment. In Canada, for example, there has been a steady increase in the participation rate of married women in the labour force (as seen in Table

7.1). While, in 1941, only 4.5% of married women in the population were employed, this figure rose to 47.4% in 1979. And, in Canada in 1979, married women represented 60% of the female labour force.[28] Similar trends have been occurring in the United States: in 1978, 55.4% of married women (with husbands present) were in the U.S. labour force.[29] Moreover, on the basis of previous increases in the participation rate of married women in the labour force, it has been predicted that by 1990, only 25% of the women who are expected to marry by that time will stay at home to care for their children full time.[30]

"I'm home . . ."

Not all married women are equally likely to hold outside employment. In the United States, for example, employment rates increase with the age of the woman's children. In 1978, 66% of married women with no children under 18 years old were in the labour force, compared with 57.9% of married women with children of school age (between 6 and 17); 41% of married women with preschool children were in the American labour force,[31] representing a substantial increase from 1950, when only 12% of that group were in the labour force.[32] In Canada in 1977, 37% of mothers with preschool children were in the labour force.[33] Although the presence of young children in the home may discourage a woman from

Table 7.1

**Married Women's Labour Force
Participation Rate in Canada[1]**

Year	Participation Rate (%)
1941	4.5
1951	11.2
1961	20.8
1971	33.0
1977	44.1
1979	47.4

[1]For 1941 and 1951 only, separated women are included with married women.

Sources: For 1941 and 1951, Canada, Ministère du Travail, Division de la main-d'oeuvre féminine, *La Femme Canadienne au Travail* (Publication No. 1). Ottawa, 1957, pp. 10 & 13.

For 1961 and 1971, Labour Canada. *Women in the Labour Force 1971: Facts and Figures.* Cat. No. L38–30. Table 9. Female population and female labour force, by marital status, showing women as a percentage of the total population and women as a percentage of the total labour force, and participation rates of women in the labour force, Canada, 1961, 1966 and 1971. Ottawa, 1972, p. 19.

For 1977, Labour Canada. *Women in the Labour Force: Facts and Figures 1977: Part I Labour Force Activity.* Cat. No. L38-30/1977-1. Table 14b. Female population and female labour force, by marital status, and participation rates of women in the labour force, Canada, 1967, 1972 and 1977. Ottawa, 1978, p. 37.

For 1979, Labour Canada. *1978-1979 Women in the Labour Force: Part I Participation.* Cat. No. L38-30/1979-1. Table 24b. Female population and female labour force, by marital status and participation rates of women in the labour force, Canada, 1969, 1974 and 1979. Ottawa, 1980, p. 69.

seeking outside employment unless she has made suitable childcare arrangements, there is a trend toward increased employment among married women. Why are more married women seeking employment? There are primarily two reasons to be considered: increasing financial need of the family and greater social acceptability of the employed mother. As Sylva Gelber, past director of Canada's Women's Bureau, put it: "[We can assume] that the vast majority of women, particularly married women with young children, who double their own burden by going out to work, are employed because of economic need (p. 7)."[34] The increased economic need for women to hold employment may be the result of the growing disparity between rich and poor workers and of the declining level of purchasing power among the poor.[35] Many married women have to work outside the home because it is the only way their families can continue to meet their financial needs. Inflation, rising expectations for the acquisition of goods, and for provision of environments that are seen as better and more stimulating for children (e.g., such as lessons, sports, equipment) no doubt also contribute to married women's increasing employment.

Dramatic increases in the acceptance of mothers holding outside employment can be seen by comparing the results of recent surveys with those of several decades ago. For example, in the thirties, only 18% of women in a national opinion survey in the United States agreed that married women should have a full-time job outside the home, and 41% disagreed.[36] In 1964, 54% of women surveyed in another study agreed that a mother who held outside employment could still establish a close relationship with her children. Within only six years, the percentage of women with this attitude increased to 73%.[37] It is clear that more and more women are coming to hold the belief that employment outside the home is compatible with having a family. In 1977, 85% of a sample of 198 unmarried female undergraduates at York University planned to have a career and children in the future.[38] However, the majority were planning either to interrupt their career to care for their preschool children on a full-time basis or to hold part-time jobs while their children were young. While there may be greater acceptance of mothers holding outside employment, women's own future employment plans seem to be affected by the ages of their prospective children.

Women's outside employment is also correlated with the number of children they have. Women in the work force have fewer children than full-time housewives, and women who plan to be employed outside the home also plan to have smaller families.[39,40] Voluntary maternal employment and small family size may coexist because both may be manifestations of a particular role definition.[41] Since psychological fulfillment is seen by these women to depend partly on their employment success, fewer children are needed for their complete psychological fulfillment. However, the majority of women who are employed out of economic necessity will have smaller families because they do not have the financial resources to raise more children. Normative expectations of smaller families in both Canada and the United States probably also contribute to the greater participation of women in the work force. With fewer children and therefore less parental responsibility, a married woman today has more opportunity to seek outside employment, since (contrary to the situation in the past) most of her adult life will not be occupied with childcare. In the United States, women born in 1880 had three or four surviving children compared to the two-child average expected for women born in 1950.[42] While in 1960, the average American family had 3.65 children, in 1974, the average family had 1.86 children.[43] And in Canada in 1976, families were having an average of 1.6 children.[44] A U.S. Census Bureau study reports that over two-thirds of women between the ages of 18 and 34 in 1976 expected to have none, one, or two children, with 47% of the total expecting to have two.[45] So although more and more young women are planning to hold outside employment, they still want to have children; on the average, their families will likely be smaller than those of the past. It is important also to examine the implications of maternal employment for the woman herself, her spouse, and their children.

Effects on the Woman. Employed wives generally enjoy better physical and psychological health than housewives.[46,47] These findings are particularly interesting, since holding outside employment may lead to guilt and anxiety about adequately fulfilling both the maternal and housewife roles and the employment role as well. But bringing home a pay cheque is a tangible symbol of competence, and employed wives have been found generally to have higher self-esteem, more self-confidence, and a greater sense of personal competence and autonomy.[48,49] While adverse effects of holding outside employment should be reduced by its psychological and economic benefits, sizeable numbers of women nevertheless experience role strain when they simultaneously occupy the roles of mother and employee — they have difficulty in fulfilling all their role obligations. When women take on employment, they are seen as taking on an additional role — that of employee — while maintaining their traditional roles of housewife and mother. Men who hold outside employment are not considered to be taking on a role extraneous to their husband/father roles. Regardless of whatever else a woman does, however, her roles as wife and mother are expected to take precedence.

Given these attitudes, it is not surprising to find that while employed mothers spend less total time with their children than do full-time housewives, they still spend more time on housework and childcare than their husbands. One researcher estimates that when both spouses are employed full time, the work week of wives (job plus housework) averages 66 to 75 hours and exceeds that of husbands by about eight hours.[50] These women are sacrificing time from other activities such as eating, sleeping, television viewing, gardening, and visiting.[51] As a result, many married women carrying a double load may be too tired and worn out to have regular sex with their husbands. This is illustrated in a letter written by a dismayed husband who was seeking advice from a columnist in a local newspaper. He writes "... Since my wife went back to work, our sex life has dropped off almost completely. She is always too tired, or the wash has to be done, or the kids are around, or she doesn't feel like it. You name it — she has every excuse in the book, including 'I'm tired and I have a headache.' There must be other guys whose wives work who have the same problem." — "FRUSTRATED". The columnist's reply invites the "frustrated" husband to share equally in the housework.

One of the effects of the work overload experienced by many employed wives and mothers is "weekend stress syndrome". This syndrome is characterized by tension, irritability, and, occasionally, physical malaise. It is most easily recognized by its periodicity: symptoms peak every Monday, Friday, and Saturday, diminish on Sunday, and are hardly noticeable from Tuesday through Thursday.[52] The syndrome presumably stems from the woman's knowledge that she actually holds not one but two jobs — she is both breadwinner and housekeeper. "Blue Monday" comes about because of the anxious feelings most people experience when anticipating another hard week at the office. But while men cheer up as the weekend approaches, employed women become tense. This is because they feel they have to catch up on all the housework they have put off during the week. If the husband does some of the housework, it does not help much because the wife still considers herself fully responsible for the housework. Many women may prefer to do everything themselves, rather than accept what they feel are the clumsy efforts of inexperienced househusbands.

The problem of role strain becomes more acute in the relatively small contingent of families where the woman is raising a family and simultaneously occupying a career role which demands a high level of commitment. While she is more likely than her less affluent counterpart to be able to hire outside help with the housework, nevertheless, she and her husband will likely show high achievement aspirations for their marriage and their children's psychological development. Such aspirations require considerable time for planned activities, both within the family and the community. Since normative expectations disproportionately place the responsibilities for children's psychological development on the mother, the extent of these burdens will likely be felt more by the woman involved in a demanding career than by the man.[53] Consequently, many women may lower their commitment level in their careers and settle for lower rewards, while strengthening their commitment to their marriage and parental roles. For many women in careers, this is one of the few ways in which they can alleviate their role strain. Unlike men, who are highly motivated in their careers, they cannot (because of societal expectations) place familial demands below those of career. While a family may accept a man's career ambitions and make the necessary adjustments, it is doubtful that the same thing would occur when it is the wife who holds high career aspirations.

Effects on the Man. While much has been written on women who are employees as well as mothers, little has been written on men who are married to employed women. Does the husband share more in performing household tasks when his wife is employed? Although studies done between 1960 and 1970 show that the number of husbands participating in housework has increased, there is little evidence that household tasks are shared equally when the wife is employed. Husbands generally contribute almost the same amount of time to family tasks whether their wives are employed or not.[54,55] Other data show that husbands' family time did increase slightly when wives were employed if a child under two was present.[56] But, in general, husbands' average time investment in family tasks remains very small and seems unaffected by the number of hours the wife is employed. It may be that husbands, while accepting their wives' employment grudgingly, may have more trouble than wives enacting nonstereotypical roles (which includes doing housework).[57] When the husband assumes the homemaking function, he is also assuming a lower-status role, which may strain his sense of status and identity.[58] The woman's expectations for her husband's greater participation in

"Your foreman is on the phone. Shall I tell him you're pumping iron?"

housework may also be ambivalent, increasing his tendency toward low involvement. On the one hand, she may resent his not sharing household tasks, particularly since she is likely suffering from work overload; on the other hand, if she regards his work in the home as inadequate, she may prefer to do everything herself. Societal attitudes give further support to the husband's relative lack of participation in the home, since many men (particularly professionals) are expected not only to take their work home, but also to use family time to recuperate from the stresses of the job. What is more, men are expected to manage their family responsibilities so that they do not interfere with their employment, and *their* families are expected to accommodate the demands of husbands' occupational role.

     Other research reports that husbands of employed wives, when compared to those married to full-time housewives, have lower marital satisfaction, greater job pressure, and poorer mental and physical health.[59] In a traditional marriage, part of the wife's role is to ensure her husband's comfort and the satisfaction of his psychological needs. However, when a wife holds outside employment herself, she may be less responsive to her husband's needs, as suggested in a study which found that husbands whose wives were employed were less satisfied with their wives as confidantes than those whose wives were full-time housewives.[60] Because of their own pressures, employed wives may be unable to provide the same level of emotional support to their husbands as full-time housewives. Not only is the employed wife less likely to cater to her husband's needs in this respect, but she may even turn to her husband for support and encouragement in *her* employment role.

In theory, the dual-earner family has its advantages, however. When two people share the breadwinner role, there should be less pressure on the man's earning capacity. As a result, the man should enjoy better physical and mental health. Is this the case in actual practice? Unfortunately, it is not always. The prescriptions of the traditional masculine role are still preventing men from appreciating the benefits of a second income. In fact, the wife's financial contributions may be seen as an erosion of the husband's conventional breadwinner role and thus become a source of resentment. This potential resentment may be exacerbated by the tendency of many husbands not to seek out fulfillment in other areas, also largely as a result of adherence to conventional gender roles. Since the man's employment role is still seen as his paramount concern, allowances are generally not made for men to take the time to expand into new family roles. However, there is some evidence that society is beginning to recognize the possibility of greater diversity in men's roles: the idea of paternity leave is now being raised in some labour negotiations. But the day when fathers are equally as likely as mothers to absent themselves from their employment to stay home and care for a sick child is still far off.

Effects on the Child. Prior to 1960, the social climate generally resisted the idea of mothers holding outside employment, the assumption being that maternal employment was synonymous with maternal deprivation. The concept of maternal deprivation arose from earlier studies which focused on the effects of extreme maternal absence or deprivation as found among children reared in institutions. In what are now considered classic studies,[61] the maternal deprivation found among these children had grave and extensive effects on a child's personality and intellectual development. But later studies indicated that the long-term effects of maternal employment on children cannot be equated with those of institutional care. In an institution such as an orphanage where there may be discontinuity in the caretakers, as well as inadequate interaction between caretaker and child, children may indeed suffer. However, where the mother shares parenting with a variety of surrogates, as is frequently the case when the mother is employed, children do not suffer, provided stable relationships and good care are provided by the substitute parent.[62,63] Where there is a high degree of continuity in caretakers, as in the case of the extended family,[64] there is further evidence that children do not suffer any adverse consequences.

A mother does not have to be with her children 24 hours a day in order to establish meaningful emotional bonds with them. The massive research literature on mother-child attachment and separation anxiety suggests little or no difference in the emotional bonds between mother and child whether the child is in daycare, at home with a babysitter, or at home with the mother.[65] Nor is there evidence to show that later difficulties in the child are determined by the mother's having been employed when the child was young. Mental health and behaviour problems can frequently be traced to serious conflicts between the parents, but not to maternal employment. One factor that has emerged as being important for a child's psychological adjustment has to do with the mother's satisfaction with her role. When a mother is relatively satisfied with what she is doing — either holding outside employment or being a full-time homemaker — the children are likely to benefit psychologically.[66] Specifically, when a mother's employment is gratifying, the mother-child relationship will likely be a warm one. Conversely, when the mother's employment is not a satisfying experience, she shows her child less affection, and she is likely to be less involved with the child altogether.[67]

The child's perceptions of men and women are also determined to a great extent by whether or not the mother is employed. There is a tendency among both sons and daughters of employed mothers to hold less traditional or less stereotypic perceptions of women and men. For example, gender-role perceptions have been examined among male and female college students to see if they varied at all as a function of their mothers' employment.[68] Gender-role perceptions were measured by having participants describe the "typical" man and woman, by checking a point along a continuum between two bipolar descriptions. In general, the positively valued stereotypes about men included items that reflected effectiveness and competence; the highly valued feminine-associated items described warmth and expressiveness. Both sons and daughters of employed mothers perceived significantly smaller differences between men and women than those with homemaker mothers. Daughters of employed mothers tended to see women as more competent and effective than did daughters of homemaker mothers; sons and daughters of employed mothers were more likely than sons and daughters of homemaker mothers to see men as warm and expressive (see Chapter 2). Evidently, children of employed women are less likely to see men and women as differing greatly in personality traits than children of homemaker mothers.

Daughters whose mothers are employed also have a greater tendency to emulate their mothers as role models. For example, adolescent daughters of employed mothers have been found to name their mothers as the people they most admired more than daughters of unemployed mothers.[69] College women whose mothers held outside employment were also more likely to name their mothers as the parent they most resembled and the one they most wanted to be like.[70] These results are to be expected, considering that gender-role stereotypes assign a lower status to women on the assumption that they are less competent. An employed mother is more likely to convey a sense of competence because she possesses fewer of the traits associated with the traditional feminine gender role and more of those associated with the higher-status masculine gender role. She may have higher status in the family because she is contributing income, thus conveying skills in areas other than the household. Since the developing girl, herself, is immersed in an educational system that values traits traditionally considered to be nonfeminine (i.e., high drive to succeed, competence, and those associated with skills outside the home), it is not surprising that she strives to model her employed mother.

But what are the effects of maternal employment on the son? How does he react to his mother's employment? Of particular importance is the boy's perception of the meaning of his mother's employment. If he thinks that his mother is employed because of his father's inadequacy ("he can't make enough money, so mother has to work"), then maternal employment may adversely affect the boy's perception of his father. In two Canadian studies, boys of lower socio-economic class were found to devalue their fathers as a result of the mother's full-time employment status.[71,72] It is possible that in a lower socio-economic class sons view their mother's employment as necessary because the father is unable to make enough money to cover necessary expenses as a result of present-day inflation. Today, even in middle-class families, the wife's income is probably seen as a requirement for the family to maintain a comfortable, but not extravagant, standard of living. In some families, then, the mother's contribution may undermine the position of the father in the children's eyes, while the mother may be viewed positively as a result of her employment.

Just as the mother's satisfaction with her role is significant in determining the quality of the mother-child relationship, it has a major influence on the daughter's future employment plans. Two studies of female British university graduates found little relationship between the mother's actual employment pattern during the respondent's childhood and the respondent's subsequent orientation toward or away from employment. However, when daughters perceived that their mothers felt satisfied in their employment role or dissatisfied as a housewife, they were most likely to have career commitments and to be employed continuously. When daughters perceived their mothers as contented housewives or dissatisfied career women, they were *least* likely to have careers or continuous employment patterns. [73,74] Thus, the mother's satisfaction with her role, whatever that may be, appears to be a critical factor in determining her attractiveness as a role model for her daughter.

The effects of maternal employment on a child constitute a multifaceted phenomenon. Whether a mother is employed outside the home because of financial necessity or whether she holds employment by choice, her effectiveness as a mother is greatly enhanced when she is satisfied by what she is doing. In addition to feeling satisfied with her employment role, a woman has to feel that childcare arrangements are suitable, so that feelings of anxiety or apprehension do not intrude on her performance in her job.

Divorce: Implications for the Individual and the Family

One of the most significant recent social developments that has undermined the traditional nuclear family is that of the increased divorce rate. Divorce involves a disruption of the relationship between the biological parents and their children — a relationship on which the traditional nuclear family is based. In the past, when couples promised in the marriage ceremony to stay together "till death [did them] part", they usually did. As a matter of fact, only 12% of women in the United States born at the turn of the century and now in their seventies have ended their first marriage in divorce.[75] Since the early 1960s, the rate of divorce has been steadily climbing in Canada, the United States, and the rest of the world. Recent statistics indicate that one out of every 2.8 marriages in the United States ends in divorce. Between 1963 and 1973, the divorce rate nearly doubled.[76] Although, traditionally, divorce has most commonly occurred in the early years of marriage, it has become increasingly frequent among older married couples. In the United States, divorces have more than doubled since 1960 among couples who have maintained relationships for periods of 15 years and longer.[77] In Canada, divorce rates nearly doubled within a nine-year period from 1969 to 1978.[78] The high North American divorce rate is without precedence in any industrialized society.

The explanation for the rather rapid increase in the divorce rate is a complex one, involving legal, technical, social, and personal factors. For one thing, legal reforms introduced within the last few decades in the United States and Canada have made divorce easier by broadening the grounds on which it can be obtained. In Canada, for example, prior to 1968, adultery was by and large the only effective ground for divorce. In 1968, liberalization of the divorce laws in Canada resulted in an extension of the grounds for divorce to include not only adultery, but also cruelty, bigamy, and various unusual sexual acts. Additional grounds were established for cases in which the spouses had been living apart, thus making it evident that there had been a permanent breakdown in their marriage. The greater life expectancy of North Americans today may also partially account for the increased divorce rate. One hundred years ago, the average North American lived 35 to 40 years. Today, the average is 70 years. While marriage for life once suggested a period of 15 to 20 years, today, a marriage may span 50 or more years. While in the past, an unsatisfactory marriage may have been terminated by the death of a spouse, this is less likely to be the case today.

The relationship between women's increasing employment and divorce is not clear. While there are those who argue that women's employment is a direct cause of divorce, others conclude that the two factors are unrelated. Since the family enjoys a total higher income when both spouses are employed, dual-earner marriages should, in fact, be conducive to greater happiness, since the spouses' quality of life should be improved as a result of a higher standard of living.[79] At the same time, when the wife is employed outside the home, she has less time for childcare, spousecare, and housework. If family members continue to hold expectations of the woman that conform to traditional gender-role demands, then their satisfactions will likely decrease when the mother is employed. This, along with the woman's work overload and her likely resulting frustration, will contribute to greater dissatisfaction and marital instability. The employed woman may also want a greater role in family decision making and may be unwilling to subordinate her needs to those of her husband, as prescribed in the traditional family. Once again, if the man tenaciously clings to stereotyped ideas of the "proper" behaviour for a wife, friction may result.

It is more likely, however, that the married woman's employment does not cause friction leading to divorce. Rather, a woman who holds outside employment has the financial resources to support herself outside marriage and therefore is more likely to consider divorce as a realistic option to an unworkable or unsatisfactory marriage. In a study of divorce rates since the turn of the century, it has been suggested that women's employment is not a cause of divorce, but that increasing divorce rates, linked to greater control of conception and smaller families, have contributed to higher rates of employment among women. Couples with small families are more likely to divorce than those with large families, and divorced women are more likely to be employed.[80] Thus, although we know that women's employment is linked in various ways to divorce, there is no evidence that increased employment of women will cause a further increase in divorce rates.

The rising divorce rate may also be partially the result of the enormous cultural and personal expectations that have been placed on the marriage relationship today as compared to the past. For many young people marrying today, marriage is expected to provide communication, understanding, personal fulfillment, eroticism, romantic love, stimulating intellectual companionship, and emotional support.[81] To the extent that the spouse is seen as not providing expected rewards in marriage, disillusionment may result, and the marriage begins to break down. A new awareness exists today that a marriage considered to be unviable can be dissolved and replaced by a more viable one. In this way, the high divorce rate may be interpreted as a pursuit of happiness, however vague that pursuit might be. High divorce rates, coupled with high remarriage rates may reflect a universal wish for compatible marriage and happy family life.[82] Three-quarters of all divorced people tend to remarry within five years,[83] with remarriage rates tending to be higher for men than for women.[84] Although many divorced women (especially those under 30) do remarry, a greater proportion (especially over the age of 30) remain divorced.[85] When a couple breaks up, it is usually the woman who retains custody of the children. This may lessen the likelihood of her remarrying since many men may not want to provide financial support for, let alone raise, another man's offspring. Women's lower remarriage rate is probably also a function of the sheer unavailability of prospective mates. While social norms condone and even encourage men to marry women who are younger than themselves, younger men are not seen as legitimate prospective mates for women. This double standard results in considerably fewer prospective mates for women, who may well find that most "older" men are already married.

Effects of Divorce on the Child

Many professionals and lay people have assumed that divorce is basically bad for children. This assumption has been based on early research in the area showing that children from dissolved marriages were more likely than those from intact marriages to be delinquent, disturbed, and low achievers. There is also a plethora of research that points to father absence as a causative factor in childhood pathological behaviour, including poor personal adjustment and inadquate gender-role identification. However, later reviews of studies of father absence and marital disruption found that the early research lacked adequate controls (for socio-economic class, for example) and did not ask the appropriate questions.[86,87] Studies of children from one- and two-parent families with comparable economic backgrounds have found few differences between the two groups on measures including school achievement, social adjustment, and delinquent behaviour.[88-90] Furthermore, a two-parent environment does not automatically ensure good childrearing patterns, and, conversely, a one-parent family does not necessarily lead to inadequate childrearing.[91,92] The issue then becomes a question of how well the family situation meets the individual child's needs. Although meeting a child's needs has typically been the joint responsibility of two parents, research evidence suggests that a single parent can shoulder this responsibility and carry it out effectively.

Single-Parent Families

The number of children being raised in single-parent families is on the rise as a result of the increasing divorce rate. In 1978, it was estimated that in the United States, more than 10 million children were living with only one parent. This represents one out of every six children under the age of 18.[93] While in Canada in 1976, close to 10% of families had single parents,[94] the comparable figure in the United States approached 7% in 1977.[95] Most sole-support families in Canada are headed by women and a little less than one-half have been estimated to be living below the poverty line.[96] The Economic Council of Canada reports that the average Canadian family headed by a man earns more than twice as much as one headed by a woman.[97] In the United States as well, the majority of single-parent families are headed by women, who tend to be considerably poorer than their male counterparts.[98]

A study of income dynamics conducted at the University of Michigan shows that marital disruption, itself, has an important effect on family income and that women who head families suffer more from loss of income than their male counterparts.[99] For example, between 1967 and 1971, families that experienced no disruption saw their income rise by 35% over the five-year period. Men who lost a wife during this period and did not remarry also had rising incomes, though they did not rise as quickly as in families where husband and wife remained together. Women who were divorced, widowed, or separated during that period experienced a loss in family income of 16.5%,[100] due partly to a loss of the husband's income and partly to low remuneration from their jobs — typically low-paying, low-status occupations — which afforded little opportunity for advancement. These women's average earnings for full-time, year-round work were only 58% of that of their male counterparts.[101] There are many other reasons why women without husbands are poor. Some of these are a greater prevalence of divorce and early death among poor families; low and irregular levels of alimony, child support, and public assistance; fewer opportunities for employment; and lower wages than those of men when employment is found. The practical problems of the sole-support mother centre around a basic financial insecurity and a subsistence level of living, which very often show no real prospect of improving. The economic plight of the sole-support mother must therefore become a main concern of policy makers. In order that women and their families are ensured an adequate economic standard of living, existing laws relating to collection of maintenance payments should be improved or new ones should be instituted. This is particularly important, since the tensions and frustrations that result from not having enough money affect the children, as well as the women, and make the task of parenting even more difficult.

Although sole-support mothers are subject to more difficulty than sole-support fathers because of their socio-economic disadvantage, there are certain problems common to all single parents. For example, one person instead of two has to provide for all the children's needs. Some of these include the provision of love, the encouragement and fostering of self-esteem in a child who may feel especially vulnerable, guilty, or angry, and the furnishing of models for the children, both of the same gender role and the absent one as well. Frequently, an employed parent may be too drained at the end of the day to meet all the child's needs. In intact families, parents can substitute for each other if one parent wants to relax, unwind, or do other things. In a single-parent family, there may not be an available parent substitute to relieve the sole parent. While in the past, members of the extended family may have been available to act as buffers between child and parent, today's isolated nuclear family frequently does not have this option. The result very often is a feeling of isolation experienced by many single parents.

The Woman as a Single Parent. For the woman who finds herself taking on all of the responsibilities of parenting, there are unique difficulties which stem from her identity as a woman. Since most women have been socialized to define their self-esteem and identity in terms of their role as a dependent in a marriage relationship, loss of a marital relationship can create psychological problems for them. Loneliness and the loss of the role of wife may cause a woman to mourn for her husband and that relationship (despite its conflicts). This is especially likely among women who have been raised to view marriage and motherhood as their ultimate careers. For them, divorce may be particularly difficult and may provoke an identity crisis, aggravated by the loss of their housewife role.[102]

Traditionally, men are accorded the right to be the head of the household, and mothers and children are expected to fall under the protection of the man in the family. Moreover, many people in our society may resist recognizing the woman in an independent or authoritative status. So both the woman's lack of socialization for independence and, very often, society's reluctance to accept her in an independent status contribute to many women's inability to exercise authority in the home. The situation is somewhat exacerbated by the woman's typically low economic status within the community, which may further prevent her children from seeing her as an authority figure.

In light of the practical, social, and psychological consequences of divorce for women, it is not surprising that divorced and separated women often experience high levels of depression, especially if they have small children.[103] However, women who lose their role as wife through separation or divorce are not all equally vulnerable to psychological distress. In a study of 253 women who were in the process of divorce, it was found that the woman's attitudes toward gender roles were a significant predictor of psychological well-being. Women who held nontraditional gender-role attitudes or whose attitudes became less traditional during the process of divorce, experienced less distress and more personal growth, had higher self-esteem, and had a greater sense of well-being and personal effectiveness than those who maintained traditional gender-role attitudes.[104] The woman who is most likely to have difficulty coping with the demands of the new situation is the one who continues to accept the "woman-in-the-home" role, whose primary orientation is toward childrearing and care of the husband, and who discounts the value of the new roles that must be assumed. While some women adapt to their new "head-of-the-household" role, they may not feel comfortable in it. They will worry about being unfeminine and may even feel guilty about not fulfilling traditional role expectations. One woman interviewed in this study said, "I don't like my job. I do it for the money, but it takes away from my time as a mother (p. 324)." On the other hand, the woman whose gender-role attitudes become less traditional in the process of divorce is likely to consider maximization of her own potential just as important as familial duties. Such attitudes were found to be associated with more favourable outcomes and less distress during divorce. So, when women divorce, their traditionally passive roles become inadequate for coping with their change in status. New independent and autonomous roles have to be learned. However, few divorced women have social support systems to facilitate this important transition. Lacking financial, social, and psychological support, the plight of the divorced, single-parent woman is indeed a difficult one. In a society where divorce rates are rapidly increasing, girls should be socialized in order to develop a sense of autonomy and independence on a par with that of their male counterparts. Otherwise, they will be unable to cope effectively in a variety of roles.

The Man as a Single Parent. Single parenthood for men is not a new social phenomenon. Prior to the 20th century, many men became single parents through the death of their wife. Numerous women died in childbirth, leaving the husband to look after the children. With rapid advances in medical technology and more widespread access to prenatal medical attention, there has been a significant decline in maternal mortality. At the present time, when a man finds himself a single parent, it is most likely to be the result of separation or divorce. When a couple experienced separation or divorce in the past, mothers were automatically granted custody of the children. Traditional folk wisdom held that regardless of any problems that the woman had in raising her children, they were "better off" with their mother than with their father. In short, the mother has typically been regarded as the "natural" person to take care of the children. Today, however, courts are required to make a genuine decision as to which parent should have custody of the children, as an increasing number of fathers are seeking and obtaining custody of their minor children. In some cases, the woman may feel that the man is better equipped financially to provide for the children than she is. While most children remain with their mothers after marriage breakdown, there has been a notable increase in the number of motherless families in recent years. The 1976 Census of Canada indicated that there were 93 585 male lone-parent families in Canada.[105] In the United States between 1970 and 1973, the number of motherless families, excluding those in which the mother had died, increased from 807 000 to 971 000, an increase of 20%.[106]

When a man becomes a single parent, he, too, must take on the roles typically enacted by two parents. While he was married, the man probably functioned primarily in the instrumental role — namely, that of bread-winner. Whether his wife was employed or not, she likely provided for many of the child's emotional needs. But when a man becomes the sole parent caring for the child, he is expected to be the emotional mainstay of the family as well as the breadwinner. Not surprisingly, one study of 20 single-parent fathers in North Carolina reports that the majority of their problems centred around the difficulties experienced in harmonizing parental roles with adult roles and responsibilities.[107] The feelings of these fathers were similar to those expressed by many employed mothers who try to reconcile their adult and primary parent roles. Fathers mentioned their lack of time and patience for children and having to be away from them more than they wanted to be. Most expressed the desire to compensate for being the sole parent present by devoting as much time as possible to their children. Some of the fathers felt that they had gained custody because they were more nurturant than their wives and, overall, felt quite comfortable in their expressive roles.

But to what extent do male single parents feel that their performance of functions typically associated with women detracts from their masculinity? In another study of 32 single-parent fathers in California, none acknowledged that he had any feelings of loss of masculinity as a result of taking on many tasks usually performed by women, such as cooking, shopping, and managing the home.[108] However, one factor emerged quite clearly from among these fathers' experiences as parents: their lack of knowledge about normal child development. This is understandable, since boys' socialization, unlike that of girls, is not directed toward the care of children. As a consequence, most men in our society are not as sensitized to a child's needs at various stages of development as are most women, nor are they psychologically prepared to be the primary parent in a family.

On the basis of the limited existing information, it appears that most single-parent fathers studied have demonstrated their willingness and ability to competently handle parenthood. The increasing numbers of men who are becoming single parents and the growing trend toward mothers holding employment outside the home indicate a need for boys and men in our society to learn how to handle tasks within the home, including training and knowledge in both childcare and home management. Contrary to the stereotypical view that men cannot express nurturance and warmth toward children, research with single-parent fathers demon-strates that not only are men capable of such expressive behaviour, but they can also be comfortable in a role requiring nurturance.

Voluntary Childlessness

Despite the many changes that have recently altered the traditional family unit, there remains considerable pressure on married people to have children. In the past, children were, in fact, considered a woman's *raison d'être*. Although couples are now having fewer children, society condones and prescribes procreation. North American prescriptions for universal parenting among married couples are rooted in the teachings of the dominant organized religions. Judaism, Catholicism, and Protestantism all present parenthood as a moral responsibility. The Catholic Church, for example, regards "marriage in the eyes of God" as a permanent union for the procreation of children. Moreover, a marriage contracted with the intent of remaining childless is regarded by many religions as invalid. Traditional Judaic teaching, for example, explicitly states that the individual is obligated to marry and reproduce.

It is generally assumed that a marriage with children is a happy one and that a childless marriage is unhappy. But studies in this area do not clearly support or refute this assumption.[109] Having children contributes significantly to some couples' marital happiness, but for others, children may disrupt an otherwise contented union. There is no doubt, however, that with the advent of children, the relationship between the man and the woman changes. For example, the presence of children can be disruptive of adult touching and, by implication, of communication.[110] Moreover, anthropologists have contended that the presence of children, particularly when the children are young, encourages a division of labour along gender-role lines, since women are still seen as primarily responsible for childcare. This may partially explain why many women, once they have children, may be persuaded to forestall previous interests and occupations for the alternative of full-time childcare. In general, childless couples probably experience less division of labour along gender-role lines than couples with children. Other differences have also been reported between couples with children and their childless counterparts. For example, childless couples are more likely to be involved in democratic patterns of interaction than those with children.[111] Research also shows that women who show a preference for no children are more likely to describe themselves as self-reliant, assertive, and less easily influenced by others.[112] It may well be that women who decide to remain childless are less traditionally feminine in the first place, as demonstrated by their personality traits. Or, being childless, and thus being less likely to experience a division of labour along traditional gender-role lines in their marriage, childless women may experience fewer restraints on their independence and assertiveness strivings.

There is evidence that voluntary childlessness as a family form is on the increase. In the United States in 1975, 32% of ever-married women under the age of 30 were childless, up from 27% in 1970 and just 20% in 1960.[113] Even if 20 to 30% of these women were childless only because they had some impairment, there remained three million married women under age 30 who had intentionally not yet had children.[114] Lifetime childlessness may be on the rise. In 1975, one-quarter of American childless wives aged 25 to 29 reported that they expected to remain childless throughout their entire lifetimes.[115] In Canada, an estimated 12% of couples have no children. Of these, it is thought that at least one-half have made a deliberate decision to avoid parenthood.[116]

While voluntary childlessness has generally been uncommon and widely disparaged, results of surveys suggest that it may be becoming more socially acceptable. For example, while the results of Gallup surveys in 1973 indicated a decrease in the percentage of Americans who favoured large families of four or more children, the percentage of Americans who considered the childless family ideal was still only 1%.[117] Results of surveys among the university educated suggest that this figure is growing. For example, a 1961 Gallup survey of 483 college women showed that 2.7% of the women interviewed favoured one child or none.[118] But, in 1971, 13% of a sample of 140 undergraduate women at the University of Michigan said that they planned to have no children.[119] In a more recent study conducted at a Canadian university, 11% of the sample of female undergraduates indicated that they planned to never have children.[120] Although it may be argued that most of these respondents, being unmarried, would likely change their minds later and decide to have children, the surveys show that voluntary childlessness is becoming more popular among college students.

Voluntary childlessness is still generally regarded as "deviant" behaviour, however. As a result, couples who choose not to have children may feel that they are stigmatized to some extent. One study of 52 voluntarily childless wives from Toronto and London, Ontario,[121] found these women tend to be negatively stereotyped. Compared with parents, they tended to be seen as unnatural, immature, abnormal, sexually incompetent, selfish, irresponsible, and unfulfilled.[122,123] As recently as 1974, a favourable portrayal of the intentionally childless featured in a newspaper in Kansas City was followed by one letter to the editor expressing sympathy for those who, "through fear or selfishness", do not have children, and by another that described them as "unsuccessful at the game of life", "immature", and "without love of one another and mankind".[124] These unfavourable attitudes toward those who choose not to have children are to be expected, considering the pronatalistic nature of this society. Nevertheless, as voluntary childlessness becomes increasingly visible, there should be a corresponding increase in its acceptability as an alternative lifestyle.

Because of the greater freedom associated with it, voluntary childlessness as a family form has been referred to as "the ultimate liberation",[125] mainly for women. The advantages to women who remain childless include having time to have a life of their own, having greater opportunity to attain equal gender-role status to that of the man in the family, and more chance for full-time pursuit of a career. Because mothers who pursue careers are still expected to put their family responsibilities first, they may experience serious limitations on the time and energy they can devote to their careers. It is important to note, however, that there exists a double standard regarding career and family responsibilities. According to this line of thinking, a woman cannot spend too much time with her family, while the family man who is no more committed to his career than the woman can ignore his family with impunity. The female professional who seems to be more absorbed in her career than her family is neither understood nor forgiven. With increasing numbers of women pursuing careers and striving for equality in their relationships with men, and with greater societal emphasis on self-actualization, voluntary childlessness is bound to increase in the future.

Implications

The traditional family, which has been a practical socio-economic unit for centuries, is rapidly becoming an "endangered species". In the past, religious teachings and a strong sense of community lent support to the nuclear family as a social unit, along with its institutionalized polarization of gender roles. The increasing social acceptability of women's employment, greater demands for homosexual rights, increasing acceptance of sexual activity both before and outside marriage, and a rising divorce rate are among the changes that have necessitated the establishment of new family forms. In contrast to the past when people lived in a traditional family unit that was regulated by a set of tried-and-true rules, today's emphasis is on the search for the family form that best suits the individual's needs. While these new forms include the common-law family, the communal family, and families headed by homosexual couples who sometimes live with children from previous heterosexual marriages, our discussion has concentrated on dual-earner families and those headed by single parents.

But socialization based on the conventional gender-role system and propagated by the traditional family has not adequately prepared men and women for the new family forms in which they may find themselves. Frequently, attitudes associated with a rigid definition of gender roles and imposed social sanctions for those who deviate from them prevent women and men from coping well with a new situation — one that may require behaviour associated with another gender role. So, for example, despite their outside employment, married women continue to shoulder the main responsibility for housework and childcare, and husbands of employed wives have not been found to share domestic chores equally with their wives. At times, they may even resent sharing the woman's income, perceiving this to be an infringement upon their traditional role as breadwinner.

Spouses who find themselves as single parents either through divorce or death sometimes experience difficulty in taking on what they perceive to be the role of the other parent. Generally, men and women with broader, less stereotypical perceptions of their own gender role have made better adjustments and have derived more benefit from their new situation. In fact, these new family forms may at times facilitate a keener awareness of the potential of less conventional gender-role behaviour — an awareness that may not have been otherwise possible.

However, gender-role conflicts produced by new family forms are still largely unresolved, partly because of inadequate alterations in government policy to accommodate these changes. It is now incumbent on government at all levels to shift direction in their policies that directly affect the family. Of particular importance here is government's policy on daycare. Despite evidence of the widespread increase in maternal employment, both in Canada and the United States, there is no comprehensive government policy on daycare in either country. Whereas countries in Western and Eastern Europe have been providing daycare for years, government-sponsored daycare in North America is still sporadic and inadequate. How can this blind spot in government policy be eliminated? The answer does not lie in denying much-needed daycare facilities in the hope that this will force women back into the home. Women will continue to seek outside employment, divorce rates will likely remain high, and families' need for good daycare will increase in the future. In the absence of good daycare, people will make whatever arrangements they can, and, in many instances, these may not meet the needs of developing children. As long as children's needs are not being met in this regard, they will be the ones who will suffer and the society of the future will also bear the consequences.

Changes are also needed in the employment sphere. People need and want more flexible work-schedules, daycare on the premises, and more time available to spend with their families. While it may have sounded outrageous in the past, today's families need such benefits as sick leave for employed parents whose children are ill, paternity leave whereby a man is given time off to devote full-time care to his family before, during, and after the birth of his baby, and job sharing, whereby a company allows two part-time workers to occupy a job usually done by one full-timer.

In many ways our society has been ill-prepared for the widespread changes that have occurred in the family. Thirty years ago, few people would have predicted them, let alone speculated as to how we would cope with the changes that have struck at the very foundation of our society. The answer lies not in adapting outmoded systems and policies developed for another generation, but in evolving new policies and social action which will allow the maximum utilization of human potential of a generation which is setting new rules for family living.

8

Employment and Gender Roles

The history of work has traditionally been that of *men* at work. This is not because women have not been working, but because their work has been more or less invisible. They have either done domestic chores or been occupied with childcare in the home. The jobs of poorer women, who have always worked outside the home (as well as in it), have been seen as less important than those of men — both by social scientists and by employers. Despite the fact that women represented nearly 40% of the Canadian employed labour force in 1979,[1] women's employment role is still regarded as secondary.

By and large, women's employment role has been sporadic when compared to that of men. What are the reasons for this? Traditionally, women's participation in the labour force has been much more responsive to the needs of employers. Until recently, conventional gender-role prescriptions have also dictated that women remain in the home, rather than seek outside employment. These are some of the factors that have led to women's more unstable employment compared to that of men. Women have also been more likely to take part-time employment and to interrupt their employment for other responsibilities, such as raising a family. Traditionally, women have formed a reserve army of labour, holding down paid jobs when seasonal or part-time employment was available or when men where taken away from their jobs during wars.[2] But women's employment during wartime was seen as a temporary measure — by government and society alike. The concessions of tax relief and daycare centres provided for employed women were withdrawn at the end of the wars. So, for example, temporary initiatives on the part of government, such as regulations restricting the employment of married women, ensured that women would return to "hearth and home" after World War II in order to lessen the problem of postwar unemployment of men.

Later, however, women started to become more visible again in the labour force. It has been mainly during the last few decades that women in both Canada and the United States have entered the labour force in great numbers.[3] Much of this increase has been due to the increasing participation of married women (see Chapter 7). The rapid growth in the corporate and government sectors and in the service industries has resulted in an enormous increase in jobs, particularly those thought to be suitable for women and which women, in fact, have filled. Since women first began entering the labour force, office positions have ranked high among the occupations thought to be appropriate for them. So, for example, one American study states:

> It seemed apparent that young women were particularly suited to office occupations. They were less expensive than men. Their more or less temporary attachment to the job made most of them less interested in advancement, which office positions usually lacked. Thousands of girls were pouring out of high schools in a rising wave that came with a higher standard of living... And while machines made high school education less necessary for occupations such as receiving and shipping clerks, junior high school was usual for filers, multigraph operators, and billing, stock, payroll, and mail clerks. For stenographers, dictating machine operators, bookkeepers, and book-keeping machine operators, office managers required senior high school education, and college for the secretarial stenographers (p. 215).[4]

Similar patterns of female employment appeared in the specialized occupations in the education, health, and industrial sectors, where the importance of physical strength had considerably diminished. At the same time, it was in these sectors that a host of part-time jobs sprang up. Coincidentally, these were precisely the jobs thought to be most appealing to married women and for which employers were most willing to hire women: service jobs, office employment, and jobs that permitted part-time schedules.

In recent years, women's traditional patterns of participation in the labour force have been altered to some extent. Later marriages, declining birthrates, increasing social acceptance of the employed mother, and rising divorce rates, have all led to the fact that full-time employment is prevalent among a growing number of women now. Women are also more likely to hold outside employment for longer periods of time. Interestingly, while women's participation in the labour force is increasing, the proportion of the male population in the labour force is actually falling, although the male population has expanded at about the same rate as the female one. Almost everywhere in the industrialized free world, including the United States, the population of men with jobs is falling.[5] This decrease for men is attributable largely to longer education, earlier retirement, and longer life spans.

In spite of women's increasing employment, they still have far to go before their employment status is on a par with that of men. The woman's sporadic employment in the past and today has an important effect on her financial condition later in life. Although 94 out of every 100 women marry, only 26 can expect to live with their husbands until death. Of the others, 15 will probably separate or divorce, and 53 will likely become widows. As women in North America tend to marry men who are slightly older than they are, and whose life expectancy is shorter than their own, a substantial number of them are bound to become widows at some point in their lives. This has important economic implications for women who have not themselves held outside employment and thus do not have the resources to adequately plan for their old age. In 1975 in Canada, for example, 45% of widows aged 55 to 64 were poor (had incomes below the poverty line), as were 66% of those over the age of 65.[6] Contrary to what many people believe, husbands' pensions seldom provide adequate income by themselves for surviving wives. All told, less than one widow in four can expect to get any regular benefits from her deceased husband's employer. Even then, what she receives will, in most cases, amount to only 50% of her husband's pension entitlement.[7] Thus, marriage does not generally provide women with financial security later in life. This, along with women's lack of employment stability and the fact that women generally live longer than men, have led to a disproportionately high number of poor women, compared to men, among the aged.

All indications are that women's participation in the labour force will likely increase in the future. While women, as well as men, usually seek employment for financial reasons, there are social and psychological rewards that are also associated with employment. To what extent are these the same for women and men, and how do they differ?

Motivation for Employment

Most of the research to date on motivation to work has been done with specific reference to men. According to one writer in the field, the employment role is perhaps a person's major link to society in that it allows the person the sense of having contributed something of value to society.[8] Other reasons for men's employment include satisfying the needs for prestige, social interaction, and social activity, and contributing to one's social and psychological identity. But why do women seek employment? Are the same kinds of rewards available to them? Traditionally, the family and the home have been seen as sufficiently rewarding to women as to preclude the necessity of their seeking fulfillment elsewhere. Indeed, the fact that the majority of women holding employment today are doing so for financial reasons does not rule out the possibility that employment can, and often does, satisfy some of the same needs in women as it does in men. Recent researchers have noted that feelings of personal contribution and social connectedness seem available to women in their jobs as well.[9,10]

However, employment is not to be equated automatically with social and psychological gratification. The fact is that the vast majority of jobs occupied by men and women are alienating. Rapid advances in technology have led to large numbers of dull, repetitive, dead-end jobs. It is in these low-status jobs (which are more likely to be held by women than men) where there is the greatest possibility of feelings of alienation and noninvolvement. Relative powerlessness in decisions affecting the employee and a lack of social meaning in the job, itself, lie at the root of worker discontent in this type of position. As reported in a U.S. Department of Health, Education and Welfare Report, "Work in America", released in December, 1972,[11] the problem is widespread and has become the subject of some concern throughout the business community. In an effort to grapple with these problems, major corporations all over the world have been devising new strategies to improve the quality of working life for the employee.

One such strategy is exemplified by the team approach to work, implemented by a new plant in Topeka, Kansas, in 1971.[12] The underlying premise of this project is that productivity will be maximized when the employee's needs are met and when the employee can identify with the success of the overall operation. The operations at this plant constitute just one example of a number of Quality of Working Life, or QWL, Programs being implemented in the United States and in Canada.

In the Topeka plant, employee involvement and responsibility have been increased through a complete reorganization of the employment setting. There are no superiors in the traditional sense. Instead, there are team leaders who have demonstrated skills in group dynamics. Status symbols are nonexistent and advancement is determined by merit. The team sets its own targets and assigns the jobs for any given day to its members. There is a single job classification with grade-level progression, which provides ample opportunity for employees to acquire multiple skills. One of the assumptions of this new system is that people have "ego" needs: they want self-esteem, a sense of accomplishment, and a chance to increase their skills. It is assumed that people will invest more in situations which allow them to meet these needs. It is also assumed that if employees are to feel satisfied in their jobs, these jobs must fill their social needs (as would be the case in the teamwork situation at Topeka), and they must be able to perceive themselves as a significant part of the whole product or end result. Such innovative approaches to changes in the employment setting demonstrate how the job can be made more satisfying for the employee and more effective for the organization as a whole. If workers are satisfied and productivity increases (as it has in many of these experiments), the organization benefits as well. However, the most important point demonstrated by the QWL Programs is that both men and women want their jobs to be satisfying.

The results of a recent U.S. survey of 23 008 male and female readers of *Psychology Today*[13] illustrate the psychological importance of employment to both women and men, over and above its economic importance. Keeping in mind that the sample surveyed tend to be younger, better educated, and higher paid than the population of the country as a whole, the results of this survey are of considerable interest. Only 9% said that they would quit their employment if they could live as comfortably as they liked for the rest of their lives; almost 75% said that they would continue to be employed; and women were as likely as men to want to continue their employment, which suggests that employment has become as important to the woman's identity as it has been to the man's. The wish for fulfillment from employment was not restricted to the middle class. Among foremen, clerical workers, and unskilled workers, many expressed feelings of being trapped, and reported that they, too, wanted a satisfying job that offered the prospect of personal growth.

Despite growing evidence that a job often satisfies the same social and psychological needs in women as in men, stereotypes about why women work outside the home continue to abound. Women are seen as holding "until" jobs — until they get married, until they have children. However, once married and having become mothers, many women find that their job income is needed in order for the family to maintain a satisfactory standard of living. While the majority of married women hold employment out of financial need, there still is considerable debate about why married women have paid jobs. It is generally held that married middle-class women who pursue interesting and challenging careers are motivated largely by a wish for psychological fulfillment. Married working-class women, however, have been considered to prefer the housewife role. This preconception, based on the belief that most working-class jobs are monotonous, unfulfilling, and psychologically unrewarding, has been challenged by recent research.

In interviews with 135 working-class women whose average family income was less than $10 000.00 a year, one study compared housewives with married women who held outside employment.[14] The employed women held jobs generally not considered to be satisfying or challenging —

clerical jobs, factory jobs, and a variety of sales and service positions. The results showed that the working-class women who were full-time home-makers were less satisfied with their lives than the women who held jobs; the housewives also tended more to see themselves as engaging in less interesting activities than their husbands. The majority of the employed women said that they would continue working at their jobs even when their children were older and even if they did not need the money. Although financial necessity forced many of these women to seek outside employ-ment and many of the jobs they held were of an alienating nature, these women, like their husbands, received much more than financial benefits from their jobs. More social interaction with other adults, greater personal autonomy, and greater power in decision making in the home were among the rewards they received that were not forthcoming from the housewife role. These results suggest that the sacrifice of time and effort on the job may be considered justification for more rights within the home itself. In this way, the woman who holds outside employment in fact gains more power in domestic matters.

In summary, then, there would appear to be a growing convergence in the needs of men and women that are satisfied by outside employment. The fact that most men and women are employed for money and that many jobs are not necessarily fulfilling in and of themselves, should not obscure the psychological needs that people seek to fulfill in their employment.

Occupational Differences between Women and Men

One of the most obvious and persistent differences between women and men lies in the number and type of occupational areas in which they are found. In general, women continue to be found in a few low-status, low-paying occupations, and data for 1979 do not reveal any substantive changes from the past. Table 8.1 gives employment distributions based on general occupational areas in Canada in 1979 with associated percentages of employed women and men. It is evident from this table that men are much more evenly distributed among the various job categories than are women. While no one occupation contains more than 11.6% of all male workers, over one-third of the employed female labour force is shown to have been in clerical occupations in 1979. Moreover, women tend to be concentrated in three main areas: the clerical, sales, and service sectors of the economy. A full 62.6% of all female employees were in these occupations, compared to 26.4% of all male employees. Comparisons with 1962 reveal that there have not been any appreciable changes since then; in that year, 61.2% of female employees were in these three areas.[15] Despite their increased participation rate in the labour force since 1962, women are increasingly entering the same occupational areas that they occupied over 15 years ago. Table 8.2 shows that from 1962 to 1979, women's represen-

Table 8.1

Percentage Distribution of Women and Men in Occupational Categories, Canada, 1979

Occupation	Percentage Distribution	
	Women	Men
	%	%
Managerial and Administrative	5.0	9.3
Natural Sciences, Engineering and Mathematics	1.1	5.1
Social Sciences	1.8	1.2
Religion	*	0.4
Teaching	6.1	3.0
Medicine and Health	8.7	1.7
Artistic and Recreational Occupations	1.2	1.5
Clerical	34.0	6.4
Sales	10.7	10.3
Service	17.9	9.7
Agriculture	2.9	6.3
Fishing, Hunting and Trapping	*	0.4
Forestry and Logging	*	0.9
Mining and Quarrying	*	0.9
Processing	1.8	5.1
Machining	0.4	4.2
Product Fabricating, Assembling and Repairing	5.6	11.6
Construction Trades	0.2	10.3
Transport Equipment Operation	0.6	6.4
Materials Handling	1.2	3.3
Other Crafts and Equipment Operating	0.6	1.8
All Occupational Categories	100.0	100.0

*Figures too small to be reliable.

Source: Labour Canada. *1978-1979 Women in the Labour Force: Part 1 Participation*. Cat. No. L38-30/1979-1. Table 9b. Employed labour force in occupational categories by sex, women as percentage of the total employed labour force, and percentage distribution of women and men, Canada, 1979. Ottawa, 1980, p. 33.

Table 8.2

Women as Percentage of the Total Employed Labour Force in Selected Occupations, Canada, 1962[1] and 1979[2]

Occupation	Women as Percentage of the Total Employed Labour Force	
	1962	1979
Clerical	62.7	77.1
Sales	35.5	39.9
Service	56.5	53.9

[1]Labour Canada. *Women in the Labour Force: Facts and Figures (1973 edition).* Cat. No. L38-3072. Table 24. Employed labour force in occupational categories, by sex, women as percentage of the total employed labour force, and percentage distribution of women and men by occupation, Canada, 1962 and 1972. Ottawa, 1974, p. 49.
[2]Labour Canada. *1978-1979 Women in the Labour Force: Part 1 Participation.* Table 9b. Ottawa, 1980, p. 33.

tation in the clerical area has actually increased. In the sales and service areas, there has been little change over the years. Continued occupational segregation can also be seen in women's participation in selected occupations over a span of seven years. In 1971, for example, women made up more than three-quarters of the employees in seven occupational categories, including stenographers and typists; personal service workers (including chambermaids and babysitters); fabricators and assemblers; graduate nurses; waiters and waitresses; nursing assistants, aides and orderlies; and telephone operators.[16] In 1978, the picture changed very little: women made up 97% of all secretaries and stenographers, 95% of all telephone operators, and 96% of all babysitters,[17] to name only a few. By contrast, in 1971, the 21 largest occupations for male employees contained less than 40% of their numbers.[18] Among these were truck drivers, janitors, accountants, sales clerks, secondary school teachers, and foremen. Likewise, most jobs in the professional and technical fields have tended to remain typed as either women's or men's work. As of 1971, more than three-quarters of elementary and kindergarten teachers, dental hygienists, librarians, physiotherapists, and dieticians were women. At the same time, more than three-quarters of university teachers, doctors, pharmacists, lawyers, industrial engineers, and dentists were men.[19]

Despite the fact that women are obtaining higher education more than in the past, for the most part, they are still entering a few stereotypical feminine professions. In 1979, for example, in Canada, one-half of the graduates with bachelor's and first professional degrees were women; two-thirds of these were in arts and education.[20] In 1979, again, women comprised approximately three-quarters or more of those receiving first degrees in social work, nursing, and household science. In comparison, for example, men still comprised about three-quarters or more of those awarded degrees in engineering and applied sciences, and dental studies and research.[21] Although about 90% of the lawyers in Canada were men in the late seventies,[22] the proportion of women aspiring to law appears to be increasing. For example, in 1978, one out of every seven lawyers practising in Canada for five years or less was a woman, compared with one out of every 14 lawyers who had been in practice for five to ten years.[23] In pharmacy, too, there has been an increase in the number of women, partly because of the opportunity for part-time work it affords. In 1979, the proportion of pharmacy degrees awarded to women reached 60%.[24] While medicine has traditionally been a profession predominantly associated with men, in recent years that picture, too, has been changing. Over 20 years ago, only 7% of all medical students were women. By the end of the 1970s, one-third of medical students in Canada were women.[25] This shows a recent trend, albeit a small one, in women's increasing visibility in a handful of professions traditionally occupied almost exclusively by men.

In the area of teaching in Canada, the distribution of men and women has not changed much over the years. As of 1977–78, for example, women were still found predominantly at the elementary school level, where 70% of the teachers were women. In contrast, nearly 70% of teachers of grades 9 and higher were men.[26] At the university level, the proportion of women found in teaching positions has actually decreased in recent years from that reported in 1931.[27] There are few women teaching in departments of engineering, applied sciences, mathematics, and the physical sciences, a finding which reflects a pattern found in the occupational sphere. Women are more likely to be found in departments of education, fine arts, humanities, and health sciences, where they are found mainly in nursing or teaching positions.[28]

By the seventies, women in both Canada and the United States began to appear in almost every job. Women now work in construction crews, drive buses and heavy trucks, operate bulldozers, and are actuaries in insurance offices. Very often, however, women who "break ground" by entering jobs that have been typically occupied by men, find implicit obstacles, not the least of which is the stipulation that the woman must demonstrate that she has more of the qualifications usually considered necessary for the job. A case in point is that of Ms. Leslee Marsellus, one of five female pilots for an American airline that employs 4500 male pilots. When she was hired in November 1977, she had already completed 4600 hours of flying time. "Most military pilots only have about 2000 hours when they go job-hunting," said Marsellus in a newspaper interview.[29] However, the fanfare given by the media to the relatively small percentage of women in jobs that have been almost exclusively occupied by men, has created a false impression of equal representation of women and men throughout the occupational sector. Women in Canada continue to be concentrated in jobs traditionally associated with women.[30] Despite the small increase in women's participation in some occupations where only men were found, occupational job segregation is still the order of the day.

Similar patterns of occupational segregation have been found in the United States, where, according to 1979 data, women accounted for 42.2% of the civilian labour force.[31] However, occupational segregation occurs here as well. In 1977 in the United States, more than two-thirds of employed women held jobs in stereotypically feminine occupations: nurses, librarians, teachers, social workers, clerical workers, and service workers.[32] While women accounted for 43% of the "professional and technical workers" in the United States in 1977,[33] over one-half of all women in this category were nurses or noncollege teachers — low-paying, low-status professions. As in Canada, more women are aspiring to the medical profession in the United States.[34] Similar increases have been observed in the percentage of women enrolled in law school.[35] Although women received 27% of doctoral degrees awarded in 1978 in the United States,[36] the proportion of women on American college faculties has hovered around 24% since 1960 — a lower share than the share they held in 1930 (27%).[37]

Despite women's increased education over the past, they are still far from being equally represented in the whole range of occupations and professions. "Prestige" occupations and professions are still seen — by both women and men — as the proper domain for men. The exclusivity which has traditionally been associated with these positions lives on, albeit in a much more subtle form, since overt discrimination is no longer tolerated in most spheres. The social structure reflected in most occupations and professions can be regarded as a microcosm of the social structure at large, where it is held that women's place is inferior to that of men. Long-held attitudes regarding the appropriate positions for men and women do not vanish overnight. Most men in their employment are unable to accept women in positions of authority or dominance over them, and women are generally more comfortable in accepting directives from men than in giving them directives. But, increasingly, women are expressing interest in learning how to exert their authority — particularly when they occupy positions that require authoritative behaviour. The growing numbers of women who want to learn how to exercise authority may partially explain women's burgeoning interest in courses in assertiveness training.

At the same time, certain jobs continue to be seen as belonging to men's domain, not because women are incapable of fulfilling the job requirements, but because many of these jobs exist in a social atmosphere somewhat similar to that of an exclusive men's club. Conventionally masculine behaviour and language and even the kinds of jokes regularly exchanged by occupants of these jobs convey the impression that the job is closed to women. Such is the case, too, when women are excluded from consideration for a particular job because, it is said, there are no bathroom facilities for them. These observations reinforce the preconception that the job in question is part of a man's world, where women have no business trespassing.

But men are also casualties of occupational segregation, which prevents them from diversifying their employment role. While it is true that there has been an increase in the number of men occupying jobs previously considered to be suitable only for women, this number remains small. Not only are these jobs judged as inappropriate for men, but they are also seen as demeaning. There is a stigma attached to people who aspire *down* the social prestige ladder in our achievement-oriented society. Men who take on "women's" jobs fall into this category. The pressures of the traditional masculine role also prevent them from entering jobs that do not allow them to "prove themselves as men" through the exercise of power and dominance — precisely those jobs traditionally held by women. Thus, social and psychological pressures prevent men and women alike from diversifying their employment role, and, as such, prevent the individual from expressing his or her potential in employment.

Employment Status: Implications for Women and Men

A perusal of the employment picture for men and women reveals that in every occupational and professional sphere, women generally occupy lower status positions, exert less power and control, and, for the most part, are not represented in positions where major decision making takes place. The vast majority of jobs held by women are dead-end positions — that is, they are not conducive to career advancement, nor are they regarded as stepping stones to more challenging jobs. Compared to the jobs and occupations held by men, those in which women are predominantly found are almost universally rated as lower in prestige. Similarly, the professions in which women predominate (i.e., nursing, social work, etc.) are regarded as less prestigious than those held mainly by men (i.e., medicine, law, engineering, etc.).

The common practice of assigning men as superiors in employment settings that are occupied largely by women limits women's upward mobility. Not only does this practice provide few, if any, role models of women in positions of authority, but it also reinforces the impression that there is little opportunity for women to be promoted through the ranks to more prestigious positions. For example, in the United States in 1980, over two-thirds of the teachers in elementary and secondary schools were women, but only slightly over one-third of the principals and other school administrators were women.[38] While most librarians are women, most chief librarians and library administrators are men. In social work, most case workers are women; most superiors are men. In advertising and

THE EVOLUTION OF MAN

journalism, most researchers are women, and the more prestigious jobs of writing usually go to men.

It has also been observed that women are almost twice as likely as men to have no control over the pacing of tasks associated with their jobs. One study[39] of white-collar workers in British Columbia, for example, found that women more often worked with machines all day, had few decisions to make, and had little involvement in the total work process. Men were found to be twice as likely as women to have jobs involving creative work. Moreover, in white-collar jobs, in manufacturing, or in trade, women have much less opportunity than men to initiate and control their work. They are seldom involved in decision making; instead, their work tends to be supportive and/or done in direct response to men or machines.[40] As in the case of white-collar work, traditional gender roles dictate that blue-collar women should be supervised by men and, in fact, they usually are.

Although there are trends toward increasing participation of women in some areas that have typically been occupied almost exclusively by men, it seems that even when women enter these fields, they tend to cluster in low-status, low-prestige positions and they rarely reach the top. In university teaching, for example, in both Canada and the United States, women tend to be concentrated in the lower ranks and are conspicuously absent from the higher, more senior positions. For example, in 1977-78, slightly more than one-third of the women holding teaching positions in Canadian universities were at the associate or full professor ranks compared to two-thirds of the male faculty. An additional one-third of the female faculty occupied the junior rank of assistant professor, and the remainder were in positions below that of assistant professor. Even taking into account the fact that men are more likely to hold doctorates, women still do not progress to the senior ranks as frequently as men. For example, in Canada in 1975-76, nearly one-third of the men holding doctorates were full professors, compared to only one-seventh of the women holding doctorates.[41] In the United States as well as in Canada, women faculty also stay at the same job level longer than men and are more often cycled out of their jobs without tenure. In 1976 in the United States, there had been no substantial change in the status of women faculty; the proportion of women at the senior levels was still the same as it was in 1960: under 10% for the full professor rank and about 17% for associates.[42] These differences in status in the university persist despite the findings that there are small or no differences in productivity between women and men holding Ph.D.s. Moreover, a study by the American Council of Education shows that, of the more than 2500 accredited institutions of higher education in the United States, only 6% had women presidents.[43]

Women's increased participation in the labour force has not been paralleled by a greater presence in corporate management or in the board room. In Canada in 1979, for example, 5% of the employed female labour force was in the managerial and administrative category, compared with 9.3% of all employed men (see Table 8.1). A study of Canadian boards of directors, including those of some 276 manufacturing and nonmanufacturing firms, found that women accounted for only 0.95% of all directors in 1976 — a negligible change from the 1973 level.[44] In both the United States and Canada, women are not found in major decision-making positions. In *Games Mother Never Taught You: Corporate Gamesmanship for Women*,[45] Harragan made some predictions about women's future opportunities for advancement to top executive positions. Basing her projections on conditions in the United States in the late seventies, when there were over 35 million women employed in full-time positions, compared to at least 57 million men, all other things being equal, she argued:

> ...it should seem safe to predict that the future chief executives of America's four million major corporations will start turning up in a ratio of one woman to every 2 or 3 men. Yet the odds against a woman becoming chief executive officer of AT & T, General Electric, Xerox, IBM, First Boston Corporation, Bank of America, Pillsbury, Revlon, CBS, or Sears, by the year 2000 are so astronomical that, in real terms, she has almost no hope. But we *know* that the reins of control will inevitably pass into the hands of men who are working side by side today with female peers (p. 9).

There is a striking parallel between the role of employee and the role of wife. In terms of selection for a job, for example, since much of women's employment requires few skills, hiring may rely more heavily on appearance than on skill. Moreover, the tasks required of most women in their jobs are very similar to those they perform in the home. This holds for both nonprofessional and professional jobs. Women's employment tasks frequently include menial ones such as washing, sewing, serving others, teaching young children, and caring for the sick, as well as playing supportive roles to others — in most cases, to the male boss. For example, the office secretary has even been referred to as "the office wife" or "the helpmate". Just as a good wife is supposed to oversee the home, attend to the menial and mundane tasks necessary for its day-to-day maintenance, and minister to her husband's needs, so the good secretary is required to tend to her boss and *his* office. Both roles require that the woman create a supportive and worry-free atmosphere so that the *man* can tend to his "important work". The secretary's role is aptly described in the following excerpt from a speech made at the meeting of the U.S. National Secretaries Association in 1967:

> Secretaries are marvelous people. They are ornamental and they are useful. They take down what you say and improve upon it. They know where to put in the double l's, the commas and the paragraphs. They hold the mad letters until tomorrow. They answer the telephone, sidetrack the bores and put through those on the important list. They

remember the birthdays and anniversaries. They remind you that it's time to get going for the lunch date. They say when you need a haircut (p. 71).[46]

The similarity between the role of secretary and that of wife is accentuated by management's widespread practice of tying the secretary's career to that of her male boss. If he gets a promotion and a bigger office, so does she, although she does not get his salary increase. But there is a double standard associated with their work. Since the boss's work, like the husband's is seen as more important and the secretary's is considered to be less important, the secretary can be constantly interrupted by phone calls and directives from her boss. On the other hand, the boss often tells her not to disturb him while he is working. Another manifestation of the ubiquitous double standard in employment spheres lies in the expectation that a secretary is to keep her personal life restricted to after 5 P.M., whereas her boss may take time off for a haircut, for example. If a secretary were to take such liberties, she could lose her job.[47]

Finally, because the requirements for the jobs held by the majority of women are usually minimal, so are the opportunities for change or development. Women are less likely than men to receive on-the-job training, which makes it more difficult for them to acquire additional skills. This situation exists partly as a result of the stereotyped attitudes that employers hold toward their female workers. For example, employers have been found to provide better job training for men than for women on the assumption that women's commitment to work is not as great and that their employment will be intermittent. In Canada in 1977, women accounted for only 28.3% of all on-the-job industrial trainees and women accounted for only 2.8% of apprenticeships for highly skilled jobs — and most of these were for hairdressing.[48] Canadian Federal Government cutbacks in job training allowances and counselling services have also contributed to lowering women's chances to qualify for well-paid jobs.[49] It is not surprising, then, that most women end their employment lives performing many of the same tasks they carried out at the outset.[50]

The statistics on women's employment paint a rather gloomy picture. Just as they have been doing for decades, women tend to hold low-status jobs more than men and seem to gravitate toward positions that offer little opportunity for promotion. In cases where women do have promotion opportunities, they appear to have less control than men over the direction of their career paths. Even in occupational areas where women predominate, it is men, not women, who are the supervisors and who take on the major decision-making positions.

Sexual Harassment. Among the possible undesirable by-products of a workplace where men almost universally have the opportunity to wield power over women is exploitation of female employees by males. Sexual harassment is only one of these possible forms of exploitation. Although the phenomenon is not new, it has only recently begun to be discussed openly. Historical accounts have given descriptions of sexual harassment of female factory workers in the latter half of the 19th century and of domestic servants, waitresses, sales clerks, and office workers in the early part of the 20th century. In *The Secret Oppression: Sexual Harassment of Working Women,* Constance Backhouse and Leah Cohen [51] define sexual harassment as including both physical and psychological elements. Leering, pinching, hugging, grabbing, pawing, and making propositions can all be forms of sexual harassment. In the case of an employer or supervisor making advances, noncompliance could put the woman's job in jeopardy. Sexual harassment by a woman's client or coworker has also been documented, and results of recent surveys indicate that sexual harassment is a pervasive feature of many employment settings. Contrary to traditional beliefs, it affects employed women of all ages, appearances, occupations, and social classes. In a *Redbook* magazine survey conducted in 1976,[52] 88% of 9000 readers reported that they had experienced some form of sexual harassment. The majority of these also reported feeling embarrassed, intimidated, and angry as a result. Other complaints included feelings of powerlessness, defeat, and impaired job performance, as well as physical complaints. In another survey conducted in 1976, this time by the Ad Hoc Group of the Equal Rights for Women Committee at the United Nations, half of the 875 women in professional and clerical positions polled, reported that they had at some time either personally experienced sexual pressure or were aware that such pressure existed within their organization.[53]

The woman who has experienced sexual harassment is in a dilemma: firstly, there usually is no place where she can lodge a complaint, and, if she does, she will likely lose her job; secondly, management is far from sympathetic to the problem. In their interviews with a cross-section of managers, personnel directors, union representatives, and policemen, Backhouse and Cohen found that there is a general denial that sexual harassment exists. When confronted with charges of making unwanted sexual advances, bosses frequently say "she asked for it".

Feminists and women's groups in both Canada and the United States point out that sexual harassment is a crime against women, an exercise of male power over a female subordinate. Since many more women are now planning to hold employment throughout their lives, they are beginning to take threats to their employment status more seriously. More women are speaking up, as demonstrated by the increasing number of complaints received by status of women groups and human rights commissions in Canada and the United States. Women's groups across North America are also exposing sexual harassment as a social problem and as a form of discrimination against women, which has heightened public awareness of the problem and caused people to treat it with the seriousness it deserves.

Are Women and Men Paid Equally?

In general, women's earnings are almost always less than those of men. Contrary to what many people believe, women rarely earn as much as men, even when they are in the same occupation, despite the existence of equal pay legislation, which prohibits differential pay rates based solely on sex. In 1979, Canadian male workers who worked mostly full time (50 to 52 weeks per year) earned $17 441.00, compared to $11 034.00 for their female counterparts (see Table 8.3). Moreover, according to data for full-time workers, there has not been any appreciable change over the decade in the difference between earnings of women and those of men. The discrepancy still holds when men's and women's earnings are examined by occupational category. Table 8.4 shows that in all occupational categories in 1979, men's annual salaries exceeded those of women. In some, women

---

Table 8.3

Median Earnings for Male and Female Full-Time[1] Workers in Canada for 1971, 1973, 1975, 1977, and 1979

Year	Male $	Female $	Female as Percentage of Male
1971	7 982	4 828	60.5
1973	9 553	5 738	60.1
1975	12 584	7 672	61.0
1977	14 977	9 246	61.7
1979	17 441	11 034	63.3

[1]A full-time worker is a person who worked, mostly full-time, 50–52 weeks in a given year.
Sources: Data for 1971, 1973, and 1975 are from Statistics Canada. *Consumer Income and Expenditure Division, Selected Tables on Earnings and Work Experience, 1971-75.* Percentage distribution of individuals by size of earnings, age and sex, 1971, 1973, 1975, Tables 4, 14, and 24, respectively. Mimeo, Ottawa, 1977.

Data for 1977 are from Statistics Canada. *Income Distributions by Size in Canada 1977.* Cat. No. 13-207. Table 70. Percentage distribution of earners by earnings groups, age, sex and full/part-time worker status, 1977. Ottawa, 1979, pp. 130-132.

Data for 1979 are from Statistics Canada. *Income Distributions by Size in Canada 1979.* Cat. No. 13-207. Table 72. Percentage distribution of earners by earnings groups, age, sex and full/part-time worker status, 1979. Ottawa, 1981, pp. 134-136.

were earning as little as about half of men's wages. In others, notably, the "professional", "clerical", and "farming, fishing, and logging" categories, women were earning somewhat more: approximately two-thirds of the amounts men were being paid.

A similar pattern emerges when weekly and hourly rates for various occupations are examined. Based on 1979 Canadian data, men's average weekly and hourly wages for various office occupations, sales positions, and factory jobs exceeded those of women in practically every case.[54] In many categories, the gap in wages between men and women doing the same job has actually increased over the past few years.

Table 8.4

Median Earnings of Male and Female Full-Time[1] Workers in Canada by Occupation[2] for 1979

Occupation	Male $	Female $	Female as Percentage of Male
Managerial	23 530	14 119	60.0
Professional	21 395	14 856	69.4
Clerical	15 986	11 010	68.9
Sales	17 192	9 661	56.2
Service	14 426	8 672	60.1
Farming, fishing, logging, etc.	10 846	7 467	68.8
Processing and machining	17, 077	9 494	55.6
Product fabrication, etc.	16 742	9 198	54.9
Construction	17 342	*	—
Transport	16 954	10 432	61.5

[1]A full-time worker is a person who worked, mostly full-time, 50–52 weeks in 1979.

[2]The classification of occupation is based on the standards developed for the 1971 Census. The occupational categories are based on the status at the time of the survey (i.e. May 1980), which may not correspond to the status during the year 1979.

*Figures too small to be reliable.
Source: Statistics Canada. Unpublished data, Survey of Consumer Finances, Ottawa, 1980.

Are women being paid less because they have less formal education? The answer is no. When incomes for women and men at different levels of education are compared, some very startling and disturbing results emerge. We find, for example, that a woman with some high school education is being paid less than a man with eight years of schooling or less (see Table 8.5). A woman with a post-secondary certificate or diploma is still being paid a lower amount than a man with some elementary school. And women with a university degree earn only slightly more than men with high school education, complete or incomplete. Comparisons of earnings of men and women with the same education produce the same discouraging results: women continue to earn less than men. The smallest percentage difference is for men and women with university degrees, and even in that category, women make only 68% of the amount that men are earning.

The persistent gap in wages between men and women is partly a function of a system which regards women as secondary wage earners. Since women are not seen as "serious" breadwinners, despite the fact that they may be sole wage earners, they are less likely to be sought out for programmes of vocational training and retraining which could upgrade

Table 8.5

Median Earnings for Male and Female Full-Time[1] Workers in Canada by Education for 1979

Education	Male $	Female $	Female as Percentage of Male
0–8 years	15 221	8 895	58.4
Some or completed high school	16 679	10 530	63.1
Some post-secondary	17 728	11 446	64.6
Post-secondary certificate or diploma	19 018	12 725	66.9
University degree	25 188	17 224	68.4

[1]A full-time worker is a person who worked, mostly full-time, 50–52 weeks in 1979.

Source: Statistics Canada. *Earnings of Men and Women: Selected Years 1967–1979.* Cat. No. 13–577. Table 6. Ottawa, 1981.

their position in the labour force. Women are very much in the minority in technical, machining, finance, and supervisory courses. Schools, guidance counsellors, and manpower training officers alike are more likely to favour men over women for their courses: the very courses that are likely to lead to better-paid, skilled jobs. The generally unchallenged stereotypes that women do not want to "get dirty" on the job, that they dislike working with machinery, and that "people don't like to work for a female supervisor", function to keep women out of training programmes. What is more, women, themselves, may accept these stereotypes unless encouraged to do otherwise. The better the job, the more training required, the less likely are the chances of a woman doing it.

Discrimination on the basis of *sex* remains the single most important factor affecting the wage gap in spite of the fact that the majority of workers in Canada are covered by the labour laws of the province in which they are employed. The labour legislation of each province is essentially similar, requiring equal pay for the same or substantially the same work, performed in the same establishment, and requiring substantially the same skill, effort, and responsibility. The wording and degree of specificity varies with each provincial law. All of these laws, however, share the same major weakness. They are virtually unenforceable. Since the majority of female employees are clustered in a handful of occupations, few men can be found doing the same work as women. How can these laws be enforced when there are almost no male stenographers, maids, telephone operators, nurses, sewing-machine operators, typists, chambermaids, and lab technicians? In one analysis[55] of the gap in wages between women and men, it was estimated that in 1974, 500 000 women in the paid labour force were excluded from protection by equal pay legislation for this reason. The numbers would be greater today.

In order to achieve equality in compensation, the principle of equal pay for work of equal value must be implemented. The present problem could be circumvented by initiating the use of job evaluations to compare positions as diverse as stenographer and male warehouse worker, for example. As of 1981, however, only Quebec employees[56] and workers under federal jurisdiction in Canada[57] were covered by such legislation; the majority of workers are unaffected by this legislation. Nevertheless, the adoption of the principle of equal pay for work for equal value would prove a significant improvement over current legislation. By facilitating comparisons between traditionally feminine and traditionally masculine jobs, adoption of this principle would increase the chances of pay equalization between the ghettoized jobs in which most women find themselves and the better-paid, male-dominated occupations.

But it is not enough to have good equal pay legislation. If the situation is to improve in the future, this legislation has to be enforced. At present, enforcement procedures are so cumbersome that individuals are discouraged from taking action, and penalties for breaking the law are so

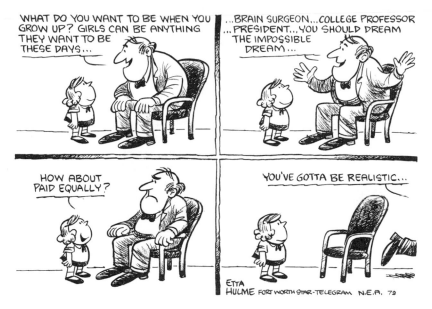

ETTA HULME FORT WORTH STAR-TELEGRAM N.E.A. 79

low as to be inconsequential. Prosecutions for violation of laws prohibiting pay discrimination in this country are extremely rare.[58] Women continue to provide cheap labour. Employers save money by employing women rather than men (when they can) because it is socially and legally acceptable to pay women less money. Since women work part time more often than men (mainly because of family responsibilities), employers save money by not having to pay their female part-time workers fringe benefits such as pensions and unemployment insurance. Moreover, when business is slack, it is easier to lay off women who may be part-time workers and who are less likely to belong to unions and consequently have lower job security. In 1977, only 26.8% of Canadian paid women employees were unionized, compared with 41.1% of the men.[59]

The most absurd rationalization of wage or financial discrimination consists in the postulate that women do not need money as much as men. If they are married, it is said, their husbands can support them. It is further argued that if they are unmarried, they do not need much money because they do not have to support a family. If this argument is carried to its logical conclusion, all people should be paid on the basis of need and the bachelor should receive less remuneration for doing the same job as the one done by a "family" man. Such a suggestion has probably never been considered by employers, let alone proposed.

Why Does the Employment Picture Differ for Women and Men?

Despite the advent of Canadian and American legislation prescribing equal employment opportunity for men and women, there has been little change in the employment picture over the past few decades. Women continue to flock into the low-status, low-paying jobs that require little job preparation, and they are conspicuously absent from management positions. While there is legislation designed to create equal opportunity, it cannot truly guarantee equal access to that opportunity. In fact, changes are needed in government policy for women to be placed on an equal footing with men in the workplace. Adequate daycare facilities, job evaluations to ensure equal pay, and incentives for employers to hire and promote women will probably not spontaneously appear either in the private or the public sector. Until new legislation reflecting these and other requirements is passed and enforced, government will be condoning social and economic discrimination against employed women.

Of course, even if improved legislation changes hiring practices, it will not automatically eliminate social and economic discrimination. Attitudes according to which women are considered unsuitable for certain types of jobs will continue to bar women from access to the training that will give them the skills necessary to take advantage of more available opportunities. Stereotyped and outmoded ideas of women's ability, held not only by employers, but also by potential female applicants themselves, will also effectively bar women from many positions. In short, the problem will continue to be similar to that raised by the Black Movement: "You can legislate against segregation but you cannot legislate integration." That is, saying that a person cannot be kept out does not ensure that the person can get in.

The persistent differences in the employment of men and women, both in status and kind, represent the culmination of the roles that society has prepared them to enact. As was discussed in Chapter 3, the differences in socialization begin early. Through toys, books, and television, children are exposed to the role models that represent what we, as a society, designate are appropriate gender-role attributes (see Chapter 4). In short, girls' socialization is largely a preparation for their role as a wife-mother. Boys, on the other hand, are taught early that some day they will be providers, and, to that end, they are encouraged to develop skills that will facilitate their success in whatever employment they eventually undertake.

Changes are needed in the socialization of girls if they are to develop the skills and abilities required for advancement in the employment sphere. But these changes are insufficient in themselves for ensuring that women will be put on an equal footing with men. Changes are also required in gender-role expectations which are so pervasive as to make the woman's presence in male-dominated spheres practically unacceptable. On the other hand, there must also be alterations in labour legislation in order to reduce social and economic discrimination, which are often accepted practices of employers, wittingly or unwittingly. Women will not achieve equality with men in the employment sphere without changes on all of these fronts.

Preparation for Employment: The Educational Experience. One of the most important influences on choice of employment goals and employment performance is the educational experience. Education and training per se not only provide people with the skills needed to perform a particular job, but also contribute to the way they view the world and perceive themselves in relation to it. Children learn very early that this is a man's world; the major participants are male and they are the ones who determine the goals and set the rules. Some investigators have noted, for example, that in the school system, there is an increasing masculinization of school subjects — that is, the higher the grade, the less frequently women are shown in textbooks. These findings are based on studies of texts used in primary and secondary schools in Quebec and Ontario.[60],[61] When women are shown, they are typically in the home, and their work is trivialized. Even in literature, in which girls excel, most books studied in high schools have male central characters. History books ignore women almost entirely, while mathematics, science, business, and economics texts are written mainly by men for male readers. One study of secondary school curricula, for example, discovered a lack of female mathematicians and scientists in school texts; problem-solving materials consistently portrayed boys in diverse activities, while girls and women were confined to sewing, cooking, and childcare. Also, only males have been depicted demonstrating the use of scientific equipment in science textbooks.[62] As is the case with books read by children (see Chapter 4), high school texts do not present girls and young women with feminine role models for anything but domestic work. Moreover, as was pointed out earlier in this chapter, nearly 70% of secondary school teachers are men. While girls' grades excel over boys' in the early, primary grades, the situation changes in high school. It has been noted that there is a parallel between the increasing masculinization of school subjects and the fact that girls' scholarly performance deteriorates with every additional year in secondary school.[63] The absence of feminine role models as teachers for "hard" subjects like mathematics, chemistry, and physics is an important factor in many girls' avoidance of the maths and the sciences. Because many young women have not taken these subjects in high school, they are unable to enter many programmes in university, particularly those leading to professional degrees such as medicine, dentistry, and engineering.

It has been observed that boys and men are more likely than girls and women to view their careers in a long-term perspective and are more likely to invest early in education and training that will likely lead to higher earnings in the future. This process begins early. In one study of high school students conducted in 1977 in Ottawa, boys had become more career-conscious than girls during their high school years;[64] most were planning ther future education to help them decide among some possible occupations. In dramatic contrast to the boys, many girls had lowered their career ambitions from grades 9 to 11 because they disliked school or were afraid of university. The majority of the girls had already settled on "female jobs" requiring little further academic training, such as nursing and semi-professional health jobs, as well as childcare, secretarial positions, and a variety of other office work.

Another obstacle to girls' occupational achievement centres around their expectations, which have been found to be quite limited. For example, one study[65] of high school students in Ontario, found that the girls' career aspirations were considerably higher than those they expected to pursue in the future. While almost half of the girls aspired to "upper class" careers (for example, physician, lawyer, architect), about 40% aspired to "nontraditional" careers (those occupied by less than 40% females). But, less than one-third actually *expected* to have an upper-class occupation in the future, and only one in four *expected* to have a non-traditional occupation. While many of these students may have held relatively high career aspirations, their expectations, which are probably more oriented toward reality, were considerably lower. Specifically, some of the girls expected to be interior designers, legal secretaries, or nurses.

Why were these students' expectations lower than their aspirations? Two possible reasons are suggested in the study. Firstly, many of the female students did not demonstrate a high degree of commitment to a career, as shown in the wish held by the majority of them (59%) to have a career *only* when their prospective children were at various stages in their education. It is possible, then, that these girls acknowledged their un-willingness to make the total commitment required by careers classified as "upper class" or even "nontraditional". Secondly, the female students generally lacked knowledge of occupations other than those traditionally occupied by women — typically low-status, low-paying positions. In this regard, they admitted that it would be difficult to make a wise decision about a prospective career in view of their lack of knowledge about many different jobs; only 9% felt that their knowledge was adequate enough to make a well-informed choice. Finally, many of these students believed a number of myths that reinforced traditional stereotypes of women's limited ability in the employment sphere, thus further limiting their expectations for occupational achievement.

Female students, compared to their male counterparts, are often less willing to forgo short-term earnings to undertake costly education that may lead to more lucrative positions at some future date. In a recent informal poll conducted among some students in an upper-level psychology course at a Canadian university, the overwhelming majority of the young women in the class said that they were planning to go into jobs traditionally occupied by women, such as dental hygiene, social work, and teaching. When one student was asked why she considered dental hygiene rather than dentistry (a more prestigious and remunerative profession), her answer was that she did not want to spend "all those years" in school and that, besides, she wanted to be able to earn her own money soon. Part of the reason why women focus on short-term rather than long-term career goals is that many of them see their main goal as marriage; they do not plan to hold outside employment while they have small children. They want a career, but they see it as intermittent. They plan to hold outside employment until they have children, to stay home to care for the children full time when the children are young, and re-enter the job market later. In the Ottawa study mentioned earlier,[66] for example, more than one-half of the girls believed that their main role in life was going to be that of a wife-mother, and they expected to stay at home full time while their children were growing up. In general, women underestimate the length of their employment. In a national survey reported in 1977 in the United States, for example, the labour market experiences of two groups of women were followed for five years, revealing that younger women (14 to 24 years old in 1968) grossly underestimated their future labour market participation when their predictions were compared with the actual employment experience of "older" women. Young white women predicted a participation rate of 29% at age 35, compared with an *actual* rate of 48% for "older" women at age 35.[67] When women underestimate their future labour market participation, they tend to invest in less education and training. In college, women tend to specialize in arts and humanities, which are less likely to lead to professions, than subjects such as science or business, which are taken predominantly by men.

Students' university experiences often contribute to and amplify the message they have been receiving thus far — namely, that women are devalued. One of the most important influences in this regard is a professor's attitudes toward female students. A professor may overtly and covertly convey to a female student that she does not belong in the university, particularly at the graduate level, simply because she is a woman. One colleague of mine, a female professor of sociology, was told during graduate school by one of her professors after a setback in her doctoral dissertation research:

"Why do you want a Ph.D.? Why don't you just give it all up and get married?"

Additional statements cited below are examples of other professors' comments which discriminate against women. These were cited by students at Western Michigan University in the United States.[68] For example, a biology professor during a class field trip passed a junk lot and said:

"Well, there's women's biggest contribution to the world."

Another professor told a woman student,

"Don't worry, with your body, you'll get whatever you want."

And still another professor was quoted as saying,

"Now that there are permapress shirts, dishwashers, and garbage disposals, women aren't needed."

Such overt displays of sexism on the part of professors in jest and seeming innocence can, and often do, undermine a female student's confidence in herself as an intellectual and a serious student. The fact that these kinds of remarks are made by respected and prestigious members of society renders them even more powerful in their potentially damaging psychological effects on female students. While it is difficult to assess how widespread these remarks are in the university setting, it is nevertheless disturbing to know that they occur at all. Moreover, the relative paucity of women on the faculties of campuses in both the United States and Canada does little to provide positive role models for female university students.

Until recently, social sciences in the university have not generally included women as part of their study. Moreover, research has shown that males are used more often than females as participants in psychological research.[69] In one study, for example, the number of participants in all-male psychological research was almost five times the number of those used in all-female research.[70] Because women's experiences did not fit neatly into the categories of behaviour accepted by scholars, they were not studied in the past. Moreover, in psychological research, the man's experience is typically seen as the prototype of all human experience, while the woman's is seen as the exception. Man, it is reasoned, includes woman. In the past, female university students learned virtually nothing about women — their culture, history, psychology, or status. This has been changing in recent years, as feminist scholars and the study of women's experience have emerged in almost all disciplines. However, much of this research has been criticized as being unscientific or as not meeting "acceptable" standards of research — those set forth by male researchers to deal primarily with men's experience from a masculine perspective. The only research that is valued conforms to these man-made standards; research that does not fit into this perspective is automatically labelled as less important. One American female social psychologist reported that her written work on attitudes toward rape victims was rejected twice by a top scholarly journal on the grounds that it did not deal with social issues and thus was not appropriate for the journal. ". . . Whether it's because I deal with women, or rape, or because I have a feminist perspective," she says, "the word is: this research is not orthodox, and therefore not important (p. 94)."[71] The subjects of rape and attitudes toward rape victims are, of course, vital social issues worthy of study. The denial of their importance by a journal such as this suggests that the study of women and particularly of social issues pertaining to them is relegated to secondary status among some scholars.

In the university, particularly, there is the danger of a female professor losing her credibility if she is "overconcerned" with women's issues. As Dr. Norma Bowen, an outstanding Canadian female professor and administrator, put it, "You tend to lose your impact if you talk about women's issues all the time. You are identified as being only concerned with women and not broader university issues (p. 3)."[72] A senior-ranking Canadian university administrator once said to a reputable female psychology professor who had just published a book on abortion, "Are you still studying women! When are you going to move on to something important?"

Nevertheless, there can be no doubt that the university, as an all-male bastion of teaching and research, is slowly being eroded. Women studies' courses have sprung up on campuses all across North America. These courses provide students with material on women which have virtually been excluded from texts in most disciplines. They also provide excellent forums for the sharing of ideas and the gathering of much-neglected facts on women, their motivations, and their place in our and other societies. However, women's studies have yet to be accorded the prestige and importance associated with studies of men. Rather than acting as a leader in the field of fostering equality between the sexes, the university has become notable for its preservation of traditional attitudes toward women and men. But if women are to have equal opportunity to attain the most prestigious occupations in our society, the university must take the lead in changing stereotyped beliefs.

Attitudes of Employers. Despite the existence of laws which prohibit sex discrimination in hiring and promotion and which prescribe equality of opportunity for men and women in employment, employers' attitudes still function as a primary obstacle to the achievement of equality in the employment setting. Numerous reports both by government agencies (notably, women's bureaus of government employment departments) and by academics continue to document stereotyped beliefs shared by employers and large segments of society about the capabilities and potential of male and female employees. Ultimately, decisions about hiring, firing, and promotion take place on an individual level, within the informal structure of the organization, and legislation can do little to modify them. And, what is worse, because these stereotyped beliefs determine an employer's behaviour toward a class of individuals (male versus female), they do not allow for individual differences within each class but assume that *all* men (or all women) will share the same motivations, abilities, strengths, and weaknesses. Some of the stereotyped beliefs commonly held about employed women and men are discussed below.

Stereotyped Beliefs about Gender-Role Differences and Employment

1. *Working women are only secondary earners, so men should be given precedence in hiring. A corollary to this assumption is that women do not have to be promoted to better paid jobs, since they do not need the*

money. To classify all women as secondary wage earners constitutes a refusal to recognize women's motivation for employment. The majority of employed women are economically compelled to work. Of the approximately 4 000 000 women in the labour force in 1975 (excluding the hidden unemployed), about 31% were single, 9% were widowed, divorced, or separated, and almost 21% were married to husbands earning $10 000.00 per year or less. These women represented about 61% of the female labour force in 1975 (see Table 8.6). Single women work to support themselves and to pay for their own education or job training. Approximately 9% of the female labour force — those who are widowed, divorced, or separated — work to support themselves. Over half of these women (191 000 estimated for 1977) are single-parent women who are responsible not only for themselves, but also for their one or more dependent children. And in 1978, of Canadian families with female heads, 53.9% reported incomes of less than $12 000.00; their average income was $13 421.00. The distribution of families with male heads had the opposite pattern, with 80.7% reporting incomes of $12 000.00 or more, and with an average income of $23 346.00.[73] It is evident from this that sole-support mothers

Table 8.6

Canadian Female Labour Force, by Marital Status and Husband's Income, 1975

	Number (000)	Percentage
Single	1 146	31.0
Married, husband earning $10 000.00 plus	1 437	38.9
Married, husband earning $10 000.00 or less	767	20.7
Widowed, divorced, separated	347	9.4
	3 697	100.0

Sources: Labour Canada. *Women in the Labour Force: Facts and Figures (1976 edition). Part 1 Labour Force Survey.* Cat. No. L38–30/1976. Table 14. Female population and female labour force, by marital status, and participation rates of women in the labour force, Canada, 1965, 1970 and 1975. Ottawa, 1977, p. 33.
Statistics Canada. *Income Distribution by Size in Canada 1975.* Cat. No. 13–207. Table 23. Percentage distribution of husband-wife families by husband's income groups, presence of children and labour force participation of wife, 1975. Ottawa, 1977, p. 51.

have to be employed just to maintain a subsistence level of living. All available data indicate that the lower the family's income (excluding the wife's earnings), the greater the likelihood that a married woman will hold employment. Many families thus escape being categorized as poor *only because* the wife is employed. Therefore, the wife's employment should be given the same importance as that of her husband.

2.   *Married women take jobs away from men.* This stereotyped belief contravenes the international principle that work is guaranteed to all citizens, not just to men, and fails to account for the fact that men and women are in different labour markets and, therefore, not in direct competition with each other. The Women's Bureau of the Ontario Ministry of Labour[74] illustrates this point very well: it reported that in March, 1975, there were 866 000 married women in the Ontario labour force. At the same time, there were 176 000 unemployed men. If all the married women left the labour force and their jobs were taken by the unemployed men, 690 000 jobs would remain vacant. Furthermore, most unemployed men do not have the education or the skills to fill many of the jobs held by married women (e.g., teachers, secretaries and nurses).

3.   *Women do not want responsibility or promotion.* The implications of this stereotyped belief are that since women are less interested than men in getting ahead, they will put forth only the minimum effort acceptable to their employer. As a result, the employer will justifiably restrict them to positions of less responsibility. There is little evidence to support this. A U.S. study using a national probability sample of 539 working women and 993 working men found a significant difference between men and women in desire to be promoted (64% of the men versus 48% of the women).[75] However, further results of the same study indicated that desire for promotion was largely the result of *expectation* of promotion. Two-thirds of all the women never expected to be promoted. Women wanted promotions as much as men when they thought they had a realistic chance of being promoted. The apparent lack of ambition among the women surveyed was often the result of their being restricted to dead-end jobs. To avoid frustration, women, like men, may well scale down their ambitions to bring them in line with the actual opportunities offered by their jobs.

4.   *Women are not as mobile as men: you cannot transfer a woman because her husband's job comes first.* According to this belief, a married woman does not have the same freedom to relocate as a man, since it is assumed that her husband would be unwilling to relocate to accommodate her job. Thus, it is held that she will refuse transfers, and promotions that involve moving. However, in the opposite case — when the man is offered a job requiring that he be transferred — his wife is expected to relocate far more willingly. While there may have been some truth in this belief in the past, it corresponds much less to present-day reality, as increasing numbers of married women are holding employment and placing greater importance on their careers. This belief also does not take

into account the large percentage of employed women who do not have husbands. For example, in 1979, 40% of the female labour force in Canada was single, separated, divorced, or widowed.[76] This preconception is further invalidated by the fact that for many jobs, the question of relocation for promotion never comes up. In a study of civilian employees of the U.S. army, for example, most employees, male and female, had never been asked to move for the job.[77] Of those civilian employees who were asked to relocate temporarily in the course of their duties, 89% of the men had always accepted, compared with 87% of the women. An employee's willingness to relocate is better viewed as a function of incentives than of sex and marital status. Where payoffs were equal for both men and women, sex would no longer be used as a basis for prediction as to whether an employee will relocate.

5.   *The appropriate roles for women are those of wife and mother.* Married women who are also mothers are perhaps faced with the greatest possibility of discriminatory action being taken against them in employment. Managers, who tend to consider that the appropriate roles of women are those of wife and mother, may be reluctant to hire or promote married women because of skepticism about their ability to balance employment and family demands. Similar reluctance is practically nonexistent when it comes to married male employees. The results of a U.S. study of a national sample of managers and executives perhaps best illustrate the double standard that is commonly used in making important decisions about male and female employees with families.[78]

Respondents in this study, managers and executives, were mailed a questionnaire in which they were provided descriptions of hypothetical organizations, asked to read a series of incidents in the form of letters depicting various organizational problems, and asked to make recommendations for hiring and promotion for positions, including managerial ones. Each incident was written in two versions: one involved a female, the other, a male. Each respondent received only one version of each incident. Some of the topics covered were the following: (1) evaluation of a married man (or woman) for a position requiring extensive travel; (2) organizational efforts to retain a valuable employee when his (her) spouse's career progress required relocation; and (3) assessments of promotability of an employee who emphasized his (her) first duty to his (her) family. The findings were that when a married male applicant was considered for a Purchasing Manager position requiring travel, evaluations were more favourable, and decisions to accept were more frequent than when the applicant was a married female. A majority of respondents felt it quite inappropriate to hire a woman for a managerial position requiring extensive travel. Furthermore, when a man married to a career woman had the opportunity to relocate to take a better job, his wife, even though a highly valued employee, was expected to give up her own job for the sake of *his* career. However, when the roles were reversed, organizational intervention was considered much more appropriate to retain a valued male employee. Perhaps one of the most interesting findings in this study relates to the managers' perceptions of male and female employees who put their family first. When a male candidate for promotion to the position of Personnel Director made the statement, "my first duty is to my family", he was evaluated favourably for the position. An equally qualified female candidate making this statement was evaluated much less favourably. The male candidate may be perceived as a wholesome person striving for a balance in his life, while the female applicant may have been perceived as lacking commitment to the job. The implications of these results are that a married woman's career progress is limited because of expectations on the part of management that her professional obligations are secondary to those of her family. Accordingly, married women would not be considered as serious candidates for promotion to better positions involving more responsibility as much as married men. Moreover, despite the collaborative efforts that the female employee may have made with her husband regarding family responsibilities, these are likely to conflict with managers' expectations, thus impeding changes that she and her husband may have made in the direction of role redefinition. This is a superior illustration of the necessity for role redefinition to take place in many spheres of the society simultaneously. It is not enough that the married couple negotiate to expand the traditional feminine gender role. Their efforts must occur within a social context that is accepting and supportive of such role redefinition if real change is to occur.

As long as stereotyped attitudes are still held toward employed men and women, equality of opportunity will not be achieved. Despite the fact that the person holding prejudiced beliefs cannot often substantiate them, they continue to function as obstacles to equality. What is more, when employers make hiring decisions on the basis of these stereotyped beliefs, very often the onus is on the individual woman to behave in ways that disprove these stereotypes. Frequently she accomplishes this by being overqualified for a position.

Room at the Top for Women?

Despite the rather dramatic increase in the numbers of North American women taking on employment, as well as the increase in their levels of education, women remain conspicuously absent from the management ranks in the corporate and government sectors. Essentially, this means that major decisions affecting the lives of millions of women and men in both Canada and the United States are still being made by only one-half of the population. An explanation for the striking absence of women from the top levels of management where major decisions are made is no doubt complex and necessitates examining factors on both the psychological and social levels. On the psychological level, for example, there are differences between women and men in achievement motivation (see Chapter 5). However, women's absence from the senior ranks of management cannot be simplistically explained by saying that women are less motivated to achieve, or that they possess a "fear of success". Rather, the systematic differential socialization experiences of girls and boys lead them to strive for excellence in different areas. Girls and women come to assess their worth as persons on the basis of how successful they are in interpersonal relationships. Thus, good interpersonal relationships come to be seen as *ends* in themselves toward which girls and women strive. Boys and men, on the other hand, learn to value achievement in intellectual and leadership roles. Their value as persons is seen as contingent also on their effectiveness in mastering skills. Viewed in this way, there are important differences between the way women and men perceive interpersonal relationships. While success in interpersonal relationships is frequently seen as an end in itself by many women, for many men, good interpersonal relationships may simply be a means to another end — namely, success within the corporate structure. As a result of women's preoccupation with the interpersonal, they may fall into the "trap" of emotional intolerance as typified by a remark such as "I don't like him, and I can't work with him". A man, on the other hand, may also dislike a particular coworker (or superior), but he may see that working with that person is just one step to be made on the way to a long-range goal or objective. In other words, men may tolerate each other in the corporate structure because they perceive that a distasteful relationship, when encountered, is simply a necessary part of a series of steps toward a goal.

There are other important psychological differences between women and men, the origins of which may also be found in their differing

---

Use of the Term Ms.

The use of the modern term Ms. is becoming more and more popular in the business and professional worlds as women show a more serious commitment to full-time careers. . . . The prefix Mrs. gives the idea that marriage is the most important function for women — if you're not Mrs. you just haven't made it. On the other hand, the use of Miss or Mrs. conveniently indicates whether a woman is "free" or not. But the term Mr., used by both bachelors and married men alike, does not make this distinction. . . . In a business setting or relationship, it makes little difference whether someone is married or single. . . . One benefit of the adoption of Ms. is that it may eventually eliminate such hackneyed questions as "Why isn't a nice girl like you married?"

From *Institute of Canadian Bankers Review*, 1972, 5, p. 14.

---

socialization experiences and which have important implications for their career progress. A book entitled *The Managerial Woman,*[79] discusses some of the differences between men and women in management to learn what factors impede women's progress through the ranks. To this end, the authors interviewed more than 100 women working as senior executives in business and industry, including women managers in the utilities, banking, and communications industries. In addition, they looked at the careers of 25 women who held top management positions. On the basis of their results, the authors suggest that because of the way in which women's perceptions differ from those of men, women are limited in the acquisition of the skills necessary to be successful in management. While men tend to see a job as a task to be completed before going on to something else, women tend to see a job as something that continues on or repeats itself from day to day. Women, then, do not as readily see themselves as moving on and up. In the same vein, while men tend to concentrate on the achievement of long-range goals, women tend to focus on the short-term, with little concern for long-term implications. This fundamental difference in perspective may be partly the result of how and when career plans are formulated. Compared to men, female executives typically make their career decisions late, between the ages of 30 and 33, when they suddenly realize that they will be employed for the rest of their lives. And, for the most part, women do not plan to have a career on a long-term basis, as men do. Men, on the other hand, bring to the management setting a clearer understanding of their own career goals and what they will have to do to get there.

In effect, the management situation consists of informal systems whose predominantly male members have a great deal in common: aspirations, expectations, and perceptions. Because their social experiences are different, few women can fit into this informal system, which is the nucleus of middle management and which plays an increasingly significant role as one ascends the corporate ladder. The authors liken corporate management to team play. Boys' experience in team sports, with its emphasis on winning as a team, prepares them for an acceptance, as adults, of the rules governing their pragmatic relationships to male colleagues in management. But the vast majority of girls have not had the "team" experience that boys get from games like football and hockey, for instance. Popular sports for girls, such as swimming, gymnastics, as well as the proverbial piano and dancing lessons taken by many girls, stress individual, not team, performance. As a result, girls are at a distinct disadvantage, compared to boys, because they have had less experience with the rules governing team play. As adults, women are less likely than men to be accepted by coworkers in management, since they have more difficulty learning to "play" the corporate game to which their male counterparts are more accustomed. Thus, if a woman shows that the quality of relationships is her most important priority, if she has no clear career objectives, if she focuses her energies on current job performance, and if she remains oblivious to the informal pressures that influence promotion, she will probably end up with "just a job" and no career.[80]

A man's socialization not only predisposes him to seek out leadership positions, but also inculcates characteristics that are required to climb the corporate ladder. A woman's socialization, in placing less emphasis on the development of these traits, encourages her to define herself more in terms of her future family than in terms of her career. This may explain why women may not as readily feel prepared to make a long-term commitment to a particular job because of an indeterminate future familial commitment she feels may be required of her. Since women are generally expected to make stronger commitments to their families than men — in terms of both time and energy — their tendency to focus on the temporary rather than on the long-term aspects of their jobs may be seen as an attempt to keep all of their options open. While it is not tolerated for men to choose marital and familial involvement over employment, such options are still available to women. Even though a growing proportion of married women are seeking and holding employment, our society still evaluates women and they value themselves largely by how well they perform in the role of wife-mother. This, coupled with the fact that women experience greater demands as parents than men do, may prevent women from setting long-term career goals. This may also explain why so many women wait until their children are grown up before they commit themselves totally to a career.

Corporate success is not possible without knowledge of certain rules. If women are to achieve equality with men in the board room, gender roles — particularly as they pertain to the familial sphere — must be redefined. As long as employed women continue to carry the burden of unequal sharing of work in the home and continue to be defined primarily in terms of their familial activity, there cannot be equality. The social role prescribed for men must also be redefined to allow men greater latitude in behaviour and expression. Of special importance is the modification of roles to ensure that men will be more likely to participate equally with women in the family. In this way, some of the social and psychological obstacles to women's advancement in the corporation could be removed. But discrimination and prejudice against women remain among the most important social reasons for women's lack of employment progress. Stereotyped attitudes held by employers and society at large continue to function as social barriers to improvement of women's status in employment. If women are to achieve equality with men in major decision making in employment, there must be an end to such discrimination.

9

Psychopathology and Gender Roles
with William G. McDonald

Typically, abnormal behaviour has been assumed to reflect mental illness or psychopathology of some kind. And the question of how to define mental illness is a difficult one. The concept of illness, whether it be physical or mental, implies deviation from defined norms or standards. These norms or standards may vary from one field or discipline to another, and across cultures and historical periods. In most subspecialities of medicine where physical disorders are treated, the structure and function of the human body are of basic interest to the medical practitioner. So, in the case of physical illness, the norm centres around the structural and functional integrity of the body. While the concept of mental illness also implies some deviation, the question is this: What are the norms involved? Here, reference is usually made to norms which are neurological, psychological, social, ethical, or legal in nature. So, for example, to say that a person is mentally ill because she is promiscuous invokes a moral judgement of a particular behaviour. Likewise, the notion that a person commits murder because of insanity illustrates the use of a legal concept as a norm of mental health. Unlike other forms of illness, in the case of mental illness, a value judgement is almost always placed on a specific kind of behaviour which is evaluated as abnormal when it exceeds the boundaries defined as acceptable. But this raises several more questions: How does psychiatry decide when a particular kind of behaviour deviates sufficiently from a norm to warrant its definition as illness, and who ultimately decides which behavioural norms are acceptable indicators of mental health? One view on the subject is that put forth by Thomas Szasz.[1] Well known for his view that mental illness is a myth, Szasz proposes that psychiatrists are essentially treating people who experience difficulties in day-to-day living. Following the lead of Szasz and others (e.g., Laing[2] and Liefer[3]), increasing numbers of people have been arguing recently that it is the psychiatrist who, as the agent of society, has the function of ensuring the status quo. The psychiatrist does this by classifying people as mentally ill, which then legitimizes the use of social controls to restrain and change their behaviour and thereby ensure their conformity to society's norms. As such, psychiatry and psychiatrists are seen as agents of the establishment, whose functions are redefined as socio-political.

While the misuse of psychiatry can be documented everywhere, nowhere is it better illustrated than in the Soviet Union,[4] where unconventional or socially deviant behaviour is redefined as psychiatrically abnormal behaviour. Here psychiatry is used in a widespread and systematic way as an expression of a deliberate governmental policy and as an agent of social repression. With the emergence of various kinds of dissent among Soviet citizens in the 1960s, people all over the world have become aware that substantial numbers of human-rights activists, religious believers, and would-be emigrants — almost all mentally healthy according to family and friends, are being declared mentally ill by Soviet psychiatrists. Their "treatment" consists of compulsory incarceration in psychiatric hospitals where they are subjected to punitive and brutal measures, apparently to eliminate their nonconformist behaviour patterns. While, admittedly, the case of the Soviet Union is an extreme one, it serves to illustrate how enormous power can be entrusted to the psychiatric profession and how that power can be abused.

On a less cynical note, contemporary psychiatrists and psychologists may be seen as helping their clients learn better methods of coping whenever their clients feel that they are not getting what they want out of life. Since the mid-1960s, greater accessibility to mental health care has made people more aware of the possible benefits to be gained from psychotherapy. Before this time, most people who were treated by the psychiatric profession tended to be severely disturbed or chronically anxious. The more contemporary emphasis on humanism and self-actualization has prompted relatively "normal" people to seek out strategies for helping them to realize their potential, enabling them to function better in interpersonal relationships and to achieve their own goals in more effective ways than in the past. In this regard, then, psychiatrists and psychologists may be seen as those who can help people become aware of the consequences of what they are doing and, at the same time, facilitate their taking responsibility for their own actions. Specific objectives may include removing maladaptive responses such as tics, phobias, or compulsions; resolving conflicts; alleviating anxiety; and facilitating the acquisition of greater self-understanding. Ideally, the therapist promotes a supportive emotional atmosphere by conveying interest, concern, and appreciation of the client's or patient's assets. The therapist may then guide the patient in methods of coping in a more constructive manner, and not uncommonly may interpret the patient's self-destructive or self-defeating behavioural patterns. In short, ideally, the therapist should offer advice and guidance within an accepting, positive, and supportive relationship with the patient.

The conditions treated by psychotherapists in the Western world fall into one of two broad categories: the neuroses and the psychoses. Many people seeking psychiatric help may be seen as suffering from some kind of neurosis. Generally speaking, these are people who are able to function more or less effectively on a daily basis but who, at the same time, are having difficulty coping in one or more areas of their lives. Generally, the neurotic is not so disturbed that he or she loses contact with reality. Rather, the neurotic who seeks psychotherapy is seen as a person who is searching for more effective ways of coping with life. The psychotic, on the other hand, is usually seen as more severely disturbed than the person with a neurotic disorder. Usually, the psychotic is one whose personality is severely disturbed and whose normal social functioning is greatly impaired. Perhaps one of the chief distinctions here is that while the neurotic may be trying desperately to cope with his or her anxiety in order to function more adequately in the world, the psychotic may be seen as someone who has lost contact with reality. Psychotics may withdraw into their own fantasy world and may fail to respond to things or people around them, or they may respond with behaviours and emotions that are inappropriate to the situation. Their thought processes may be disturbed to the extent that they experience delusions (e.g., false beliefs) or hallucinations (e.g., imagining smells, voices, or sights). It is chiefly for these reasons that the psychotic is more likely to require hospitalization than the neurotic individual.

It is generally held today that the aetiology of psychopathology is organic and/or functional. Organic factors causing psychopathology are of a physiological nature and may include such things as brain disease, drug or alcoholic poisoning, or neurological impairment. Functional factors causing psychopathology are psychological in nature and have occurred as a result of learning. So, for example, a disturbed relationship with one or both parents can be a functional cause of psychopathology because it involves faulty learning to relate to others in early relationships. Functional factors such as these are considered to have their roots in the person's life experiences. The idea that abnormality has psychological causes is a relatively new one which emerged along with the disciplines of psychiatry and psychology in the late 19th century. Before then, "madness" was explained in a variety of different ways.

An Historical View of Gender-Role Differences and Psychopathology

Throughout history, there has been a tendency to see different symptoms of mental illness as unique to either women or men. The first "medical" approaches to abnormality emerged in ancient Egypt, Greece, and Rome. The ancient theories, although largely erroneous by today's standards, attempted to explain symptoms in terms of physical malfunctioning. Interestingly, the symptoms thought to be unique to women were more frequently discussed than those seen as unique to men. One syndrome the Ancients frequently associated with women included lethargy, physical pain, paralysis, and/or sensory impairment. The *Kahun Papyrus*, which includes Egyptian medical records dating from about 1900 B.C., discusses these:

"a woman who loves bed; she does not rise and does not shake it,"
another woman "who is ill in seeing" and has a pain in her neck, a third
"woman pained in her teeth and jaws " (p. 3).[5]

Often, women's symptoms were attributed to a disorder of the female sex
organs, specifically to the belief that the uterus had detached and wandered
to the various affected parts of the body. Hippocrates, the famous Greek
physician of the 5th century B.C., termed the syndrome *hysteria,* after the
Greek word for uterus. The hallmark of hysteria is physical pain or
physical impairment for which there is no apparent physical cause,
although a variety of other symptoms, such as indifference to the pain, may
also be present. Although the uterine theory has been abandoned, the term
"hysteria" is still used today to describe the same set of symptoms, and the
diagnosis continues to be given more often to women than to men. Regarding the ancient writings, it is unclear whether hysteria was associated with
women because they really displayed more hysterical symptoms than men,
or because women's actual physical complaints were more often er-
roneously labelled "hysterical".

   While ancient writings focused on physical or bodily symptoms in
women (e.g., pain, numbness, paralysis), they described men's symptoms
more in terms of intellectual aberrations. This was related to a long-
standing attitude according to which men were associated with the intellect
and women, with the body. Plato, the Greek philosopher of the 5th century
B.C., in the *Timaeus,* emphasized the "downfall of reason" as the hallmark of derangement in men.   Plato's philosophy regarding women
pointed to the physical-hysterical symptoms discussed by Hippocrates and
the Egyptians,[6] and continued to influence Western European views of
mental illness into the 18th century and beyond. In fact, 19th century
scientists were even hard put to dispel the uterine notions of hysteria
inspired by Plato.[7]

   Early theories of the aetiology of abnormal behaviour in both men
and women often concentrated on the sex organs and sexual activity (or
lack of it). This focus can be noted in theories espoused by both the early
Greeks and the early Romans. So, for example, Plato wrote that the sex
organs of both sexes were "animals", meaning that the sex organs had a life
and spirit independent of the rest of the body. For men, it was thought that
too much sexual activity, or lack of it, could cause the "animal" to become
rebellious and masterful over the mind. This would cause the "downfall of
reason" thought to be characteristic of derangement in men:

   ... but he is mad, and is at the time utterly incapable of any participation in reason. He who has the seed about the spinal marrow too
   plentiful and overflowing, like a tree overladen with fruit, has many
   throes ... and is for the most part of his life deranged, because his
   pleasures and pains are so very great; his soul is rendered foolish ...
   (p. 161).[8]

There is a similarity between Plato's theory that sex organs were "animals" and the earlier uterine theory of hysteria. It was agreed that, for women, failure to bear children and thus fulfill their "natural" function, caused the "animal" (the uterus) to become discontented and angry, and, hence, to wander throughout the body. The animal's "rebellion" in women was seen as the cause of physical symptoms similar to those first described by the Egyptians. Of women, Plato wrote:

> ...the animal within them is desirous of procreating children, and when remaining unfruitful long beyond its proper time, gets discontented and angry, and wandering in every direction through the body, closes up the passages of the breath, and, by obstructing respiration, drives them to extremity, causing all varieties of disease...(p. 162).[9]

The idea that sexual inactivity led to symptoms of mental illness flourished in ancient Rome. Galen, a Roman physician of the 2nd century A.D., considered sexual abstinence to be bad for both sexes. Galen believed that both men and women expelled a type of semen during orgasm and that the semen rid the body of toxic impurities. If retained, the toxic semen would cause hysterical symptoms in women and sadness and loss of appetite in men. Galen thought that women had an advantage over men in that menstruation was another way in which the body could expel impurities. Men, lacking menstruation, had to rely more on the regular ejaculation of semen.[10]

With the spread of Christianity throughout the Roman world, spiritual explanations of abnormal behaviour replaced those of a physical nature. St. Augustine, in the 4th century A.D., attributed symptoms to demon-possession. "Demonology" flourished in Europe throughout the Middle Ages and into the 17th century. Moreover, Galen's ideas about the dangers of sexual abstinence were reversed. Mediaeval Christianity considered sexual abstinence to be a moral virtue which protected the individual from demon possession. Sexual indulgence, on the other hand, was thought to reflect moral weakness, vulnerability to possession, and, hence, to the strange symptoms the demon caused. Disturbed individuals were accused of being sexually indulgent not only with other humans, but also with the demons themselves.[11] A common belief at this time held that deranged people, supposedly in league with the demon world, were involved in witchcraft (i.e., devil-worship and evil magic). The "cure" for witchery was frequently the "cleansing" of the soul through drowning or burning. The condemnation of witchcraft culminated in Kramer and Sprenger's *Malleus Maleficarum*, a treatise commissioned by the Pope, which was written in Germany in 1484 and sparked widespread witchhunts in Europe for more than the next hundred years. Those accused of witchcraft were almost exclusively women. If a man displayed unusual behaviour, or impotence, the cause was believed to be the spell of a female witch. The belief that women were more prone to demon possession and witchcraft may be traced to Judeo-Christian teachings which held that

women were inherently morally weaker: women were the initiators of
"Original Sin", since it was Eve who yielded to the serpent's temptation.[12]
Women were thus believed to be more vulnerable to the devil's temptation,
to sexual indulgence, and to becoming witches. According to Kramer and
Sprenger

> [women are] more credulous . . . more impressionable, and more ready
> to receive the influence of a disembodied spirit . . . .
>   All witchcraft comes from carnal lust, which is in women insati-
> able . . . . (p. 114–116).[13]

There is, then, consistency between the view of men put forth by
Kramer and Sprenger and that of the Ancients — namely, that men were
the more "reasonable" creatures. Women were seen as more passionate,
more gullible, more impressionable, and, above all, more bodily — in this
case, "carnal". In this regard, the symptoms of witchcraft discussed by
Kramer and Sprenger were frequently bodily in nature. For example, body
numbness, which today might be diagnosed as an hysterical symptom, was
often interpreted as a sign of witchcraft, as were any unusual blemishes on
the body.[14]

With the gradual emergence of medical science during the 16th
century, belief in witchcraft came under criticism. However, the notions of
men's greater rationality and women's more physical and emotional
nature, persisted. The view that women were more impressionable and
vulnerable to witchcraft was translated into the belief that women were
weaker and more prone to emotional disturbance. The belief that women
were basically emotional creatures can be seen as the basis of the widely
held Victorian concept of "the vapours", which included symptoms such as
fainting spells, temper tantrums, and whims.[15] During the 19th century,
there was a tendency to focus on intellectual distress as a sign of madness in
men. For women, emotional and psychosomatic symptoms remained
salient. Edward Jarvis, an American physician of the mid-19th century,
described the symptoms of "madness" in the men of his time:

> . . . excess of study, excessive devotion to various interests and
> pursuits, and anxiety about political or other success . . . . Men are
> more devoted to books, and investigations, and theories. They are
> more ungoverned [than women] in their ambition and eagerness to
> accomplish their purposes of gaining knowledge or for the
> advancement of science (p. 55).[16]

Men's symptoms are pictured in terms of excessive ambition and
intellectual activity. The causes, Jarvis stated, were social pressures that
were "driving men mad" — that is, the tremendous economic, industrial,
and scientific growth of 19th-century America.[17] Clearly, Jarvis' implication was that men were expected by society to play a much more active role
in the building of the new nation than were women. Although Jarvis
admitted that men's sex drive could contribute to the development of

mental illness in them, he saw social pressures as the primary cause, a view that has persisted until today. Treatment required the relief of pressure through leisure, relaxation, decreased expectations, and social reform.

In the 19th century, women were generally viewed as having more emotional and bodily symptoms than men, including depression, nervousness, phobias, tantrums, and a host of psychosomatic complaints. Egotism and distaste for domestic duties were also seen as symptoms of an impending nervous breakdown. Women's symptoms, unlike those of men, were traced more to physical than social factors. Women's emotional and psychosomatic distress was believed to stem from the female reproductive system and its cycles, as well as from a generally weak nervous system. Nineteenth-century physicians often pointed to menopause, menstrual irregularities, or masturbation as the aetiology of mental illness. In such cases, "treatments" included castration (clitorectomies), hysterectomies, and ovarectomies. Surgical solutions to emotional problems in women also appear to have been widespread in 19th-century America.[18] This was in marked contrast to the treatments prescribed for men, which included relief from social pressure, but certainly not castration. In cases where overstimulation of the weak female nervous system was blamed for their symptoms, women were advised to avoid education and reading and encouraged instead to develop "feminine virtue" through rest, religion, and passivity.[19,20]

This brief historical view of how gender-role differences in mental illness have been perceived has important implications for contemporary views of men and women and, particularly, how we perceive the "basic nature" of men and women today. As will be seen in this chapter, women continue to be associated with disturbances which are primarily emotional in nature, the aetiology of which is seen in physiological factors. Likewise, men are still viewed as less emotional than women and tend to be associated today more with intellectual aberrations. As it did in the 19th century, conventional wisdom today tends to place greater emphasis on "social pressures" as causes of men's disturbance than on physiological changes per se.

The way in which "disturbed" individuals have been treated historically also has important implications for students of gender-role differences. In the past, people regarded as insane were subjected to horrendous treatment. Floggings, various kinds of torture, and even murder, were considered appropriate "treatments" of madness.[21] People regarded as mad were perceived as threats and so were segregated or punished because, in the main, they were thought to have been responsible for their own suffering. This kind of thinking about deranged people persisted until fairly recent times when it was replaced by the view that these people were "sick" and thus not responsible for their behaviour. The idea that deranged people were sick rather than sinful is due in part to the efforts of an 18th-century French physician, Philippe Pinel, who released

Insane Asylum: Crowded Ward of the New York Lunatic Asylum, Blackwell's Island, 1868

asylum inmates from their chains and treated them with kindness.[22] He believed that the slogan "Liberty, Equality, Fraternity" should apply to the asylum inmates and, along with others, played a key role in pressuring the French government to treat asylum inmates in a more humane fashion. His primary contribution was to change society's attitude toward the insane so that they could come to be considered as sick human beings deserving medical treatment. Unfortunately, Pinel's concept also led to a tendency to regard *any* kind of abnormal behaviour as "sick" and has caused the "sickness" concept to lose credibility for some — notably, Thomas Szasz, who, as mentioned earlier, has criticized the psychiatric profession for its tendency to enforce conformity in its treatment of patients. The "sickness" concept as it emerged in psychiatry has also resulted in a disproportionately greater number of women being "treated" than men.[23] To some extent, this may be a reflection of the fact that it is more socially acceptable for women to be emotional and to explore emotional turmoil. It may also be linked to the greater dependency associated with the feminine gender role. Since it is more acceptable for women to be dependent, seeking help (including psychiatric help for mental illness) would appear to be more congruent with feminine gender-role expectations than with those associated with the masculine gender role. Nevertheless, this raises another important question: Who suffers more from mental illness: men or women?

Who Is Sicker: Men or Women?

It is generally held that women suffer from psychopathology far more than men. This conclusion is based on information from a variety of sources. Firstly, it has been reported that women use mental health services more than men. For example, Phyllis Chesler reports in *Women and Madness*[24] that the official statistics on mental illness in the United States showed a considerably larger involvement of women than men with psychiatry. During the 1960s adult women constituted the majority of patients in psychiatric wards, private hospitals, and public outpatient clinics. At the same time, Chesler reports, more women than men were confined in state and county hospitals. Similar conclusions were reached by Gove and Tudor[25] in their review of previous studies that used various methods of estimating rates of men and women who were mentally ill in the United States. They argue that the information on first admissions to mental hospitals, psychiatric treatment in general hospitals, psychiatric out-patient clinics, private outpatient psychiatric care, the practices of general physicians, and community surveys all indicate that more women than men are mentally ill. Furthermore, they argue that the higher rate of mental illness among women is a relatively recent phenomenon, having emerged since about World War II. Before the war, men had higher rates of mental illness. Other research reports that female patients are in therapy more than twice as long as male patients.[26] It is well known that women also take more tranquilizers and psychotropic drugs* than men. [27-29] All of these statistics have been interpreted to mean that women are therefore more prone to mental illness than men. Is this, in fact, the case?

Recently, this conclusion has been challenged. The methodological bases of studies that have been frequently quoted to suggest that women are more prone to mental illness have been questioned. One of the problems involves the inconsistency from study to study in the definition of mental illness. So, for example, Gove and Tudor's analysis defines

---

Psychotropic drugs are those which affect mental processes and which stimulate, sedate, or otherwise change behaviour.

mental illness in a very narrow sense. They define psychopathology as a disorder which involves personal distress and/or mental disorganization that is not caused by an organic or toxic condition. In their view, mental illness is a disorder of mental or emotional processes which is not part of an organic disease and does not result from using drugs or alcohol. They also exclude from their definition personality disorders because they consider that those experiencing these disorders do not themselves suffer from mental distress, thus not conforming to their definition of a mental disorder. The way Gove and Tudor have defined mental illness excludes from consideration most of those disorders in which men tend to predominate.[30] According to U.S. statistics, these include obsessional neurosis (where obsessive thoughts and compulsive urges occupy so much time and take up so much of the person's energy that they seriously interfere with daily life), alcoholism, drug addiction, and various deviant sexual compulsions such as transvestism, fetishism, sadism, and masochism.[31] In Canada, too, mental disorders such as alcoholism, alcoholic psychosis, personality disorders, sexual deviation, and drug dependence continue to be predominantly male disorders, while neuroses and affective psychosis (exaggerated deviations of mood) remain predominantly female disorders.[32]

Essentially, then, women and men appear to differ considerably in the kinds of psychopathology to which they are prone. So, for example, while women may be more likely to be diagnosed as neurotic, men are seen more often in sociopathic categories — that is, men engage in more antisocial behaviour. Compared to men's diagnoses, there is a tendency for women's diagnoses to be grouped into categories which focus on their emotional states.[33] Female patients are found to be depressed, to have suicidal thoughts, and to attempt suicide more often (men actually succeed at suicide more often). Male patients are more assaultive and more likely to act out antisocial urges such as robbery, rape, and homicide. In the past, however, sociopathy (as typically found in men) was seen as psychopathology by some investigators and excluded from the definition of psychopathology by others, with the result that findings showing differences between women's and men's rates of mental illness have not always been comparable. Since about World War II, clinical diagnostic instruments used to identify certain conditions of mental illness have tended to be biased towards the kinds of conditions associated with mental illness in women. For example, the psychiatric screening devices used to select men for military service during the war were based on symptom checklists relying on self-report. These are precisely the diagnostic instruments that record the negative self-perceptions and mood states more typically found in women. Because of these methodological considerations, then, we cannot conclude simply that women are sicker than men. Rather, it would make more sense to ask, just what is it in the life experiences of women and men that predispose them to different kinds of psychopathology?

Marital Status, Gender Roles, and Psychopathology

Although being a man or a woman does not, in itself, predispose a person to mental disturbance, different combinations of sex, gender role, and marital status reveal significant differences. In recent times, married women have consistently appeared to be more prone to psychopathology than either single women or married men. On the other hand, single, widowed, and divorced men have higher rates of various forms of psychopathology than their female counterparts. It has been shown that married women are more likely than the unmarried to report somatic symptoms indicative of psychological distress, even when they are not patients.[34] Married women who are not employed have been shown to be at the highest risk for psychological disorders: they have the highest rates of entry into psychiatric treatment of any occupational group; they request (and receive) the greatest quantity of prescribed mood-modifying drugs;[35] and they report the highest incidence of symptoms such as nervousness, nightmares, dizziness, and headaches.[36] A review of studies of mental health impairment found that married women, when compared with either single women or married men, show greater mental disturbance.[37] Overall, more married than single women have been reported to be passive, phobic, and depressed. Twice as many married women as married men have reported that they felt a nervous breakdown impending, and many more married women than married men have been found to experience psychological and physical anxiety, as well as immobilization.[38]

What is it about marriage that leads to married women's greater vulnerability to psychopathology? The implications of having children in our culture, particularly the stress associated with the presence of young children, is one possible cause that has received considerable attention. In a major Quality of Life Survey conducted in the United States in the 1970s,[39] for example, there was a considerable difference found in the reported satisfaction with life as a whole between young, married, childless women (89% satisfied) and married women with young children (65% satisfied). The same study found that indications of psychological stress were greatest for both men and women during the early parental life stage. In our culture, the woman is thought to be more responsible than the man for the care and emotional well-being of the children. Apparently, this is the case even when the mother holds full-time outside employment (see Chapters 7 and 8). Because primary childcare falls more heavily on the mother, with relatively little participation by others, including the father, it is to be expected that women would experience the stress associated with having children more than men. The toll is apparently greatest among full-time housewives who stay at home to care for the children. This was illustrated in a study[40] that examined mental health among three groups: unemployed housewives, employed wives, and employed husbands. A general measure of mental health was obtained by asking respondents how often they had experienced 14 different psychiatric symptoms during the past few weeks. The symptoms included feeling anxious about something; being bothered by special fears; feeling that people are saying things behind your back, and feeling so depressed that it interferes with your daily activities. Husbands showed the fewest psychiatric symptoms and thus manifested the best mental health of the three groups; employed housewives reported slightly more psychiatric symptoms, while unemployed housewives reported the most.

In the same study, additional findings suggested some of the factors that may have been responsible for the observed differences among the groups. Three additional factors were assessed in these groups: the rate of demands perceived to be made of the respondent; extent of desire to be alone; and self-reported loneliness. On all three measures, employed husbands tended to have the lowest scores and unemployed housewives, the highest, while employed housewives scored between the other two groups. The unemployed housewife's feelings would seem to have been caused by an immersion in the world of children, with its incessant demands and lack of time for oneself, lack of adult interaction, and lack of opportunity to use instrumental skills such as those associated with a job. There is also a strong relationship between these factors and the development of psychiatric symptoms. Taken together, these findings would suggest that being continually immersed in the world of children with their continual demands and the relative lack of meaningful adult contacts and sources of fulfillment other than children can lead to a greater vulnerability to psychiatric symptoms.

The paradox here is apparent. Marriage and children are supposed to be greater sources of psychological fulfillment for women than for men. Yet, the evidence would suggest that marriage and, in particular, the early child-rearing period, are associated with greater vulnerability to psychopathology in women. While marriage and parenthood may be desirable goals in themselves, they involve major life changes and thus may contribute to overall stress, thereby increasing the risk of mental disturbance. It has been argued that life changes, both positive and negative life events, may be stressful.[41–43] Surveys of large populations have found that the number of life changes reported is related to symptom level. This holds true regardless of the sex, social class, age, or ethnicity of those studied. The life events studied may be summarized under 11 major headings including School, Work, Love and Marriage, Having Children, Family, Residence, etc. When asked to judge each life event in terms of the magnitude of the life change involved, women were more likely than men to judge events relating to marriage and childbirth as being of greater magnitude.[44] It has also been found that women report being exposed to more life changes than men,[45] and that they are also more sensitive to changes in the life events of others.[46] All of this would lead to more stress for women with young children than for their male counterparts.

It is also quite possible that women entering marriage are not aware of the many life changes which marriage will bring, nor are they equipped with prior knowledge to deal with them. Not being prepared for these changes should lead to feelings of lack of control or power in dealing with critical life events. There is also evidence that loss of power can lead to psychiatric symptoms,[47] and studies of traditional marriages suggest that wives are expected to give up their power to their husbands.[48] When children are young, housewives are expected in our society to put aside their own needs and respond to their children's needs on demand. Being isolated most of the day from other adults and adult relationships may also contribute to a feeling of alienation from the "real world" and worry about loss of ability to deal with it.

The case of the employed mother is particularly interesting. Despite the problem of role strain frequently experienced by the employed mother and the disproportionate amount of time she invests in the home and in childcare compared to her husband (see Chapter 7), the employed mother still enjoys better physical and psychological health than the full-time housewife.[49–52] This may be partially accounted for by the fact that the stress associated with having children may be less for the employed mother, since on the average, she has fewer children than her unemployed counterpart.[53,54] More importantly, however, the employed mother has other avenues of self-expression available to her, which likely contribute to her overall feelings of control or power. Unlike changes at home, for which she may not have been prepared, the employed mother's work situation is a relatively structured one where the rules of interaction are formalized and where she is armed with skills for performing a particular job. Although the stress arising from the demands associated with family life may be similar in some ways for both the employed and the unemployed mother, the employed mother's greater feeling of control associated with her employment may attenuate that stress to some extent. Unlike her unemployed counterpart, however, the employed mother has a buffer between herself and her children — namely, her job, assuming, of course, that the woman is relatively satisfied that her children are receiving adequate care in her absence.

An additional and significant factor is that, unlike her efforts in the home, the employed mother's work outside the home is rewarded with pay — tangible evidence of a job well done. And in society's view, holding outside remunerative employment is generally of greater value than occupying a nonremunerative job (e.g., that of housewife), which supposedly requires little skill (at least according to the popular view). To some extent, women themselves probably internalize this view, which may explain why employed mothers have a more positive image of themselves than housewives.[55] The rise in the number of women sharing the provider role, (see Chapter 8), has been accompanied by the beginning of mutual accommodation of certain changes in the roles enacted by men and women in marriage. The good-provider role that men enacted in the past has, along with its prerogatives, undergone profound change.[56] The wife who is now sharing the provider role with her husband feels justified in making demands today that she did not make in the past. In short, her power has increased. With greater opportunity for jobs outside the home as alternatives to an existing marriage, married women today may be more likely to assert themselves in the home and insist on more equitable decision making than is typically the case in the more traditional family.[57] Thus, because of her greater power, the employed mother is less vulnerable to psychopathology, particularly those conditions which tend to be found to be disproportionately high among women, including neuroses, depression, and psychosomatic disorders.

While most studies show that married women in general have higher rates of symptomatology, the situation is reversed in the case of people who are single (never-married), divorced, or widowed. In each instance, men show more psychopathology than women. In the case of single people, what this may mean is that a single man who is mentally impaired is less likely to marry than his female counterpart. In our society, we still expect the man to play a more active role in premarital courtship, while the woman generally is expected to enact a more passive role. This may account for the findings of one study that the mental health of the man, not that of the woman, was related to the progress of the courtship among college student couples who were engaged or going steady.[58] Because the man is expected more than the woman to show initiative and take an active role during courtship, a man with mental disturbance may be less likely to be able to live up to these expectations. This may explain the findings of another study that female schizophrenics were more likely to marry than male schizophrenics.[59] The male schizophrenic may lack the necessary social skills and initiative needed and expected in the primary breadwinner role typically assigned to the man in the family. He may simply be unable to seek and hold a job.

Another possible reason for differences in the mental health of single men and women centres around the person's ability to establish and maintain satisfying interpersonal relationships. The availability of satisfying interpersonal relationships should contribute positively to an individual's personally satisfying self-conception. While the single man may have many more business and/or professional ties than his female counterpart, these relationships are less likely to have the same extent of psychological meaning that a purely social relationship has. There is also evidence that single men do not experience as much satisfaction from their social relationships as single women. In his studies of loneliness, Vello Sermat and his coworkers[60] have developed a scale for measuring loneliness: the Differential Loneliness Scale (DLS). This is an instrument designed to yield an overall indicator of the extent to which people are satisfied or dissatisfied with their social relationships. A person's score on this scale is based on the quality and stength of his/her interpersonal networks and support systems in four areas: (1) the romantic-sexual; (2) friendships; (3) relationships with family members, and (4) social groups and the larger community. Results of overall DLS scores and of subscale scores have been reported for men and women who differ in marital status. In a sample of over 400 single Canadians whose average age was 21 to 22 years, it was found,[61] for example, that single men tended to have higher overall scores on the DLS scale (indicating greater dissatisfaction with their relationships) than single women, and higher scores on the "Romantic-Sexual", "Family", "Friends", and "Groups" subscales. What this suggests then, is that single men tend not only to have fewer relationships than single women, but also to be more dissatisfied with relationships, specifically those that involve romance (or sexual activity), family, friends, and groups. These findings are expected in view of differential socialization pressures, which encourage women, more than men, to develop the ability to establish and maintain close relationships as ends in themselves. As a result, the single woman is usually more capable than her male counterpart of establishing such relationships and finding meaning in them, thus giving her a greater sense of "social relatedness" than is usually found in the single man. A person who has such meaningful relationships is less vulnerable to feelings of alienation and the resulting emotional or psychological problems than the more socially isolated one. Single men, then, are more vulnerable to developing psychological problems in part because they have fewer satisfying emotional relationships.

Men benefit psychologically more from marriage than women because it provides them with an intimate relationship that they may not find elsewhere. In fact, the prescribed way for men to satisfy their emotional needs is by attempting to establish an intimate heterosexual relationship, usually in a marriage. Women have more flexibility in the ways by which they can satisfy their emotional needs. They are more likely to have other emotionally satisfying relationships — with family members, as well as with same-sex friends. In marriage, men are also receiving more pragmatic benefits than women, in the form of meals, laundry, and housecleaning, since it is the wife who takes major responsibility for housework (see Chapter 7). In both psychological and practical ways, then, men derive more benefit from marriage than women do. This may partially explain why married men are less prone to psychopathology than married women.

By the same token, loss of a spouse through either death or divorce may have greater deleterious effects on men's mental health than on women's. In fact, there is evidence to show that men are more vulnerable to various forms of mental illness than women in divorce and after a spouse's death.[62-66] For example, Canadian statistics for first hospitalization for psychiatric disorders in 1977 show that married men had the lowest rates (255 per 100 000 population), and divorced and widowed men, the highest (770 per 100 000).[67] Among both men and women, divorce has been found to be associated with higher rates of emotional disturbance than marriage. There also seems to be a relationship between emotional problems and marital unhappiness. For example, it has been found that happily married people tend to have very high levels of psychological well-being and that those who are unhappily married have lower levels. But it is difficult to know whether emotional problems in marriage cause marital unhappiness or whether marital unhappiness and marital breakdown cause emotional problems. One possibility is that the high incidence of emotional problems among divorced people reflects a causal relationship from emotional problems or mental illness in marriage to marital disintegration and, finally, to divorce.[68] Yet, studies on married people consistently find that married men are mentally healthier than married women. It is after divorce that the opposite situation occurs, and divorced men are shown to have higher rates of mental disturbance than women. One possible reason is that women are able to cope better after divorce than are men. One study found that while divorce is associated with increased mental disturbance among both women and men, divorced men are more impaired, with only one man out of 25 as compared with one woman out of 14 being symptom free.[69]

Alcoholism, or addiction to alcohol, has been associated particularly with divorced men, as shown in statistics from Canada and Finland. In the population hospitalized for psychiatric problems in Canada in 1974, divorced men in the 20-to-39 age bracket had an alcoholism rate of 698 (per 100 000 population) compared to a rate of 93 for divorced women and a rate of 99 for unmarried men.[70] In a Finnish study, mortality rates were examined by marital status and cause of death in men and women in the working-age population for the years 1969 to 1971. When mental disorders were examined, alcoholism was found to be the main single cause of death. And while married men had the lowest rates, divorced men had the highest.[71] These statistics, however, do not allow us to disentangle alcoholism as a cause of marital breakdown or as a response to it. In the case of a marriage that is no longer satisfying, a man may use excessive amounts of alcohol as a means of coping with an intolerable situation. Furthermore, it is more socially acceptable for men to drink heavily than for women because drinking has traditionally been associated with the masculine gender role. In some circles, in fact, the amount of alcohol a man can consume while remaining sober is regarded as a measure of his masculinity. But the man who uses excessive amounts of alcohol as a means of coping is putting a further drain on his marriage and his relationship with his children.[72] Addiction to alcohol may, then, be a strong contributing factor to marital breakdown. Alcoholism may also occur as a response to the stress and social isolation that result after a marriage has broken down.

One of the main problems with which a divorced man has to cope is that of social isolation. Since women generally retain custody of the children after divorce, most divorced men will likely lose the continuity of relationships they had in their nuclear family. Having a greater sense of interdependence herself, the wife was probably the one who took the initiative in establishing and maintaining social relationships with extended family and friends. While men may have made acquaintances outside the family, these would have tended to fulfill business or practical needs, rather than emotional ones. During the marriage, the wife probably functioned as her husband's liaison with the world of interpersonal, purely "social" (as opposed to business) relationships, for which he may not have had either the time or the skills. As a result of divorce, the man will likely lose many stable emotional ties with both family and friends, in addition to his marital relationship, which, in turn, will lead to social isolation and vulnerability to psychological problems. Finally, a divorced man is less prepared to cope with the daily tasks of housekeeping than a divorced woman, which adds to the amount of stress that men experience through divorce.

Loss of a spouse through death also results in greater vulnerability to mental and emotional problems in men than in women. Death of a spouse, especially for men, may result in suicidal behaviour, as has been documented by various investigations in the United States.[73-76] In Finland, too, widowers have been found to have the highest rate of suicide, and married men, the lowest. Women's suicide rates, in comparison, were considerably lower.[77] Social isolation and its psychological effects have been singled out as key factors leading to mental disturbance and suicide, particularly among elderly male widowers. The social isolation referred to here may have begun during the man's marriage if he retired. At retirement, he likely lost much of his social esteem, which depended heavily on his occupational role and his relationships with coworkers. As a result, the man may have come to depend even more heavily on his marital partner for personal meaning and social significance. With the loss of his wife, the widower probably lost many of his contacts with family and community which his wife had maintained. Research has found that the elderly widower is less likely than a widow or a married man or woman to have relations living in his community or to belong to community organizations.[78] The elderly widower will therefore have more difficulty than an elderly widow in finding meaningful substitute relationships for the one he had with his wife. According to this line of reasoning, unless new relationships are substituted for the old, death of a spouse can lead to intense social and personal disorganization and possibly to suicide. The elderly widow, on the other hand, has a greater opportunity for role continuity. Interacting with relatives and participating in various formal and informal relationships, she is in a much better position to substitute other relationships for the marital one she lost — relationships that are meaningful enough to prevent her developing psychopathological symptoms.

To summarize, then, our comprehension of the differences in men's and women's mental illness patterns is greatly increased when marital status and marital roles are taken into account. Because men and women react differently both in marriage and after marital breakdown, their mental and emotional problems can also be expected to vary considerably, depending on their marital status.

Gender Roles and Specific Mental Disorders

It is evident that men and women are vulnerable to different kinds of emotional problems and mental disorders. Marital status, as we have seen, predisposes women and men to different kinds of disorders. We will now turn to an examination of specific mental disorders and how they differ in women and men. Differences in gender roles and the societal expectations associated with these roles play a major part in the aetiology of a particular disorder.

Alcoholism

Traditionally, drinking alcoholic beverages has been associated with men and male camaraderie. The man who boasted, "I can drink you under the table" and then proceeded to do so was using alcohol to confirm and exhibit his virility. A man's social standing among his male friends may depend on the extent to which he can imbibe large quantities of alcohol without any visible signs of drunkenness. The transformation in men's personality as a result of drunkenness is well known. Frequently, men who get drunk are frightening because their behaviour becomes aggressive and hostile. So, when men drink excessively, the behavioural and personality changes that result may be labelled "exaggerated masculinity". The drunk may be even more frightening because he seems to have lost control and is behaving irrationally. At other times, however, when men drink excessively, they may become less stereotypically masculine in their personality and behaviour and more stereotypically feminine, as evidenced in some men's greater passivity and withdrawal behaviour under the influence of alcohol. This kind of reaction may be particularly puzzling when the man in question is typically (in his nondrunk state) very "masculine" in his behaviour. In a drunken state, the man can act out many repressed and often forbidden impulses. The process is somewhat similar to what happens to some men when they experience a breakdown in their mental health. With men who tend toward greater activity, dominance, and aggressiveness, a breakdown in mental health may lead to the adoption of a pattern of behaviour characterized by passivity, withdrawal, submissiveness, and retreat from exposure to danger.[79] Conversely, an inhibited and passive male may display impulsive and aggressive behaviour during a breakdown.

The study of female alcoholism is more problematic, as accurate statistics on female alcoholism rates are difficult to obtain. In the past, research on alcoholism tended to be limited mainly to men,[80] and little investigation was conducted on the female alcoholic. In contrast, the seventies have seen a rather significant increase in interest in the female alcoholic. However, it is still almost impossible to determine the actual rate of female alcoholism. Traditionally, women with drinking problems have remained more hidden than men, thus making it very difficult to estimate the extent of female alcoholism. Estimates vary, ranging from a ratio of six males for every one female,[81] to a ratio of 3:1,[82] down to a 1:1 ratio.[83] Hospital admissions for 1977, as reported by Statistics Canada, show a ratio of more than four males for every one female for alcoholism, and 6:1 for alcoholic psychosis.[84] Because of greater societal permissiveness and a relaxation of social mores regarding drug taking in general, women have begun drinking earlier, and they drink more.[85] However, serious drinking problems among women remain untreated and unrecognized[86] because society is still less accepting of the woman who drinks heavily than it is of her male counterpart. So studies show that the woman who drinks a lot is subject to greater criticism than the drinking man.[87] No doubt, society's attitude toward the female alcoholic may effectively prevent a woman from seeking help for her drinking problem. Furthermore, because of the prevailing condemnation of the female alcoholic, a physician who has a female alcoholic patient, usually middle class, may shield her from detection, as may her husband and her family.[88]

Gender Roles and Motivation to Drink. In general, women and men have been found to drink for different reasons. In contrast to male drinkers, who are most frequently found drinking "with the boys", women who drink heavily tend to do so alone in their homes. A substantial proportion of heavy female drinkers are housewives[89] who drink to relieve boredom, loneliness, and frustration.[90] For the housewife, frustration may emerge out of expectations that there is more in life than merely being a good wife, mother, and homemaker — expectations which derive from her educational experiences and which, in all likelihood, prepared her for a wider range of alternatives than those presented exclusively in the home.

In men, the progression of alcoholism usually occurs over an extended period of time. While both women and men who use alcohol excessively do so to cope with psychological stress, the process by which this occurs is more gradual for men. Undoubtedly, this is due to the greater acceptance of heavy drinking in men. Assuming that drinking has become a way of life for a man, by the time his role changes to that of husband or father, his drinking may no longer be tolerated.[91] Unfortunately, by this time, the man may not have mastered other techniques for coping with stress, having, in effect, typically relied on alcohol.

Patterns of alcoholism are different for women. For one thing, they usually begin their drinking later in life than men, and alcoholism among women often develops over a shorter period — usually in a few years.[92] Women's dependence on alcohol is frequently a response to a crisis situation such as a death or separation from someone who is close to them.[93,94] Women are more likely than men to drink "to settle their nerves", "to forget pressures", "to overcome loneliness", and "to get to sleep at night".[95] The fact that men and women do differ so much in their motivation to drink has important implications for the kind of treatment they receive from their physicians and therapists.

Physicians' Reactions to the Alcoholic. The female alcoholic (more than her male counterpart) will often turn to her physician for help not for her alcoholism, but for her physical and emotional problems.[96-98] Not surprisingly, female alcoholics have been found to have a higher rate of diagnosed depression than male alcoholics.[99,100] Society, in general, and physicians, in particular, may be more willing to see women as mentally ill than as alcoholic,[101] further evidence of the prevalent double standard of acceptance of alcoholism in women and men. Thus, a physician may wittingly or unwittingly rationalize or overlook a woman's drinking. This is especially true when the woman is a member of the same socio-economic class as that of the doctor — namely, the middle class. Unable to find a physical problem, and denying or being unaware of the woman's drinking problem, the physician may prescribe a drug for the woman's nerves or for her "change of life".[102,103] As will be seen later, the tendency of physicians to prescribe psychotropic drugs more for women than for men goes beyond the alcoholic population and extends into the general population as well.

Familial Relationships and the Alcoholic. Compared with the general population, alcoholics and especially female alcoholics, have a higher rate of dissolved and unstable marriages. The incidence of broken marriages among female alcoholics has been reported to range from 24 to 67%.[104-106] In further research, more than twice as many married alcoholic women as married alcoholic men recorded a "poor" relationship with their current spouse.[107] This was indicated by the extent to which married male and female alcoholics felt they could discuss personal problems with their spouses. Whereas 38% of the alcoholic men living with their spouses listed their wives as those with whom they most often discussed personal problems, only 18% of the married alcoholic women listed their husbands. The husband's heavy drinking may have been a factor here which prevented alcoholic women from discussing personal problems with their husbands, since various studies report that female alcoholics often choose alcoholics or heavy drinkers as husbands. A much smaller proportion of alcoholic men tend to be married to heavy drinkers.[108-110]

Treatment. Finally, it is important to note that treatment methods originally designed for alcoholic men are not necessarily effective with alcoholic women. One study, for example,[111] found that alcoholic women saw individual therapy as being more helpful, while men ranked group therapy as more important. This may be because a woman's heavy drinking is more likely than a man's to be related to a specific crisis event. In contrast, learning to use alcohol to cope with everyday stress is a more gradual process for men, usually occurring over many years. In order for women to recover, they may have to work through the feelings and conflicts associated with a particular life crisis. To this end, an empathetic individual therapist would be invaluable. For men, however, recovery may necessitate mainly the learning of new norms for coping — norms which will replace those that advocated drinking as a means of obtaining psychological relief. What better way to develop these norms than in a group situation in which the emphasis is placed on the development of better coping skills? Group therapy may also be more important for men because it provides the male alcoholic with interpersonal support, which may not be available elsewhere. On the other hand, because women are more likely to be involved in close interpersonal relationships outside therapy, they may not need the interpersonal support available in group therapy to the same extent.

In summary then, it can be seen that alcoholism in men and in women should be treated as separate phenomena. A woman is less likely to acknowledge her heavy drinking, as are the woman's physician and family. The pattern of the development of alcoholism differs in men and women and so do the reasons for drinking. Finally the most effective type of therapy for alcoholics depends very much on their patterns of inter-personal relationships — patterns which, in turn, depend on whether they are women or men.

Schizophrenia

Schizophrenia is a form of mental illness, usually defined as a psychosis, where there is some degree of personality disorganization, loss of ability to evaluate reality, and an inability to relate appropriately to others. One of the salient features of schizophrenia is the afflicted person's disordered thought processes. It may frequently be difficult for another person to understand the schizophrenic's behaviour and speech and the schizophre-nic sometimes experiences delusions, or false belief systems, such as taking on the identity of Napoleon, Queen Victoria, etc. Another example of a false belief system is the feeling among some paranoid schizophrenics that the whole world is plotting to kill them. The schizophrenic person may also experience auditory and visual hallucinations, such as voices which criticize or instruct the person to do something. Hallucinations may also involve misperceptions of the size and shape of the person's own body. When schizophrenics experience hallucinations, they cannot, in effect, distinguish between fantasy thoughts and reality. Classical schizophrenic symptoms include the "flattened affect", most evident in the more advanced stages of the disorder, in which there is an absence of readily communicable feelings, especially of positive or optimistic feelings about life. While the schizophrenic may display anxiety or even rage, at times, "flatness" is expressed as an inability to experience anything positive about social interactions. This finally leads to total withdrawal from reality, including personal contacts and relationships.[112] In general, schizophrenia is diagnosed more frequently in men than in women. An examination of statistics between 1949 and 1951 reveals that schizophrenia, particularly between the ages of 15 and 30, occurs more frequently among men.[113] Later reviews agree that schizophrenia and obsessive-compulsive reactions are more prevalent among men.[114] Statistics Canada reports that, in 1977, approximately 60% of first hospitalizations for schizophrenia were male.[115] This differential diagnosis of schizophrenia in men and women may be partially explained by differences between them in gender-role identity. In this society, achievement in some type of meaningful work and the successful performance of a challenging task are seen as crucial for the development of masculine identification. It has been noted that men who are diagnosed as having some kind of emotional disorder often show more "feminine" patterns of behaviour such as passivity, withdrawal, submissiveness, and retreat from possible danger.[116] Most schizophrenic reaction patterns are characterized by withdrawal from contact with people, particularly close interpersonal relationships, excessive passivity, and obsessive-compulsivity. Moreover, schizoid men — men considered to be borderline schizophrenic cases — are more likely to be ushered into treatment than are similar women because these men are less able to conform to the expectations of the masculine gender role as traditionally defined in our society. So, schizoid men, who may be unable to hold a regular job because of their mental condition, may be more readily identified as schizoid and thus have a better chance of receiving treatment than women in a similar mental state. In contrast, the marginally functioning woman may also be quiet and passive, but she will not as likely be diagnosed as schizoid or even schizophrenic because her behaviour is more in line with that expected of a traditional woman.

While men are more often diagnosed as schizophrenic than women, the true incidence of schizophrenia is being questioned generally in North American psychiatry.[117] For example, there has been a trend to use a schizophrenic diagnosis for conditions which might be more accurately labelled as bipolar affective disorders — that is, conditions in which there are wide swings of mood from depression and lethargy to euphoria and overactivity. Because of problems relating to the definition of schizophrenia, it is difficult, if not impossible, to accurately estimate the true prevalence of the condition.

Depression

Depression is one of the most common forms of mental disturbance. It can vary considerably in severity from a mild transient sadness to a severe state of depression where the person withdraws totally from reality and social relationships. Often the depressed person is apathetic, loses interest in

van GOGH, Vincent.
Sorrow. (1882 November)
Transfer lithograph, printed in black.
Composition: 15 3/8 x 11 3/8".

Sheet: 18 1/2 x 14 3/4".
Collection, The Museum of Modern Art, New York.
Purchase.

people and surroundings, experiences a loss of energy and appetite, and feels guilty. The person suffering from depression may also feel life is no longer worthwhile and may attempt to commit suicide. In general, women suffer from depression more than men. This disturbance is so widespread among North American women that it has been referred to as "the common cold of psychiatric disorders".[118] Throughout history, the depressed condition has frequently been portrayed in women. Van Gogh's *Sorrow* is a case in point (see above). While the consensus is that women suffer more from depression than men, the *sex* ratio (female:male) of people diagnosed as depressed varies from about 2:1[119,120] to an estimated 6:1.[121] Several explanations have been offered to account for the preponderance of women suffering from depression. One explanation sees the cause in women's disadvantaged social status compared to that of men. The housewife role, when occupied exclusively, can lead to anxiety and depression, a postulate that is confirmed by research findings that, in general, full-time housewives are more depressed than women who hold outside employment.[122,123] This sociological explanation is based on the premise that the full-time housekeeping role, with its low social status, its frustrating nature, its overly close emotional tie-up with personal attachments, its noncompetitive nature, and its isolation, leads, not surprisingly, to depression. One reason that employment outside the home may provide a protection against depression is that it alleviates boredom, increases social contacts with other adults, and improves self-esteem and economic circumstances.[124] This may explain the findings of one study that employed women recovered more quickly from depression than did housewives, even when they were employed out of economic necessity.[125]

Other social factors must also be considered in order to develop an understanding of the causes of depression. Educational and income levels are two important social influences here. It has been reported that women with low education and low income, compared to men, are especially vulnerable to depression.[126] It has also been found that working-class married women were five times more likely to become depressed than middle-class women.[127] Four factors were found to contribute to this class difference: loss of a mother in childhood; three or more children under the age of 14 at home; absence of an intimate and confiding relationship with a husband or boyfriend, and lack of full- or part-time employment outside the home. But employment per se may not protect the working-class housewife from depression. For example, some research has shown that among those most at risk for depression were the poorly educated married women with children, who also held low-status, low-paying jobs.[128] These were also women who, for various reasons, were unable to turn to their husbands for help. These women were possibly at greater risk of depression simply because of the greater number of demands being made of them. On the one hand, they had to fulfill all the responsibilities associated with the feminine gender role at home, since the expectations of the working-class family tend to be more traditional. On the other hand, they had to cope with the stresses of their dead-end jobs. Despite the many demands made of them, these women could not get practical or emotional assistance from their husbands. All of this contributed to overwhelming feelings of helplessness often associated with depression. Other factors can contribute to depression, however, and it is a phenomenon that knows no class boundaries. Educated, middle-class women who have the "luxury" of working in the home as full-time housewives are also at high risk for developing depression.

Gender-role differences in the socialization of girls and boys have been seen as contributing to differences in vulnerability to depression observed in women and men of all classes. In their socialization, girls are encouraged more than boys to define themselves in terms of their inter-personal relationships, with the result that women come to see them as ends in themselves. Moreover, a woman's self-worth relies more directly than a man's on success in establishing meaningful interpersonal relation-ships. Thus, a woman may feel that she is valuable, likable, lovable, or significant only to the extent that she is loved by or is significant to another person.[129] According to this argument, loss of a close relationship, whether it be with a lover, husband, child, or friend, may be more likely to result in depression in the woman than in the man, since these relationships have greater psychological significance for her.

While this explanation is plausible, it does not take into account important findings discussed earlier. Men, too, may experience psycho-logical problems as a result of loss of a marital relationship through death or divorce. A man's self-acceptance and self-worth are less directly dependent on others' approval, but he, too, needs interpersonal ties in order not to become alienated. Since he is less likely than his wife to have cultivated close interpersonal relationships, the loss of the wife through death or divorce may also represent the loss of one of the few emotional relationships he had. This can lead to his social isolation and resulting psychological problems. However, as was pointed out earlier in this chapter, this disturbance is more likely to take the form of sociopathy, alcoholism, or self-destructive behaviour than depression. The particular forms of psychopathology most commonly experienced by women and men are consistent with gender-role prescriptions. Depression, more commonly associated with women, tends to be characterized by passivity and inactivity and thus is more congruent with feminine gender-role prescriptions for behaviour. The kinds of psychopathology found more in men — sociopathy, and various forms of self-destructive behaviour — are more aggressive behavioural forms and are thus more congruent with the masculine gender role.

Feminine gender-role socialization further contributes to women's greater vulnerability to depression in its emphasis on familial relation-ships, to the exclusion of all others, as important sources of gratification. Middle-aged women may suffer psychologically when they lose their maternal role — particularly if they had viewed that role as the only one of importance to them. In one study, for example, hospitalized women who had a diagnosis of depression were found more likely to have suffered a recent maternal role loss than were nondepressed hospitalized women.[130] The women who had overprotective or overinvolved relationships with their children were more likely to be depressed in their postparental period than were women who did not have such relationships. When children left home, housewives also had a higher rate of depression than employed women. Presumably, employed women were less affected, since they had another role as a vehicle for self-fulfillment.

Another explanation of the cause of depression invokes psychological factors and is integrally related to explanations based on gender-role differences. The concept of "learned helplessness",[131,132] which was developed in animal experimentation, has been employed to gain understanding of depression in women. In the original research, dogs were placed in situations in which they could not avoid electric shock, no matter what response they made. When these dogs were later placed in situations in which a particular response could have prevented an electric shock, they failed to show the necessary response. It is suggested that these dogs' experience with uncontrollable situations led them to become helpless in dealing with subsequent situations. Applying this paradigm to human depression, the main points of the theory are these:

1. helplessness is the defining symptom of depression;
2. helplessness can be acquired by learning that one's responses are unrelated to one's rewards and punishments; and
3. helplessness can be treated or prevented by learning under what conditions one's responses are effective in producing desired results.

The concept of learned helplessness is similar to the concept of powerlessness frequently experienced by women as a result of their lower social and economic status relative to men. Not only are women, compared to men, exposed to more situations where they have little control over what happens to them, but their socialization also trains them to be helpless.

An examination of socialization practices typically employed with boys and girls reveals certain consistent differences regarding the administration of positive and negative sanctions. For example, at all ages, boys receive *both* more positive and more negative feedback than do girls. While some argue that boys receive more punishment from their mothers because they "need" it more,[133] others report a greater incidence of negative control of boys' behaviour despite the frequency of the child's resistive behaviour.[134] A review[135] of studies which comprised mainly teachers of children of several different age levels concludes that boys also receive more positive feedback than girls. So it would appear that boys are getting more evaluation — both positive and negative — than are girls. Could it be that boys are more attention getting? Or are they more interesting than girls? The answer is that boys are probably seen as more interesting in a society that, by fiat, values the male and masculinity more than the female and femininity.

Because boys, compared to girls, receive more evaluative feedback of their behaviour, they have more opportunity to learn which behaviours should be retained (those that are rewarded) and which should be eliminated from their repertoire (those that are punished). Having a greater opportunity to learn which behaviours lead to positive consequences, boys are more likely to learn how to manipulate their immediate environment to their own advantage. Boys should be less prone to developing learned helplessness, since they are more likely to learn those conditions under which their responses produce a desirable result. Conversely, as we have seen, girls generally receive less evaluation — both positive and negative — than boys. Since girls' behaviour is less likely to produce evaluative consequences, they have less opportunity to learn which behaviours will allow them to manipulate their environment to their advantage. Being more likely to learn that their behaviour is unrelated to reward and punishment, girls are more prone to developing learned helplessness. Other factors associated with socialization practices employed with girls and boys probably contribute further to the difference between them in the potential for developing learned helplessness. For example, the greater encouragement of dependent behaviour in girls and the selective rewarding of aggressive behaviour in boys[136] are probably important antecedents of these differences. Thus, differences in depression between women and men can be traced to different socialization practices used with girls and boys — practices which may lead to different levels of learned helplessness, a defining symptom of depression.

Other explanations for the preponderance of women suffering from depression include hypotheses involving biological susceptibility arising from genetic or endocrine factors. For example, research so far suggests that there may be a genetic factor in depression, making it more likely for women to inherit a predisposition for this kind of mental disturbance.[137-139] While the research in this area has interesting possibilities, at this stage, the findings are in need of further examination. The evidence from genetic studies is inconclusive.

Observations that clinical depression tends to occur in association with certain major events in the woman's reproductive cycle have led to the hypothesis that female sex hormones are somehow implicated. It has been noted that depression in women is much more common at times of endocrine hormonal change, including the premenstrual, postpartum, and menopausal stages.[140,141] In particular, depression, anxiety, and irritability have been found to increase during times when a woman is experiencing a tremendous drop in estrogen production: before menstruation, just after childbirth, and during menopause. These three physical states also correlate with an enormous drop in progesterone. Any discussion of the role of hormones in the aetiology of depression is problematic, however. The fact that mood changes are correlated with hormonal variations does not mean that hormones are actually the cause of the changes. The contribution of psychological and cultural factors to a woman's emotional state during these life stages must not be underestimated. The role of hormonal factors in depression is still being debated, and the evidence is far from conclusive, as is discussed later in this chapter.

Postpartum Depression. After having undergone childbirth, women may experience postpartum depression. The symptoms which accompany this stage may include depression, crying spells, restlessness, fatigue, and irritability.[142,143] Postpartum depression may last from one or two months to one year or more. It has been estimated that the incidence of these symptoms ranges from 30 to 60%.[144] While, for most women, post-partum depression usually takes the form of a mild and transient depression, for others, it can be quite severe. More than 4000 women (one in every 1000 women who give birth) are hospitalized each year in the United States because of postpartum disturbance. The number of women estimated in one report to be permanently incapacitated is at least 20% (or 800 women).[145] Another report states that 12½% of the women admitted to the State Hospital in Washington were admitted within 6 months of a delivery or had previously been admitted within 6 months of a delivery.[146]

What accounts for postpartum depression? Is it a normal occurrence? Are all women equally susceptible to it? Is there evidence for hormonal changes as a cause of postpartum depression? As was mentioned earlier, severe drops in hormones (i.e., estrogen or progesterone) appear to be correlated with the onset of depression. Although correlational studies do not allow us to point directly to hormonal changes as the cause of postpartum depression, the medical community generally regards the dramatic reduction in these hormones as factors in triggering the depression so often documented after birth. Further research has found that women with severe postpartum depression were sometimes also found to have thyroid difficulties. These women made recoveries when treated with thyroid compounds.[147] It is important to point out, however, that hypothyroidism, in itself, will probably not cause severe mental disturbance. Research suggests that there may be an interactional relationship between lowered thyroid functioning and psychological factors. For example, in one study, new mothers, who were hospitalized for psychiatric problems were found to have lower thyroid activity than is normal following childbirth. These women were also found to have more negative attitudes toward motherhood, as well as social stresses that were not found in a control group.[148] What these results suggest, then, is that an interaction between physiological and psychological factors may be involved in the aetiology of postpartum depression.

Lack of sleep (both during pregnancy and after the infant is born) appears to contribute to depression as well. In particular, the loss of REM (rapid eye movement) sleep and the disturbance in dream patterns typically found during the final stage of pregnancy and after parturition can lead to emotional disturbance.[149] Rapid eye movements are associated with dreaming and, according to many sources, are needed for psychological replenishment. Here, as in earlier discussions of the role of physiological factors in the onset and maintenance of depression, other factors must be taken into account. For example, the mother who can share infant care with others should have greater opportunity to catch up on her sleep than her counterpart who, because of lack of help, has difficulty finding large enough blocks of time during which the infant does not require her attention and care.

While endocrine changes undoubtedly play a role in the aetiology of postpartum depression, a direct causal link between them has not been empirically demonstrated. However, there exist many possible social psychological causes.[150] One of the most important of these is the assignment of sole or primary responsibility for childcare to the mother. This usually involves cutting her off from the help of others in an isolated household and requiring her to give the child round-the-clock attentive care. Regardless of whatever else a woman has done in the past, once she becomes a mother, caring-for-baby is now supposed to become her primary, if not exclusive, interest. Interestingly, motherhood as we know it at present is a unique institution. Throughout most of human history, as in most parts of the world even today, adult women have been and are regarded as too valuable in their work capacity to be spared only for child-care.[151] Moreover, if the woman drops out of the labour force, either as a result of social pressure or because of necessity, she may find that she has exchanged an equal relationship with her mate for a more traditional one.[152] The rather abrupt shift in social status from an independent wage earner pursuing her own interests in the company of other adults to that of a dependent housewife engaged in repetitive domestic tasks while being deprived of adult company for much of the day, may result not only in resentment toward spouse and baby, but also in depression. And research shows that women who experience conflicts about becoming mothers are more likely to have a prolonged labour and postpartum depression.[153,154]

On the whole, our society has no adequate support system for the new mother. In other societies today, as in the past, the extended family, including other women who themselves have given birth, are on hand not only to give the new inexperienced mother regular relief from the chores associated with a new baby, but also to provide emotional support and advice to a confused and probably frightened woman. Probably at no other time in a woman's life are emotional support and gentle encouragement needed as much as after she returns home from hospital with her newborn baby. However, the decline of the extended family in recent decades has resulted in fewer opportunities for practical and emotional assistance for the new mother. While fathers may be participating more today in infant care than did their counterparts in the past, the father, for the most part, is not at home all day and cannot be counted on for regular relief. And, as expected, research shows that women have fewer emotional postpartum difficulties when they have received support from others (in terms of helpful suggestions) and when their husbands have attended special instruction classes on childcare.[155]

In order to understand the phenomenon of postpartum depression, then, it is important to take into account physiological, sociological, and social psychological factors. While it is generally agreed that endocrine changes are involved in postpartum depression, if any specific endocrine abnormality is involved, the mechanism is not completely understood.[156] In the past, the tendency was to attribute emotional disturbance after birth purely to physiological factors; today the emphasis tends to be on social factors related to the new mother's role, such as her change in status and the relative lack of support she experiences.

Suicide

In this society, the acts of suicide and attempted suicide are regarded as functions of mental disturbance. Often preceded by depression, suicide is associated with feelings that life is not worth living and hopelessness related to an inability to solve one's life's problems. In many societies, suicide and attempted suicide are regarded as illegal. We may ask, ironically, How does one punish the successful offender?

Patterns of suicide and suicide attempts among men and women show dissimilarities reflective of psychological differences. In every society, men have higher rates of successful suicide than women,[157] and women *attempt* suicide more than men.[158,159] Men succeed in committing about two and one-half to three times as many suicides as women.[160] In Canada, in 1977, men committed 2459, or 74%, of suicides, while women committed 858, or 26%, of suicides.[161] Men tend to be more successful than women because they are more apt to use violent and aggressive means of self-destruction such as firearms, explosives, and cutting instruments. Women, on the other hand, prefer less aggressive methods involving poison in the form of drugs or gas.[162,163] These differences are entirely in line with those generally associated with masculine and feminine gender roles. However, with the continuation of current trends among women toward greater aggressiveness and more violent crime, it is likely that aggressive means of suicide among women will also become more common.[164]

Why, we may ask, do women make more attempts at suicide than men? It has been argued that women's higher rates of attempted suicide are related to the fact that their dependency needs are more widely accepted than those of men.[165] According to this view, women use suicide attempts as a means to gain fulfillment of frustrated dependency needs. Witness the attention and concern usually shown the unsuccessful suicide. Men, on the other hand, are much less likely to ask for help because this is considered to be a sign of weakness and decreased masculinity.

Another explanation of the preponderance of female attempted suicide views attempted suicide as a weapon to manipulate relationships where no other means exists.[166] Women may substitute suicide attempts for the physical ways by which men can and frequently do gain power over women. One should not underestimate attempted suicide as a means of influencing others, particularly since its psychological effects can be more profound and longer lasting than those of physical power.

Gender-role differences also emerge from an examination of suicide rates for various marital statuses. The lowest suicide rates occur among married people, intermediate rates are found among the widowed and single, and the highest rates occur among the divorced. While there are higher rates of suicide for men in all of these categories, the disparity for men across marital categories is much greater than for women.[167] For example, between the ages of 25 and 64, single women in the United States are 47% more likely to commit suicide than married women; but single men are 97% more likely to commit suicide than married men. And while the suicide rate for widowed women is about twice that for married women, the rate for widowed men is over four times that for married men. The suicide statistics for men and women suggest that, as in the case of mental disturbance in general, loss of a spouse has more debilitating effects on men than on women. In the case of single people, it may be that mentally unstable men who are more prone to suicide may be less likely to get married in the first place. As discussed earlier, the single man may have less satisfying and intimate relationships than his female counterpart, which would make him more vulnerable to the personal disorganization and feelings of alienation that often give rise to suicide. The high rate of suicide among widowers may be the result of a similar kind of emotional isolation.

Premenstrual and Menstrual Distress

Premenstrual tension is a well-known phenomenon — the physical and psychological distress experienced by many women both before and during their periods has been well documented. Usually, the symptoms include irritability, depression, bloated feelings, and headaches during the four to five days preceding the onset of the menses. Mood changes have also been documented according to the phase of the cycle. In one study,[168] for example, mood was assessed daily in a group of 20 married women who were not pregnant and in a comparison group of pregnant women. The most euphoric mood typically occurred during the time between the end of menses and ovulation, followed by a gradual decline of mood from mid-cycle to the premenstrual phase, with the most negative moods occurring in the premenstrual and early menstrual phases. Besides depression, negative moods included anxiety, irritability, and feelings of low self-esteem. Although research suggests that many women experience negative physical and psychological changes at these times, it is difficult to obtain reliable estimates of just how prevalent these changes are in the female population. Estimates of the incidence of these symptoms range from 25 to 100%.[169] Research using reports of 150 women found that there was a wide range of unpleasant and uncomfortable physical symptoms associated with premenstrual depression and irritability.[170] Sixty-nine percent of this sample was affected by premenstrual irritability, depression occurred in 63%, and both occurred together in just less than half of the sample.

However, research reporting correlations between premenstrual factors and symptoms presents difficulties in that it is based on self-report data. In this type of study, the woman is asked to report how much she experienced "this or that" symptom. As in any self-report measure, the results may be subject to distortions because the respondents will tend to make their answers conform with what they believe they are supposed to feel.[171] Such biases are particularly likely to occur when women know they are participating in a study of menstruation and its effects. In this kind of study, a woman's responses may be influenced by social desirability: she may report reactions and symptoms that she believes are generally regarded as normal for a menstruating woman even though she herself may not experience them. It is important to be aware of these methodological problems when interpreting the research reported in this area.

Others have suggested that the changes associated with the menstrual cycle may lead to more severe debilitation. For example, one study[172] frequently cited in this area found that during the four premenstrual days and the four menstrual days of the cycle, there occurred nearly half of the crimes committed by women, half of the attempted suicides for women, half of women's accidents, and half of their hospital admissions. These rates represent about twice the rate that would be expected if all of these events were distributed equally over the cycle. While some have argued that these data provide evidence of the causal relationship between the menstrual cycle and certain deviant behaviours, others caution against drawing any definitive conclusions from these data because of certain methodological problems. For example, some of the correlations reported are based on biased samples of respondents — criminal women. Just because criminal women are more likely to commit crimes when they are premenstrual does not mean that all women, when premenstrual, will become criminals. Nor does the research mean that women in general will become sick, have an accident, or attempt suicide when they are premenstrual.

The idea that premenstrual tension is the result of some aspect of biochemical fluctuation or imbalance has come under attack in recent years. The design of research in this area does not permit any definitive conclusions to be drawn about the relationship between sex hormones and behaviour. This was stated most eloquently by one researcher in the area:

> Yet each of these studies [on premenstrual tension] is inadequate as a *test* of such a hypothesis.... Possible confounding variables such as the respondents' attitudes about the influence of the menstrual cycle on behaviour, the type of behaviour chosen for study (bursts of creative energy vs. crimes of violence) and the environmental events which may be operative are neither measured nor controlled. Physical symptoms are treated only as the markers of biochemical change and never as the triggers for a culturally meaningful belief system or the independent sources of personal stress. Little attention is given to the specification of physiological mechanisms by which biochemistry can

produce behaviours as diverse as suicide attempts and the craving for sweets. In short, so many unanswered questions remain that one is tempted to suggest that traditional menstrual cycle researchers have themselves been influenced by common cultural stereotypes about the raging hormones behind women's "unpredictable" behaviour and that their so-called scientific conclusions are a somewhat more elaborate way to exert social control by reinforcing the medicalization of women's normal biological functioning (pp. 219-220).[173]

Culture and the psychological significance it attaches to menstruation can, indeed, contribute greatly to a woman's reactions during the menstrual cycle. In this society, menstruation traditionally has been associated with being dirty, and has been labelled an undesirable event, frequently associated with taboos and restrictions.[174,175] In one study[176] of mood shifts associated with the menstrual cycle in 30 young adult women, the theme of anxiety relating to menstruation emerged in two areas. One type of anxiety appeared in the form of helplessness, of being controlled by the bodily processes. The second area of anxiety stemmed from the belief that menstruation was dirty and dangerous.

If people generally hold negative attitudes about menstruation and if the woman herself *expects* to feel badly both before and during menstruation, it is not surprising to find women showing symptoms of depression and irritability at these times. The evidence relating mood changes in premenstrual tension to sex hormones is questionable, however. While hormonal fluctuations have been implicated in the appearance of premenstrual tension, the mechanism by which this occurs has not been explained. No study so far has correlated changes in behaviour with female sex hormones using modern endocrinological methods. It would be more fruitful to regard premenstrual tension as the result of the interaction between biological and social psychological factors than as the direct result of hormonal fluctuations. This approach would take into account the fact that menstruation occurs within a social psychological environment where attitudes and expectations — held by the woman and by society — play a major role in the appearance of any psychological symptoms.

Menopause

While the term "menopause" technically means the cessation of menstruation, it is generally used to refer to physiological and/or psychological changes that occur at mid-life — changes or symptoms often associated with the gradual cessation of ovarian functioning that occurs with aging. The term "climacteric" is also used, though less frequently, to refer to these changes. In women, the physiological changes that occur during menopause may be described as follows: as ovarian functioning decreases, estrogen and progesterone levels decline, and menstrual cycles eventually stop; ovulation ceases, and the woman becomes infertile. The diminished level of hormones also results in atrophy of certain tissues, particularly the external genitalia and breasts, which are normally supported by estrogen. It has generally been thought that the menopausal woman may experience physical symptoms such as hot flashes and breast pains, as well as psychological symptoms such as irritability, crying spells, depression, confusion, and an inability to concentrate very long on anything. Headaches, dizziness, and pounding of the heart are further symptoms that may be found among women undergoing the menopause.[177] While all women may experience some of these symptoms, for most, they are relatively transient. However, it has been estimated that about 10 to 15% of women have physical or emotional problems serious enough to cause them to seek medical or psychiatric help.[178] Others argue, however, that the menopause itself does not lead to an increased incidence of depressive states. This was the conclusion of a major epidemiologic study[179] in Sweden where more than 800 women aged 38 to 60 were surveyed between 1968 and 1970 to determine possible changes in mental health during the menopause. It found no significant differences in the incidence rates for mental illness or depressive states as a function of menopause. Neither was there any evidence that characteristic personality or emotional changes took place.

While the term menopause is sometimes used to describe the physical and psychological changes that men undergo at mid-life, the question of whether or not there is a *male* "menopause" is still being debated today. For some, about 15% of older men, there is a condition called the male climacteric, characterized by a sharp drop in hormone production which can lead to impotence.[180] This syndrome can, however, be effectively treated by hormone therapy. For most men, testosterone (the hormone that contributes to a man's aggressiveness, virility, and sexuality) decreases very gradually with age. Because the reduction in hormonal level is so gradual and less extreme than it is in women, men's secondary sex characteristics and genitals do not deteriorate swiftly.[181] The average man in his mid-years should not suffer from impaired sexual activity or impotence because of a radical change in hormone production.[182]

There are other factors to consider besides the physical ones in any discussion of menopause or mid-life changes. Of particular importance are the psychological factors that come into play during this phase — especially in a society such as this one, which stresses, if not worships, youth. Psychologically (and physically) the menopause signals the end of a woman's reproductive ability. The noted psychoanalyst Helene Deutsch[183] described the menopause as "a struggle for the preservation of femininity now in process of disappearance (p. 477)", "the closing of the gates (p. 478)". She, along with psychoanalysts of her time, saw menopausal women as losing their beauty and their feminine emotional life. While this extreme view is being challenged today, the onset of middle age is usually perceived by women in terms of events within the family, most commonly, children leaving home. Research on women suggests that the way a woman reacts psychologically to the menopause depends on cultural practices and attitudes toward menopause, women's emotional investment in the maternal role, and the availability of other roles. For example, in a study[184] on middle-aged women that was mentioned earlier in the section on depression, it was found that women who were very involved with their children ("my life is my children") and who had lost their role as full-time mother became quite depressed. On the basis of interviews with women who were psychiatrically hospitalized, it was suggested that the woman whose sense of self is derived *mainly* from the role of mother and who lacks other roles as vehicles of self-fulfillment is in a stressful position when the children depart. As a result, the woman suffers a significant loss of self-esteem. This study further showed that Jewish women, who are often in the role of "supermother", feel this role loss the most and thus may be most vulnerable to depression during mid-life. Employed women who were also mothers were less affected, since they had another role. (This finding was discussed earlier in this chapter, in the section on depression.)

Healthy women, however, do not experience psychological disruption as they move through the menopause.[185] One study[186] in which postmenopausal women aged 45 to 55 years were given an "Attitudes toward Menopause Checklist" found that most of the women experienced a "recovery", and were feeling calmer and more confident than when they were younger. Moreover, for the healthy woman, the menopause is a stage of life which could signal the end of fears of pregnancy, freedom from the demands of childbearing and rearing of children, and the beginning of a new stage of life where instrumental goals (i.e., getting a job) may become important. At the same time, their personalities may become more autonomous, aggressive, and cerebral. Having carried out her nurturant role as a mother and spent years of catering to the needs of her family, this may be the time when a woman can pursue activities and interests of her own. The postmenopausal years can be exciting and vigorous ones, indeed!

Having established that men generally do not experience drastic drops in the male hormone level at mid-life, is it still possible to consider the existence of a "menopause" in men? According to some researchers,[187] a mid-life crisis does occur in men (aged 35 to 45 years), and it is a predictable developmental stage which most men experience at about the age of 40, although some are affected in their late thirties, and others, not until their fifties. It is usually characterized by agitation, restlessness, and some confusion and doubts about their job, goals, and family. To understand just what most men experience at this time, it is important to examine the traditional masculine role into which most North American men have been socialized. As has been pointed out earlier, most men, especially those of the middle class, have come to value hard work and success as ways of proving themselves as men. Moreover, the conventional masculine role stresses achievement and prescribes hard work and denial of feelings as the only means of "making it up the success ladder". These are precisely the characteristics which may lead to heart attacks, ulcers, strokes, and premature death in many men. For the majority of middle-class men, 40 is the age at which careers are on the line. This is usually the time when society judges the man as a success or a failure. The man also makes this sort of judgement of himself. At the same time the man is beginning to see the rewards of hard work, dedication, and self-denial as smaller, and the pressures as larger than what he had been led to expect. The man at mid-life frequently experiences a lower energy level than previously and, not surprisingly, may find his body less responsive to the demands he has customarily placed on it. The days of instant erection are probably in the past as well.

Having reached the stage where he must confront his own mortality, the mid-life man may go in one of two opposite directions. Some men may turn to escapism, denial of what is happening through excessive use of alcohol, and through compulsive sexual liaisons with younger women — ways of denying their aging and asserting their waning sense of masculinity. But, as some have argued, the mid-life stage can lead to new opportunities for personality growth.[188] The man may now feel that he has lived in such a way as to try to "make it" in the traditional manner — he has sought goals and pursued activities appropriate to the masculine mystique. However, mid-life could represent the end of this kind of striving and the beginning of a search for something new. At mid-life, many middle-class men discover that their total dedication to the pursuit of success has left them less than whole. Having tried to fulfill the prescriptions of the traditional masculine role and having done so with varying degrees of success, many men in mid-life may attempt to discover meaning in interpersonal relationships — an option that they may not have felt was available to them in their younger days when they were "climbing the ladder of success". Being dissatisfied with their one-sided personality, many men may even experience a reversal in personality traits:

> intent on living out the potentials and pleasures they had relinquished in earlier years, men begin to move toward the passivity, sensuality, and tenderness previously repressed in the service of productivity (p. 123).[189]

In addition to her loss of the maternal role, the contemporary woman may experience something akin to the male mid-life crisis. Having internalized middle-class values of achievement, the housewife who is approaching mid-life may suddenly feel overwhelmed and anxious by her lack of status in society. These feelings are likely exacerbated by media messages which imply that unless the modern woman seeks "fulfillment" in employment outside the home, her life has been "wasted" in the roles of wife and mother. All these influences lead to loss of self-esteem and development of feelings of depression in the middle-aged woman who has spent most of her adult years working exclusively in the home. As for the career woman in her forties and early fifties, she, like her male counterpart, may ask herself questions about her achievements in her employment. Any remorse she may have about her career would be exacerbated by practical obstacles to her employment progress, which frequently take the form of sex discrimination.

A person's reactions to menopause can best be understood within the context of traditional roles and the extent to which individuals can extricate themselves from the constraints and demands of these roles. While earlier research assumed a direct causal relationship between cessation of menses and the appearance of psychiatric symptoms in women, it has been shown more recently that the phase coinciding with the menopause may be associated with significant life events, such as departure of children from the home. These social and psychological events may have more impact on women than the cessation of menses. Furthermore, there is no conclusive evidence that women are at a greater risk for depression during the menopausal period.[190] Healthy men and women passing through mid-life can progress to a new and exciting stage, in which they are not as pressured to perform as a "real" woman or man. With women freed from childbearing and childrearing, their nurturant role can be supplanted by other roles that allow them to express their own needs and abilities — those that were likely suppressed when their families were young. Without the pressure to serve others that was likely present during the previous 20 years or more, women in mid-life can turn to new interests for which there was neither time nor energy before. For men to survive the mid-life period and be able to go on to a fuller and richer stage, they, too, must be able to extricate themselves from the demanding expectations associated with the masculine gender role and open themselves to new ideas and feelings, which heretofore had been denied expression by both society and themselves.

Gender-Role Differences and Psychotherapy

While psychotherapy is often seen as a form of medical treatment, it differs from other kinds of medical treatment in important ways. Firstly, the symptoms for which the psychotherapeutic "patient" is treated are in marked contrast to those typically encountered in other medical treatment. For example, the physician's patient frequently presents some concrete symptom or *clear* physical abnormality, such as a broken leg, gall stones, or an ingrown toenail. Psychiatric patients, however, are usually found to be suffering from more vague, less tangible symptoms, such as emotional conflict, stress, and depression, all of which are subjective and emotional conditions. While feelings or affective states are associated to some degree with all illnesses, they tend to be the most salient symptoms of psychiatric disorders.

In general, more women than men obtain psychiatric treatment for emotional disorders. This disparity occurs partly as a result of the differential meanings of "sickness" for males and females found in this society. Being sick does not, in itself, have the same implications for women as for men. Generally speaking, since it is more culturally appropriate or acceptable for women to express their problems and their feelings, it is probable that more women than men disclose their emotional problems.[191,192] Women do not have as much fear of being labelled "sick" as do men. In the case of men, the sick role is regarded as a sign of weakness that may diminish their masculinity. When we hear that women are more "emotional" than men, this does not mean that emotionalism is exclusively a female characteristic. It simply means that society is more accepting of

"I've told you again and again — women will never be equal to men because they get too damn emotional about everything!!"

women's display of the full range of their feelings. In men, only limited displays of emotion are considered acceptable. Men are generally expected to be stoic — once again, a trademark of masculinity. Because women can overtly express emotional complaints, and can identify them in themselves more readily than men without fear of being labelled "weak", it is not surprising to discover that there are more psychiatric labels for women's feelings and behaviours than for men's.

Women's greater likelihood to seek psychotherapy may also result, in part, from the way they perceive and interpret their moods. For example, women have been found more than men to hold themselves responsible for unhappy moods.[193] People who feel they are responsible for their own unhappiness are more likely to seek psychotherapy. Those who can blame factors external to themselves for their unhappiness are less likely to seek help, since they can rationalize that, after all, there is not much *they* can do to improve their unhappy mood if other factors are held to be responsible. These differences in patterns of symptom expression in men and women may thus lead to differences between them in help seeking. Some researchers, for example, have found significant differences between men and women in severity of depression manifested before help seeking: men appeared to be much more reluctant to seek help for depression in general, and were more likely to report that they would never seek psychotherapy for depression.[194,195] A further reason for these differences in help seeking can be seen in the differential importance of dependency for masculine and feminine gender roles. Since it is more acceptable for women than men to be dependent, seeking help (of any kind) would appear to be more congruent with feminine role expectations. A woman who experiences personal problems will interpret these as signs of psychiatric symptoms more readily than a man and will be encouraged to seek psychiatric help for them. In general, then, women can be said to be more accepting of the role of patient, particularly the role of psychiatric patient.

Medication and Psychotherapy

There is evidence that women, compared to men, receive more drug prescriptions for mental disorders. For example, in a study of 1.5 million prescriptions written by general practitioners in Australia, 80% were for mental disorders, most commonly for depressive neurosis; the drugs were issued far more frequently for women than for men.[196] In the United States, one study found in 1973 that women received 67% of the prescriptions for psychotropic drugs,[197] and another study revealed that women were prescribed significantly more psychotropic medication than men: for the age groups 30 to 44 and 45 to 59, the ratio of drug prescriptions for women to men was 2:1.[198]

Why do women receive more mood- and mind-altering medication? Women are diagnosed more frequently than men as suffering from some kind of emotional or nervous disorder and thus are seen as "needing" more medication. But, even when they have the same diagnostic label, male and female psychiatric patients probably receive different drug treatment. For example, in one study[199] where clinicians were asked to evaluate hypothetical patients on a number of measures related to diagnosis, prognosis, and treatment recommendations, the *same* depressed patient was rated as in need of medication significantly more often by those clinicians who were told the patient was a woman than by clinicians who were told the patient was a man. Since there is no evidence that female patients are generally more disturbed than their male counterparts,[200] why should women receive disproportionately more mood- and mind-altering drugs? Feminine gender-role stereotypes held by physicians may influence them to over-prescribe drugs for women. For example, it has been reported that physicians are willing to prescribe tranquilizers for housewives because "they need not be alert".[201] And it is not surprising to find that use of prescribed tranquilizers is especially high among suburban women,[202] since many physicians have been found to endorse daily use of a strong sedative by housewives.[203] Moreover, when medication is prescribed for men who are diagnosed as neurotic depressive, its purpose is to allay the anxiety that is seen to be interfering with their basic ability to function adequately. Women with the same diagnosis and the same self-description are treated significantly longer with mood-elevating drugs.[204]

To understand why women receive more psychotropic drugs, it is useful to look at medical advertisements. In one study,[205] 73% of physicians rated advertisements in medical journals as important to them as sources of information on drugs. Using an in-depth content analysis of medical advertisements from four leading medical journals, other research[206] recorded the following findings: psychogenic illnesses, such as anxiety, depression, or insomnia, were associated with female patients, and nonpsychogenic illnesses, which refers to all other conditions, were associated with men; within the psychogenic drug category, alone, women were shown as having diffuse emotional symptoms, while men were shown with anxiety from pressures at work or from associated physical illness; and, in general, the images of women and men conformed to cultural stereotypes. Women tended to be portrayed as emotional, irrational, and complaining. Men, on the other hand, were shown as nonemotional, rational, and stoic. It is difficult to say precisely just how much advertising influences a physician's behaviour. However, one may speculate that since they reflect cultural stereotypes about women and men, probably confirming the stereotypes held by the physician, and since they provide a recurrent biased approach to the subject of drug prescription, drug advertisements may have a significant influence on physicians' differential treatment of male and female patients.

Psychotherapy and Ideology

Most kinds of psychotherapy involve a relationship — usually long-term — between a patient or a client and a therapist. Patients enter psychotherapy with the expectation that the therapist will help them solve their problems, thus enabling them to lead happier, more productive lives. As patients discuss their problems, a therapist interprets in accordance with his or her own biases, which, of course, include beliefs concerning appropriate behaviour for women and men. In recent years, there has been a considerable increase in concern with discrimination on the basis of sex and with unfavourable aspects of gender-role stereotyping in therapy. Psychiatry and the mental health professions in general have been criticized for their sexist beliefs and practices — that is, those which manifest discrimination against women. Interest in the whole issue of sex bias in therapy has become more prevalent in the professions of psychiatry and psychology. Both the American[207] and Canadian Psychological Associations[208] have established or endorsed task forces and committees which have shown that sex bias is quite prevalent in the delivery of psychological services to women. Moreover, the popularity of women's self-help groups and counselling advertised as feminist or nonsexist is evidence of the seriousness with which such attacks have been taken.[209]

A great deal of research has been undertaken during the 1970s to determine the nature and extent to which sex bias permeates clinical practice. One of the most influential investigations in this area is the work of Broverman and her associates,[210] which suggests that psychotherapists hold a "double standard" of mental health for men and women. That is, the ideal personality is held to be the masculine one. If women conform to the norms of the ideal feminine personality, they are perceived as less healthy than men who conform to the masculine ideal. In their study, which has received wide citation in both the research literature and the popular press, 79 psychologists, psychiatrists, and social workers were asked to describe a mature, healthy, socially competent male, female, or adult (sex unspecified) in terms of a list of well-known stereotypical gender-role characteristics. The results were that the clinical judgement of optimal mental health varied with the stated sex of the person being judged. Clinicians were likely to judge the healthy woman as more submissive, less independent, less aggressive, more emotional, less objective, and less adventurous than her male counterpart. The clinicians were also less likely to attritube traits characteristic of a healthy adult (sex unspecified) to a mentally healthy woman than to a healthy man. According to the results of this study, there tend to be two standards of mental health: one for adult men and adult people and another for adult women. Mental health practitioners view mental health in terms of a masculine model. In other words, the paradigm of well-being is represented by masculine traits.

Although the Broverman study has had a great influence on views in the area of mental illness and gender-role differences, it can be criticized on a number of grounds. For example, the clinicians doing the ratings may not have thought that women were less healthy, as Broverman argues, but that exaggerated feminine traits were. Furthermore, if the clinicians assumed that the word "adult" referred to a man — a widespread assumption that reflects the sexism in language usage — then Broverman's conclusions could be questioned. In later research,[211] Broverman's results were not replicated, suggesting that the concept of the "healthy adult" is coming to correspond more with the androgynous person, who possesses both feminine and masculine traits. One of the criticisms repeatedly levelled against the Broverman study is that it fails to show that different standards of mental health actually contributed to differential treatment of women and men in the practice of therapy. Differential judgement does not automatically prove differential treatment.

There is other evidence, however, that the behaviour of mental health personnel with female and male patients corresponds to a double standard of health. For example, studies of how patients were treated in a private hospital found that, while diagnosis was related to length of hospitalization for male patients, it was not a good predictor variable for female patients.[212] This research showed, further, that over time, female patients were seen as becoming healthier than male patients.[213] And while staff ratings of psychopathology for men were closely related to the type of referral recommendations made, staff ratings for the women were unrelated to the referral. Women who were referred for further hospitalization were found to be younger than those who were discharged, and tended to be single and unemployed. But marital and employment status were unrelated to the male referral recommendations.

Further evidence of bias comes from a 1975 U.S. nationwide survey[214] of psychologists engaged in the practice of psychotherapy and provides at least anecdotal evidence of the biases affecting women in four major areas: fostering the traditional feminine role and discouraging innovations in gender-role behaviour; holding biased expectations of women and devaluing them; using psychoanalytic concepts in a sexist way (e.g., assertiveness and ambition in female patients are sometimes equated with penis envy); responding to female patients as sex objects, including engaging in seduction. Thus, evidence suggests that bias against women is still very much a part of the practice of psychotherapy. However, recent research suggests that trends may be beginning to change. In one study, male middle-aged therapists saw both positively valued and negatively valued stereotypically feminine characteristics as unhealthy and "a problem for their female clients".[215] Other evidence indicates that both male and female therapists are starting to become more egalitarian.[216,217] There is, then, a trend toward less sexism beginning to appear in psychotherapy. A major review of 25 studies conducted in the area of sex-related differences in psychological/psychiatric assessment and treatment concludes that a large and possibly diminishing minority of clinicians holds separate standards of mental health for men and women.[218] While there is growing evidence that therapists are starting to become more egalitarian in their treatment of women, most of the data, both clinical and anecdotal, continue to suggest that there is still considerable sexism in therapeutic relationships involving female patients.

The Woman-Patient

Psychotherapy typically involves a female patient and a male therapist, since more men than women are psychiatrists and clinical psychologists. Female patients tend to prefer a male therapist, partly because, along with many men, they distrust women in authority roles. According to Phyllis Chesler's[219] analysis, the traditional psychotherapeutic encounter is just one more example of an unequal relationship, in which the woman is dominated, in this case, by the therapist. Although it may be argued that men in therapy also have submissive and dependent relationships with their therapists (especially in institutional settings), it could be an even greater problem for women, because of their socially prescribed role. Chesler likens psychotherapy to marriage: both emphasize individual, rather than collective, solutions to women's unhappiness. In psychotherapy, the woman-patient is encouraged to talk by a therapist whom she perceives as her superior. The woman who deviates from the traditional feminine gender role "needs fixing", according to this view, and it is the therapist's goal to bring his patient to terms with her feminine role. In short, according to feminist critiques of traditional psychotherapy, psychiatric ideologies interpret the world for women in such a way as to create a special demand for psychiatry among women, especially among those of the middle and upper middle class.

The belief held by therapists that restoration to health for women is achieved by adjustment to the traditional feminine gender role may cause women serious difficulties. While the female patient is urged to act and think in stereotyped ways, the evidence around her indicates that psychological traits associated with traditional femininity are not as highly valued in our society as those associated with masculinity. The status and role toward which she is encouraged to strive are likewise less valued and are not seen as commanding as much respect as those associated with men.

In general, the ideology of psychoanalysis has been detrimental to women (see Chapter 3). Freud's view that "anatomy is destiny" is well known. Although inconsistencies have been noted among many of the ideas about women in traditional psychoanalysis, as expounded by Freud, his views have had a major impact on clinicians and their conception of women. For example, women who compromise their maternal role in favour of more "masculine" pursuits, such as a career, are sometimes said to be suffering from an unresolved case of penis envy — a condition which has also been seen as the cause of competitiveness in female patients. In addition, Freud's idea that women have a less well-developed conscience than men because they cannot resolve the Oedipal conflict (see Chapter 3) has been no less influential than his idea that clitoral sexuality has to be substituted with vaginal sexuality for a woman to achieve true femininity (see Chapters 3 and 6).

Neo-Freudians have also held biased views about female patients. Many authoritative and influential analytic thinkers, such as Erik Erikson, Bruno Bettelheim, and Melanie Klein have emphasized the importance of mothering, not only to a woman's happiness, but also to the emotional health of children. For example, according to Erik Erikson, "women spend their whole lives searching for a man to fill their inner space with a baby."[220] Erich Fromm[221] also defined personality using gender- and sex-typed concepts. While he saw femininity as receptive, realistic, maternal, and productive, he described masculinity as being characterized by penetration, activity, and adventurousness. For the most part, these analyses are extensions of long-standing cultural conceptions of women and men.

Of all modes of therapy, psychoanalysis is the most negative toward women. Karen Horney was one of the few psychoanalysts who departed from this negative outlook in any substantial way. Differing from Freud in the way she regarded penis envy (see Chapter 3), she suggested that men recognize women's superior creative power in their ability to bear and nurse children. This "womb envy" is expressed by men in the form of disparagement of women's natural achievements and glorification of the practical accomplishments of men. Men, she argued, compensate for their inability to bear children through work, art, and other creative ambitions, as well as by belittling women.[222]

In the past, psychoanalytically inclined therapists tended to rely on theories of human behaviour based largely on biological factors. As a result of theoretical changes, however, they are becoming more eclectic in their approach. In combining ideas derived from cognitive-developmental and learning theory as well, many of these therapists are paying more attention than they did in the past to the influence of social and cognitive factors and their role in emotional disturbance in women. There is also evidence that these therapists sometimes recognize the changing roles of women and men that, at times, they may even compare women favourably with men.[223–225]

If therapy for women is to be effective, however, all therapists must be constantly aware of the changes occurring in women's roles. By acting on the basis of outmoded stereotypes regarding the traditional feminine role, therapists cannot respond effectively to women's problems, nor can they be sensitive to problems that are linked to the continuing transformation of the feminine gender role. Not surprisingly, the symptoms that women are presenting in psychotherapy have changed considerably over the last few decades. One study,[226] for example, has compared a sample of 50 female patients, one-half of whom were treated between 1953 and 1956, and the other half, between 1973 and 1976. Women in the first group tended to seek treatment for problems with sexual behaviour (including frigidity), marriage, and childrearing. The most prominent symptom in ten of these patients related to desperation in finding a husband. In contrast, among the problems present in women seeking therapy in the seventies, those pertaining to sexual behaviour played a much less important role in marital conflicts. Most of those who were seeking a husband had already been divorced; several others were looking only for a better sexual partner. Many of the problems of women seeking help in the seventies centred around conflict about professional versus personal identity, divorce, and extramarital affairs. In contrast to the women seeking help in the fifties, women patients in the seventies often perceived marriage as a trap. For female patients in the seventies, anxieties emerged which were a direct result of greater role proliferation. These women, more than their counterparts in the past, experienced anxiety on entering new jobs, about their job performance and about their ability to assert themselves.

In short, greater freedom of choice in women's personal and employment lives has resulted in new anxieties. Women today have more freedom to choose to remain single, to remain childless, and to devote themselves to a career. With the dramatic rise in the divorce rate and the increase in single female parents, women are being required more than in the past to carry on autonomous lives. Since many women are mothers or wives or lovers, *and* they are also working outside the home, they more frequently have to act in multiple roles. Lack of skills in their new roles, a paucity of feminine role models for those new roles, together with relatively high expectations for performance in all their spheres of activity contribute to anxieties unique to contemporary women.

The Man-Patient

Far less has been written about the unique disadvantages of the male patient, both in the popular press and in the research literature. Although there has been much verbiage about the dependency of the female patient, women have no monopoly on the submissive role. The type of dependency that can develop in men has been aptly depicted in *One Flew over the Cuckoo's Nest*, a film based on the book by Ken Kesey. Men can be reduced to a childish, dependent, and submissive position in an institution, even when the therapist is a woman. While traditional therapy places the therapist in a position of authority and reinforces the patient's dependent role, it is doubtful that any therapy which diminishes the patient's responsibility can benefit a person of either sex. Freud recounted that many men have conflicts regarding male authority figures, often considering the male therapist to be a father image. Like his female counterpart, the male patient is seen as "regressing" to a childish position, which is considered to be necessary for therapist and patient to work through parental conflicts. Once awareness of the conflicts is achieved, in many forms of therapy the patient is helped or guided in rebuilding a more adequate lifestyle and developing better coping mechanisms. The problem enters, however, when therapists, because of their own biases, foster an artificial or gender-role stereotyped course of growth. This can occur as readily in the case of the male as in the case of the female patient.

The masculine gender role has undergone profound changes in recent years, and many men are experiencing conflict between "traditional" and "modern" roles.[227] As children, most boys are socialized into a role that values and encourages physical prowess, emotional coolness (except perhaps for impulsive expressions of anger), distance from women and bonding with male peers. The "modern" adult role for men emphasizes intellectual, rather than physical, skills, pragmatic relationships with other men, and emotional tenderness with women. Recent changes in the feminine gender role, resulting in women showing more assertiveness and dominance at home and in the employment sector, have also led to contradictory role expectations for men, which place them in a bind: they are not sure how to express themselves in various situations. The tried-and-true

"I know what you're up to, Henry. You're trying to impress me by being sensitive and compassionate. But I think you're faking it, Henry — only an idiot would cry every time Elmer Fudd gets blown up!"

ways that men have used in "dealing with" women are not only inappropriate today, but, in many instances, they simply do not work anymore. More and more women are meeting men on their own ground. This presents a dilemma for the man socialized to be chivalrous in his relationships with women. While in the past, men's relationships with women meant that the man either dominated or helped the woman, today's norms prescribe equal relationships between men and women. As a result of anxiety about these contradictory demands on them, men may react, at times, by being aggressive toward women, "putting women down" or criticizing them, for example. Furthermore, the sexual demands of "liberated" women can cause anxiety in men that can result in impotence and sexual dysfunctions.[228] The control a man feels he should have in sexual encounters is threatened when the woman takes the sexual initiative (see Chapter 6).

In short, contemporary conflicts for many men arise from their relationships with women who have felt the impact of feminism. Since the influences on women also affect men, changes in the woman's gender role require parallel changes in the man's. To accommodate the new directions that women's gender role is taking, men will have to accept women as equals in employment settings, share power with them in heterosexual relationships, including marriage, and become more involved in family roles. While men are required to give up power to women in certain areas, they will have more freedom to make gains in other areas. The expansion of the feminine gender role has also suggested possibilities for expansion for the masculine gender role. As mentioned at several points throughout this book, traditional gender-role prescriptions for men have given them less opportunity than women to develop intimate interpersonal relationships and a sense of interdependence. But, this too may be changing.

Now that men are beginning to feel less pressure to dominate their relationships with women, they will be freer to express and satisfy their interpersonal needs, thus experiencing rewards and fulfillment that were not possible in the past. The expansion of the masculine gender role should therefore result in greater possibilities for self-expression in men. As the past two decades have seen significant changes in the role of women in employment and in the family, future decades are likely to witness a significant movement toward change and development of the masculine gender role.

Alternative Forms of Therapy

Whether they are held consciously or unconsciously, therapists' beliefs and assumptions about gender roles and gender-role differences have a significant influence on the behaviour of the patient. Most experiences and interactions with the patient are interpreted and evaluated within this system of beliefs — beliefs which, very often, are sexist. The growing awareness of sexism in psychotherapy, along with an increase in feminist consciousness among researchers and practitioners in the mental health field, have resulted in a proliferation of alternative forms of therapy. The emphasis here is not on helping the patient recover from illness, but on fostering personal growth in a client. Based on the assumption that environmental, rather than biological, factors play a major part in precipitating problems for the individual, these forms of therapy allow for the consideration of gender roles and their effects. Finally, they de-emphasize the therapist as an authority, instead, espousing an equal relationship between therapist and client.

Feminist Therapy. In feminist therapy, feminist values and goals have been incorporated into psychotherapy for women. In line with the belief that personal change and socio-political change are inextricably linked, feminist therapy helps the client become aware of the social and political context of her psychological problems. The relationship between treatment goals and social change is emphasized through discussion of how social roles influence the client's problems. Social change is considered a necessary counterpart of personal change.[229] In feminist therapy the client becomes aware of the extent to which social forces have shaped her life, her lifestyle, and her means of coping. During the process of developing awareness, the client may express anger and frustration as she realizes that her problems are not the result of her own actions (as she may have been led to believe), but are caused in part by being a woman in a sexist society. However, the strategies selected by feminist therapists emphasize the client's own responsibility in reshaping her life to bring her greater satisfaction. Women are encouraged to discover their personal strengths, to achieve a sense of independence, to view themselves as equals in interpersonal relationships, and to trust and respect other women. In the process, the therapist helps the client to recognize the choices that are realistically available to her. At times, nothing short of a complete change of lifestyle will allow the client to take advantage of her revised perception of what she values in life. Through discussion, the therapist helps the client recognize the consequences of the choices available to her. It is up to the client to take the risks necessary to experience self-growth.

While the goal of feminist therapy is similar to that of other therapy in that it is oriented toward alleviating distress, feminist therapy differs in that it views gender roles as a major factor contributing to emotional problems — particularly the pressures on women to submit to the prescriptions of the status quo. For the most part, women tend to judge themselves in terms of how adequately they fulfill the requirements of the roles they hold in relation to others — those of wife, mother, daughter, for example. In feminist therapy, the client is encouraged to challenge her traditional identity and to seek new definitions of self which are more independent and autonomous.

Self-Help Groups. Another outgrowth of the feminist movement has been the development of self-help groups, which are based on the principle of collective, rather than hierarchical, structures and the sharing of responsibility. In these groups, power is shared among the group members, rather than being concentrated in a therapist because of the belief that if women are to change the oppressive aspects of their lives, the oppressive aspect of therapy must be modified as well. Consciousness-raising (CR) groups are one example of such self-help groups. Small groups of women meet on a regular basis, without a male or female therapist, to share their common experiences. As with feminist therapy, they proceed from the assumption that environmental, rather than biological, factors play a major role in the client's problems. Through participation in CR groups, greater awareness can be developed about the social meaning of being a woman in this society. It has been suggested that participation in CR groups has resulted in remarkable changes in self-perceptions, goals, and lifestyle.[230] CR groups can also help many women rid themselves of the belief that the problems they have are the result of their own actions, thus destroying the patterns of guilt and self-destructive behaviour which have traditionally characterized women.

Although CR groups are predominantly attended by women, men have also participated in this form of self-help. In CR groups, men learn to become aware of the implications that the masculine gender role holds for them. Through discussion with others, men are encouraged to examine the restrictions of their roles. For example, some of the objectives of a CR group for men might include clarifying that men are discouraged from expressing their feelings, increasing men's awareness of their needs for intimacy, and stressing the importance of and learning how to express caring more adequately.[231]

While there is little systematic information about the prevalence and usefulness of CR groups, the little available evidence suggests that they are helpful. Their popularity suggests further that they are providing a necessary service. It is important to point out that self-help groups are suited mainly to people who are functioning reasonably well in their everyday lives, but who are interested in developing increased personal awareness and psychological growth. Persons who are psychotic or who are suffering from debilitating neurotic symptoms would require a more structured form of therapy.

Androgyny as a Model of Mental Health

Traditional assessments of the relationship between gender roles and psychological health have gone on the assumption that healthy individuals are those who adopt conventional masculine or feminine roles. Sandra Bem has challenged these traditional notions, arguing that our current system of role differentiation serves to prevent women and men from developing as full and complete human beings (see Chapter 2). She has argued further that for fully effective and healthy human functioning, both masculinity and femininity must be integrated into a more balanced, androgynous personality. The idea of an androgynous model of mental health goes all the way back to Carl Jung who talked about the animus (a masculine aspect) and the anima (a feminine aspect) being integrated into everyone's personality (see Chapter 2). The androgynous person (male or female) is one who identifies with both desirable masculine and feminine characteristics. Such persons might regard themselves as both dominant and yielding, and analytical yet sensitive to the needs of others, for example. According to this model, people possessing both masculine and feminine traits are better able to cope with a wider variety of situations and are therefore better adapted to deal with complex environments. The concept of androgyny as an alternative to strive for has been enthusiastically endorsed both within and outside academic circles. The concept has been so popular that it has permeated most alternatives to traditional forms of psychotherapy. For many people, androgyny equals mental health.[232]

Recently, however, the notion of androgyny as the basis of sound mental health has been challenged on a variety of grounds. First, while an androgynous view of mental health necessitates a balance between femininity and masculinity in one person, it has frequently been demonstrated that masculine individuals score as high as androgynous ones on scales assessing self-concept and personal adjustment.[233],[234] Other research has shown that when male and female university students describe themselves, level of masculinity is the major contributing factor to their self-esteem.[235] Such results are expected in our culture where "masculine" traits are more socially desirable and are generally perceived as having higher status than "feminine" ones. Moreover, it may be difficult for people of either sex to achieve a flexible balance of characteristics because of the unbalanced pressures from cultural norms and the greater evaluation of "masculine" traits.

One reason why several studies have reported better psychological adjustment among androgynous and masculine people than among those who describe themselves as more feminine, derives from the type of sample employed. Most research studying the relationship between gender roles and psychological health has been conducted with college students as participants. In a college environment, maximal rewards would appear to accrue to those who possess "masculine" characteristics, as the emphasis in this context is on achievement, competition, and ambition.[236] The relationship between gender typing and mental health is quite different when people other than college students are studied. For example, in one study conducted by Hoffman and Fidell,[237] in which middle-class women between the ages of 20 and 59 were participants, feminine women did not make more frequent health-related visits, nor were they more neurotic than androgynous and masculine women. Androgynous individuals, then, do not always enjoy better mental health. At times, gender-typed people (who are either highly masculine or highly feminine) may show good adjustment in settings which call for gender-role-appropriate behaviour. However, gender-typed people may show signs of maladjustment when they find themselves in situations calling for behaviour appropriate to another gender role. The Hoffman-Fidell study illustrates this very well. Hoffman and Fidell found that masculine and androgynous women were more likely than their feminine counterparts to hold outside employment and to associate satisfaction with their employment. Stereotypically feminine women, on the other hand, were more likely to take full responsibility for childcare and housework, which were associated with satisfaction for them. It is likely, then, that the degree of concordance among gender-role self-description, life circumstances, and perceived sources of satisfaction is the critical factor. In effect, there was a good match between the gender-role descriptions of women in this study and their life circumstances. In most cases, their sources of satisfaction also fit their gender role. The question still remains, however, as to whether gender-typed people select situations which support their gender-role-appropriate behaviour or whether such situations shape people to be gender-typed.[238] In summary, then, androgyny is not always equated with good psychological adjustment. Conversely, traditional gender typing is not always equated with neuroticism.

Originally, the concept of androgyny was introduced to help eliminate gender-role bias and stereotyping. However, according to its present definition, it will probably not accomplish these goals because it is derived from a comparison of degrees of femininity and masculinity. Rather than decreasing reliance on gender roles, as traditionally defined, the concept of androgyny may, in fact, be increasing the salience of gender roles as primary ways of evaluating others.[239] If real change is to be achieved in the way people evaluate each other, behaviours and attitudes must be perceived without reference to whether they are "feminine" or "masculine". Finally, androgyny cannot substitute for social change.[240] Even if our society were composed totally of androgynous people, it is questionable that discrimination on the basis of sex would cease. While the concept of androgyny may help people adjust to a particular situation, it cannot be regarded as an agent of change. The feminist goal is to restructure society so that individuals are not restricted on the basis of their gender role or their sex, and to this end, feminists have called for an elimination of gender roles.

Summary and Implications

Since the beginning of recorded history, being male or female has been one of the most significant defining characteristics of a person. Sex and gender not only determine the kinds of experiences people have, but they also significantly influence the way people perceive and act toward each other. Moreover, socio-cultural expectations have been integrated into elaborate gender-role systems which have had an enormous impact on all areas of psychological and social functioning.

Scientific inquiry into the nature of the psychological differences between women and men is not new. In the past, this inquiry was directed primarily at justifying women's inferior and subordinate position in society. The assumption was that the ways in which women differed from men reflected some basic intrinsic differences between them. The fact that women had fewer resources and less power than men, was taken to be a perfectly natural phenomenon. More recently, however, research has shown that there are far fewer psychological differences between women and men than was previously thought. Increasingly, we are learning that, when differences are found, they are not the result of inborn factors but, rather, a reflection of the influence of the social environment.

What Is the Difference?

There are biological differences between the sexes: menstruation, pregnancy, and ejaculation, for example, are sex-specific phenomena and result in psychological patterns of reactions unique to women or men. However, despite their biological origins, recent research has shown that psychological reactions associated even with these phenomena are subject to change through social learning and experience. It has also been demonstrated that environmental factors have an impact on psychological phenomena which are partially biological in origin, such as visual spatial ability and aggression. In addition, most of the behaviour usually assumed to be more characteristic of either women or men and linked to one specific gender role, has been shown, overwhelmingly, to result primarily from social learning.

The ideology underlying the definition of the two gender roles consists of unequal valuation: one of the most consistent themes to be found in psychological theory and research is that the masculinity of men is more valued than the femininity of women. Surveys of interaction between women and men — whether in the home, the workplace, or in educational institutions — reveal that the male is more powerful. Male dominance is due to the universal ascription of higher status to the masculine gender role. At the same time, there exists a political distribution of personality characteristics which assigns one set of characteristics to the masculine gender role and another set to the feminine one. By assigning instrumental traits such as dominance, independence, and competitiveness to the masculine gender role, and socio-emotional traits such as nurturance, affiliation, and sensitivity to the feminine gender role, this system prescribes traits for women and men that facilitate performance of activities that are differentially valued by society. So, for example, economic success and the exertion of power are seen as important accomplishments in our society and the traits associated with the masculine gender role facilitate achievement of these goals. The role assigned to women, on the other hand, prescribes traits which prepare its members for activities that have less value according to society's standards — namely, mothering, caretaking, and serving others. What is more, the nature of the cultural assignment of traits along gender-role lines facilitates the dominance of men over women. So, for example, socialization of girls prescribes greater expression of emotion, and where women are encouraged to express themselves, men are expected to be stolid and impassive. This puts women at a distinct disadvantage in any interaction with men. Since women are socialized to care about interpersonal relationships more than men are, women are rendered more vulnerable. In a sentimental relationship, the person who cares less can exploit the person who cares more.[1] Thus, women's relatively greater "caring" and emotional openness result in their having less potential power in relationships.

Behaviours prescribed for women and girls tend to be seen as immature and ineffective, while those prescribed for men and boys are seen as mature and effective. Boys are taught strategies for coping effectively with their environment and, at the same time, are expected to develop feelings of self-confidence and independence. Girls frequently fail to develop a sense of mastery and effectance, since they receive inadequate encouragement in early independence strivings. One of the effects of femininity, as it is prescribed by the gender role, is the inhibition of independence behaviour, with the result that passivity and dependence become the major features associated with the behaviour of someone who is stereotypically feminine. Although women are also given greater opportunity than men to develop interdependence, there are few situations in which this will put them on an equal footing with men, let alone achieve a position of dominance. The caring, openness, and willingness to compromise that are also part of interdependence most frequently place women at a disadvantage in sentimental, business, or intellectual relationships where men are involved.

Traditional psychological theory and research have had little to say about women. As was mentioned in Chapter 1, much of traditional psychology has been developed using male participants, resulting in the fact that psychological theory is applicable mainly to the male experience, which many researchers have regarded as the norm. Until recently, it has been assumed that experimental results based on males can be generalized to everyone, while those from females can be generalized to women only.[2,3] Moreover, the preconception that males are *more* representative of the human race than are females permeates psychological research and theory. Traditional psychology, like other social sciences, can be described by the following characteristics (pp. 118-119)[4]:

1. Women are to a large extent ignored, yet conclusions and theories are phrased in such general terms that they purport to be applicable to all of humanity.
2. If women are considered, they tend to be considered only in so far as they are important for and related to men, not by virtue of their own importance as human subjects.
3. Where both sexes are considered, the male is generally taken as the norm, the female as the deviation from the norm.
4. Sexist content is mirrored in sexist language, as reflected, for instance, in the use of the generic he and the generic man.
5. Sexist science is full of preconceived notions concerning a masculine and feminine nature. Consequently, identical behaviours or situations involving women and men are described and analysed differently according to sex. In other words, we find a consistent double standard within sexist science.
6. By using sexist notions of human nature, and employing a double standard in interpreting findings, sexist science itself becomes one contributing factor in the maintenance of the sex structure from which it arose in the first place and in which it is grounded.

Since many existing psychological theories reflect prevailing values and biases of men, their applicability to the study of women's experience is questionable. What is needed, then, is a new theoretical model that would more accurately reflect the reality of women's psychology, as well as their experience.

The Feminist Perspective in Psychology

The feminist perspective acknowledges the limited scope of the traditional psychological approach vis-à-vis women and proposes the incorporation of alternative approaches, which will yield a model for a psychology of *human* behaviour that is relevant to women as well as to men.[5] It has become increasingly evident, according to the feminist view, that women's behaviour and psychological experiences cannot be understood without taking into account the political aspects associated with the situations in which they occur. As was discussed earlier, there are distinct political elements associated with the concept of gender roles which must be studied in interaction with social and situational factors in order for women's behaviour to be understood.[6] Feminist therapists, aware of the impact of the socio-political environment on the behaviour and well-being of women, study women's economic, political, and historical position in society in order to understand their psychology. They have also pointed to the inadequacies of the hierarchical authority model of the therapist-patient relationship which, in reinforcing the dominance of the therapist, does not assist women in freeing themselves from authority figures.

The approach needed for the study of human behaviour is one which takes into account the socio-political implications of gender roles as they interact with situational factors in their influence on behaviour and cognitions. Only in this way can we begin to gauge the reasons for any psychological differences we observe between women and men. The psychology of human behaviour with a feminist perspective is characterized further by the following aspects: pointing out "new" phenomena; reinterpreting traditional notions and/or bodies of data; and determining the applicability of established theories to a "new" realm of data.[7]

"New" Psychological Phenomena. Because traditional psychology has been based primarily on men's experience, it has failed to deal with many psychological phenomena associated with women. Feminist psychology has pointed to psychological phenomena that are "new" in the sense that they have not been dealt with in existing psychological theory and research. These "new" psychological phenomena thus represent a challenge to traditional psychology and point to the need for extensive revision of existing psychological theory if it is to deal with all of humankind and not just half.

Among the kinds of research that have traditionally excluded women is the study of achievement motivation (discussed in Chapter 5). Based on research with male participants, an elaborate theory of achievement motivation was developed in the fifties. But, as was pointed out earlier, the model failed to account for certain achievement phenomena in women. Research undertaken later with both female and male participants revealed that there were differences not only in their achievement patterns, but also in the way they viewed the causes of their successful achievements. Research findings showed, for example, that when men are successful at a task, they tend to attribute their success to internal factors, particularly to their ability; on the other hand, women attribute their successful achievement to external factors, such as luck.[8-10] Reactions to failure have also been found to differ between female and male participants. Women and girls, more than men and boys, are likely to attribute their failures to their lack of ability.[11,12] These findings have important implications for the way women and girls view their achievements. Because they are less likely than their male counterparts to accept personal responsibility for their successful achievements, as would be the case when success is attributed to luck, women and girls should feel less pride from their success than men and boys. The findings cited above also have implications for how women and girls perceive their future achievement attempts. If someone believes she has failed in the past because of lack of ability, she will likely be unmotivated to try again in the future since, she may reason, her ability level will probably remain unchanged and she will likely fail again in future achievement attempts. These findings are clearly of significance in any explanation of women's underrepresentation among high achievers in professional, artistic, political, and academic spheres.

Another "new" phenomenon that has emerged relatively recently has to do with the way women and men are evaluated. Research has shown that often the behaviour of males and females, even when objectively identical, is not evaluated in the same way. In Chapter 5, findings were cited which indicated that women are judged as less competent than men, even when they possess the same objective qualifications.[13-15] And, not surprisingly, what often happens is that women learn to expect to be less competent than men, the expression of which may constitute a self-fulfilling prophecy. Many of the psychological phenomena associated with women that are emerging in recent research can be understood better when viewed within an existing societal perspective which sees "masculine" as almost uniformly higher in status than "feminine".[16]

Reinterpretation of Traditional Ideas and Data. Recent research and theoretical discussion from a feminist perspective have also provided reinterpretation not only of certain traditional notions in psychology, but also of specific bodies of research data. It is generally held that the psychology of women is more dependent on biological factors than is that of men. So psychological phenomena such as premenstrual tension, postpartum depression and reactions to menopause have traditionally been attributed solely to biological factors. More recently, however, these phenomena have been reinterpreted within a social psychological context where the impact of expectations, changing social roles, and a person's psychological reactions to significant life events are seen as important aetiological factors (see Chapter 9). This is not to deny the influence of factors associated with female physiology. However, it is becoming increasingly evident that even *sex*-specific phenomena are not immune to the influence of socio-cultural factors.

Along the same lines, it has been held, traditionally, that females, are more able to care for the young than are males, simply because of their physiological make-up. In Chapter 2 it was observed that while it is possible that hormones associated with pregnancy, childbirth, and lactation may contribute to a *readiness* to care for the young, there is little information available about the role of hormones in initiating and maintaining maternal behaviour in humans. Research has demonstrated that "new" fathers are capable of engaging in as much or even more nurturant behaviour toward their newborns as are mothers.[17] Additional data suggest that responsivity toward infants can be enhanced by early and continued exposure to the newborn.[18] Not only are males capable of nurturant behaviour, but they can also enjoy being parents. However, there are socio-political factors which must be taken into account in explanations of men's lesser involvement in infant caretaking. Caring for the young, particularly maintenance tasks such as feeding, bathing, and changing diapers, are defined as "women's work". Because of the norms of male deference, many men may regard these tasks as demasculinizing not only because they constitute work typically assigned to women, but also because work on women's turf may be seen as inherently degrading. Thus, in explaining division of labour along gender-role lines, even when it involves sex-related behaviour, it is necessary to take into account factors and influences associated with the immediate environment as well as the socio-political context in which the behaviour occurs.

A feminist approach has also been taken in a reinterpretation of a body of data relating to women's experience in interpersonal interactions. Women's functions have been seen largely as centring around the activities of nurturing and caring for others; the qualities of nurturance and interpersonal sensitivity have been viewed as signs of weakness both by society at large and by traditional psychology. In one review, feminist scholars have reinterpreted a body of data relating to interpersonal interaction and conclude that the social competence of women is superior to that of men in the interpersonal domain.[19] This review examined the psychological literature on nonverbal behaviour, communication styles, proxemics or personal space, influence and power tactics, eye contact, and differences in specific social behaviours. These are some of the gender-role differences found in the literature and cited in this review, many of which were interpreted originally as reflecting positively on men and/or as evidence of women's weaknesses: that women are generally better listeners than men, that women's speech patterns in contrast to men's reflect emotional involvement, that women are more likely to be rewarding to others in interpersonal interactions, that women's communications are more likely to contain interpersonal information, while men discuss nonhuman topics, and that women are generally more empathetic than men.[20]

In their review, the authors redefined competent behaviours as those resulting in positive consequences for all of those involved in an interpersonal interaction. Incompetent behaviours were redefined as those resulting in negative consequences for either their recipient(s) or their instigator. Their conclusions were that

> females surpass males in
> 1.   being more attentive to social stimuli;
> 2.   being more accurate decoders of social stimuli;
> 3.   being more effective encoders of social messages;
> 4.   being more responsive to variations in social input;
> 5.   having language and speech patterns which indicate greater complexity and interpersonal sensitivity; and
> 6.   showing prosocial patterns as opposed to antisocial patterns of social behaviour (p. 148).

In short, reinterpretation of existing psychological data reveals that women have greater interpersonal social competence than men. Contrary to conclusions drawn in the past, when women's interpersonal behaviour was assumed to reflect weaknesses of various kinds, this reinterpretation of the data points to the strengths associated with their interpersonal behaviour.

Based on the "male" model which values differential power and hierarchical structures of dominance, many theories in traditional psychology, when applied to human interactions, perceive the individual as acting against or on other people in order to achieve personalistic goals, while at the same time precluding the possibility of mutuality in relationships.[21] In contrast, a feminist perspective views interpersonal behaviour within a context where harmonious mutuality is seen as a positive aspect of interaction. Viewed from this perspective, women's greater nurturance, interpersonal sensitivity, and their interdependence skills in general, are not seen negatively, as in the past, but are redefined as being of positive value because they promote harmonious and communal relationships between people.

Applicability of Established Theories to "New" Data. The feminist approach has also resulted in discussions and investigations which have used well-established theories to explain some aspect of women's psychology or behaviour. Women's greater vulnerability to depression, for example, has been explained using the theory of "learned helplessness".[22] In the research on which the idea of learned helplessness was based, dogs were placed in experimental situations in which none of their responses could assist them in avoiding electric shock. When the dogs were later placed in situations where they could have prevented an electric shock by a particular response, they failed to show the necessary response; in other words, they became "helpless". The same phenomenon appears in humans. Exposure to conditions where the individual is presented with a series of insoluble problems or inescapable punishment results in expectations that responding is independent of reinforcement.[23] When individuals (both animals and human beings) are placed in situations where none of their actions produces the desired outcome, their behaviour bears a striking resemblance to that of an individual who is described as depressed.[24] A review of differential socialization practices used with girls and boys suggests further that girls may be rendered more predisposed to developing learned helplessness than boys. In general, research which examines socialization practices employed by parents and teachers suggests that the behaviour of girls is less likely to be followed by *both* positive and negative reinforcement than that of boys.[25,26] In this regard, Maccoby and Jacklin,[27] in their review of socialization practices employed with girls and boys, say, "In some situations, boys appear to be more attention-getting, either because they do more things calling for adult response or because parents and teachers see them as having more interesting qualities or potential (p. 335)." Since boys receive more evaluative feedback fr behaviour, both positive and negative, they are more likely to e the opportunity of learning to manipulate their environment to achieve a desirable result. Since girls are less likely to receive evaluative feedback of their behaviour, they are less likely to learn how to effectively manipulate their environment, and thus may be more prone to learned helplessness (see Chapter 9).

Other psychological phenomena associated with women have been analyzed within the context of role theory. For example, it has been noted recently that increasing numbers of married women are holding outside employment while also raising a family. The concept of role strain has been invoked to explain the difficulties experienced by many women in fulfilling all the obligations associated with the roles of wife and mother and also the role of employee. When married women work outside the home, they are seen as taking on the additional role of employee, while maintaining the traditional roles of wife and mother, which are still supposed to take precedence (see Chapter 7). Because normative expectations associated with the parenting role do not stress the role of father as much, men do not experience this type of role strain to the same degree. This kind of conceptual analysis, then, enables us to identify the sources and types of women's conflicting behavioural expectations, particularly in those who are both mothers and employees, and, as such, constitutes the first step in resolving a dilemma experienced by increasing numbers of women.

The issues discussed here are examples of the direction in which a feminist approach has expanded traditional psychological theory and inquiry in ways that can deal with feminine psychology as well as women's experience. But we do not need special laws and theories to deal with the psychology of women. Women's behaviour and psychology, as well as those of men, can be explained using existing theories, provided that these theories are modified in ways that take into account biological, social, and political factors — separately and in combination with each other.

Feminist Psychology and the Interdisciplinary Approach. Much of the new material on women and psychology is characterized by an interdisciplinary orientation drawing on social, political, cultural, biological, and historical material. A substantial number of publications pertaining to women and psychology (both in Canada and the United States) appears in interdisciplinary journals, and courses dealing with the psychology of women are often offered in interdisciplinary women's studies programmes.[28] The practice of integrating biological, historical, and sociopolitical factors with psychological material follows from the view that a person's psychology and personal experience cannot be understood outside their contexts. This view, however, represents a deviation from the major methodological approach held as ideal in mainstream psychology. As one observer has said,[29] psychology demonstrates "physics envy" in its attempts to mould a science of behaviour, using a methodology imported from the "hard" sciences which emphasizes control and manipulation of variables. Often referred to as the "masculine" approach to science, this type of methodology relies on the laboratory experiment, which is directed toward the study of the interrelationships of variables in their "purest" form. This involves simplifying or "purifying" complex psychological variables by lifting them out of their real-life context and importing them into the laboratory. "Extraneous" variables are controlled or held constant and only one or two variables are manipulated and studied in isolation. One writer in the field refers to this practice as "context stripping"[30] where psychological variables that are studied in the laboratory experiment are stripped of the complexity that characterizes them in the real world. Thus, the laboratory experiment, as it has been used in psychology, ". . . requires removing people from their natural embeddedness in their 'normal' human milieus, focuses on isolated bits of the behaviour of individuals, and precludes attention to social, cultural, and historical contexts (p. 4)."[31] Moreover this type of approach as used in the study of interpersonal relationships, for example, obscures the fact that interpersonal relations at the individual level are embedded in and reflect social roles and the institutions in which they are found.[32] The feminist view, on the other hand, acknowledges the connections between the individual's experience and social roles and maintains that understanding of psychological phenomena is not possible without a full appreciation of the influence of the socio-political factors that are frequently embedded in the social roles people enact daily. In this way, though often mistakenly accused of being narrower in focus than traditional psychological inquiry, the feminist perspective is much broader in its approach.

Prospects for the Future

The last two decades have seen significant changes in the feminine gender role. The expansion of the role assigned to women has resulted in the increased availability to women of lifestyle choices that were not only unthinkable in the past, but which were not feasible for most women. Voluntary childlessness, living with a man before or instead of marriage, and simultaneously occupying mothering and employment roles, are just some of the options that have recently become more accessible to women. But the expansion of women's lifestyle choices has not resulted in equality between the sexes as originally expected. The persistence of gender-role stereotypes and their unrealistic behavioural prescriptions frequently function as obstacles that prevent women and men from expanding their roles. And without this role development, equality between the sexes will never be realized in the family, employment, and political sectors.

Changes in the masculine gender role are required not only to accommodate those that have occurred in the feminine one, but also to allow men to fulfill their needs. Recent research in the area of women's studies has led to an awareness that the masculine role is often unrealistic and restrictive in its behavioural and psychological prescriptions, a fact which has important psychological implications for men and their relationships with women. The stress associated with the pressures for achievement and independence which emanate from the masculine gender role, often precludes the expression of interdependence, the ability to express interpersonal needs in emotional relationships. The masculine gender role may be seen, then, as denying men the opportunity of experiencing a significant aspect of human social existence. This may lead not only to men's greater vulnerability to certain forms of psychopathology, but also to a widening of the chasm frequently observed between women's and men's experiences. While women continue to be more interdependent than men, there is a growing awareness of men's need to develop greater interdependence. The direct benefits of greater psychological health and growth would, in themselves, be vastly rewarding. Greater interdependence in men would also bridge the gap that often separates the experiences of women and men, thus increasing the likelihood of more harmonious and satisfying relationships between the sexes.

But if both women and men are to have greater opportunity to realize their human potential, the socialization practices that parents use with their developing youngsters must be revised. Girls and boys have the same capability to develop independence strivings, qualities of interdependence, and behaviours that promote harmonious relationships. If parents reward children of both sexes to the same extent in all these areas, they will have had a great part in furthering the development of complete human beings. They will also be demonstrating that awareness of, and expression of, emotional needs can coexist with independence in one person — boy or girl. Parallel changes are called for in the presentation of symbolic models through media such as books and television. Since these media have such an intense impact on children's development, the creators of books and programmes for children have an obligation to eliminate gender-role stereotypes and to present males and females in more flexible roles. By being exposed to nonstereotypical role models, young children will get the message that their behaviour need not to be restricted by the standards associated with traditional gender roles.

The perpetuation of gender-role stereotypes also characterizes the educational system from elementary school to university. If the purpose of education is to encourage and foster the individual's creative and intellectual strivings without regard to artificial limits, that purpose is not being served when gender-role standards are employed as salient dimensions for evaluating behaviour and achievement. Thus, the need for revision of socialization forms is widespread, existing in the family, the media, and the educational system itself.

From a psychological perspective, there can be no doubt, then, that gender roles must be abolished if all individuals are to have the opportunity to achieve their full human potential. But discrimination on the basis of sex remains one of the most significant obstacles to the achievement of social and political equality between the sexes. The abolition of gender roles will not, in itself, ensure equality between the sexes. To believe that females differ from males is one thing. To believe that females differ from males in ways that render them inferior to males, is quite another. It is precisely this kind of reasoning that is at the heart of most social and political discrimination. Whether this belief is held at the conscious or nonconscious level, it is contrary to the principles held as ideal in any democratic society. It also functions as an obstacle to the full social participation of more than one-half of humankind. While there is some evidence that this belief system is beginning to be eroded, we still have a long way to go in order to achieve a society which does not use gender and sex as bases for evaluating people and their potential.

References

Introduction   1

1.   Eichler, M. *The Double Standard: A Feminist Critique of Feminist Social Science*. London: Croom Helm Ltd., 1980.

2.   Woolley, H.T. Psychological literature: A review of the recent literature on the psychology of sex. *Psychological Bulletin,* 1910, *7,* 335–342.

3.   Carlson, E. R., and Carlson, R. Male and female subjects in personality research. *Journal of Abnormal and Social Psychology,* 1961, *61,* 482–483.

4.   Dan, A. J., and Beekman, S. Male versus female representation in psychological research. *American Psychologist,* 1972, *27,* 1078.

5.   Weisstein, N. Psychology constructs the female, or the fantasy life of the male psychologist. In M. H. Garskof (Ed.). *Roles Women Play: Readings toward Women's Liberation.* Belmont, California: Brooks/Cole, 1971, pp. 68–83.

6.   Greenglass, E. R., and Stewart, M. The under-representation of women in social psychological research. *The Ontario Psychologist,* 1973, *5,* 21–29.

7.   Pyke, S. W., and Stark-Adamec, C. Canadian feminism and psychology: The first decade. *Canadian Psychology,* 1981, *22,* 38–54.

8.   Stark-Adamec, C. (Ed.). *Sex Roles: Origins, Influences, and Implications for Women.* Montreal: Eden Press Women's Publications, 1980.

Gender-Role Differences:
Stereotypes, Behaviour and Biology   **2**

1.   Vaughter, R. M. Review essay: Psychology. *Signs,* 1976, *2,* 120–146.

2.   Unger, R. K. Toward a redefinition of sex and gender. *American Psychologist,* 1979, *34,* 1085–1094.

3.   Graham, J. M., and Stark-Adamec, C. Sex and gender: The need for redefinition. *Resources for Feminist Research,* 1980, *9,* 7.

4.   Vaughter, 1976.

5.   Unger, R. K., and Denmark, F. L. (Eds.). *Woman: Dependent or Independent Variable?* New York: Psychological Dimensions, Inc., 1975.

6.   Slaby, R. G., and Frey, K. S. Development of gender constancy and selective attention to same-sex models. *Child Development,* 1975, *46,* 849–856.

7.   Thompson, S. K. Gender labels and early sex-role development. *Child Development,* 1975, *46,* 339–347.

8.   Kagan, J. *Understanding Children.* New York: Harcourt, Brace, Jovanovich, 1971.

9.   Rosenkrantz, P. S., Vogel, S. R., Bee, H., Broverman, I. K., and Broverman, D. M. Sex-role stereotypes and self-concepts in college students. *Journal of Consulting and Clinical Psychology,* 1968, *32,* 287–295.

10.   Broverman, I. K., Vogel, S. R., Broverman, D. M., Clarkson, F. E., and Rosenkrantz, P. S. Sex-role stereotypes: A current appraisal. *Journal of Social Issues,* 1972, *28,* 59–78.

11.   Rosenkrantz et al., 1968.

12.   Turner, B. F., and Turner, C. B. The political implications of social stereotyping of women and men among black and white college students. *Sociology and Social Research,* 1974, *58,* 155–162.

13. Kagan, J. Acquisition and significance of sex typing and sex role identity. In M. L. Hoffman and L. W. Hoffman (Eds.). *Review of Child Development Research*, vol. 1. New York: Russell Sage, 1964, pp. 137–167.

14. Der-Karabetian, A., and Smith, A. J. Sex-role stereotyping in the United States: Is it changing? *Sex Roles*, 1977, *3*, 193–198.

15. MacBrayer, C. T. Differences in perception of the opposite sex by males and females. *Journal of Social Psychology*, 1960, *52*, 309–314.

16. Der-Karabetian and Smith, 1977.

17. Rosenkrantz et al., 1968.

18. Vogel, S. R., Broverman, I. K., Broverman, D. M., Clarkson, F. E., and Rosenkrantz, P. S. Maternal employment and perception of sex-roles among college students. *Developmental Psychology*, 1970, *3*, 384–391.

19. Maccoby, E. E., and Jacklin, C. N. *The Psychology of Sex Differences*. Stanford, California: Stanford University Press, 1974.

20. Dawe, H. C. An analysis of two hundred quarrels of preschool children. *Child Development*, 1934, *5*, 139–157.

21. Jersild, A. T., and Markey, F. V. Conflicts between preschool children. *Child Development Monograph*, 1935, no. 21.

22. McCandless, B. R., Bilous, B., and Bennett, H. L. Peer popularity and dependence on adults in preschool age socialization. *Child Development*, 1961, *32*, 511–518.

23. Beller, E. K., and Neubauer, P. B. Sex differences and symptom patterns in early childhood. *Journal of Child Psychiatry*, 1963, *2*, 414–433.

24. Beller, E. K. Personality correlates of perceptual discrimination in children. Unpublished progress report, 1962.

25. Serbin, L. A., O'Leary, K. D., Kent, R. N., and Tonick, I. J. A comparison of teacher response to the pre-academic and problem behaviour of boys and girls. *Child Development*, 1973, *44*, 796–804.

26. Pedersen, F. A., and Bell, R. Q. Sex differences in preschool children without histories of complications of pregnancy and delivery. *Developmental Psychology*, 1970, *3*, 10–15.

27. Omark, D. R., Omark, M., and Edelman, M. Dominance hierarchies in young children. Paper presented at the meeting of

the International Congress of Anthropological and Ethnological Sciences, Chicago, 1973.

28. Denmark, F. L., and Diggory, J. C. Sex differences in attitudes toward leaders' display of authoritarian behaviour. *Psychological Reports,* 1966, *18,* 863–872.

29. Maccoby and Jacklin, 1974.

30. Terman, L. M., and Tyler, L. E. Psychological sex differences. In L. Carmichael (Ed.). *Manual of Child Psychology,* 2nd ed. New York: Wiley, 1954, pp. 1064–1114.

31. Omark et al., 1973.

32. Munroe, R. L., and Munroe, R. H. Effect of environmental experience on spatial ability in an East African society. *Journal of Social Psychology,* 1971, *83,* 15–22.

33. Speer, D. C., Briggs, P. F., and Gavolas, R. Concurrent schedules of social reinforcement and dependency behaviour among four-year-old children. *Journal of Experimental Child Psychology,* 1969, *8,* 356–365.

34. Greenglass, E. R. A cross-cultural study of the child's communication with his mother. *Developmental Psychology,* 1971, *5,* 494–499.

35. Golightly, C., Nelson, D., and Johnson, J. Children's dependency scale. *Developmental Psychology,* 1970, *3,* 114–118.

36. Baltes, P. B., and Nesselroade, J. R. Cultural change and adolescent personality development. *Developmental Psychology,* 1972, *7,* 244–256.

37. Whiting, B. B., and Pope, C. P. A cross-cultural analysis of sex differences in the behaviour of children aged three through eleven. *Journal of Social Psychology,* 1973, *91,* 171–188.

38. Hovland, C.I., and Janis, I. L. (Eds.). *Personality and Persuasability.* New Haven: Yale University Press, 1959.

39. Kagan, J., and Moss, H. A. *Birth to Maturity: A Study in Psychological Development.* New York: Wiley, 1962.

40. Lindzey, G., and Goldberg, M. Motivational differences between males and females as measured by the TAT. *Journal of Personality,* 1953, *22,* 101–117.

41. Sears, R. R., Whiting, J., Nowlis, V., and Sears, P. Some child rearing antecedents of aggression and dependency in young children. *Genetic Psychology Monographs,* 1953, *47,* 135–234.

42. Siegel, A. E., Stolz, L. M., Hitchcock, E. A., and Adamson, J. Children of working mothers and their controls. *Child Development*, 1959, *30*, 533–546.

43. Bardwick, J. M., and Douvan, E. Ambivalence: The socialization of women. In V. Gornick and B. K. Moran (Eds.). *Woman in Sexist Society*. New York: Basic Books, 1971, pp. 225–241.

44. Terman and Tyler, 1954.

45. Walker, R. N. Some temperament traits in children as viewed by their peers, their teachers, and themselves. *Monographs of the Society for Research in Child Development*, 1967, *32*.

46. Hannah, R., Storm, T., and Caird, W. K. Sex differences and relationship among neuroticism, extraversion, and expressed fears. *Perceptual and Motor Skills*, 1965, *20*, 1214–1216.

47. Sarason, S. B., Lighthall, F. F., Davidson, K. S., Waite, R. R., and Ruebush, B. K. *Anxiety in Elementary School Children*. New York: Wiley, 1960.

48. Mendelsohn, G. A., and Griswold, B. B. Anxiety and repression as predictors of the use of incidental cues in problem solving. *Journal of Personality and Social Psychology*, 1967, *6*, 353–359.

49. Baltes and Nesselroade, 1972.

50. Cowen, E. L., Zax, M., Klein, R., Izzo, L. D., and Trost, M. A. The relation of anxiety in school children to school record, achievement and behavioural measures. *Child Development*, 1965, *36*, 685–695.

51. Maccoby and Jacklin, 1974.

52. Sarason, S. B., Hill, K. T., and Zimbardo, P. G. A longitudinal study of the relation of test anxiety to performance on intelligence and achievement tests. *Monographs of the Society for Research in Child Development*, 1964, *29*, no. 98.

53. Hill, K. T., and Sarason, S. B. The relation of text anxiety and defensiveness to test and school performance over the elementary-school years. *Monographs of the Society for Research in Child Development*, 1966, *31*, no. 104.

54. Lekarczyk, D. T., and Hill, K. T. Self-esteem, test anxiety, stress, and verbal learning. *Developmental Psychology*, 1969, *1*, 147–154.

55. Money, J., and Ehrhardt, A. A. *Man and Woman, Boy and Girl*. Baltimore: The Johns Hopkins University Press, 1972.

56.   Ibid.

57.   Jost, A. A new look at the mechanism controlling sex differen-
       tiation in mammals. *Johns Hopkins Medical Journal,* 1972,
       130, 38–53.

58.   Moulton, R. A survey and reevaluation of the concept of penis envy.
       Contemporary Psychoanalysis, 1970, *7,* 84–104.

59.   Ibid.

60.   Sherfey, M. J. *The Nature and Evolution of Female Sexuality.* New
       York: Random House, 1972.

61.   Money, J., Hampson, J. G., and Hampson, J. L. Imprinting and
       the establishment of gender role. *Archives of Neurology and
       Psychiatry,* 1957, *77,* 333–336.

62.   Money, J., Hampson, J. L., and Hampson, J. G. An examination of
       some basic sexual concepts: The evidence of human herma-
       phroditism. *Bulletin of the Johns Hopkins Hospital,* 1955,
       97, 301–319.

63.   Money and Ehrhardt, 1972.

64.   Money, J., and Tucker, P. *Sexual Signatures: On Being a Man or a
       Woman.* Boston: Little, Brown, 1975.

65.   Ibid.

66.   Money et al., 1957.

67.   Money and Ehrhardt, 1972.

68.   Ibid.

69.   Money, J. Prenatal hormones and postnatal socialization in gender
       identity differentiation. In J. K. Cole and R. Dienstbier
       (Eds.). *Nebraska Symposium on Motivation 1973.* Lincoln:
       University of Nebraska Press, 1974, pp. 221–295.

70.   Stoller, R. J. *Sex and Gender: On the Development of Masculinity
       and Femininity.* New York: Science House, 1968.

71.   Diamond, M. A critical evaluation of the ontogeny of human sexual
       behaviour. *Quarterly Review of Biology,* 1965, *40,* 147–175.

72.   Ibid.

73.   Young, W. C., Goy, R. W., and Phoenix, C. H. Hormones and
       sexual behaviour. *Science,* 1964, *143,* 212–218.

74.   Ehrhardt, A. A., and Baker, S. W. Hormonal aberrations and their
       implications for the understanding of normal sex differentia-

tion. Paper presented at the meeting of the Society for Research in Child Development, Philadelphia, 1973.

75. Edwards, D. A. Early androgen stimulation and aggressive behaviour in male and female mice. *Physiology and Behaviour,* 1969, *4,* 333–338.

76. Weitz, S. *Sex Roles: Biological, Psychological, and Social Foundations.* New York: Oxford University Press, 1977.

77. Maurer, C. D. The effects of sex, parental status, and relationship of opponent on physical aggression and hostility of married subjects. *Dissertation Abstracts International,* 1973, *33,* 4518B (University Microfilms no. 73–6627).

78. Straus, M. A., Gelles, R. J., and Steinmetz, S. K. Violence in the family: An assessment of knowledge and research needs. Paper presented at the meeting of the American Association for the Advancement of Science, Boston, 1976.

79. Gelles, R. J. Child abuse as psychopathology. *American Journal of Orthopsychiatry,* 1973, *43,* 611–621.

80. Gil, D. G. *Violence against Children.* Cambridge, Massachusetts: Harvard University Press, 1970.

81. Rosenblatt, J. S. The development of maternal responsiveness in the rat. *American Journal of Orthopsychiatry,* 1969, *39,* 36–56.

82. Bowlby, J. *Attachment.* New York: Basic Books, 1969.

83. Lorenz, K. *Studies in Animal and Human Behaviour,* vol. 1. Cambridge, Massachusetts: Harvard University Press, 1970.

84. Rosenblatt, 1969.

85. Ibid.

86. Wortis, R. P. The acceptance of the concept of the maternal role by behavioural scientists: Its effects on women. *The American Journal of Orthopsychiatry,* 1971, *41,* 733–746.

87. Parke, R. D., and O'Leary, S. E. Family interaction in the newborn period: Some findings, some observations, and some unresolved issues. In K. Riegel and J. Meacham (Eds.). *The Developing Individual in a Changing World,* vol. 2. The Hague: Mouton, 1976, pp. 653–663.

88. Bell, R. Q. Stimulus control of parent or caretaker behaviour by offspring. *Developmental Psychology,* 1971, *4,* 63–72.

89. Thomas, A., Chess, S., Birch, H. G., Hertzig, M. E., and Korn, S. *Behavioural Individuality in Early Childhood.* New York: New York University Press, 1963.

90. Stannard, U. Adam's rib or the woman within. *Transaction,* 1970, *8,* 24–35.

91. Farrell, W. *The Liberated Man.* New York: Random House, 1974.

92. Harford, T. C., Willis, C. H., and Deabler, H. L. Personality correlates of masculinity-femininity. *Psychological Reports,* 1967, *21,* 881–884.

93. Mussen, P. H. Long-term consequences of masculinity of interests in adolescence. *Journal of Consulting Psychology,* 1962, *26,* 435–440.

94. Cosentino, F., and Heilbrun, A. B., Jr. Anxiety correlates of sex-role identity in college students. *Psychological Reports,* 1964, *14,* 729–730.

95. Gall, M. D. The relationship between masculinity-femininity and manifest anxiety. *Journal of Clinical Psychology,* 1969, *25,* 294–295.

96. Sears, R. R. Relation of early socialization experiences to self-concepts and gender role in middle childhood. *Child Development,* 1970, *41,* 267–289.

97. Bem, S. L. Androgony vs. the tight little lives of fluffy women and chesty men. *Psychology Today,* 1975, *9,* 58–59, 61–62.

98. Jung, C. G. *Two Essays on Analytical Psychology.* Trans. R. F. C. Hull. New York: Pantheon Books, 1953. (Originally published, 1943.)

99. Bem, S. L. The measurement of psychological androgyny. *Journal of Consulting and Clinical Psychology,* 1974, *42,* 155–162.

100. Ibid.

101. Bem, S. L. Sex role adaptability: One consequence of psychological androgyny. *Journal of Personality and Social Psychology,* 1975, *31,* 634–643.

102. Bem, S. L. Probing the promise of androgyny. In A. G. Kaplan and J. P. Bean (Eds.). *Beyond Sex-Role Stereotypes: Readings toward a Psychology of Androgyny.* Boston: Little, Brown, 1976, pp. 48–62.

103. Maffeo, P. A. Conceptions of sex role development and androgyny: Implications for mental health and for psychotherapy.

Journal of the American Medical Women's Association, 1978, *33,* 225–230.

104. Bem, S. L., and Lenney, E. Sex typing and the avoidance of cross-sex behaviour. *Journal of Personality and Social Psychology,* 1976, *33,* 48–54.

105. Bem, S. L., Martyna, W., and Watson, C. Sex typing and androgyny: Further explorations of the expressive domain. *Journal of Personality and Social Psychology,* 1976, *34,* 1016–1023.

106. Bem, 1975. See footnote #101.

107. Jones, W. H., Chernovetz, M. E., and Hansson, R. O. The enigma of androgyny: Differential implications for males and females? *Journal of Consulting and Clinical Psychology,* 1978, *46,* 298–313.

108. Pyke, S. W. Androgyny: A dead end or a promise. In C. Stark-Adamec (Ed.). *Sex roles: Origins, Influences, and Implications for Women.* Montreal: Eden Press Women's Publications, 1980, pp. 20–32.

109. Ibid.

110. Rebecca, M., Hefner, R., and Oleshansky, B. A model of sex-role transcendence. *Journal of Social Issues,* 1976, *32,* 197–206.

111. Kaplan, A. G., and Bean, J. P. Conclusion/From sex stereotypes to androgyny: Considerations of societal and individual change. In *Beyond Sex-Role Stereotypes: Readings toward a Psychology of Androgyny,* pp. 383–392.

112. Bem, 1976.

Socialization of Girls and Boys: How Gender Roles Are Acquired ## 3

1. Mead, M. *Sex and Temperament in Three Primitive Societies.* New York: William Morrow, 1935.

2. Fortune, W. F. Arapesh warfare. *American Anthropologist,* 1939, *41,* 22–41.

3. D'Andrade, R. G. Sex differences and cultural institutions. In E. E. Maccoby (Ed.). *The Development of Sex Differences.* Stanford, California: Stanford University Press, 1966, pp. 174–204.

4. Sontag, L. W., Steele, W. G., and Lewis, M. The fetal and maternal cardiac response to environmental stress. *Human Development,* 1969, *12,* 1–9.

5. Cited in Hoffman, L. W. Changes in family roles, socialization, and sex differences. *American Psychologist,* 1977, *32,* 644–657.

6. Condry, J., and Condry, S. Sex differences: A study of the eye of the beholder. *Child Development,* 1976, *47,* 812–819.

7. Rubin, J. Z., Provenzano, F. J., and Luria, Z. The eye of the beholder: Parents' views on sex of newborns. *American Journal of Orthopsychiatry,* 1974, *44,* 512–519.

8. Moss, H. A. Sex, age, and state as determinants of mother-infant interaction. *Merrill-Palmer Quarterly,* 1967, *13,* 19–36.

9. Yarrow, L. J., Rubenstein, J. L., and Pedersen, F. A. Dimensions of early stimulation: Differential effects on infant development. Paper presented at the meeting of the Society for Research in Child Development, 1971.

10. Lewis, M. State as an infant-environmental interaction: An analysis of mother-infant behaviour as a function of sex. *Merrill-Palmer Quarterly,* 1972, *18,* 95–121.

11. Garai, J. E., and Scheinfeld, A. Sex differences in mental and behavioural traits. *Genetic Psychology Monographs,* 1968, *77,* 169–299.

12. Minton, C., Kagan, J., and Levine, J. A. Maternal control and obedience in the two-year-old. *Child Development*, 1971, *42*, 1873–1894.

13. Pedersen, F. A., and Robson, K. S. Father participation in infancy. *American Journal of Orthopsychiatry*, 1969, *39*, 466–472.

14. Maccoby, E. E., and Jacklin, C. N. *The Psychology of Sex Differences*. Stanford, California: Stanford University Press, 1974.

15. Lewis, 1972.

16. Goldberg, S., and Lewis, M. Play behaviour in the year-old infant: Early sex differences. *Child Development*, 1969, *40*, 21–31.

17. Rheingold, H. L., and Cook, K. V. The contents of boys' and girls' rooms as an index of parents' behaviour. *Child Development*, 1975, *46*, 459 463.

18. Lansky, L. M. The family structure also affects the model: Sex-role attitudes in parents of preschool children. *Merrill-Palmer Quarterly*, 1967, *13*, 139–150.

19. Fling, S., and Manosevitz, M. Sex typing in nursery school children's play interests. *Developmental Psychology*, 1972, *7*, 146–152.

20. Block, J. H. Another look at sex differentiation in the socialization behaviours of mothers and fathers. In J. A. Sherman and F. L. Denmark (Eds.). *The Psychology of Women: Future Directions in Research*. New York: Psychological Dimensions, 1978, pp. 29–87.

21. Maccoby and Jacklin, 1974.

22. Ban, P., and Lewis, M. Mothers and fathers, girls and boys: Attachment behaviour in the one-year-old. Paper presented at the meeting of the Eastern Psychological Association, New York, April, 1971.

23. Rebelsky, F., and Hanks, C. Fathers' verbal interaction with infants in the first three months of life. *Child Development*, 1971, *42*, 63–68.

24. Goodenough, E. W. Interest in persons as an aspect of sex difference in the early years. *Genetic Psychology Monographs*, 1957, *55*, 287–323.

25. Lansky, 1967.

26. Tasch, R. J. The role of the father in the family. *Journal of Experimental Education*, 1952, *20*, 319–361.

278 References

27. Van Gelder, L., and Carmichael, C. But what about our sons? *Ms.*, 1975, *4*, 52–56, 94–95.

28. Maccoby and Jacklin, 1974.

29. Block, J. H. Issues, problems, and pitfalls in assessing sex differences: A critical review of the psychology of sex differences. *Merrill-Palmer Quarterly*, 1976, *22*, 283–308.

30. Block, 1978.

31. Fagot, B. I. How parents reinforce feminine role behaviours in toddler girls. Paper presented to the National Conference on Feminist Psychology: Research, theory and practice. Association for Women in Psychology, St. Louis, Missouri, February, 1977.

32. Callard, E. D. Achievement motive in the four-year-old and its relationship to achievement expectancies of the mother. Unpublished doctoral dissertation, University of Michigan, 1964.

33. Hoffman, 1977.

34. Fagot, 1977.

35. Ibid.

36. Block, 1978.

37. Lynn, D. B. *The Father: His Role in Child Development*. Monterey, California: Wadsworth, 1974.

38. Freud, S. 1933. The dissection of the psychical personality. In J. Strachey (Ed. and Trans.). *New Introductory Lectures on Psychoanalysis*. New York: Norton, 1965, pp. 57–80.

39. Freud, S. 1923. The ego and the id. In J. Strachey (Ed.). *The Standard Edition of the Complete Psychological Works of Sigmund Freud*, vol. 19. London: The Hogarth Press, 1961, pp. 3–66.

40. Freud, 1933. See footnote #38.

41. Freud, S. 1933. Anxiety and instinctual life. In *New Introductory Lectures on Psychoanalysis*, pp. 81–111.

42. Freud, S. 1933. Femininity. In *New Introductory Lectures on Psychoanalysis*, pp. 112–135.

43. Freud, S. 1925. Some psychological consequences of the anatomical distinction between the sexes. In J. Strachey (Ed. and Trans.). *The Collected Papers of Sigmund Freud*, vol. 5. New York: Basic Books, 1959, pp. 186–197.

44. Ibid.

45. Freud, 1933. See footnote #42.

46. Ibid.

47. Millett, K. *Sexual Politics.* New York: Doubleday, 1970. Copyright 1969, 1970 by Kate Millett. Reprinted by permission of Doubleday & Company, Inc.

48. Shafer, R. Problems in Freud's psychology of women. In H. P. Blum (Ed.). *Female Psychology: Contemporary Psychoanalytic Views.* New York: International Universities Press, 1977, pp. 331–360.

49. Money, J., and Ehrhardt, A. A. *Man and Woman, Boy and Girl.* Baltimore: The Johns Hopkins University Press, 1972.

50. Sherman, J. A. *On the Psychology of Women: A Survey of Empirical Studies.* Springfield, Illinois: C. C. Thomas, 1971.

51. Masters, W. H., and Johnson, V. E. *Human Sexual Response.* Boston: Little, Brown, 1966.

52. Deutsch, H. *The Psychology of Women: A Psychoanalytic Interpretation,* vol. I. New York: Grune and Stratton, 1944.

53. Deutsch, H. *The Psychology of Women: A Psychoanalytic Interpretation,* vol. II. New York: Grune and Stratton, 1945.

54. Horney, K. 1926. The flight from womanhood. In K. Horney. *Feminine Psychology.* New York: Norton, 1973, pp. 54–70.

55. Horney, K. 1935. The problem of feminine masochism. In K. Horney. *Feminine Psychology,* pp. 214–233.

56. Bandura, A., and Huston, A. C. Identification as a process of incidental learning. *Journal of Abnormal and Social Psychology,* 1961, *63,* 311–318.

57. Hetherington, E. M. A developmental study of the effects of sex of the dominant parent on sex-role preference, identification, and imitation in children. *Journal of Personality and Social Psychology,* 1965, *2,* 188–194.

58. Hetherington, E. M., and Frankie, G. Effects of parental dominance, warmth, and conflict on imitation in children. *Journal of Personality and Social Psychology,* 1967, *6,* 119–125.

59. Parsons, T. Family structure and the socialization of the child. In T. Parsons and R. F. Bales (Eds.). *Family, Socialization, and Interaction Process.* New York: Free Press, 1955, pp. 35–131.

60. Slater, P. E. Parental role differentiation. *The American Journal of Sociology,* 1961, *67,* 296–308.

61.   Mischel, W. A social-learning view of sex differences in behaviour. In *The Development of Sex Differences,* pp. 56–81.

62.   Mussen, P. H. Early sex-role development. In D. A. Goslin (Ed.). *Handbook of Socialization Theory and Research.* Chicago: Rand McNally, 1969, pp. 707–731.

63.   Bandura, A. Vicarious processes: A case of no-trial learning. In L. Berkowitz (Ed.). *Advances in Experimental Social Psychology,* vol. 2. New York: Academic Press, 1965, pp. 1–55.

64.   Bandura, A., Ross, D., and Ross, S. Transmission of aggression through imitation of aggressive models. *Journal of Abnormal and Social Psychology,* 1961, *63,* 575–582.

65.   Bandura, A., and Walters, R. H. *Social Learning and Personality Development.* New York: Holt, Rinehart & Winston, 1963.

66.   Maccoby and Jacklin, 1974.

67.   Mischel, W. Sex-typing and socialization. In P. H. Mussen (Ed.). *Carmichael's Manual of Child Psychology,* vol. II, 3rd ed. New York: Wiley, 1970, pp. 3–72.

68.   Kohlberg, L. A cognitive-developmental analysis of children's sex-role concepts and attitudes. In *The Development of Sex Differences,* pp. 82–173.

69.   Mussen, 1969.

70.   White, S. The learning theory approach. In P. H. Mussen (Ed.). *Carmichael's Manual of Child Psychology,* vol. I, 3rd ed. New York: Wiley, 1970, pp. 657–701.

71.   Endler, N. S., Boulter, L. R., and Osser, H. (Eds.). *Contemporary Issues in Developmental Psychology,* 2nd ed. New York: Holt, Rinehart & Winston, 1976, pp. 1–10.

Other Agents of Gender Role Socialization   **4**

1. McCracken, G., and Walcutt, C. E. *Basic Reading* (Lippincott, 1963), California State Department of Education, 1969.

2. Ibid.

3. O'Donnel, M. *Around the Corner.* New York: Harper and Row, 1966.

4. Mead, M. Research in contemporary cultures. In H. Guetzkow (Ed.). *Groups, Leadership and Men.* Pittsburgh: Carnegie Press, 1951, pp. 106–118.

5. Weitzman, L. J., Eifler, D., Hokada, E., and Ross, C. Sex-role socialization in picture books for preschool children. *American Journal of Sociology,* 1972, *77,* 1125–1150.

6. Women on Words and Images. *Dick and Jane as Victims: Sex Stereotyping in Children's Readers.* Princeton, New Jersey: Women on Words and Images, 1975.

7. Vukelich, C., McCarty, C., and Nanis, C. Sex bias in children's books. *Childhood Education,* 1976, *52,* 220–222.

8. Weitzman et al., 1972.

9. Women on Words and Images, 1975.

10. Lieberman, M. R. "Some day my prince will come": Female acculturation through the fairy tale. *College English,* 1972, *34,* 383–395.

11. Ibid.

12. Wright, V. The rape of children's minds: A survey of the most frequently used grades 1, 2 and 3 readers in the Borough of North York. Interim Report no. 2, Ad Hoc Committee Respecting the Status of Women in the North York System, June 3, 1975.

13. Weitzman et al., 1972.

14.   Frasher, R., and Walker, A. Sex roles in early reading textbooks. *Reading Teacher,* 1972, *25,* 741–749.

15.   Beach, D. L. Fun with Dick and Jane. *Spectrum,* 1971, *47,* 8–9.

16.   Women on Words and Images, 1975.

17.   Ibid.

18.   Pyke, S. W. Children's literature: Conceptions of sex roles. In W. E. Mann and L. Wheatcroft (Eds.). *Canada: A Sociological Profile.* Toronto: Copp Clark, 1976, pp. 158–171.

19.   Ibid.

20.   Lieberman, 1972.

21.   Frasher and Walker, 1972.

22.   O'Donnell, R. W. Sex bias in primary social studies textbooks. *Educational Leadership,* 1973, *31,* 137–141.

23.   Pyke, 1976.

24.   Vukelich et al., 1976.

25.   Women on Words and Images, 1975.

26.   Ibid.

27.   Ibid.

28.   Wright, 1975.

29.   *The Baltimore Sunday Sun,* May 23, 1971.

30.   McGraw-Hill Book Company. Guidelines for equal treatment of the sexes. *Elementary English,* 1975, *52,* 725–733.

31.   *The Globe and Mail* (Toronto), October 5, 1972.

32.   Women on Words and Images, 1975.

33.   Labour Canada. *1978–1979 Women in the Labour Force; Part 1 Participation.* Cat. no. L38–30/1979–1. Table 1b. Population, labour force, and participation rates, by sex, Canada, 1969, 1974 and 1979. Ottawa, 1980, p. 11.

34.   Labour Canada. *1978–1979 Women in the Labour Force: Part 1 Participation.* Table 24b. Female population and female labour force, by marital status and participation rates of women in the labour force, Canada, 1969, 1974 and 1979. Ottawa, 1980, p. 69.

35.   Statistics Canada. *Canada Year Book 1978–79.* Cat. no. CS11–202/

1978. Table 4.28. Families by family structure, 1966, 1971 and 1976. Ottawa, 1978, p. 164.

36. Statistics Canada. *Vital Statistics,* vol. II. *Marriages and Divorces 1979.* Cat. no. 84–205. Table 10. Divorces granted and rates per 100 000 population and per 100 000 married women 15 years and over, with per cent change from previous year, Canada and provinces, 1975–1979. Ottawa, 1981, pp. 16–17.

37. Women on Words and Images, 1975.

38. McClelland, D. C. *The Achieving Society.* Princeton, New Jersey: Van Nostrand, 1961.

39. McArthur, L. Z., and Eisen, S. V. Achievements of male and female storybook characters as determinants of achievement behaviour by boys and girls. *Journal of Personality and Social Psychology,* 1976, *33,* 467–473.

40. Pyke, 1976.

41. Nielsen, A. C. Quoted in Waters, H. F. What T.V. does to kids. *Newsweek,* February 21, 1977, 62–70.

42. Barnouw, E. *A History of Broadcasting in the United States, vol. III–1953: The Image Empire.* New York: Oxford University Press, 1972.

43. Spock, B. Quoted in Waters, 1977. See footnote #41.

44. Berkowitz, L. *Aggression: A Social Psychological Analysis.* New York: McGraw-Hill, 1962.

45. Bandura, A., and Walters, R. H. *Social Learning and Personality Development.* New York: Holt, Rinehart & Winston, 1963.

46. Liebert, R. M., Neale, J. M., and Davidson, E. S. *The Early Window: Effects of Television on Children and Youth.* New York: Pergamon, 1973.

47. Levinson, R. M. From Olive Oyl to Sweet Polly Purebread: Sex role stereotypes and televised cartoons. *Journal of Popular Culture,* 1975, *9,* 561–572.

48. Busby, L. J. Defining the sex-role standard in network children's programs. *Journalism Quarterly,* 1974, *51,* 690–696.

49. Levinson, 1975.

50. Ibid.

51. Busby, 1974.

52. Ibid.

53. Dohrmann, R. A gender profile of children's educational T.V. *Journal of Communication,* 1975, *25,* 56–65.

54. Ibid.

55. Barcus, F. E. Saturday children's television. A report of T.V. programming and advertising on Boston commercial television. Prepared for Action for Children's Television, Newton, Massachusetts, July, 1971.

56. McArthur, L. Z., and Eisen, S. V. Television and sex-role stereotyping. *Journal of Applied Social Psychology,* 1976, *6,* 329–351.

57. Ibid.

58. Frueh, T., and McGhee, P. E. Traditional sex role development and amount of time spent watching television. *Developmental Psychology,* 1975, *11,* 109.

59. Beuf, A. Doctor, lawyer, household drudge. *Journal of Communication,* 1964, *24,* 142–145.

60. McArthur and Eisen, 1976. See footnote #56.

61. Grambs, J. D., and Waetjen, W. B. *Sex: Does It Make a Difference?* Belmont, California: Wadsworth, 1975.

62. Kenyon, G. S. Attitude toward sport and physical activity among adolescents from four English-speaking countries. In G. Luschen (Ed.). *The Cross-Cultural Analysis of Sports and Games.* Champaign, Illinois: Stipes, 1970, pp. 138–155.

63. Grambs and Waetjen, 1975.

64. Levy, B. The school's role in the sex-role stereotyping of girls: A feminist review of the literature. *Feminist Studies,* 1972, *1,* 5–23.

65. Ibid.

66. Tobias, S. The problem: Math anxiety and math avoidance. The Solution: Reentry mathematics. *American Association for Higher Education Bulletin,* 1979, *32,* 1, 3–4, 13–14.

67. Donahue, T. J., and Costar, J. W. Counselor discrimination against young women in career selection. *Journal of Counseling Psychology,* 1977, *24,* 481–486.

68. Chasen, B. Sex-role stereotyping and prekindergarten teachers. *Elementary School Journal,* 1973–74, *74,* 220–235.

69. Ricks, F. A., and Pyke, S. W. Teacher perceptions and attitudes which foster or maintain sex role differences. *Interchange,* 1973, *4,* 26–33.

70. Serbin, L. A., and O'Leary, K. D. How nursery schools teach girls to shut up. *Psychology Today,* 1975, *9,* 56–57, 102–103.

71. Levy, 1972.

72. Pollack, J. H. Are teachers fair to boys? *Today's Health,* 1968, *46,* 21.

73. Minuchin, P. P. Sex differences in children. *The National Elementary Principal,* 1966, *46,* 45–48.

Gender-Role Differences in Cognitive Ability and Achievement   **5**

1.   Maccoby, E. E., and Jacklin, C.N. *The Psychology of Sex Differences.* Stanford, California: Stanford University Press, 1974.

2.   Jacklin, C.N. Epilogue. In M.A. Wittig and A.C. Petersen (Eds.). *Sex-Related Differences in Cognitive Functioning.* New York: Academic Press, 1979, pp. 357–371.

3.   Bock, R. D., and Kolakowski, D. Further evidence of sex-linked major gene influence on human spatial visualizing ability. *American Journal of Human Genetics,* 1973, *25,* 1–14.

4.   Corah, N. L. Differentiation in children and their parents. *Journal of Personality,* 1965, *33,* 300–308.

5.   Hartlage, L. C. Sex-linked inheritance of spatial ability. *Perceptual and Motor Skills,* 1970, *31,* 610.

6.   Vandenberg, S. G., and Kuse, A. R. Spatial ability: A critical review of the sex-linked major gene hypothesis. In *Sex-Related Differences in Cognitive Functioning,* pp. 67–95.

7.   Maccoby and Jacklin, 1974.

8.   de Wolf, V. *High School Mathematics Preparation and Sex Differences in Quantitative Abilities.* Spokane, Washington: Educational Assessment Center Project no. 523, 1977.

9.   Fennema, E., and Sherman, J. A. Sex-related differences in mathematics achievement, spatial visualization and affective factors. *American Educational Research Journal,* 1977, *14,* 51–71.

10.   Witkin, H. A., Dyk, R. B., Faterson, H. F., Goodenough, D. R., and Karp, S. A. *Psychological Differentiation: Studies of Development.* New York: Wiley, 1962.

11.   Maccoby and Jacklin, 1974.

12.   Sherman, J. A. Problem of sex differences in space perception and

aspects of intellectual functioning. *Psychological Review,* 1967, *74,* 290–299.

13. Witkin, H. A., Birnbaum, J., Lomonaco, S., Lehr, S., and Herman, J. L. Cognitive patterning in congenitally totally blind children. *Child Development,* 1968, *39,* 767–786.

14. Maccoby and Jacklin, 1974.

15. Witkin et al., 1962.

16. McClelland, D. C. Wanted: A new self-image for women. In R. J. Lifton (Ed.). *The Woman in America.* Boston: Beacon, 1964, pp. 173–192.

17. Maccoby and Jacklin, 1974.

18. Ibid.

19. Fennema and Sherman, 1977.

20. Fox, L. H. Gifted girls: Scientists and mathematicians of the future. Paper presented at the meeting of the National Association for Gifted Children, Kansas City, Missouri, October, 1976.

21. Fox, L. H. Women and the career relevance of mathematics and science. *School Science and Mathematics,* 1976, *26,* 347–353.

22. Sells, L. Cited in Tobias, S. The problem: Math anxiety and math avoidance. The solution: Reentry mathematics. *American Association for Higher Education Bulletin,* 1979, *32,* 3 ff.

23. Maccoby and Jacklin, 1974.

24. Sherman, J. A. *On the Psychology of Women: A Survey of Empirical Studies.* Springfield, Illinois: C. C. Thomas, 1971.

25. Fennema, E. Influence of selected cognitive, affective and educational variables on sex related differences in mathematics learning and studying. In J. Shoemaker (Ed.). Women and Mathematics: Research Perspectives for Change. (N.I.E. Papers in Education and Work: No. 8) Washington, D.C., Education and Work Group, The National Institute of Education, U.S. Department of Health, Education and Welfare, 1977.

26. Sherman, J. A. The effect of genetic factors on women's achievement in mathematics. In Women and Mathematics: Research Perspectives for Change. See footnote #25.

27. Fox, L. H. The effects of sex role socialization on mathematics par-

288 References

ticipation and achievement. In Women and Mathematics: Research Perspectives for Change. See footnote #25.

28. Milton, G. A. Five studies of the relation between sex role identification and achievement in problem solving. Technical Report no. 3, Dept. of Industrial Admin., Department of Psychology, Yale University, 1958.

29. Pedersen, D. M., Shinedling, M. M., and Johnson, D. L. Effects of sex of examiner and subject on children's quantitative test performance. *Journal of Personality and Social Psychology,* 1968, *10,* 251–254.

30. Tobias, S. Math anxiety: Why is a smart girl like you counting on your fingers? *Ms.,* 1976, *5,* 56–59 ff.

31. Fox, L. H., Tobin, D., and Brody, L. Sex-role socialization and achievement in mathematics. In *Sex-Related Differences in Cognitive Functioning,* pp. 303–332.

32. Fox et al., 1979.

33. Maccoby and Jacklin, 1974.

34. Ibid.

35. Ibid.

36. Greer, G. *The Obstacle Race: The Fortunes of Women Painters and Their Work.* London: Secker and Warburg, 1979.

37. *The Toronto Star,* October 12, 1979.

38. Helson, R. M. Creativity in women. In J. A. Sherman and F. L. Denmark (Eds.). *The Psychology of Women: Future Directions in Research.* New York: Psychological Dimensions, 1978, pp. 553–604.

39. Helson, R. M. Women mathematicians and the creative personality. *Journal of Consulting and Clinical Psychology,* 1971, *36,* 210–220.

40. Fasteau, M. F. *The Male Machine.* New York: McGraw-Hill, 1974. Copyright © 1974 by Marc Fiegen Fasteau. Reprinted by permission of the publisher.

41. McClelland, D. C., Atkinson, J. W., Clark, R. A., and Lowell, R. L. *The Achievement Motive.* New York: Appleton-Century-Crofts, 1953.

42. Ibid.

43. McClelland, D. C., Clark, R. A., Roby, T. B., and Atkinson, J. W. The projective expression of needs. IV. The effect of the need for achievement on thematic apperception. *Journal of Experimental Psychology,* 1949, *39,* 242-255.

44. Atkinson, J. W., and Litwin, G. H. Achievement motive and test anxiety conceived as motive to approach success and motive to avoid failure. *Journal of Abnormal and Social Psychology,* 1960, *60,* 52-63.

45. Atkinson, J. W. (Ed.). *Motives in Fantasy, Action, and Society.* Princeton, New Jersey: Van Nostrand, 1958.

46. Entwisle, D. R. To dispel fantasies about fantasy-based measures of achievement motivation. *Psychological Bulletin,* 1972, *77,* 377-391.

47. Veroff, J., Wilcox, S., and Atkinson, J. W. The achievement motive in high school and college-age women. *Journal of Abnormal and Social Psychology,* 1953, *48,* 103-119.

48. Atkinson, 1958.

49. McClelland, D. C. *The Achieving Society.* Princeton, New Jersey: Van Nostrand, 1961.

50. Field, W. F. The effects on thematic apperception of certain experimentally aroused needs. Cited in *The Achievement Motive,* p. 80.

51. Maccoby and Jacklin, 1974.

52. Stein, A. H., and Bailey, M. M. The socialization of achievement orientation in females. *Psychological Bulletin,* 1973, *80,* 345-366.

53. Deaux, K. *The Behavior of Women and Men.* Monterey, California: Brooks/Cole, 1976.

54. Horner, M. S. Sex differences in achievement motivation and performance in competitive and noncompetitive situations. Unpublished doctoral dissertation, University of Michigan, 1968.

55. Horner, M. S. Femininity and successful achievement: A basic inconsistency. In Bardwick, J. M., Douvan, E., Horner, M. S., and Gutmann, D. *Feminine Personality and Conflict.* Belmont, California: Brooks/Cole, 1970, pp. 45-74. Copyright © 1970 by Wadsworth Publishing Company, Inc. Reprinted by permission of Brooks/Cole Publishing Company, Monterey, California 93940.

56. Horner, M. S. Toward an understanding of achievement-related conflicts in women. *Journal of Social Issues,* 1972, *28,* 157–176.

57. Tresemer, D. Fear of success: Popular, but unproven. *Psychology Today,* 1974, *7,* 82–85.

58. Ibid.

59. Deaux, 1976.

60. Monahan, L., Kuhn, D., and Shaver, P. Intrapsychic versus cultural explanations of the "fear of success" motive. *Journal of Personality and Social Psychology,* 1974, *29,* 60–64.

61. Cherry, F., and Deaux, K. Fear of success versus fear of gender-inappropriate behavior. *Sex Roles,* 1978, *4,* 97–101.

62. Stein and Bailey, 1973.

63. Goldberg, P. A. Are women prejudiced against women? *Transaction,* 1968, *5,* 28–30.

64. Pheterson, G. I., Kiesler, S. B., and Goldberg, P. A. Evaluation of the performance of women as a function of their sex, achievement, and personal history. *Journal of Personality and Social Psychology,* 1971, *19,* 114–118.

65. Fidell, L. S. Empirical verification of sex discrimination in hiring practices in psychology. *American Psychologist,* 1970, *25,* 1094–1098.

66. Feldman-Summers, S., and Kiesler, S. B. Those who are number two try harder: The effects of sex on attributions of causality. *Journal of Personality and Social Psychology,* 1974, *30,* 846–855.

67. Deaux, 1976.

68. Frieze, I., and Bar-Tal, D. Achievement motivation and gender as determinants of attributions for success and failure. Unpublished manuscript, University of Pittsburgh, 1974.

69. Parsons, J. Sex differences in attributional patterns and expectancy for success. Paper presented at the meeting of the Eastern Psychological Association, New York, 1975.

70. Kukla, A. Attributional determinants of achievement-related behavior. *Journal of Personality and Social Psychology,* 1972, *21,* 166–174.

71. Weiner, B. *Theories of Motivation.* Chicago: Markham, 1972.

72. Weiner, B., and Kukla, A. An attributional analysis of achievement motivation. *Journal of Personality and Social Psychology,* 1970, *15,* 1–20.

73. Weiner, B., and Potepan, P. A. Personality correlates and affective reactions towards exams of succeeding and failing college students. *Journal of Educational Psychology,* 1970, *61,* 144–151.

74. Weiner, 1972.

75. Feather, N. T. Attribution of responsibility and valence of success and failures in relation to initial confidence and task performance. *Journal of Personality and Social Psychology,* 1969, *13,* 129–144.

76. Simon, J. G., and Feather, N. T. Causal attributions for success and failure at university examinations. *Journal of Educational Psychology,* 1973, *64,* 46–56.

77. McMahan, I. D. Sex differences in causal attribution following success and failure. Paper presented at the meeting of the Eastern Psychological Association, New York, 1971.

78. Frieze, I. Studies of information processing and the attributional process in achievement-related contexts. Unpublished doctoral dissertation, University of California, Los Angeles, 1973.

79. McMahan, 1971.

80. Nichols, J. Causal attributions and other achievement-related cognitions: Effects of task, outcome, attainment value, and sex. *Journal of Personality and Social Psychology,* 1975, *31,* 379–389.

81. Peplau, L. A. Impact of fear of success and sex-role attitudes on women's competitive achievement. *Journal of Personality and Social Psychology,* 1976, *34,* 561–568.

82. Hoffman, L. W. Early childhood experiences and women's achievement motives. *Journal of Social Issues,* 1972, *28,* 129–155.

Human Sexuality: Implications for Gender-Role Differences   **6**

1.   Millett, K. *Sexual Politics*. New York: Doubleday, 1970. Copyright 1969, 1970 by Kate Millett. Reprinted by permission of Doubleday & Company, Inc.

2.   Brecher, E. M. *The Sex Researchers*. New York: The New American Library, 1971.

3.   Kern, S. *Anatomy and Destiny: A Cultural History of the Human Body*. New York: Bobbs-Merrill, 1975.

4.   Williams, J. H. *Psychology of Women: Behaviour in a Biosocial Context*. New York: Norton, 1977.

5.   Kern, 1975.

6.   Hayes, A. *Sexual Physiology of Woman*. Boston: Peabody Medical Institute, 1869.

7.   Ellis, H. *Studies in the Psychology of Sex*. New York: Random House, 1936.

8.   Freud, S. 1905. *Three Essays on the Theory of Sexuality*. New York: Avon, 1965.

9.   Fancher, R.E. *Psychoanalytic Psychology: The Development of Freud's Thought*. New York: Norton, 1973.

10.   Reiss, I. L. Changing sociosexual mores. In J. Money and H. Musaph (Eds.). *Handbook of Sexology*. Amsterdam: Elsevier/North-Holland Biomedical Press, 1977, pp. 311–325.

11.   Kinsey, A. C., Pomeroy, W. B., Martin, C. E., and Gebhard, P. H. *Sexual Behaviour in the Human Female*. Philadelphia: W. B. Saunders, 1953.

12.   Kantner, J. F., and Zelnik, M. Sexual experience of young unmarried women in the United States. *Family Planning Perspectives*, 1972, *4*, 9–18.

13. Kinsey, A. C., Pomeroy, W. B., and Martin, C. E. *Sexual Behaviour in the Human Male*. Philadelphia: Saunders, 1948.

14. Hunt, M. *Sexual Behaviour in the 1970's*. Chicago: Playboy Press, 1974.

15. Bell, R. R., and Chaskes, J. B. Premarital sexual experience among coeds, 1958 and 1968. *Journal of Marriage and the Family*, 1970, *32*, 81–84.

16. Christensen, H. T., and Gregg, C. Changing sex norms in America and Scandinavia. *Journal of Marriage and the Family*, 1979, *32*, 616–627.

17. King, K., Balswick, J. O., and Robinson, I. E. The continuing premarital sexual revolution among college females. *Journal of Marriage and the Family*, 1977, *39*, 455–459.

18. Burgess, E. W., and Wallin, P. *Engagement and Marriage*. Philadelphia: J. B. Lippincott, 1953.

19. Kinsey et al., 1953.

20. Terman, L. M. *Psychological Factors in Marital Happiness*. New York: McGraw-Hill, 1938.

21. Hunt, 1974.

22. Ibid.

23. Hobart, C. W. Changing orientations to courtship: A study of young Canadians. In W. E. Mann (Ed.). *Social and Cultural Change in Canada*, vol. 2. Toronto: Copp Clark, 1970, pp. 272–295.

24. Hobart, C. W. Sexual permissiveness in young English and French Canadians. *Journal of Marriage and the Family*, 1972, *34*, 292–303.

25. Ibid.

26. Greenglass, E. R., Levitt, K., and Borovilos, R. Factors related to coital experience and contraceptive use in unmarried women. Submitted for publication to *Archives of Sexual Behaviour*, 1981.

27. Perlman, D. The sexual standards of Canadian university students. In D. Koulack and D. Perlman (Eds.). *Readings in Social Psychology: Focus on Canada*. Toronto: Wiley, 1973, pp. 139–160.

28. King et al., 1977.

29.   Ibid.

30.   Greenglass et al., 1981.

31.   Sorensen, R. C. *Adolescent Sexuality in Contemporary America.*
      New York: World Publishing, 1973.

32.   Ibid.

33.   Zelnik, M., and Kantner, J. F. Sexual and contraceptive experience
      of young unmarried women in the United States, 1976 and
      1971. *Family Planning Perspectives,* 1977, *9,* 55–71.

34.   Sorensen, 1973.

35.   Zelnik and Kantner, 1977.

36.   Badgley, R. F., Caron, D. F., and Powell, M. G. Report of the
      Committee on the Operation of the Abortion Law. Ottawa,
      1977.

37.   Zelnik and Kantner, 1977.

38.   Kantner and Zelnik, 1972.

39.   Cowell, C. A. The adolescent and contraception. In *An Exploration
      of the Limitations of Contraception.* Don Mills, Ontario:
      Ortho Pharmaceutical Canada Ltd., 1976, pp. 34–42.

40.   Guyatt, D. E. Adolescent sexuality: Implications for social work.
      Family Planning and Social Work. Ottawa: Department of
      National Health and Welfare, 1977, pp. 176–209.

41.   Tanner, J. M. *Education and Physical Growth.* London: University
      of London Press, 1961.

42.   Keniston, K. Psychological development and historical change.
      Journal of Interdisciplinary History, 1971, *2,* 329–345.

43.   Kinsey et al., 1953.

44.   Reiss, I. L. Premarital sexual standards. In C. B. Broderick and J.
      Bernard (Eds.). *The Individual, Sex, and Society.* Baltimore:
      The Johns Hopkins Press, 1969, pp. 109–118.

45.   Roundup of Current Research. *Transaction,* 1971, *8,* 14–16.

46.   Hunt, 1974.

47.   King et al., 1977.

48.   Rainwater, L. Some aspects of lower class sexual behaviour.
      Journal of Social Issues, 1966, *22,* 96–108.

49.   Pietropinto, A., and Simenauer, J. *Beyond the Male Myth.* Scarbo-

rough, Ontario: The New American Library of Canada, 1978.

50. Ibid.

51. "J". *The Sensuous Woman.* New York: Lyle Stuart, 1969.

52. Gordon, M., and Shankweiler, P. J. Different equals less: Female sexuality in recent marriage manuals. In A. Skolnick and J. H. Skolnick (Eds.). *Intimacy, Family, and Society.* Boston: Little, Brown, 1974, pp. 163–175.

53. Barbach, L. G. *For Yourself— The Fulfillment of Female Sexuality: A Guide to Orgasmic Response.* New York: Doubleday, 1975.

54. Laws, J. L. Toward a model of female sexual identity. *Midway,* 1970, *11,* 39–75.

55. Hubbard, S. D. An overview of female sexuality. *The Humanist,* 1976, *36,* 9, 17–19.

56. May, R. *Love and Will.* New York: Norton, 1969.

57. Ibid.

58. Bardwick, J. M. Psychological factors in the acceptance and use of oral contraceptives. In J. T. Fawcett (Ed.). *Psychological Perspectives on Population.* New York: Basic Books, 1973, pp. 274–305.

59. Ginsberg, G., Frosch, W., and Shapiro, T. The new impotence. *Archives of General Psychiatry,* 1972, *26,* 218–222.

60. Bach, G. R., and Goldberg, H. *Creative Aggression.* New York: Avon, 1975.

61. *Chatelaine,* 1980, *53,* 47, 169–170 ff.

62. Koedt, A. The myth of the vaginal orgasm. Pittsburgh: KNOW, 1970.

63. Robinson, M. N. *The Power of Sexual Surrender.* New York: Signet, 1959.

64. Greenland, C. Is there a future for human sexuality? In B. Schlesinger (Ed.). *Sexual Behaviour in Canada: Patterns and Problems.* Toronto: University of Toronto Press, 1977, pp. 279–290.

65. Masters, W. H., and Johnson, V. E. *Human Sexual Response.* Boston: Little, Brown, 1966.

66.   Pomeroy, W. B. The male orgasm. *Cosmopolitan,* 1976, *180,* 203–
      205 ff.

67.   Hite, S. *The Hite Report.* New York: Dell, 1976.

68.   Slater, P. E. Sexual adequacy in America. In C. Gordon and G.
      Johnson (Eds.). *Readings in Human Sexuality: Contempo-
      rary Perspectives,* 2nd ed. New York: Harper and Row,
      1980, pp. 87–89.

69.   Coleman, J. S. Female status and premarital sexual codes.
      American Journal of Sociology, 1966, *72,* 217.

70.   Lipman-Blumen, J. Preliminary thoughts on reconceptualizing the
      area of family structure. Paper presented to the Merrill-
      Palmer conference on Reconceptualizing Family Sociology
      in the Light of Sex Role Research. Detroit, Michigan,
      November, 1975.

71.   Slater, 1980.

72.   Greer, G. *The Female Eunuch.* London: MacGibbon and Kee,
      1971.

73.   Ibid. Reprinted by permission of Granada Publishing Limited and
      McGraw-Hill Book Co.

74.   Ibid. Reprinted by permission of Granada Publishing Limited and
      McGraw-Hill Book Co.

75.   Kinsey et al., 1953.

76.   Bell, R. R. Changing aspects of marital sexuality. In S. Gordon and
      R. W. Libby (Eds.). *Sexuality Today and Tomorrow:
      Contemporary Issues in Human Sexuality.* Belmont:
      Wadsworth, 1976, pp. 213–218.

77.   Tavris, C., and Sadd, S. *The Redbook Report on Female Sexuality.*
      New York: Dell, 1977.

78.   Bell, 1976.

79.   Tavris and Sadd, 1977.

80.   Ibid.

81.   Bell, 1976.

82.   Kinsey et al., 1953.

83.   Hunt, 1974.

84.   Tavris and Sadd, 1977.

85.   Bell, 1976.

86. Ibid.

87. Byrne, D. A pregnant pause in the sexual revolution. *Psychology Today,* 1977, *11,* 67–68.

88. Kantner and Zelnik, 1972.

89. Zelnik and Kantner, 1977.

90. Sorensen, 1973.

91. U.S. Department of Health, Education, and Welfare. *Advanced Data.* From Vital and Health Statistics of the National Center for Health Statistics. Contraceptive utilization in the United States: 1973 and 1976. Washington, D. C., 1978.

92. Statistics Canada. *Vital Statistics,* vol. 1 — *Births 1972.* Cat. no. 84–202. Table 5. Live births by sex and rates, Canada and provinces, 1921–1972. Ottawa, 1974, p. 54.

93. Statistics Canada. *Vital Statistics,* vol. 1 — *Births 1972.* Table 11. Illegitimate births, Canada and provinces, 1921–1972. Ottawa, 1974, p. 75.

94. Statistics Canada. *Vital Statistics,* vol. 1 — *Births and Deaths 1978.* Cat. no. 84–204. Table 7. Number of live births by marital status and age of mother, Canada, 1978. Ottawa, 1980, p. 10.

95. Dominion Bureau of Statistics. *Vital Statistics 1960.* Cat. no. 84–202. Table 14. Illegitimate births, Canada and provinces, 1921–1960, and Table 16. Live births by age of parents, Canada, 1960. Ottawa, 1962.

96. Statistics Canada. *Therapeutic Abortions 1978.* Cat. no. 82–211. Table 42. Female teenage (15 – 19 years) population, therapeutic abortions among teenage females and abortion rate per 1000 females of the same age, by province, Canada, 1978. Ottawa, 1980, p. 88.

97. Badgley et al., 1977.

98. Bragonier, J. R. Viewpoints: Why do unmarried women fail to use contraception? *Medical Aspects of Human Sexuality,* 1973, *7,* 154–158 ff.

99. Ibid.

100. Howard, J. M., and LeRiche, N. G. H. A survey of teenage attitudes to sex and contraception in Kingston. Queens University, Kingston, Ontario, 1975.

101. Shah, F., Zelnik, M., and Kantner, J. F. Unprotected intercourse among unwed teenagers. *Family Planning Perspectives,* 1975, *7,* 39–43.

102. Kantner and Zelnik, 1972.

103. Werner, A. Sex questions asked by college students. *Medical Aspects of Human Sexuality*, 1975, *9*, 32, 35 ff.

104. Lipper, I., Cvejic, H., Benjamin, P., and Kinch, R. A. Abortion and the pregnant teenager. *Canadian Medical Association Journal*, 1973, *109*, 852–856.

105. Wolf, S. R. Psychosexual problems associated with the contraceptive practices of abortion-seeking patients. *Medical Aspects of Human Sexuality*, 1973, *7*, 169–171 ff.

106. Simon, N. M. Viewpoints: Why do unmarried women fail to use contraception? *Medical Aspects of Human Sexuality*, 1973, *7*, 162 ff.

107. Byrne, 1977.

108. Monsour, K. J., and Stewart, B. Abortion and sexual behaviour in college women. *American Journal of Orthopsychiatry*, 1973, *43*, 804–814.

109. Ibid.

110. Lundy, J. R. Some personality correlates of contraceptive use among unmarried female college students. *Journal of Psychology*, 1972, *80*, 9–14.

111. Ibid.

112. Kar, S. B. Individual aspirations as related to early and late acceptance of contraception. *Journal of Social Psychology*, 1971, *83*, 235–245.

113. Goldsmith, S., Gabrielson, M. O., Gabrielson, I., Mathews, V., and Potts, L. Teenagers, sex and contraception. *Family Planning Perspectives*, 1972, *4*, 32–38.

114. Kapor-Stanulovic, N., and Lynn, D. B. Femininity and family planning. *Journal of Sex Research*, 1972, *8*, 286–297.

115. Bardwick, 1973.

116. Ibid.

117. U.S. Bureau of the Census. *Statistical Abstract of the United States 1980*. No. 103. Legal abortions — Number, rate per 1000 women 15–44 years old, and abortion/live births, ratio by state of occurrence: 1973 to 1978. Washington, D. C., 1980.

118. Statistics Canada. *Therapeutic Abortions, Canada*. Advance Information 1978. Cat. no. 82-211-P. Table 1. Canadian residents

obtaining abortions in Canada, 1973–1978. Ottawa, 1979, p. 13.

119. Statistics Canada. *Therapeutic Abortions 1978*. Ottawa, 1980, p. 20, *and* Statistics Canada. *List of Canadian Hospitals 1978*. Cat. no. 83–201. Number of operating hospitals and their bed capacities, by type of hospital and province, 1978. Ottawa, 1978, pp. 12–13.

120. Forssman, H., and Thuwe, I. One hundred and twenty children born after application for therapeutic abortion refused. *Acta Psychiatrica Scandinavica,* 1966, *42,* 71–88.

121. McCance, C., Olley, D. C., and Edward, V. Long-term psychiatric follow-up. In G. Horobin (Ed.). *Experience with Abortion.* London: Cambridge University Press, 1973, pp. 245–300.

122. Osofsky, J. D., Osofsky, H. J., and Rajan, R. Psychological effects of abortion: With emphasis upon immediate reactions and follow-up. In H. J. Osofsky and J. D. Osofsky (Eds.). *The Abortion Experience: Psychological and Medical Impact.* New York: Harper and Row, 1973, pp. 188–205.

123. Patt, S., Rappaport, R., and Barglow, P. Follow-up of therapeutic abortion. *Archives of General Psychiatry,* 1969, *20,* 408–414.

124. Osofsky et al., 1973.

125. Smith, E. M. A follow-up study of women who request abortion. *American Journal of Orthopsychiatry,* 1973, *43,* 574–585.

126. Addelson, F. Induced abortion: Source of guilt or growth? *American Journal of Orthopsychiatry,* 1973, *43,* 815–823.

127. Schneider, C. Review of psychological literature. In *Abortion in the Seventies.* Proceedings of the Western Regional Conference on Abortion. Denver, Colorado, February, 1976.

128. Greenglass, E. R. Therapeutic abortion and psychiatric disturbance in Canadian women. *Canadian Psychiatric Association Journal,* 1976, *21,* 453–460.

129. Jansson, B. Mental disorders after abortion. *Acta Psychiatrica Scandinavica,* 1965, *41,* 87–110.

130. Simon, N. M., Senturia, A., and Rothman, D. Psychiatric illness following therapeutic abortion. *American Journal of Psychiatry,* 1967, *124,* 97–103.

131. Ekblad, M. Induced abortion on psychiatric grounds: A follow-up study of 479 women. *Acta Psychiatrica et Neurologica Scandinavica,* Supplement 99, 1955.

132. Greenglass, E. R. Therapeutic abortion, fertility plans, and psychological sequelae. *American Journal of Orthopsychiatry,* 1977, *47,* 119–126.

133. Smith, 1973.

134. Ekblad, 1955.

135. Aren, P. On legal abortion in Sweden: Tentative evaluation of justification of frequency during the last decade. *Acta Obstetricia et Gynecologica Scandinavica, 37,* Supplement 1, 1957.

136. Greenglass, E. R. *After Abortion.* Don Mills, Ontario: Longman, 1976.

137. Ibid.

138. Ibid.

139. Riddle, D., and Morin, S. F. Psychology and the gay community. *Journal of Social Issues,* 1978, *34,* 1–142.

140. Morin, S. F., and Schultz, S. J. The gay movement and the rights of children. *Journal of Social Issues,* 1978, *34,* 137–148.

141. Karr, R. Homosexual labelling: An experimental analysis. Unpublished doctoral dissertation, University of Washington, 1975.

142. McDonald, G. J., and Moore, R. J. Sex-role self-concepts of homosexual men and their attitudes toward both women and male homosexuality. *Journal of Homosexuality,* 1978, *4,* 3–14.

143. Mannion, K. Female homosexuality: A comprehensive review of theory and research. JSAS *Catalogue of Selected Documents in Psychology,* 1976, *6,* 44.

144. Freedman, M. *Homosexuality and Psychological Functioning.* Monterey: Brooks/Cole, 1971.

145. Wolff, C. *Love between Women.* New York: Harper and Row, 1971.

146. Riess, B. F. New viewpoints on the female homosexual. In V. Franks and V. Burtle (Eds.). *Women in Therapy: New Psychotherapies for a Changing Society.* New York: Brunner/Mazel, 1974, pp. 191–214.

147. Morin, S. F. Heterosexual bias in psychological research on lesbianism and male homosexuality. *American Psychologist,* 1977, *32,* 629–637.

148. Kinsey et al., 1948.

149. Kinsey et al., 1953.

150. Ford, C. S., and Beach, F. A. *Patterns of Sexual Behaviour.* New York: Harper and Row, 1951.

151. Ibid.

152. Hooker, E. The adjustment of the male overt homosexual. *Journal of Projective Techniques,* 1957, *21,* 18–31.

153. Hooker, E. Male homosexuality in the Rorschach. *Journal of Projective Techniques,* 1958, *22,* 33–54.

154. Hoffman, M. *The Gay World.* New York: Basic Books, 1968.

155. Hooker, 1957.

156. Hooker, E. Homosexuality. In J. Livingood (Ed.). *National Institute of Mental Health Task Force on Homosexuality: Final Report and Background Papers.* Washington, D.C., 1972.

157. Marmor, J. *Sexual Inversion: The Multiple Roots of Male Homosexuality.* New York: Basic Books, 1965.

158. Szasz, T. The product conversion — From heresy to illness. In J. A. McCaffrey (Ed.). *The Homosexual Dialectic.* Englewood Cliffs, New Jersey: Prentice-Hall, 1972, pp. 101–120.

159. McDonald, G. J. Misrepresentation, liberalism and heterosexual bias in introductory psychology textbooks. *Journal of Homosexuality,* 1981, *6,* 45–60.

160. American Psychological Association. Proceedings of the American Psychological Association for the year 1974. *American Psychologist,* 1975, *30,* 620–651.

161. McDonald, 1981.

162. Ibid.

163. Bardwick, J. M. *The Psychology of Women: A Study of Bio-Cultural Conflicts.* New York: Harper and Row, 1971.

164. Bardwick, J. M., and Douvan, E. Ambivalence: The socialization of women. In V. Gornick and B. K. Moran (Eds.). *Woman in Sexist Society.* New York: Basic Books, 1971, pp. 225–241.

165. Broverman, I. K., Broverman, D. M., Clarkson, F. E., Rosenkrantz, P. S., and Vogel, S. R. Sex-role stereotypes and clinical judgments of mental health. *Journal of Consulting and Clinical Psychology,* 1970, *34,* 1–7.

166. Steffensmeier, D., and Steffensmeier, R. Sex differences in reac-

tions to homosexuals: Research continuities and further developments. *The Journal of Sex Research,* 1974, *10,* 52–67.

167. Rich, A. Compulsory heterosexuality and lesbian existence. In C. R. Stimpson and E. S. Person (Eds.). *Women: Sex and Sexuality.* Chicago: University of Chicago Press, 1980, pp. 62–91.

168. Ibid.

169. Peplau, L.A. What homosexuals want. *Psychology Today,* 1981, *15,* 28–34; 37–38.

170. Loney, J. Background factors, sexual experiences and attitudes toward treatment in two "normal" homosexual samples. *Journal of Consulting and Clinical Psychology,* 1972, *38,* 57–65.

171. Peplau, 1981.

172. Mannion, 1976.

173. Peplau, 1981.

174. Rich, 1980.

175. Ibid.

176. McDonald, 1981.

177. Gibson, G. G. *By Her Own Admission.* New York: Doubleday, 1977.

The Family and Gender Roles 7

1. Rubin, Z. *Liking and Loving: An Invitation to Social Psychology.* New York: Holt, Rinehart & Winston, 1973.

2. Walster, E. Passionate love. In B. I. Murstein (Ed.). *Theories of Attraction and Love.* New York: Springer, 1971, pp. 85–99.

3. Rubin, 1973.

4. Knox, D. H., Jr., and Sporakowski, M. J. Attitudes of college students toward love. *Journal of Marriage and the Family,* 1968, *30,* 638–642.

5. Rubin, Z. The social psychology of romantic love, doctoral dissertation, University of Michigan, 1969 (University Microfilms, no. 70–4179).

6. Fengler, A.P. Romantic love in courtship: Divergent paths of male and female students. *Journal of Comparative Family Studies,* 1974, *5,* 134–139.

7. Greenglass, E. R., and Devins, R. Factors related to marriage and career plans in unmarried women. *Sex Roles,* 1982, *8,* 57–71.

8. U.S. Bureau of the Census. *Census of the Population 1970.* vol. 1. *Characteristics of the Population* (Part A, Number of inhabitants). Washington, D.C., 1972.

9. Nilson, L. B. The social standing of a housewife. *Journal of Marriage and the Family,* 1978, *40,* 541–548.

10. Eichler, M. The prestige of the occupation housewife. In P. Marchak (Ed.). *The Working Sexes.* Vancouver: Institute of Industrial Relations, 1977, pp. 151–175.

11. In Bernard, J. *The Future of Motherhood.* New York: Penguin, 1974.

12. Ibid.

13.   Minturn, L., and Lambert, W. L. *Mothers of Six Cultures: An-
      tecedents of Child Rearing.* New York: Wiley, 1964.

14.   Birnbaum, J. A. Life patterns, personality style and self-esteem in
      gifted family oriented and career committed women. Un-
      published doctoral dissertation, University of Michigan,
      1971.

15.   Blood, R. O., and Wolfe, D. M. *Husbands and Wives: The
      Dynamics of Married Living.* New York: The Free Press,
      1960.

16.   Meissner, M., Humphreys, E. W., Meis, S. M., and Scheu, W. J. No
      exit for wives: Sexual division of labour and the culmina-
      tion of household demands. *Canadian Review of Sociology
      and Anthropology,* 1975, *12,* 424–439.

17.   Vanek, J. Time spent in housework. *Scientific American,* 1974, *231,*
      116–120.

18.   Nickols, S. Work and housework: Family roles in productive activi-
      ty. Paper presented at the meeting of the National Council
      on Family Relations, New York, 1976.

19.   Lopata, H. *Occupation: Housewife.* New York: Oxford Univer-
      sity Press, 1971.

20.   Rebelsky, F., and Hanks, C. Fathers' verbal interaction with infants
      in the first three months of life. *Child Development,* 1971,
      42, 63–68.

21.   Kotelchuck, M. The nature of the child's tie to his father. Un-
      published doctoral dissertation, Harvard University,
      Cambridge, Massachusetts, 1972.

22.   Ban, P., and Lewis, M. Mothers and fathers, girls and boys: Attach-
      ment behaviour in the one-year-old. *Merrill-Palmer
      Quarterly,* 1974, *20,* 195–204.

23.   Meissner et al., 1975.

24.   Cogswell, B. E., and Sussman, M. B. Changing family and marriage
      forms: Complications for human service systems. *The
      Family Coordinator,* 1972, *21,* 505–516.

25.   *U.S. Statistical Abstract, 1977.* Cited in *Ms.,* 1978, *7,* 43.

26.   Ibid.

27.   Goodman, E. Excerpted from a speech given at the Association of
      National Advertisers. In *Ms., 1979, 7,* 54.

28. Labour Canada. *1978-1979 Women in the Labour Force: Part 1 Participation.* Cat. no. L38-30/1979-1. Table 5b. Percentage distribution of women and men in the population and labour force, by marital status, Canada, 1969, 1974 and 1979. Ottawa, 1980, p. 21.

29. U.S. Department of Labour. Bureau of Labour Statistics, unpublished tabulations from the March 1978 Current Population Survey. Cited in Smith, R. E. The movement of women into the labour force. In R. E. Smith (Ed.). *The Subtle Revolution: Women at Work.* Washington, D.C.: The Urban Institute, 1979, pp. 1-29.

30. Smith, R. E. The movement of women into the labour force. In *The Subtle Revolution: Women at Work,* pp. 1-29.

31. U.S. Department of Labour, 1978. See footnote #29.

32. Van Dusen, R. A., and Sheldon, E. B. The changing status of American women: A life cycle perspective. *American Psychologist,* 1976, *31,* 106-116.

33. *The Toronto Star,* September 25, 1979.

34. Gelber, S. M. The underemployed, underpaid third of the labour force. In S. M. Gelber, Women's Bureau, Ottawa, Information Canada, 1972, pp. 7-12.

35. Johnson, L. A. *Income, Disparity and Impoverishment in Canada Since World War II.* Toronto: New Hogtown Press, 1973.

36. Oppenheimer, V. K. *The Female Labour Force in the United States: Demographic and Economic Factors Governing Its Growth and Changing Composition.* Berkeley: University of California, 1970.

37. Mason, K. O., Czajka, J. L., and Arber, S. Changes in U.S. women's sex-role attitudes, 1964-1974. *American Sociological Review,* 1976, *4,* 573-596.

38. Greenglass and Devins, 1982.

39. Moore, K. A., and Hofferth, S. L. Women and their children. In *The Subtle Revolution: Women at Work,* pp. 125-157.

40. Hoffman, L. W., and Hoffman, M. L. The value of children to parents. In J. T. Fawcett (Ed.). *Psychological Perspectives on Population.* New York: Basic Books, 1973, pp. 19-76.

41. Ibid.

42. Moore and Hofferth, 1979.

43. *Ms.*, 1978, *7*, 62.

44. Statistics Canada. *1976 Census of Canada*. Vol. 4. *Families: Families by Number of Children*. Cat. no. 93–823. Table 11. Families, children at home and average number of children per family, for Canada and provinces and municipalities of 5000 population and over, 1971 and 1976. Ottawa, 1978, pp. 11:1–11:11.

45. U.S. Department of Commerce. Bureau of the Census. Fertility of American Women, June 1976, *Current Population Reports,* series P–20, #308, Table 5. Washington, D.C., 1977, p. 15.

46. Feld, S. Feelings of adjustment. In F. I. Nye and L. W. Hoffman (Eds.). *The Employed Mother in America*. Chicago: Rand McNally, 1963, pp. 331–352.

47. Birnbaum, 1971.

48. Feldman, H., and Feldman, M. *The Relationship between the Family and Occupational Functioning in a Sample of Rural Women*. Ithaca, New York: Department of Human Development and Family Studies, Cornell University, 1973.

49. Ohlbaum, J. S. Self-concepts, value characteristics and self-actualization of professional and non-professional women. Unpublished doctoral dissertation, United States International University, San Diego, California, 1971.

50. Walker, K.E. Household work time: Its implication for family decisions. *Journal of Home Economics,* 1973, *65,* 7–11.

51. Meissner et al., 1975.

52. Szinovacz, M. Cited in "Health Matters," *Family Health,* 1978, *10,* 18.

53. Johnson, F. A., and Johnson, C. L. Role strain in high commitment career women. *Journal of the American Academy of Psychoanalysis,* 1976, *4,* 13–36.

54. Meissner et al., 1975.

55. Robinson, J., Juster, T., and Stafford, F. Americans' Use of Time. Ann Arbor, Michigan: Institute for Social Research, 1976.

56. Walker, K. E. Time spent by husbands in household work. *Family Economics Review,* 1970, *4,* 8–11.

57. Fogarty, M. P., Rapoport, R., and Rapoport, R. N. *Sex, Career and Family*. London: George Allen and Unwin, 1971.

58.　Burke, R. J., and Weir, T. Relationships of wives' employment status to husband, wife and pair satisfaction and performance. *Journal of Marriage and the Family,* 1976, *38,* 279–287.

59.　Ibid.

60.　Burke, R. J., and Weir, T. Husband-wife helping-relationships: The "mental hygiene" function in marriage. *Psychological Reports,* 1977, *40,* 911–925.

61.　Bowlby, J. *Maternal Care and Mental Health.* Geneva: World Health Organization, 1951.

62.　Rutter, M. Parent-child separation: Psychological effects on the children. *Journal of Child Psychology and Psychiatry and Applied Disciplines,* 1971, *12,* 233–260.

63.　Yudkin, S., and Holme, A. *Working Mothers and Their Children.* London: Michael Joseph, 1963.

64.　Mead, M. A cultural anthropologist's approach to maternal deprivation. In *Deprivation of Maternal Care: A Reassessment of Its Effects.* Geneva: World Health Organization, 1962.

65.　Bronfenbrenner, U. Research on the effects of day care on child development. In *Toward a National Policy for Children and Families.* National Academy of Sciences Advisory Committee on Child Development, Washington, D. C., 1976.

66.　Hoffman, L. W. Effects on Child. In L. W. Hoffman and F. I. Nye, *Working Mothers: An Evaluative Review of the Consequences for Wife, Husband, and Child.* San Francisco: Jossey-Bass, 1974, pp. 126–166.

67.　Hoffman, L. W. Mother's enjoyment of work and effects on the child. *Child Development,* 1961, *32,* 187–197.

68.　Vogel, S. R., Broverman, I. K., Broverman, D. M., Clarkson, F. E., and Rosenkrantz, P. S. Maternal employment and perception of sex-roles among college students. *Developmental Psychology,* 1970, *3,* 384–391.

69.　Douvan, E. Employment and the adolescent. In *The Employed Mother in America,* pp. 142–164.

70.　Baruch, G. K. Maternal role pattern as related to self-esteem and parental identification in college women. Paper presented at the meeting of the Eastern Psychological Association, Boston, Massachusetts, 1972.

71.　Kappel, B. E., and Lambert, R. D. Self worth among the children of working mothers. Unpublished manuscript. University of Waterloo, 1972.

72. Propper, A. M. The relationship of maternal employment to adolescent roles, activities, and parental relationships. *Journal of Marriage and the Family*, 1972, *34*, 417–421.

73. Rapoport, R., and Rapoport, R. N. Early and later experiences as determinants of adult behaviour: Married women's family and career patterns. *British Journal of Sociology*, 1971, *22*, 16–30.

74. Fogarty et al., 1971.

75. Smith, L. G., and Smith, J. R. Divorce and remarriage: Trends and patterns in contemporary society. In J. Money and H. Musaph (Eds.). *Handbook of Sexology*. Amsterdam: Elsevier/North-Holland Biomedical Press, 1977, pp. 551–561.

76. Herman, S. J. Women, divorce, and suicide. *Journal of Divorce*, 1977, *1*, 107–117.

77. Smith and Smith, 1977.

78. Ambert, A.-M. *Divorce in Canada*. Don Mills, Ontario: Academic Press, 1980.

79. Hofferth, S. L., and Moore, K. A. Women's employment and marriage. In *The Subtle Revolution: Women at Work*, pp. 99–124.

80. Michael, R. T. Factors affecting divorce: A study of the Terman sample. National Bureau of Economic Research Working Paper no. 147, Stanford, California, 1976.

81. Singer, L. J. Divorce and the single life: Divorce as development. *Journal of Sex and Marital Therapy*, 1975, *1*, 254–262.

82. Norton, A. J., and Glick, P. C. Marital instability: Past, present, and future. *Journal of Social Issues*, 1976, *32*, 5–20.

83. Kargman, M. W. There ought to be a law! The revolution in divorce law. *The Family Coordinator*, 1973, *22*, 245–248.

84. Vital Statistics, 1974. Cited in Smith and Smith, 1977. See footnote #75.

85. Carter, H., and Glick, P. C. *Marriage and Divorce: A Social and Economic Study*. Cambridge, Massachusetts: Harvard University Press, 1970.

86. Brandwein, R. A., Brown, C.A., and Fox, E. M. Women and children last: The social situation of divorced mothers and their families. *Journal of Marriage and the Family*, 1974, *36*, 498–514.

87. Herzog, E., and Sudia, C. E. *Boys in Fatherless Families*. U.S. Department of Health, Education, and Welfare, Children's Bureau, no. 72–33. Washington, D.C., 1971.

88. Burchinal, L. Characteristics of adolescents from unbroken, broken, and reconstituted families. *Journal of Marriage and the Family*, 1964, *26*, 44–51.

89. Murchison, N. Illustration of the difficulties of some children in one-parent families. In M. Finer (Ed.). Report of the Committee on One-Parent Families. London, 1974.

90. Thomas, M. M. Children with absent fathers. *Journal of Marriage and the Family*, 1968, *30*, 89–96.

91. Nye, F. I. Child adjustment in broken and in unhappy unbroken homes. *Marriage and Family Living*, 1957, *19*, 356–361.

92. Hill, R. Social stresses on the family. In M.B. Sussman (Ed.). *Sourcebook in Marriage and the Family*, 3rd ed. Boston: Houghton, 1968, pp. 440–451.

93. *Ms.*, 1978, *7*, 62.

94. Statistics Canada. *Canada Year Book 1978–79*. Cat. no. CS11–202/ 1978. Table 4.28. Families by family structure, 1966, 1971 and 1976. Ottawa, 1978, p. 164.

95. *U.S. Statistical Abstract, 1977*. Cited in *Ms.*, 1978, *7*, 43.

96. Advisory Council on the Status of Women. One-parent family. Ottawa, 1977.

97. *Ms.*, 1978, *7*, 20.

98. In the U.S. in 1977, husband-wife households had a median income of $17,570. For households with no spouse present, the median income for those with a male householder [male head] was $10,520. compared to $6,330. for those with a female householder [female head] (U.S. Bureau of the Census. *Money Income in 1977 of Households in the United States. Current Population Reports*, Series P–60, no. 117. Washington, D.C., 1978).

99. Duncan, G. J., and Morgan, J. N. *Five Thousand American Families: Patterns of Economic Progress*, vol. 3. Ann Arbor, Michigan: Institute for Social Research, 1975.

100. Morgan, J. N. *Five Thousand American Families: Patterns of Economic Progress*, vols. 1 and 2. Ann Arbor, Michigan: Institute for Social Research, 1973.

101. U.S. Bureau of the Census. *Money Income in 1973 of Family and Persons in the United States. Current Population Reports,* Series P-60, no. 97. Washington, D.C., 1975.

102. Lopata, H. *Widowhood in an American City.* Cambridge, Massachusetts: Schenkman, 1973.

103. Guttentag, M. Women-to-women services: Alternative services in mental health. Unpublished manuscript, Harvard University, Cambridge, Massachusetts, 1976.

104. Brown, P., and Manela, R. Changing family roles: Women and divorce. *Journal of Divorce,* 1978, *1,* 315–328.

105. Statistics Canada. *1976 Census of Canada. Supplementary Bulletins: Housing and Families. Lone Parent Families.* Cat. no. 93–833. Table 5. Lone parent families by sex, mobility status and age of parent, showing family size and composition and school attendance of children, for Canada, 1976. Ottawa, 1978, pp. 5:1–5:6.

106. U.S. Department of Commerce. *Statistical Abstract of the United States,* 95th Ed. Social and Economic Statistics Administration, Bureau of the Census. Washington, D.C., 1974, p. 43.

107. Orthner, D. K., Brown, T., and Ferguson, D. Single-parent fatherhood: An emerging family life style. *The Family Coordinator,* 1976, *25,* 429–437.

108. Mendes, H. A. Single fathers. *The Family Coordinator,* 1976, *25,* 439–444.

109. Veevers, J. E. The social meaning of parenthood. *Psychiatry,* 1973, *36,* 291–310.

110. Rosenblatt, P. C. Behavior in public places: Comparisons of couples accompanied and unaccompanied by children. *Journal of Marriage and the Family,* 1974, *36,* 750–755.

111. Veevers, J. E. Voluntary childlessness: A review of issues and evidence. *Marriage and Family Review,* 1979, *2,* 1–26.

112. Silka, L., and Kiesler, S. Couples who choose to remain childless. *Family Planning Perspectives,* 1977, *9,* 16–17; 20–25.

113. U.S. Bureau of the Census. Fertility of American women, June, 1975. *Current Population Reports,* Series P-20, no. 301, Table 17. Children ever born by age and marital status of woman, by race and Spanish origin for June 1975 and April 1970, and race for April 1960. Washington, D.C., 1976.

114. Silka and Kiesler, 1977.

115. U.S. Bureau of the Census. Fertility history and prospects of American women, June 1975. *Current Population Reports*, Series P-20, no. 228, Table 3. Additional births expected and lifetime births expected by wives 18 to 39 years old, by age, race and Spanish origin: June 1975. Washington, D.C., 1976.

116. Veevers, J. E. The violation of fertility mores: Voluntary child-lessness as deviant behaviour. In C. L. Boydell, C. F. Grind-staff, and P. C. Whitehead (Eds.). *Deviant Behaviour and Societal Reaction.* Toronto: Holt, Rinehart & Winston, 1972, pp. 571–592.

117. Hoffman, L.W. The employment of women, education, and fertility. *Merrill-Palmer Quarterly*, 1974, *20*, 99–119.

118. Blake, J. Demographic science and the redirection of population policy. In M. C. Sheps and J. C. Ridley (Eds.). *Public Health and Population Change.* Pittsburgh: University of Pittsburgh Press, 1965, pp. 41–69.

119. Cited in Hoffman, 1974. See footnote #117.

120. Greenglass and Devins, 1982.

121. Veevers, J. E. Voluntarily childless wives: An exploratory study. *Sociology and Social Research*, 1973, *57*, 356–366.

122. Ibid.

123. Veevers, 1972.

124. Cited in Silka and Kiesler, 1977. See footnote #112.

125. Movius, M. Voluntary childlessness — The ultimate liberation. *The Family Coordinator*, 1976, *25*, 57–63.

Employment and Gender Roles   **8**

1.   Labour Canada. *1978–1979 Women in the Labour Force: Part 1
        Participation.* Cat. no. L38–30/1979–1. Table 8. Employed
        and unemployed labour force, and rate of unemployment, by
        sex, Canada, 1978 and 1979. Ottawa, 1980, p. 29.

2.   Armstrong, P., and Armstrong, H. *The Double Ghetto: Canadian
        Women and Their Segregated Work.* Toronto: McClelland
        and Stewart, 1978.

3.   During the last few decades, the participation rate of women in the
        Canadian labour force has more than doubled, going from
        23.4% in 1931 (Labour Canada. *Women in the Labour
        Force: Facts and Figures* [*1973 edition*]. Cat. no. L38–3072.
        Table 86. Women as percentage of the labour force, and
        labour force participation rates of women and men, Canada,
        June, 1931 to 1972. Ottawa, 1974, p. 227), to 48.9% in 1979
        (Labour Canada. *1978–1979 Women in the Labour Force:
        Part 1 Participation.* Table 1b. Population, labour force, and
        participation rates, by sex, Canada, 1969, 1974 and 1979.
        Ottawa, 1980, p. 11). In the U.S., while only 18% of women
        were in the labour force in 1890 (Smith, R. E. The movement
        of women into the labour force. In R. E. Smith (Ed.). *The
        Subtle Revolution: Women at Work.* Washington, D.C.:
        The Urban Institute, 1979, pp. 1–29), 51.5% of women were
        in the labour force in 1979 (U.S. Department of Commerce,
        Bureau of the Census. *Statistical Abstract of the United
        States 1980.* No. 654. Civilian labour force and participation
        rates, by sex, by state: 1976 and 1979. Washington, D.C.,
        1980, p. 395.)

4.   Baker, E. F. *Technology and Women's Work.* New York: Colum-
        bia University Press, 1964.

5.   Smith, 1979. Cited in footnote #3.

6.   National Council of Welfare. Women and Poverty. A report by the
        National Council of Welfare, Ottawa, 1979.

7. Ibid.

8. Kahn, R. The meaning of work: Interpretations and proposals for measurement. In A. Campbell and P. E. Converse (Eds.). *The Human Meaning of Social Change.* New York: Russell Sage, 1972, pp. 159–204.

9. Argyle, M. *The Social Psychology of Work.* Baltimore: Penguin, 1972.

10. Seashore, S., and Taber, T. Job satisfaction indicators and their correlates. *American Behavioural Scientist,* 1975, *3*, 333–368.

11. Cited in Booker, C. Alienation in the quiet factory. *The Labour Gazette,* 1974, *January,* 41–44.

12. Denyer, J. Quality of working life — What is it all about? *Women's Bureau Newsletter,* 1974, *4*, no. 3.

13. Renwick, P. A., and Lawler, E. E. What you really want from your job. *Psychology Today,* 1978, *11*, 53–65; 118.

14. Ferree, M. M. Working-class jobs: Housework and paid work as sources of satisfaction. *Social Problems,* 1976, *23*, 431–441.

15. Labour Canada. *Women in the Labour Force: Facts and Figures (1973 edition).* Table 24. Employed labour force in occupational categories, by sex, women as percentage of the total employed labour force, and percentage distribution of women and men by occupation, Canada, 1962 and 1972. Ottawa, 1974, p. 49.

16. Armstrong and Armstrong, 1978.

17. *The Toronto Star,* October 19, 1979.

18. Armstrong and Armstrong, 1978.

19. Ibid.

20. Statistics Canada. *Education in Canada: A Statistical Review for 1979–80.* Cat. no. 81–229. Table 8. Bachelor's and first professional degrees, by specialization and sex, Canada, 1974–1979. Ottawa, 1981, pp. 65-68.

21. Ibid.

22. Young Lawyers' Section of the Canadian Bar Association. Demographic Survey of Canadian Lawyers #1 1978–79. Toronto, 1979.

23. Ibid.

24. Statistics Canada. *Education in Canada: A Statistical Review for 1979–1980.* Table 8. Ottawa, 1981.

25. Ryten, E. Enrolment in Canadian Medical Schools, 1977/78 and 1978/79. *ACMC/AFMC Forum*, 1978–1979, *12*, 4–10.

26. Statistics Canada. *Education in Canada: A Statistical Review for 1977–78.* Cat. no. 81–229. Table 35. Summary of full-time teachers, by level and sex, Canada and provinces, 1977–78. Ottawa, 1979, pp. 128–129.

27. In 1931, women made up approximately 19% of the teaching staff in Canadian universities and colleges, 17% in 1941, 18% in 1953, and around 13% during the 1960s. In 1972–73, approximately 13% of the full-time teaching staff of Canadian universities were women (Boyd, M. Rank and salary differentials in the 1970's: A comparison of male and female full-time teachers in Canadian universities and colleges. Ottawa: Association of Universities and Colleges of Canada, 1979). By 1979–80, the proportion of female full-time university teachers was approximately 14% (Statistics Canada. *Education in Canada: A Statistical Review for 1979–1980.* Table 35. Summary of full-time teachers, by level and sex, Canada and provinces, 1979–80. Ottawa, 1981, pp. 168–169).

28. Boyd, 1979. See footnote #27.

29. *The Miami Herald*, January 27, 1980.

30. Armstrong and Armstrong, 1978.

31. U.S. Department of Commerce, Bureau of the Census. *Statistical Abstract of the United States 1980.* No. 652. Labour force and employment: 1947 to 1980. Washington, D.C., 1980, p. 394.

32. U.S. Department of Labour, Bureau of Labour Statistics, 1977. Cited in Barrett, N.S. Women in the job market: Occupations, earnings, and career opportunities. In *The Subtle Revolution: Women at Work*, pp. 31–61.

33. U.S. Department of Labour, Bureau of Labour Statistics, *Employment and Earnings*, 24, (February 1977). Washington, D.C., p. 39.

34. In the U.S. in 1977, 22.4% of all medical students and almost one-quarter of first-year medical students were women (*Los Angeles Times*, February 6, 1977).

35. The percentage of women enrolled in law school in the U.S. increased from 4% in 1960 to 19% in 1974 (Parrish, J.B. Women in professional training — An update. *Monthly Labour Review*, 1975, *98*, 49–50).

36. *The Chronicle of Higher Education*, 1979, *19,* 16.

37. Bernay, E. Gazette: News from all over. Affirmative inaction. *Ms.,* 1978, *7,* 87–90.

38. U.S. Department of Labour, Bureau of Labour Statistics. *Employment and Earnings January 1981.* Cat. no. 70–11379. Table 23. Employed persons by detailed occupations, sex, and race, 1980. Washington, D.C., 1981, pp. 180–181.

39. Marchak, P. The Canadian labour farce: Jobs for women. In M. Stephenson (Ed.). *Women in Canada.* Toronto: New Press, 1973, pp. 202–212.

40. Armstrong and Armstrong, 1978.

41. Boyd, 1979. See footnote #27.

42. Bernay, 1978.

43. Ibid.

44. Ferrari, L. A. Canadian directorship practices: A profile. Ottawa, The Conference Board in Canada, 1977.

45. Harragan, B. L. *Games Mother Never Taught You: Corporate Gamesmanship for Women.* New York: Rawson, Wade, 1977 Copyright © 1977 by Betty Lehan Harragan. Reprinted with the permission of Rawson Associates.

46. Bird, C. *Born Female: The High Cost of Keeping Women Down.* New York: Simon and Schuster, 1968. Copyright© 1968 by Caroline Bird. Reprinted by permission of Russell & Volkening as agents for the author.

47. Booker, 1974.

48. Canadian Committee on Learning Opportunities for Women. Cutbacks to training allowances and outreach programs: Their impact on women. A brief presented to representatives of the Liberal, New Democratic and Progressive Conservative Parties. Toronto, 1979.

49. *The Globe and Mail* (Toronto), May 12, 1979.

50. Smuts, R. W. *Women and Work in America.* New York: Schocken, 1971.

51. Backhouse, C., and Cohen, L. *The Secret Oppression: Sexual Harassment of Working Women.* Toronto: Macmillan, 1978.

52. Ibid.

53. Ibid.

54. Labour Canada. *1978–1979 Women in the Labour Force: Part II Earnings of Women and Men.* Cat. no. L38–30/1979–2. Ottawa, 1981.

55. McDonald, L. Wages of work: A widening gap between women and men. *Canadian Forum,* 1975, *55,* 4–7.

56. Quebec Charter of Human Rights and Freedoms, Bill 50, 1975, as amended 1976, Bill 56.

57. Canadian Human Rights Act, 1978.

58. McDonald, 1975.

59. Labour Canada. *Women in the Labour Force: Facts and Figures 1977: Part III Miscellaneous.* Cat. no. L38–30/1977–3. Table 4. Paid workers and union members in selected industries, union members as percentage of paid workers, women as percentage of total union members, by sex, Canada, 1977. Ottawa, 1980, p. 11.

60. Dunnigan, L. Analyse des stéréotypes masculins et féminins dans les manuels scolaires au Québec. Quebec, Quebec Status of Women Council, 1975.

61. Fischer, L., and Cheyne, J. A. Sex roles: Biological and cultural interactions as found in social science research and Ontario educational media. Toronto: Ontario Ministry of Education, 1977.

62. Trecker, J. L. Sex stereotyping in the secondary school curriculum. *Phi Delta Kappan,* 1973, *55,* 110–112.

63. Fischer and Cheyne, 1977.

64. Russell, S. J. Sex role socialization in the high school: A study in the perpetuation of patriarchal culture. Unpublished doctoral dissertation, University of Toronto, 1978.

65. Glaze, A. Factors which influence career choice and future orientations of females: Implications for career education. Unpublished doctoral dissertation, University of Toronto, 1979.

66. Russell, 1978.

67. U.S. Department of Labour, Employment and Training Administration. *Women and Work.* Manpower Research Monograph no. 46, p. 15. Washington, D.C., 1977.

68. Association of American Colleges. Project on the Status and Education of Women. On Campus with Women, #7, December, 1973.

69. Carlson, E. R., and Carlson, R. Male and female subjects in personality research. *Journal of Abnormal and Social Psychology*, 1961, *61*, 482–483.

70. Greenglass, E. R., and Stewart, M. The under-representation of women in social psychological research. *The Ontario Psychologist*, 1973, *5*, 21–29.

71. Crawford, M. Climbing the ivy-covered walls. *Ms.*, 1978, *7*, 61–63; 91–94.

72. Bowen, N. Quoted in Tausig, C. Women academics: Little change in status over past decade. *University Affairs,* 1979, *November,* 2–3.

73. Labour Canada. *1978–1979 Women in the Labour Force: Part II Earnings of Women and Men.* Table 11. Percentage distribution of families by income group and sex of head, Canada, 1977 and 1978. Ottawa, 1981, p. 47.

74. Ontario Ministry of Labour, Women's Bureau. *Women in the Labour Force: "Fact and Fiction".* Fact Sheets, no. 1. 1978.

75. Crowley, J. E., Levitin, T. E., and Quinn, R. P. Seven deadly half-truths about women. *Psychology Today*, 1973, *6,* 94–96.

76. Labour Canada. *1978–1979 Women in the Labour Force: Part I Participation.* Table 5b. Percentage distribution of women and men in the population and labour force, by marital status, Canada, 1969, 1974 and 1979. Ottawa, 1980, p. 21.

77. The utilization of civilian women employees within the Department of the Army: Civilian Personnel Pamphlet CPP79. Washington, D.C.: Department of the Army, 1973.

78. Rosen, B., Jerdee, T. H., and Prestwich, T. L. Dual-career marital adjustment: Potential effects of discriminatory managerial attitudes. *Journal of Marriage and the Family*, 1975, *37*, 565–572.

79. Hennig, M., and Jardim, A. *The Managerial Woman.* New York: Pocket Books, 1978.

80. Ibid.

Psychopathology and Gender Roles 9

1. Szasz, T. *The Myth of Mental Illness*. New York: Harper and Row, 1961.

2. Laing, R. D. *The Politics of Experience and the Bird of Paradise*. Baltimore: Penguin, 1967.

3. Liefer, R. The medical model as ideology. *International Journal of Psychiatry*, 1970, *9*, 13–21.

4. Block, S., and Reddaway, P. *Russia's Political Hospitals: The Abuse of Psychiatry in the Soviet Union*. Southampton: Camelot Press, 1977.

5. Veith, I. *Hysteria: The History of a Disease*. Chicago: University of Chicago Press, 1965.

6. Ehrenwald, J. (Ed.). *The History of Psychotherapy: From Healing Magic to Encounter*. New York: Jason Aronson, 1976, pp. 157–168.

7. Ibid.

8. Plato. *Timaeus*. In *The History of Psychotherapy: From Healing Magic to Encounter*, pp. 157–168.

9. Ibid.

10. Veith, 1965

11. Ibid.

12. Ehrenwald, 1976, pp. 105–124.

13. Ibid.

14. Veith, 1965.

15. Ibid.

16. Barker-Benfield, G. J. *The Horrors of the Half-Known Life: Male Attitudes toward Women and Sexuality in Nineteenth-Century America*. New York: Harper and Row, 1976.

17. Ibid.

18. Ibid.

19. Bullough, V. I. *Sex, Society, and History.* New York: Science History Publications, 1976.

20. Bromberg, W. *From Shaman to Psychotherapist.* Chicago: Henry Regnery, 1975.

21. Zilboorg, G., and Henry, G. W. *A History of Medical Psychology.* New York: Norton, 1941.

22. Alexander, F. G., and Selesnick, S. T. *The History of Psychiatry.* New York: Harper and Row, 1966.

23. Chesler, P. Patient and patriarch: Women in the psychotherapeutic relationship. In V. Gornick and B. K. Moran (Eds.). *Woman in Sexist Society.* New York: Basic Books, 1971, pp. 362–392.

24. Chesler, P. *Women and Madness.* New York: Doubleday, 1972.

25. Gove, W. R., and Tudor, J. F. Adult sex roles and mental illness. *American Journal of Sociology,* 1973, *78,* 812–835.

26. Fabrikant, B. The psychotherapist and the female patient: Perceptions, misperceptions and change. In V. Franks and V. Burtle (Eds.). *Women in Therapy: New Psychotherapies for a Changing Society.* New York: Brunner/Mazel, 1974, pp. 83–109.

27. Chaiton, A., Spitzer, W. O., Roberts, R. S., and Delmore, T. Patterns of medical drug use — A community focus. *Canadian Medical Association Journal,* 1976, *114,* 33–37.

28. Cooperstock, R., and Sims, M. Mood-modifying drugs prescribed in a Canadian city: Hidden problems. *American Journal of Public Health,* 1971, *61,* 1007–1016.

29. Parry, H. J., Balter, M. B., Mellinger, G. D., Cisin, I. H., and Manheimer, D. I. National patterns of psychotherapeutic drug use. *Archives of General Psychiatry,* 1973, *28,* 760–783.

30. Dohrenwend, B. P., and Dohrenwend, B. S. Sex differences and psychiatric disorders. *American Journal of Sociology,* 1976, *81,* 1447–1454.

31. Lewis, H. B. *Psychic War in Men and Women.* New York: New York University Press, 1976.

32. Statistics Canada. *Mental Health Statistics,* vol. 1. *Institutional Admissions and Separations 1977.* Cat. no. 83–204. All

institutions, first admissions, 1977. Table 4. Diagnostic class, by sex and age. Ottawa, 1980, pp. 42–43.

33. Smith, D. E. The statistics on mental illness: (What they will not tell us about women and why). In D. E. Smith and S. J. David (Eds.). *Women Look at Psychiatry.* Vancouver: Press Gang, 1975, pp. 73–119.

34. Seiden, A. M. Overview: Research on the psychology of women. II. Women in families, work, and psychotherapy. *The American Journal of Psychiatry*, 1976, *133*, 1111–1123.

35. New York Narcotic Addiction Control Commission. *Differential drug use within the New York State Labour Force: An assessment of drug use within the general population*, Albany, 1971.

36. Lief, H. I. Sexual counseling. In S. L. Romney, M. J. Gray, A. B. Little, J. A. Merrill, E. J. Quilligan, and R. Stander (Eds.). *Gynecology and Obstetrics: The Health Care of Women.* New York: McGraw-Hill, 1975, pp. 526–548.

37. Bernard, J. The paradox of the happy marriage. In *Woman in Sexist Society*, pp. 145–162.

38. Ibid.

39. Campbell, A., Converse, P. E., and Rodgers, W. L. *The Quality of American Life: Perceptions, Evaluations, and Satisfactions.* New York: Russell Sage Foundation, 1976.

40. Gove, W. R., and Geerken, M. R. The effect of children and employment on the mental health of married men and women. *Social Forces*, 1977, *56,* 66–76.

41. Holmes, T. H., and Masuda, M. Life change and illness susceptibility. In J. P. Scott and E. C. Senay (Eds.). *Separation and Depression: Clinical and Research Aspects.* Washington, D.C.: American Association for the Advancement of Science, 1973, pp. 161–186.

42. Dohrenwend, B. S. Life events as stressors: A methodological inquiry. *Journal of Health and Social Behaviour,* 1973, *14,* 167–175.

43. Dohrenwend, B. S., Krasnoff, L., Askenasy, A. R., and Dohrenwend, B. P. Exemplification of a method for scaling life events: The PERI Life Events Scale. *Journal of Health and Social Behaviour,* 1978, *19*, 205–229.

44. Ibid.

45. Dohrenwend, B. S. Social status and stressful life events. *Journal of Personality and Social Psychology*, 1973, *28*, 225–236.

46. Dohrenwend, B. S. Anticipation and control of stressful life events: An exploratory analysis. Paper presented at the meeting of the Eastern Psychological Association, New York, April, 1976.

47. Marecek, J. Powerlessness and women's psychological disorders. *Women and Psychotherapy*, 1976, *12*, 50–54.

48. Bernard, 1971.

49. Ibid.

50. Radloff, L. Sex differences in depression: The effects of occupation and marital status. *Sex Roles*, 1975, *1*, 249–265.

51. Birnbaum, J. A. Life patterns, personality style and self-esteem in gifted family oriented and career committed women. Unpublished doctoral dissertation, University of Michigan, 1971.

52. Feld, S. Feelings of adjustment. In F. I. Nye and L. W. Hoffman (Eds.). *The Employed Mother in America*. Chicago: Rand McNally, 1963, pp. 331–352.

53. U.S. Bureau of the Census. Fertility of American women: June, 1976. *Current Population Reports*, series, P–20, no. 308. Table 5. Washington, D.C., 1977.

54. Moore, K. A., and Hofferth, S. L. Women and their children. In R. E. Smith (Ed.). *The Subtle Revolution: Women at Work*. Washington, D.C.: The Urban Institute, 1979, pp. 125–157.

55. Feld, 1963.

56. Bernard, J. The good-provider role: Its rise and fall. *American Psychologist*, 1981, *36*, 1–12.

57. Heer, D. M. The measurement and bases of family power: An overview. *Marriage and Family Living*, 1963, *25*, 133–139.

58. Murstein, B. I. The relationship of mental health to marital choice and courtship progress. *Journal of Marriage and the Family*, 1967, *29*, 447–451.

59. Farina, A., Garmezy, N., and Barry, H., III. Relationship of marital status to incidence and prognosis of schizophrenia. *Journal of Abnormal and Social Psychology*, 1963, *67*, 624–630.

60. Schmidt, N., and Sermat, V. Measuring loneliness in different relationships. Submitted for publication to *Journal of Personality and Social Psychology*, 1981.

61. Sermat, V. Unpublished research report to the Social Sciences and Humanities Research Council of Canada, 1978.

62. Gurin, G., Veroff, J., and Feld, S. *Americans View Their Mental Health*. New York: Basic Books, 1960.

63. Srole, L., Langner, T. S., Michael, S. T., Opler, M. K., and Rennie, T. A. C. *Mental Health in the Metropolis*. New York: McGraw-Hill, 1962.

64. Garai, J. E. Sex differences in mental health. *Genetic Psychology Monographs*, 1970, *81*, 123–142.

65. Berardo, F. M. Survivorship and social isolation: The case of the aged widower. *The Family Coordinator*, 1970, *19*, 11–25.

66. Bock, E. W., and Webber, I. L. Suicide among the elderly: Isolating widowhood and mitigating alternatives. *Journal of Marriage and the Family*, 1972, *34*, 24–31.

67. Statistics Canada. *Mental Health Statistics*, vol. 1. *Institutional Admissions and Separations, 1977*. Table 11. Marital status, by diagnostic class, sex and age. Ottawa, 1980, pp. 66–71.

68. Briscoe, W. Divorce and psychiatric disease. *Archives of General Psychiatry*, 1973, *29*, 119–125.

69. Srole et al., 1962.

70. Unpublished figures on first hospitalizations obtained from the Health Division of Statistics Canada in 1976. Cited in Ambert, A.-M. *Divorce in Canada*. Don Mills, Ontario: Academic Press, 1980.

71. Koskenvuo, M., Sarna, S., and Kaprio, J. Cause-specific mortality by marital status and social class in Finland during 1969–1971. *Social Science and Medicine*, 1979, *13A*, 691–697.

72. Ambert, 1980. See footnote #70.

73. Berardo, F. M. Social adaptation to widowhood among a rural-urban aged population. Washington Agricultural Experiment Station Bulletin 689. College of Agriculture, Washington State University, 1967.

74. Berardo, F. M. Widowhood status in the United States: Perspective on a neglected aspect of the family life-cycle. *The Family Coordinator,* 1968, *17*, 191–203.

75. Berardo, 1970.

76. Bock and Webber, 1972.

77. Koskenvuo et al., 1979.

78. Bock and Webber, 1972.

79. Garai, 1970.

80. Schuckit, M. A. The alcoholic woman: A literature review. *Psychiatry in Medicine*, 1972, *3*, 37–43.

81. Lindbeck, V. L. The woman alcoholic: A review of the literature. *The International Journal of the Addictions*, 1972, *7*, 567–580.

82. Fraser, J. The female alcoholic. *Addictions*, 1973, *20*, 64–80.

83. Senseman, L. A. The housewife's secret illness. *Rhode Island Medical Journal*, 1966, *49*, 40–42.

84. Statistics Canada. *Mental Health Statistics*, vol. 1. *Institutional Admissions and Separations 1977*. Table 11. Ottawa, 1980.

85. Lindbeck, 1972.

86. Bell, R. G. Cited in Fraser, 1973. See footnote #82.

87. Fraser, 1973.

88. Birchmore, D. F., and Walderman, R. L. The woman alcoholic: A review. *The Ontario Psychologist*, 1975, *7*, 10–16.

89. Fraser, 1973.

90. Bell, R. G. Cited in Fraser, 1973. See footnote #82.

91. Mulford, H. A. Women and men problem drinkers: Sex differences in patients served by Iowa's Community Alcoholism Centers. *Journal of Studies on Alcohol*, 1977, *38*, 1624–1639.

92. Fraser, 1973.

93. Ibid.

94. Mulford, 1977.

95. Ibid.

96. Schuckit, M. A., and Morrissey, E. R. Drug abuse among alcoholic women. *American Journal of Psychiatry*, 1979, *136*, 607–611.

97. Lindbeck, 1972.

98. Johnson, M. W., Devries, J. C., and Houghton, M. I. The female alcoholic. *Nursing Research*, 1966, *15*, 343–347.

99.   Winokur, G., and Clayton, P. J. Family history studies. IV. Comparison of male and female alcoholics. *Quarterly Journal of Studies on Alcohol*, 1968, *29*, 885–891.

100. McLachlan, J. F. C. Classification of alcoholics by an MMPI actuarial system. *Journal of Clinical Psychology*, 1975, *31*, 145–147.

101. Curlee, J. A. A comparison of male and female patients at an alcoholism treatment center. *The Journal of Psychology*, 1970, *74*, 239–247.

102. Fraser, 1973.

103. Mulford, 1977.

104. Lisansky, E. S. Alcoholism in women; social and psychological concomitants. I. Social history data. *Quarterly Journal of Studies in Alcohol*, 1957, *18*, 588–623.

105. Winokur and Clayton, 1968.

106. Curlee, 1970.

107. Mulford, 1977.

108. Ibid.

109. Kinsey, B. A. *The Female Alcoholic: A Social Psychological Study*. Springfield, Illinois: Charles C. Thomas, 1966.

110. Rosenbaum, B. Married women alcoholics at the Washingtonian Hospital. *Quarterly Journal of Studies in Alcohol*, 1958, *19*, 78–89.

111. Curlee, J. A. Sex differences in patient attitudes towards alcoholism treatment. *Quarterly Journal of Studies on Alcohol*, 1971, *32*, 643–650.

112. Buss, A. *Psychopathology*. New York: Wiley, 1966.

113. Malzberg, B. Age and sex in relation to mental disease. *Mental Hygiene*, 1955, *39*, 196–206.

114. Garai, 1970.

115. Statistics Canada. *Mental Health Statistics*, vol. 1. *Institutional Admissions and Separations 1977*. Table 4. Ottawa, 1980.

116. Garai, 1970.

117. Seiden, 1976.

118. Scarf, M. *The Toronto Star*, October 15, 1980.

119. Weissman, M. M., and Klerman, G. L. Sex differences and the epidemiology of depression. *Archives of General Psychiatry*, 1977, *34*, 98–111.

120. Statistics Canada. *Mental Health Statistics*, vol. 1. *Institutional Admissions and Separations 1977*. Table 5. Detailed Diagnosis, by sex. Ottawa, 1980, pp. 44–47.

121. Scarf, M. *Unfinished Business: Pressure Points in the Lives of Women*. New York: Doubleday, 1980.

122. Radloff, 1975.

123. Brown, G., Bhrolchain, M., and Harris, T. Social class and psychiatric disturbance among women in an urban population. *Sociology*, 1975, *9*, 225–254.

124. Weissman and Klerman, 1977.

125. Mostow, E., and Newberry, P. Work role and depression in women: A comparison of workers and housewives in treatment. *American Journal of Orthopsychiatry*, 1975, *45*, 538–548.

126. Radloff, 1975.

127. Brown et al., 1975.

128. Guttentag, M. Women-to-women services: Alternative services in mental health. Unpublished manuscript, Harvard University, Cambridge, Massachusetts, 1976.

129. Scarf, M. The more sorrowful sex. *Psychology Today*, 1979, *12*, 45–52, 89–90.

130. Bart, P. B. Depression in middle-aged women. In *Woman in Sexist Society*, pp. 163–186.

131. Seligman, M. E. P. Depression and learned helplessness. In R. J. Friedman and M. M. Katz (Eds.). *The Psychology of Depression: Contemporary Theory and Research*. Washington, D.C.: V. H. Winston, 1974, pp. 83–113.

132. Seligman, M. E. P. *Helplessness: On Depression, Development and Death*. San Francisco: W. H. Freeman, 1975.

133. Maccoby E. E., and Jacklin, C. N. *The Psychology of Sex Differences*. Stanford, California: Stanford University Press, 1974.

134. Serbin, L. A., O'Leary, K. D., Kent, R. N., and Tonick, I. J. A comparison of teacher response to the pre-academic and problem behaviour of boys and girls. *Child Development*, 1973, *44*, 796–804.

135. Maccoby and Jacklin, 1974.

136. Serbin, L. A., and O'Leary, K. D. How nursery schools teach girls to shut up. *Psychology Today*, 1975, *9*, 56–57; 102–103.

137. Perris, C. Abnormality on paternal and maternal sides: Observations in bipolar (manic-depressive) and unipolar depressive psychoses. *British Journal of Psychiatry*, 1971, *118*, 207–210.

138. Helzer, J. E., and Winokur, G. A family interview study of male manic depressives. *Archives of General Psychiatry*, 1974, *31*, 73–77.

139. Weissman and Klerman, 1977.

140. Bardwick, J. M. *The Psychology of Women: A Study of Bio-Cultural Conflicts.* New York: Harper and Row, 1971.

141. Pollitt, J. *Proceedings of the Royal Society of Medicine*, 1977, *70*, 145.

142. Hamburg, D. A., Moos, R. H., and Yalom, I. D. Studies of distress in the menstrual cycle and the postpartum period. In R. P. Michael (Ed.). *Endocrinology and Human Behaviour.* London: Oxford University Press, 1968, pp. 94–116.

143. Hamilton, J. A. *Postpartum Psychiatric Problems.* St. Louis: Mosby, 1962.

144. Sherman, J. A. *On the Psychology of Women: A Survey of Empirical Studies.* Springfield, Illinois: Charles C. Thomas, 1971.

145. Butts, H. F. Postpartum psychiatric problems: A review of the literature dealing with etiological theories. *Journal of the National Medical Association*, 1969, *62*, 224–227.

146. Larsen, V. L. et al. Attitudes and stresses affecting perinatal adjustment. Final report, National Institute of Mental Health Grant MH–01381–01–02, September 1, 1963, to August 31, 1966.

147. Hamilton, 1962.

148. Larsen et al., 1966.

149. Williams, B. Sleep needs during the maternity cycle. *Nursing Outlook,* 1967, *15*, 53–55.

150. Parlee, M. B. Psychological aspects of menstruation, childbirth, and menopause. In J. A. Sherman and F. L. Denmark (Eds.). *The Psychology of Women: Future Directions in Research.* New York: Psychological Dimensions, 1978, pp. 181–238.

151. Bernard, J. *The Future of Motherhood.* New York: Penguin, 1974.

152. The Boston Women's Health Book Collective. *Our Bodies Ourselves,* 2nd ed. New York: Simon and Schuster, 1976.

153. Uddenberg, N., Fagerström, C. F., and Hakanson-Zaunders, M. Reproductive conflicts, mental symptoms during pregnancy and time in labour. *Journal of Psychosomatic Research,* 1976, *20,* 575–581.

154. Meares, R., Grimwade, J., and Wood, C. A possible relationship between anxiety in pregnancy and puerperal depression. *Journal of Psychosomatic Research,* 1976, *20,* 605–610.

155. Gordon, R. E., Kapostins, E. E., and Gordon, K. K. Factors in post-partum emotional adjustment. *Obstetrics and Gynecology,* 1965, *25,* 158–166.

156. Weissman and Klerman, 1977.

157. Gibbs, J. Suicide. In R. Merton and R. Nisbet (Eds.). *Contemporary Social Problems,* 3rd ed. New York: Harcourt, Brace & World, 1971, pp. 281–321.

158. Stengel, E. *Suicide and Attempted Suicide.* Baltimore: Penguin, 1964.

159. Shneidman, E. S., and Farberow, N. L. Statistical comparisons between attempted and committed suicides. In N. L. Farberow and E. S. Shneidman (Eds.). *The Cry for Help.* New York: McGraw-Hill, 1965, pp. 19–47.

160. Garai, 1970.

161. Statistics Canada. *Causes of Death.* Cat. no. 84–203. Deaths from each cause for provinces by sex, and Canada by sex and age, 1977. Ottawa, 1980, pp. 124–126.

162. Garai, 1970.

163. Rudestam, K. E. Stockholm and Los Angeles: A cross-cultural study of the communication of suicidal intent. *Journal of Consulting and Clinical Psychology,* 1971, *36,* 82–90.

164. Rudestam, K. E. Personal communication, 1981.

165. Garai, 1970.

166. Stengel, 1964.

167. Gove, W. R. Sex, marital status and suicide. *Journal of Health and Social Behaviour,* 1972, *13,* 204–213.

168. Garron, D., and Shekelle, R. Mood, personality, and the menstrual cycle. Paper presented at the meeting of the Western Psychological Association, 1973.

169. Sherman, 1971.

170. Sutherland, H., and Stewart, I. A critical analysis of the premenstrual syndrome. *Lancet*, 1965, *1*, 1180–1193.

171. Parlee, M. B. Stereotypic beliefs about menstruation: A methodological note on the Moos Menstrual Distress Questionnaire and some new data. *Psychosomatic Medicine*, 1974, *36*, 229–240.

172. Dalton, K. *The Premenstrual Syndrome.* Springfield, Illinois: Charles C. Thomas, 1964.

173. Koeske, R. D. Theoretical/conceptual implications of study design and statistical analysis: Research on the menstrual cycle. In C. Stark-Adamec (Ed.). *Sex Roles: Origins, Influences and Implications for Women.* Montreal: Eden Press Women's Publications, 1980, pp. 217–232. Reprinted by permission of Eden's Press Women's Publications. Copyright © 1980.

174. Frieze, I., Parsons, J. E., Johnson, P. B., Ruble, D. N., and Zellman, G. L. *Women and Sex Roles: A Social Psychological Perspective.* New York: Norton, 1978.

175. May, R. R. Mood shifts and the menstrual cycle. *Journal of Psychosomatic Research,* 1976, *20*, 125–130.

176. Ibid.

177. Bardwick, 1971.

178. Shafer, N. Helping women through the change of life. *Sexology,* 1970, *36*, 54–56.

179. Hallstrom, T. *Mental Disorder and Sexuality in the Climacteric.* Goteberg, Sweden: Orstadius Biktryckeri AB, 1973.

180. Mayer, N. *The Male Mid-Life Crisis: Fresh Starts After Forty.* Scarborough, Ontario: The New American Library of Canada, 1979.

181. Bardwick, 1971.

182. Masters, W. H., and Johnson, V. E. *Human Sexual Inadequacy.* Boston: Little, Brown, 1970.

183. Deutsch, H. *The Psychology of Women: A Psychoanalytic Interpretation*, vol. II. New York: Grune and Stratton, 1945.

184. Bart, 1971.

185. Williams, J. H. *Psychology of Women: Behaviour in a Biosocial Context.* New York: Norton, 1977.

186. Neugarten, B. L. Women's attitudes toward the menopause. *Vita Humana,* 1963, *6,* 140–151.

187. Levinson, D. J., Darrow, C. M., Klein, E. B., Levinson, M. H., and McKee, B. The psychosocial development of men in early adulthood and the mid-life transition. In D. F. Ricks, A. Thomas, and M. Roff (Eds.). *Life History Research in Psychopathology,* vol. 3. Minneapolis: University of Minnesota Press, 1974, pp. 243–258.

188. Ibid.

189. Mayer, 1979.

190. Weissman and Klerman, 1977.

191. Phillips, D. L., and Segal, B. E. Sexual status and psychiatric symptoms. *American Sociological Review,* 1969, *34,* 58–72.

192. Dohrenwend, B. P., and Dohrenwend, B. S. Reply to Gove and Tudor's comment on "Sex Differences and Psychiatric Disorders". *American Journal of Sociology,* 1977, *82,* 1336–1345.

193. Calhoun, L. G., Cheney, T., and Dawes, A. S. Locus of control, self-reported depression, and perceived causes of depression. *Journal of Consulting and Clinical Psychology,* 1974, *42,* 736.

194. Padesky, C., and Hammen, C. Help-seeking for depression: Sex differences in college students. Unpublished manuscript, University of California, Los Angeles, 1977.

195. Padesky, C., and Hammen, C. Pattern of coping with depression. Unpublished manuscript, University of California, Los Angeles, 1977.

196. Rowe, I. L. Prescriptions of psychotropic drugs by general practitioners. *Medical Journal of Australia,* 1973, *1,* 642–644.

197. Fidell, L. S. Put her down on drugs: Prescribed drug usage in women. Paper presented at the meeting of the Western Psychological Association, Anaheim, California, April, 1973.

198. National Disease and Therapeutic Index. *Annual Report.* Ambler, Pennsylvania: Lea, 1970.

199. Stein, L. S., Fox, M. M., and Luepnitz, D. Therapists' judgments of prognosis, severity of disturbance, and treatment needs as a function of patients' sex. Unpublished manuscript, University of Rochester, 1974.

200. Stein, L. S., Del Gaudio, A. C., and Ansley, M. Y. A comparison of female and male neurotic depressives. *Journal of Clinical Psychology*, 1976, *32*, 19–21.

201. Brodsky, C. M. The pharmacotherapy system. *Psychosomatics*, 1971, *11*, 24–30.

202. Mellinger, G. D. Psychotherapeutic drug use among adults: A model for young drug users. *Journal of Drug Issues*, 1971, *1*, 274–285.

203. Linn, L. S. Physician characteristics and attitudes toward legitimate use of psychotherapeutic drugs. *Journal of Health and Social Behaviour*, 1971, *12*, 132–140.

204. Stein et al., 1976.

205. Linn, L. S., and Davis, M. S. Physicians' orientation toward the legitimacy of drug use and their preferred source of new drug information. *Social Science and Medicine*, 1972, *6*, 199–203.

206. Prather, J., and Fidell, L. S. Sex differences in the content and style of medical advertisements. *Social Science and Medicine*, 1975, *9*, 23–26.

207. Report of the Task Force on Sex Bias and Sex-Role Stereotyping in Psychotherapeutic Practice. *American Psychologist*, 1975, *30*, 1169–1175.

208. Report of the Task Force on the Status of Women in Canadian Psychology. *Canadian Psychological Review*, 1977, *18*, 3–18.

209. Zeldow, P. B. Sex differences in psychiatric evaluation and treatment: An empirical review. *Archives of General Psychiatry*, 1978, *35*, 89–93.

210. Broverman, I. K., Broverman, D. M., Clarkson, F. E., Rosenkrantz, P. S., and Vogel, S. R. Sex-role stereotypes and clinical judgments of mental health. *Journal of Consulting and Clinical Psychology*, 1970, *34*, 1–7.

211. Harris, L. H., and Lucas, M. E. Sex-role stereotyping. *Social Work*, 1976, *21*, 390–395.

212. Doherty, E. G. Length of hospitalization in a short-term therapeutic community: A multivariate study of sex across time. *Archives of General Psychiatry*, 1976, *33*, 87–92.

213. Doherty, E. G. Are differential discharge criteria used for men and women psychiatric inpatients? *Journal of Health and Social Behaviour*, 1978, *19*, 107–116.

214. Report of the Task Force on Sex Bias and Sex-Role Stereotyping in Psychotherapeutic Practice, 1975.

215. Cowan, G. Therapist judgments of clients' sex-role problems. *Psychology of Women Quarterly*, 1976, *1*, 115–124.

216. Gomes, B., and Abramowitz, S. I. Sex-related patient and therapist effects on clinical judgment. *Sex Roles*, 1976, *2*, 1–13.

217. Fabrikant, 1974.

218. Zeldow, 1978.

219. Chesler, 1972.

220. Erikson, E. Inner and outer space: Reflections on womanhood. *Daedalus,* 1964, *93*, 582–606.

221. Fromm, E. *The Art of Loving*. New York: Harper and Row, 1956.

222. Horney, K. 1926. The flight from womanhood. In K. Horney. *Feminine Psychology*. New York: Norton, 1973, pp. 54–70.

223. Moulton, R. Some effects of the new feminism. *The American Journal of Psychiatry*, 1977, *134*, 1–6.

224. Symonds, A. Neurotic dependency in successful women. *The Journal of the American Academy of Psychoanalysis*, 1976, *4*, 95–103.

225. Wittkower, E. D., and Robertson, B. M. Sex differences in psychoanalytic treatment. *American Journal of Psychotherapy*, 1977, *31*, 66–75.

226. Moulton, 1977.

227. Pleck, J. H. The male sex role: Definitions, problems, and sources of change. *Journal of Social Issues*, 1976, *32*, 155–164.

228. Moulton, 1977.

229. Marecek, J., and Kravetz, D. Women and mental health: A review of feminist change efforts. *Psychiatry*, 1977, *40*, 323–329.

230. Kirsh, B. Consciousness-raising groups as therapy for women. In *Women in Therapy: New Psychotherapies for a Changing Society*, pp. 326–354.

231. Nelson, R. C., and Segrist, A. E. Raising the male consciousness through group experiences. *The School Counselor*, 1976, *24*, 93–101.

232. Stark-Adamec, C., Graham, J. M., and Pyke, S. W. Androgyny and mental health: The need for a critical evaluation of the theoretical equation. *International Journal of Women's Studies*, 1980, *3*, 490–507.

233. Erdwins, C., Small, A., and Gross, R. The relationship of sex roles to self-concept. *Journal of Clinical Psychology*, 1980, *36*, 111–115.

234. Jones, W. H., Chernovetz, M. E., and Hansson, R. O. The enigma of androgyny: Differential implications for males and females. *Journal of Consulting and Clinical Psychology*, 1978, *46*, 298–313.

235. Antill, J. K., and Cunningham, J. D. Self-esteem as a function of masculinity in both sexes. *Journal of Consulting and Clinical Psychology*, 1979, *47*, 783–785

236. Lenney, E. Concluding comments on androgyny: Some intimations of its mature development. *Sex Roles*, 1979, *5*, 829–840.

237. Hoffman, D. M., and Fidell, L. S. Characteristics of androgynous, undifferentiated, masculine, and feminine middle-class women. *Sex Roles,* 1979, *5*, 765–781.

238. Lenney, 1979.

239. Stark-Adamec et al., 1980.

240. Unger, R.K. *Female and Male: Psychological Perspectives.* New York: Harper and Row, 1979.

Summary and Implications   **10**

---

1.   Ross, E. A. *Principles of Sociology*. New York: Century, 1921.

2.   Greenglass, E. R., and Stewart, M. The under-representation of women in social psychological research. *The Ontario Psychologist*, 1973, *5*, 21–29.

3.   Schwabacher, S. Male versus female representation in psychological research: An examination of the *Journal of Personality and Social Psychology*, 1970, 1971. *Catalogue of Selected Documents in Psychology*, 1972, *2*, 20–21.

4.   The characteristics describing a sexist psychology are taken from Eichler, M. *The Double Standard: A Feminist Critique of Feminist Social Science*. London: Croom Helm Ltd., 1980. Eichler was describing aspects of sexist science.

5.   Vaughter, R. M. Review essay: Psychology. *Signs*, 1976, *2*, 120–146.

6.   Ibid.

7.   These three headings are taken from a discussion of the directions that feminist psychology is taking in a paper by Parlee, M. B. Review essay: Psychology. *Signs*, 1975, *1*, 119–138.

8.   Deaux, K. *The Behaviour of Women and Men*. Monterey, California: Brooks/Cole, 1976.

9.   Frieze, I., and Bar-Tal, D. Achievement motivation and gender as determinants of attributions for success and failure. Unpublished manuscript, University of Pittsburgh, 1974.

10.   Parsons, J. Sex differences in attributional patterns and expectancy for success. Paper presented at the meeting of the Eastern Psychological Association, New York, 1975.

11.   McMahan, I. D. Sex differences in causal attribution following success and failure. Paper presented at the meeting of the Eastern Psychological Association, New York, 1971.

12.   Nichols, J. Causal attributions and other achievement-related cognitions: Effects of task, outcome, attainment value, and sex. *Journal of Personality and Social Psychology*, 1975, *31*, 379–389.

13.   Goldberg, P. A. Are women prejudiced against women? *Transaction*, 1968, *5*, 28–30.

14.   Pheterson, G. I., Kiesler, S. B., and Goldberg, P. A. Evaluation of the performance of women as a function of their sex, achievement, and personal history. *Journal of Personality and Social Psychology*, 1971, *19*, 114–118.

15.   Fidell, L. S. Empirical verification of sex discrimination in hiring practices in psychology. *American Psychologist*, 1970, *25*, 1094–1098.

16.   Unger, R. K. Male is greater than female: The socialization of status inequality. *The Counseling Psychologist*, 1976, *6*, 2–9.

17.   Parke, R. D., and O'Leary, S. E. Family interaction in the new-born period: Some findings, some observations, and some unresolved issues. In K. Riegel and J. Meacham (Eds.). *The Developing Individual in a Changing World,* vol. 2. The Hague: Mouton, 1976, pp. 653–663.

18.   Rosenblatt, J. S. The development of maternal responsiveness in the rat. *American Journal of Orthopsychiatry*, 1969, *39*, 36–56.

19.   Wine, J. D., Moses, B., and Smye, M. D. Female superiority in sex difference competence comparisons: A review of the literature. In C. Stark-Adamec (Ed.). *Sex Roles: Origins, Influences, and Implications For Women.* Montreal: Eden Press Women's Publications, 1980, pp. 148–163.

20.   Ibid. Reprinted by permission of Eden Press Women's Publications. © 1980.

21.   Wine, J. D. Models of human functioning: A feminist perspective. Paper presented at the meeting of the Institute on Women of the Canadian Psychological Association, Toronto, 1981.

22.   Seligman, M. E. P. Depression and learned helplessness. In R. J. Friedman and M. M. Katz (Eds.). *The Psychology of Depression: Contemporary Theory and Research.* Washington, D.C.: V. H. Winston, 1974, pp. 83–113.

23.   Hiroto, D. S., and Seligman, M. E. P. Generality of learned helplessness in man. *Journal of Personality and Social Psychology,* 1975, *31*, 311–327.

24. Miller, W. R., and Seligman, M. E. P. Depression and learned helplessness in man. *Journal of Abnormal Psychology*, 1975, *84*, 228–238.

25. Serbin, L. A., O'Leary, K. D., Kent, R. N., and Tonick, I. J. A comparison of teacher response to the pre-academic and problem behaviour of boys and girls. *Child Development*, 1973, *44*, 796–804.

26. Maccoby, E. E., and Jacklin, C. N. *The Psychology of Sex Differences*. Stanford, California: Stanford University Press, 1974.

27. Ibid.

28. Pyke, S. W., and Stark-Adamec, C. Canadian feminism and psychology: The first decade. *Canadian Psychology*, 1981, *22*, 38–54.

29. Interview with R. Hogar. Cited in *APA Monitor*, 1979, *10*, 4–5.

30. Mishler, E. G. Meaning in context: Is there any other kind? *Harvard Educational Review*, 1979, *49*, 1–19.

31. Wine, 1981.

32. Parlee, M. B. Review essay: Psychology and women. *Signs*, 1979, *5*, 121–133.

Author Index

Index